Oil Exploration, Diplomacy, and Security in the Early Cold War

The importance of oil for national military–industrial complexes appeared more clearly than ever in the Cold War. This volume argues that the confidential acquisition of geoscientific knowledge was paramount for states, not only to provide for their own energy needs, but also to buttress national economic and geostrategic interests and protect energy security.

By investigating the postwar rebuilding and expansion of French and Italian oil industries from the second half of the 1940s to the early 1960s, this book shows how successive administrations in those countries devised strategies of oil exploration and transport, aiming at achieving a higher degree of energy autonomy and setting up powerful oil agencies that could implement those strategies. However, both within and outside their national territories, these two European countries had to confront the new Cold War balances and the interests of the two superpowers.

Roberto Cantoni is a Postdoctoral Research Fellow within the Security Studies Chair at CERI, Sciences Po, and an Associate Researcher at LATTS—IFRIS, France. In 2014 he defended his PhD on oil exploration, diplomacy and security at the University of Manchester, UK. In the same year he won the Society for the History of Technology's Levinson Prize. He currently works on the politics of epistemic vulnerability in the nuclear age.

Routledge Studies in Modern European History

For a full list of titles in this series, please visit www.routledge.com.

34 **Meanings and Values of Water in Russian Culture**
Edited by Jane Costlow and Arja Rosenholm

35 **Italy and Its Eastern Border, 1866–2016**
Marina Cattaruzza

36 **Franco–Israeli Relations, 1958–1967**
Gadi Heimann

37 **(Re)Constructing Communities in Europe, 1918–1968**
Senses of Belonging Below, Beyond and Within the Nation-State
Edited by Stefan Couperus and Harm Kaal

38 **Order and Insecurity in Germany and Turkey**
Military Cultures of the 1930s
Emre Sencer

39 **Green Landscapes in the European City, 1750–2010**
Edited by Peter Clark, Marjaana Niemi, and Catharina Nolin

40 **Resistance Heroism and the End of Empire**
The Life and Times of Madeleine Riffaud
Keren Chiaroni

41 **The Summer Capitals of Europe, 1814–1919**
Marina Soroka

42 **German Reunification**
Unfinished Business
Joyce E. Bromley

43 **Oil Exploration, Diplomacy, and Security in the Early Cold War**
The Enemy Underground
Roberto Cantoni

Oil Exploration, Diplomacy, and Security in the Early Cold War

The Enemy Underground

Roberto Cantoni

Routledge
Taylor & Francis Group
New York London

First published 2017
by Routledge
605 Third Avenue, New York, NY 10017

and by Routledge
2 Park Square, Milton Park, Abingdon, Oxon, OX14 4RN

First issued in paperback 2021

Routledge is an imprint of the Taylor & Francis Group, an informa business

Library of Congress Cataloging-in-Publication Data
CIP data has been applied for.

Typeset in Sabon
by codeMantra

Publisher's Note
The publisher has gone to great lengths to ensure the quality of this reprint but points out that some imperfections in the original copies may be apparent.

ISBN 13: 978-0-367-27529-7 (pbk)
ISBN 13: 978-1-138-69290-9 (hbk)

To my parents Giovanni and Nunzia

Contents

	List of Figures	ix
	Preface	xi
	Acknowledgments	xv
	List of Acronyms and Archive Codes	xvii
	Introduction	1
1	The Allied Shadow: International Pressures and the Italian Oil Industry	33
2	From Iraq to Africa: The Quest for French Energy	76
3	Oil Diplomacy in Wartime Algeria	119
4	The Midstream Shift	168
5	Transnational Counterattack Against Soviet Oil Plans	211
	Conclusion	247
	Bibliography	257
	Index	285

List of Figures

1.1	Enrico Mattei (1906–1962).	35
1.2	The Po Valley (shadowed).	37
2.1	The area included in the *Red Line Agreement.*	79
2.2	Pierre Guillaumat (1909–1991).	82
2.3	Map of oil exploration permits allocated and applied for in the Sahara by 1952.	104
3.1	Ahmed Ben Bella in the US in 1962. On his left, US President John F. Kennedy.	120
3.2	Geophysical activity in Algeria (1952–1965).	126
3.3	Map of exploration permits in the Algerian Sahara in early 1957.	131
3.4	Development of Saharan oil production in million tons (1957–1965). 'Bassin de Polignac' refers to Southern Sahara; 'Zone Centre-Nord' to Central and Northern Sahara.	139
3.5	Evolution of exploration permits by surface area in the Sahara (in thousand km^2).	140
4.1	Monthly variations in seismograph and gravimeter crew-months in the US.	176
4.2	World seismic activity #1 (1947–1962).	177
4.3	World seismic activity #2 (1949–1961).	177
4.4	The BRP and affiliates: geophysical activity (number of crew-months) in the franc zone (1951–1965).	179
4.5	AGIP and affiliates: geophysical activity (1945–1962).	179
4.6	West European pipelines operating or under construction in 1960.	190
4.7	The Algerian pipeline system in 1962.	195
5.1	The Soviet pipeline system in late 1960.	213
5.2	The European branch of the Soviet pipeline system (Druzhba) in 1962.	214
5.3	Dependence on Soviet Bloc oil in NATO European countries in 1960.	225

Preface

When asked to think about important developments in the Cold War standoff between the United States and the Soviet Union, many images may come to mind: the Berlin blockade and airlift, the first Soviet atomic test in 1949, the creation of NATO and the Warsaw Pact, the start of the space age with Sputnik I's launch in 1957, the Cuban Missile Crisis in 1962, and the escalation of the Vietnam War in the 1960s that fueled the explosive civilian protests of 1968.

The struggle to supply energy to Western nations does not come as quickly to mind. But perhaps it should. Just as landing humans on the Moon during the Apollo 11 mission of 1969 has become emblematic of East–West competition and conflict at the heart of the Cold War, future generations may see as a key issue of the second half of the twentieth century the search for cheap, reliable energy to sustain burgeoning industrial development. Already a major concern of combatants during World War II, discovering and maintaining sufficient energy reserves became a national security worry for the West (indeed, all industrial nations) during the first decades of the Cold War. Producing sufficient energy remains no less vital today.

Energy availability is a difficult issue to grasp. It is most tangibly felt when it is absent—as, for instance, in the 1973 oil crisis, which precipitated one of the most severe international diplomatic, political, and cultural shocks of the Cold War era. Energy, technological, and economic systems are closely intertwined, and any society that lacks ample sources of energy is destined to remain poor. While a variety of natural resources have historically been utilized for energy—wood, whale oil, and coal powered the first industrial revolution of the nineteenth century—the most important fuel for modern civilization is petroleum (oil, in American English). Because oil has a high energy density compared to coal, and is liquid (hence more easily transported), oil has fueled the modern era of automobiles, aviation, and armies. As a result, countries around the world became addicted to oil-derived energy: since the start of World War II, wars have not only been fought with it, at times they have been waged *over* it—the Iran–Iraq War (1980–1988) and the Gulf War (1990–1991) are just two examples.

In this original, deeply researched book, historian Roberto Cantoni explores an important story little appreciated until now: how, in the first decades of the Cold War, leaders in France and Italy sought to utilize national petroleum reserves to heighten their standing and influence among Western nations. Oil might not seem an ideal weapon for the politicians or petroleum industry kingpins in these countries to brandish: as World War II ended, their refineries were in ruins, pipelines and pumps rusting and unusable. Allied officials occupying Italy wanted to create a free-market system to manage petroleum reserves that would benefit Anglo-American oil while aiding Western security in general (rather than rebuilding Italy), while French petroleum companies were dominated by large multinational firms, and French President Charles de Gaulle was incensed at the weakness of France's energy portfolio. But discoveries of rich natural gas deposits in Italy enabled Enrico Mattei—a larger-than-life energy entrepreneur—to rebuild Italian petroleum holdings, becoming a popular hero and the most powerful man in Italy. As a key ally in Western Europe, France was shielded by the US State Department, which scuttled plans by giant international oil firms to gain control over French oil. In the end, Cantoni argues, both Italy and France transformed energy resources into diplomatic triumphs—for instance, making it possible for the Soviet Union to construct a giant oil pipeline to Italy in the late 1960s that allowed Soviet oil to flow into Western Europe, despite deep misgivings by NATO leaders.

The most important insights that Cantoni provides are about the Algerian War, which lasted from 1954 to 1962. This protracted conflict, also known as the Algerian War of Independence, pitted Algerian nationalist fighters against French troops as France sought to maintain its century-long dominance over its vast colony in North Africa. Prior accounts have treated the Algerian War as part of the wave of decolonization in the wake of World War II, one of the most important global political transformations of the twentieth century. That it was. But as Cantoni demonstrates, the Algerian conflict was also a multinational affair involving Italian, US, and other nations with African interests. In 1954, geophysical prospectors had discovered a natural gas field in a mountainous region in southern Algeria bordering the shifting sands of the Sahara Desert called Djebel Berga. To the victor would go the spoils: not simply political power, but access to valuable hydrocarbon reserves. A race to locate additional deposits followed the Djebel Berga discovery. When US and Italian interests wanted to gain advantage, as the war intensified, they sought secret information about newly identified oilfields not only from career diplomats but also from petroleum experts and engineers, all the while trying to assess the political allegiances of these individuals. Understanding the Algerian War, Cantoni argues, requires us to look beyond traditional diplomatic channels to clandestine flows of geoscientific intelligence. In the process, he reveals a new and surprising twist in our understanding of Cold War technology and diplomacy.

Cantoni has worked tirelessly to tell this hard-won story. He was a history detective in the best sense of the term. Rebuffed by administrators in a key geophysics company archive (where he was allowed to see only glossy advertising posters and triumphal pamphlets rather than the board meeting minutes and field reports he had requested), he successfully worked his way through voluminous collections at various branches of the French National Archives. There he discovered—and ultimately gained access to—previously classified documents on the "Mattei Affair" created by the French Secret Service. To better understand French involvement in the Algerian War (where relevant files remained sealed, for the conflict remains sensitive in France to this day), Cantoni traveled to Italian archives, where he successfully obtained confidential French documents already declassified there. In one frustrating moment, Cantoni's heart leaped when he glimpsed a folder labeled "Documents prepared for the GPRA [the Algerian nationalist fighters] with a view to Evian [the French–Algerian Peace Conference in the early 1960s]." But when he opened the folder, only a handful of anodyne post-Evian documents remained. Parts of this tantalizing story still remain hidden.

What matters is how much more we now know about "oily deals" early in the Cold War. Cantoni's book expands our understanding of the politics of energy resources during the Cold War, as well as the role of scientific and technical intelligence-gathering in realms far removed from atomic and chemical espionage. It merits attention from historians of foreign policy, energy, and technology alike.

Ronald E. Doel
Associate Professor of History
Florida State University

Acknowledgments

I would like to acknowledge the European Research Council, whose generous grant made this project and my extended archival research possible; the Centre for the History of Science, Technology and Medicine (CHSTM) at the University of Manchester, whose members accepted my PhD research proposal; the Laboratoire, Techniques, Territoires et Sociétés (LATTS) and the Institut Francilien Recherche Innovation Société (IFRIS), whose precious financial and logistic support allowed me to work on the adaptation of my thesis to this monograph.

For their greatly valued advice, I would like to thank my PhD supervisor, Simone Turchetti; my co-supervisors, Vladimir Jankovic and James Sumner; my viva examiners, Jeff Hughes and Ron Doel; *History and Technology*'s Editor-in-Chief, Martin Collins; and *Technology and Culture*'s Editor-in-Chief, Suzanne Moon.

Very welcome feedback and advice came also from the members of the TEUS project scattered around France, Spain, Sweden, and the UK, with whom I shared more than just conferences and video-meetings: feeling part of a small but international and dedicated community was a fantastic stimulus for my research. My gratitude therefore goes to Matthew Adamson, Soraya Boudia, Lino Camprubí, Néstor Herran, Sebastian Grevsmühl, Peder Roberts, Sam Robinson, and Leucha Veneer.

Many librarians and archivists were extremely helpful in assisting my research. They include staff from: in the UK, the British National Archives at Kew; in Belgium, the NATO Archives in Brussels (Eudes Nouvelot and Johannes Geurts in particular); in France, Archives diplomatiques du Ministère des Affaires étrangères at La Courneuve, Archives historiques du Groupe ELF/Total at Courbevoie (Benoît Doessant and Clémentine Pedenon in particular), Archives CGG Veritas at Massy, Archives nationales at Pierrefitte-sur-Seine, Archives nationales d'outre-mer in Aix-en-Provence, Centre de documentation de l'Institut français du pétrole at Rueil-Malmaison; in Italy, Archivio storico-diplomatico del Ministero degli Affari esteri in Rome; Archivio storico ENI at Pomezia (Anna Landolfi in particular); Archivio tecnico ENI, Associazione pionieri e veterani ENI (Enrico Orsini in particular) and ENI Corporate University, at San Donato Milanese; in the US, National Archives and Records Administration at College Park, Maryland.

Max Novick, Robert Langham and Michael Bourne of Routledge scrupulously followed the phases of development of this work, and I owe to their support the smooth process that led from my book proposal to this publication.

I would also like to thank Francesco Guidi for an interview he granted me at ENI's San Donato offices; Stuart Butler, Adriano Cantoni and Sam Robinson for helping me with archival documentation; Márton Fábok, for his reading suggestions; my Master 2's supervisor at Université Paris 7, Guillaume Lachenal, who stirred my interest in resource diplomacy and postcolonial history; Mario Di Giovanni, for introducing me to the beauty of history many years ago; John Crisp, for proofreading this work. In addition, I would like to thank Raquel, Paul and Bart. Thanks to them I became a historian instead of a linguist.

Last, but certainly not least, I would like to thank my family for their support, encouragement and packages of coffee; and all the people who, consciously or unconsciously, contributed to make this publication possible.

Earlier versions of the following chapters have been published previously. Permission to publish this material is gratefully acknowledged.

Chapter 2—Cantoni, Roberto, and Leucha Veneer. "Underwater and Underground: Gatekeeping Oil Exploration during the Cold War." In *The Surveillance Imperative: The Rise of the Geosciences during the Cold War*, edited by Simone Turchetti and Peder Roberts, 45–66. London: Palgrave Macmillan, 2014.

Chapter 3—Cantoni, Roberto. "The Enemy Underground: Geostrategic Intelligence and the War in Algeria". *History and Technology* 32, no. 1 (2016): 33–69.

Chapter 4—Cantoni Roberto, "Breach of Faith? Italian–Soviet Cold War Trading and ENI's 'International Oil Scandal.'" *Quaestio Rossica* 4 (2015): 180–98.

Chapter 5—Cantoni, Roberto. "What's in a Pipe? Transnational Negotiation of a 'Strategic' Item". *Technology and Culture* 58, no. 1 (2017): 67–96; Cantoni, Roberto. "Transnational Reactions to the Soviet Oil Offensive (1960–2)." In *Cold War Energy: A Transnational History of Soviet Oil and Gas*, edited by Jeronim Perovic, 131–61. London: Palgrave Macmillan, 2017.

List of Acronyms and Archive Codes

Acronyms

AGIP	Azienda generale italiana petroli
AIOC	Anglo-Iranian Oil Company
ARAMCO	Arabian-American Oil Company
BRP	Bureau de recherches de pétrole
CFP	Compagnie française des pétroles
CGG	Compagnie générale de géophysique
CIA	Central Intelligence Agency
CIP	Comitato italiano petroli
CREPS	Compagnie de recherches et d'exploitation de pétrole au Sahara
CTRP	Comitato tecnico ricerche e produzione
DICA	Direction des carburants
ECA	Economic Cooperation Administration
ECONAD	Committee of Economic Advisers
EEC	European Economic Community
ENI	Ente nazionale idrocarburi
ERP	European Recovery Program
FLN	Front de libération nationale
GPRA	Gouvernement provisoire de la République algérienne
GPRF	Gouvernement provisoire de la République française
IFP	Institut français du pétrole
IPC	Iraq Petroleum Company
NAC	North Atlantic Council
NATO	North Atlantic Treaty Organization
NEDC	Near East Development Corporation
OCRS	Organisation commune des régions sahariennes
RAP	Régie autonome des pétroles
SDECE	Service de documentation extérieure et de contre-espionage
SNE	Soyuznefteexport
SNPA	Société nationale des pétroles d'Aquitaine
[SN]REPAL	Société nationale de recherche et d'exploitation de pétrole en Algérie

SOCONY	Standard Oil Company of New York
SONJ	Standard Oil Company of New Jersey
UN	United Nations

Archive Codes

ADMAE	Archives diplomatiques du Ministère des Affaires étrangères [Fra]
AHTOTAL	Archives historiques du Groupe Total [Fra]
Amemb	US Embassy
AN	Archives nationales [Fra]
ANOM	Archives nationales d'outre-mer [Fra]
ASENI	Archivio storico Eni [Ita]
ASMAE	Archivio storico-diplomatico del Ministero degli Affari esteri [Ita]
Britemb	British Embassy
DS	Department of State [USA]
FO	Foreign Office [UK]
Fremb	French Embassy
Itemb	Italian Embassy
MAEF	Ministère des Affaires étrangères [Fra]
MAEI	Ministero degli Affari esteri [Ita]
NARA	National Archives and Records Administration [USA]
NATOA	NATO Archives [Bel]
TNA	The National Archives [UK]

Introduction

> At 5.40 am, Murielle, 46, the on-site emergency nurse at In Amenas gas plant was getting dressed in her bedroom. Her working day was due to start at 6 am. [...] But at 5.50 am [...] she was jolted by the "piercing sound" of the gas plant's fire alarm. [...] [A]n engineer [...] shouted: "Terrorists! Terrorists! It's a terrorist attack!"[1]

On 16 January 2013, a commando of around thirty terrorists, linked to the multinational militant Islamist organization Al-Qaeda, erupted into the Tiguentourine gas plant near In Amenas, Algeria, taking hostage its eight hundred personnel and triggering what came to be known as the 'Algerian hostage crisis.' Run by British Petroleum (BP), the Norwegian Statoil and the Algerian national company SONATRACH, the plant accounted for 10 percent of Algeria's colossal natural gas production. It is situated in the east of the country, in the middle of the Sahara desert, 1,300 kilometers from Algiers and a few dozen kilometers from the Libyan border, from where the militants are believed to have made their incursion into Algeria. The terrorists demanded an end to French military operations against Islamist groups in northern Mali, initiated a few days earlier, in return for the safety of the hostages. The crisis ended four days later when, following frantic diplomatic activity involving no less than ten states, the Algerian Special Forces penetrated the site. By the time the situation was resolved, almost forty foreign hostages, an Algerian security guard, and nearly all the militants had been killed.[2]

That the terrorist attack took place at In Amenas was not a coincidence. The site was targeted not only because of its geographical specificity, but also because of its symbolic value. The militants knew that, because of the large number of countries with citizens working at the Algerian plant, their raid would catalyze worldwide media and diplomatic attention. Furthermore, Algeria is the fourth largest natural gas supplier to Europe, so the resulting abrupt halt in natural gas output would affect the economies of many European countries. The In Amenas attack revealed the vulnerability of Western interests in the region in the hydrocarbons sector, and focused attention on a fundamental geostrategic theme, namely the intimate connection between hydrocarbons, international diplomacy, and energy security.

Oil is a significant factor in geostrategic thinking. The development of alternative forms of energy and growing interest in eco-sustainability, together with frequent news about environmental catastrophes caused by accidents at oil production facilities—of which BP's 2010 Deepwater Horizon oil spill in the Gulf of Mexico is only one of the most recent and significant examples—may prompt predictions of an end to the oil era.[3] However, oil production has peaked and declined a number of times in the past, and debates about future reliance on oil, linked to the concept of 'peak oil,' have occurred more than once since the 1920s. While fossil fuels are bound by their non-renewability ultimately to become an obsolete source of energy, this process may take time, depending on global, national, and local energy governance policies.

As new technologies are developed that make extraction of oil and gas from non-conventional reservoirs (such as shale oil and gas, oil sands, tight oil, oil from pre-salt geological layers) economically and technically viable, it seems fair to predict that unless major changes in global energy governance occur, fossil fuels may remain the world's main source of energy for decades yet, and oil and gas may maintain their role as geopolitical issues, as well as generators of security issues. These kinds of forecasts, however, are the task of scenario-makers and energy analysts. On the other hand, one of the aspects energy historians can help to elucidate is the continuity between past and present dynamics relating to hydrocarbons.

This work is framed in the context of the early Cold War. It focuses on two European countries, France and Italy, in their struggle to acquire energy independence from established transnational oil companies. I investigate two interconnected aspects: first, the role played by oil prospecting and surveillance in the quest for national security, defined by historian Melvyn Leffler as "actions deemed imperative to protect domestic core values from external threats."[4] While US national security policy has been a subject of scholarly attention since the 1960s, there has been less focus on this area in regard to European states. Second, I show how oil diplomacy has been not only the job of official diplomats, but also of oil technicians and technocrats, who have themselves acted as policymakers and diplomatic operators.

While these multiple roles have already been noted by Ronald Doel and Allan Needell, who explored connections between scientists and the military, I will argue that this is also the case in a field where scientific intelligence-gathering is less directly linked to military aspects, namely the petroleum industry.[5] In the remainder of this introduction, I will explain the importance of oil and oil prospecting in the postwar historical context, review the existing literature and clarify in what way my study enriches current scholarship in the relevant fields of knowledge. Contextually, I will situate my work theoretically within the interconnecting frameworks of a transnational history of science and technology, and the diplomacy of natural resources.

Why Oil Prospecting?

Oil is the most widespread source of high-density energy in the world. Its role as a universal energy currency, already significant for military operations during the two World Wars, became even more evident with the inception of the Cold War. Fundamental in fueling the transportation industry and heating houses, oil is also very versatile, as can be seen from the huge variety of synthetic products made available by the petrochemical industry from the 1950s onward. Since then, plastics and other mass-consumption oil derivatives have spread swiftly into everyday life. Establishing conditions for accessing the world's oil-rich regions is therefore a necessity for the economic, energy, and military security of nation states. Being able to effectively monitor the subsoil for oil and to control flows of oil, are geopolitical imperatives, not only for the security of individual states, but also for their capacity to exercise leverage on the security of other countries.

More specifically, the power to regulate oil flows—and thus prices—provides the capacity to wield decisive influence over the military–industrial complexes and economies of enemies and allies alike. Consequently, the worldwide struggle for exploration concessions and for directly or indirectly securing control of territories crucial to the passage of oil, have been the chief causes of repeated diplomatic clashes in the past, and remain so today. This was also the case during the Cold War with conflicts between, but also within, the world's main ideological blocs. An inconsistent flow of oil, besides undermining its military planning, could affect a country's economic strength. The ready availability of oil could also reduce strategic threats: it is true that Cold War confrontation would be quintessentially nuclear, but controlling oil supplies also enabled the massive provision of energy for non-military purposes.

Oil discoveries are not simply the result of individual exercises in data collection, but of years of scientific and technological activities, industrial failures and successes, and the high public and private financial investment associated with them. All these factors made geoscientific intelligence—that is, the possibility of accessing restricted data on geological and geophysical surveys, as well as on exploration technologies—inestimably precious. Favoring one prospecting method over another; possessing more reliable technologies than a rival company; or owning confidential information on the geological prospects of an area, might mean all the difference between one company making an oil discovery and another drilling a dry well.

The very same instruments that fail in one area might lead to a finding in another. Even more importantly, the diverse uses of geophysics—that is, the study of the earth using quantitative physical methods—made it valuable for purposes other than prospecting for natural resources. The physical principles underlying oil exploration seismology, for example, were the same as those employed in monitoring nuclear explosions.[6] Geophysics had been growing in importance as an academic discipline since the early twentieth century, notably in the US, home to the world's most prominent geophysical companies. It required support from a costly high-tech industry: it employed cutting-edge technologies that not all countries aspiring to a role in the oil world were capable of developing. Those that were not, had to borrow technologies from other countries or acquire the necessary knowledge abroad. This affected the confidentiality of company activities, and the autonomy of companies, in obvious ways.

Indeed, the previous consideration can be extended beyond geophysical technologies: the power with which states were endowed by the availability of oil resources necessitated a high degree of secrecy, including information gathered in exploration operations. When a country's energy security is at stake, and the possession or lack of certain data can critically affect it, and when such data cannot be obtained by overt means, surveillance comes into play. Overt or covert monitoring activities can thus be deployed over other countries' prospecting operations, technical expertise, corporate trading strategies, or diplomatic relations.

Surveillance in terms of both geophysical exploration and intelligence-gathering was therefore an essential element of oil security, one often neglected in the existing literature on the history of oil exploration.[7] Oil surveillance operations also caused conflicts between the diplomats, company managers, government officials, and geoscientists of different countries. As political scientist Robert Jervis more generally shows in what he termed 'the security dilemma,' the bolstering of energy security through surveillance activities by one government made its neighbors feel less assured of their own security.[8]

In reading this work the reader may find that, while I stress the relevance of the geosciences as a whole, I place considerably more emphasis on geophysics than on geology, and may legitimately ask why this is the case. Of course, geology is an essential part of the machinery of exploration, and its use historically preceded that of geophysics. The justification for my choice is the increasingly greater degree of confidence that companies have placed in geophysics compared with geology since the late 1940s. Naomi Oreskes and Ronald Doel argue that this shift was the result of a change in methodological and epistemic expectations, which prioritized physics and highly mathematized fields over more empirical ones. Geophysics, seen as based on more quantitative and more theoretically grounded data, and on the measurement of the physical properties of the earth, came to be considered more 'scientific' than geology. Especially after World War II, trust in quantitative methods gradually displaced reliance on more qualitative methods, and this occurred not only in the sciences but also more generally, in public life, as demonstrated by historian Theodore Porter.[9]

However, Oreskes and Doel note that geophysics was not intrinsically 'better' than geology. The shift was part of a broader move from the field to the laboratory, "which reflected an idealization of the epistemic values of exactitude and control that laboratory work embodies." The two historians also emphasize that the needs of Cold War military patrons greatly contributed to the exploitation of geophysics, especially in the US, resulting in increased funds for geophysical studies in research institutes, new instrumental practices, and more professional opportunities for individuals trained in these techniques.[10] I will return to this point later. Another factor was that the big role of technology in geophysical applications gave it much more weight in corporate balance sheets than geology, thereby asserting the predominance of American manufacturers on the world market: European companies soon became dependent on US technology to carry out geophysical prospecting. All these factors resulted in an increasingly wider application of geophysical techniques worldwide. By the early 1950s, geophysics had come to be regarded by oil prospectors as the discipline that had the last word before embarking on drilling operations. As a result, it took a prominent place in oil exploration, while geological studies remained an essential preliminary activity.[11]

Transnationalism of the Oil Industry

In light of the multiple domains in which oil is relevant, and in particular the role of the technosciences in the oil exploration industry, it seemed conceptually appropriate to situate my work within a hybrid theoretical framework, straddling the transnational history of technology and the history of resource diplomacy. Indeed, hardly anything epitomizes the concept of 'transnational' better than the oil industry.[12] Although the headquarters of world oil companies may be physically located in national spaces, their activities span the globe and know no borders, to the point that they possess powers—not to mention budgets—that can easily exceed those of national states. The dynamics of the oil industry, involving "movements and forces that cut across national boundaries" in terms of goods, people, ideas, words, capital, might, and institutions, make it an excellent candidate for a transnational historical study.[13]

In fact, the cross-border characteristics just outlined refer not only to the fact that a company based in one country may carry out its prospecting work in another country; it also extends to the mobility of corporate personnel and of the technologies employed, which are frequently the object of exchanges. The notion of transnationalism in technoscience has received much attention in the last fifteen years, used in many different contexts, and with diverse meanings. On the one hand, some have felt the need to warn against its indiscriminate use. On the other, considering the prominence of national narratives even in internationally oriented studies, some scholars have questioned whether a genuinely transnational perspective has ever been adopted.[14] While I am aware of the hazards of such a fluid concept, there seems to be no other viable conceptual framework in which to research oil matters. The very physical qualities of this natural resource, as well as the historical development of infrastructures conceived to carry it from one global area to another—namely pipelines and tankers—clearly demonstrate this. In addition, it is necessary to go beyond comparative history if one intends to explain cross-border flows of technical knowledge and not just national adaptations of foreign technologies.

I am therefore not going simply to compare the development of Italian and French oil exploration industries, but will also use these two countries' oil deals as a starting point to describe a more complex transnational scenario, in which French and Italian strategies and interests intertwined with those of other countries. These deals presented two facets: openly, they addressed urgent economic need, while secretly they were decisive in economic and military affairs, and/or energy security. An important consequence of the double nature of these deals was mutual mistrust between national agencies. In oil matters, Western alliances proved fragmentary, affected as they were by conflicting national interests.

In order to understand how a transnational perspective may afford us a better grasp of the mechanisms of knowledge production and the function of technoscience in global affairs, we need to focus on the "hybrid domains (scientific and geopolitical at the same time) in which flexible identities (the scientist-diplomat-politician) operate."[15] This geopolitical dimension of science-making was already very clear to the administration of US President Harry Truman, in the aftermath of World War II: technoscience was to be employed as a tool of US foreign relations. The new strategy was typified by a report from the Director of the US Office of Scientific Research and Development, and Presidential Science Advisor, Vannevar Bush, author of *Science—The Endless Frontier.* Bush suggested that basic science could contribute to European economic growth, social wellbeing and, eventually, military strength in the troubled postwar context.[16] Of course this was not to be a mere act of philanthropy. Centering his analysis on this use of science in foreign policy, in his seminal monograph on the role of the US in the postwar reconstruction of European science, John Krige argues that, by collaborating with European countries where classificatory standards were less restrictive, US policymakers intended to benefit American industry by acquiring future European innovations for North American scientists.[17]

In this context, part of the US funds provided by the 1948 European Recovery Program (ERP) was used for the reconstruction of European science. Although the Plan had originally been directed toward short-term reconstruction and political stability, this was the new direction suggested by Bush and other figures within the US military establishment. Without strong underlying scientific capability, they argued, economic growth and national security could not be achieved.[18] The American initiative found fertile ground in Europe. By analyzing US involvement in the creation of the European Centre for Nuclear Research (CERN) in Geneva, and the role of US private foundations and the North Atlantic Treaty Organization (NATO) in European science reconstruction, Krige has convincingly shown that American hegemony was co-produced by both US and European policymakers and scientists, at the time materialistically thirsty for financial help and advocating the principle of scientific universalism.

In 1949, in line with Bush's approach, the American physicist and engineer Lloyd Berkner, a scientific statesman familiar with the US Research and Development Board's policies, was asked by the State Department to produce a survey of the department's responsibilities in the field of science. The following year he released the *Science and Foreign Relations* report, recommending that US scientists participate more in meetings abroad and that foreign scientists be encouraged to attend US symposia, in order to keep channels open for the movement of scientists and their ideas. The consulting scientists would play an important part in determining the policies of the State Department, and would be attachés with full diplomatic status. Notwithstanding the neutral face value of this proposal, Berkner specified in a secret supplement to his report that the new officials' activities would have to include intelligence-gathering, while a second confidential report circulating through the State Department justified scientific internationalism as a means of reinvigorating US science.[19]

The close relationship between science, foreign policy, and intelligence-gathering is also brought to the fore in Doel's work on the role of scientists as policymakers, advisers, and intelligence agents. This aspect was further developed in Needell's book on Berkner's life as a scientist and policymaker. In both Doel's and Needell's cases, however, the focus of the narrative is the United States. Instead, I focus on two European countries which, due to their lesser position in Cold War dynamics in comparison with the two superpowers, could not count on world power politics to articulate their intelligence-gathering operations.[20] The case of oil shows that Krige may be correct in emphasizing collaboration, since both French and Italian companies were assisted by US agencies or individual technicians. The latter, however, used collaboration as a way of controlling foreign advances, and this activity was further reinforced, in keeping with Doel's arguments, by networks of US geoscientists and intelligence agents operating in Europe.

With the publication of Gabrielle Hecht's *The Radiance of France*, the view of scientists as policymakers was transposed to the other side of the Atlantic. Hecht's monograph, a historical and sociological account of the birth and development of the French military and civilian nuclear program, and of its technological and diplomatic tensions, introduces the concepts of 'technopolitics' to characterize the "strategic practice of designing or using technology to constitute, embody, or enact political goals," and of 'technopolitical regime' to characterize "the tight relationship among institutions, the people who run them, their guiding myths and ideologies, the artifacts they produce, and the technopolitics they pursue."[21] Hecht applies these concepts to the conflicts and negotiations characterizing relations between the French nuclear sector's two main institutions, the Atomic Energy Commission (*Commissariat à l'énergie atomique*), responsible for the general scientific and military aspects of the nuclear program, and *Électricité de France*, the public utility responsible for the production, transmission, and distribution of electricity. She analyzes the role played by French identity in the shaping of postwar industrial reconstruction, and shows how French technocrats conducted their relations according to their different technopolitical viewpoints.[22]

Technology, Hecht claims, is not a tool of politics, but a mode of politics. Technology and politics are not two parallel lines that at some points may deviate from their path and cross, but two permanently intertwined lines. Conceptualizations of French identity and the meaning given to national technoscientific prowess as a way of restoring France to its earlier greatness are central to my study. Together with the consolidation of postwar economies, postcolonial humiliation, and underdevelopment in science, the reconstitution of national identities and strength mattered in Europe as much as the increasing tensions between the superpowers.[23] Inspired by Hecht's analysis, my story shows how, within Italy and France, the creation of new oil agencies was prompted by technopolitical shifts from conservative to aggressive policies, enacted by men with very clear ideas about what a national state should or should not do with regard to the development of its energy security. Technological development was seen as a way of implementing specific strategies to position Italy and France in the Cold War scenario. Whereas, in the French situation, oil history appears by and large to replicate Hecht's nuclear narrative, in the Italian case the country aspired to assert a new role in international relations after Fascism. Through the 'Neo-Atlanticist policy,' designed by the Christian Democrat left wing in the 1950s to boost Italy's autonomy from the US in foreign politics, it was hoped this new position could be attained.

Although I know of no parallel work to Hecht's on the Italian situation, technopolitical connections have indeed been explored: for example, Barbara Curli's study on the Italian nuclear project investigated the confrontational dynamics between politicians, technocrats, and scientists on Italy's conflicting nuclear projects. Simone Turchetti's work on the Italian Communist physicist, Bruno Pontecorvo, who after getting involved in the US research and development project that produced the first nuclear weapons during World War II—the Manhattan Project—moved to the British Atomic Energy Research Establishment, and then defected to the Soviet Union, elucidates the relations between nuclear science, security, and politics in the early days of the Cold War. Significantly in terms of scientist-mediated technological transfer between disciplines, Turchetti highlights how Pontecorvo's expertise originated in his work in applied nuclear geophysics, using neutrons to prospect for oil in the US before engaging in the Manhattan Project.[24]

Because of the prevalence of nuclear narratives in Cold War history of science, technicians operating in the oil and gas business may not have enjoyed the resonance of scientists like Pontecorvo. Nevertheless, they were a professional category characterized by similar geographic fluidity. The transnational trajectory of the Italian geophysicist Antonio Bucarelli is a case in point. In the late 1940s, Bucarelli started working for the public agency, General Italian Oil Company (*Azienda generale italiana petroli*, AGIP). In 1950 he accepted a job offer from the American oil company Gulf Oil, thus leaving AGIP. He later left Gulf and joined the US Western Geophysical Company (WGC), which employed him on surveys for the Italian private company, Montecatini, one of AGIP's competitors.[25] Professional paths of a similar intricacy were not at all exceptional in the oil industry. Technician-mediated transfers of knowledge between companies were the rule rather than the exception, and had obvious implications in terms of information-gathering. For a company, acquiring a technician also meant acquiring intelligence on the methods employed and the data collected by its competitors.

The Technopolitics of Natural Resources

Approaching the history of Cold War from the perspective of resource diplomacy and technopolitics facilitates connections with the history of decolonization. Beyond global-scale two-bloc tensions, postcolonial perspectives have revealed the importance of the involvement of third powers as agents in Cold War politics, and highlighted the processes of co-constructed hegemony within the Cold War's most influential transnational organizations. In general, however, we find in Cold War literature on resource diplomacy a high prevalence of nuclear narratives centered on uranium, whereas other minerals are left to the expertise of economists and political scientists: this is particularly the case with oil.[26] The few publications that have focused on the technopolitics of other natural resources from a historical viewpoint are all very recent. Lino Camprubí has investigated international collaborations in prospecting in the Western Sahara during the 1960s, in connection with the role of Moroccan, French, Spanish, and American interests in the world market for phosphates. Leucha Veneer and I have explored French and British responses to pressures on oil security in the first half of the Cold War, revealing how these two former imperial powers reacted to the discovery of oil in their own territories. We have shown how these countries mobilized their surveillance and diplomatic apparatuses to gain and retain control of, or access to, oil in Algeria in the 1950s and in the North Sea in the 1960s.[27]

Significant contributions to uranium diplomacy include Jonathan Helmreich's work on the secret efforts of the US and the UK to monopolize the Western world's supplies of uranium and thorium during and in the immediate aftermath of World War II. The two countries pursued a policy of negotiations with Belgium, Brazil, the Netherlands, and Sweden, during which, Helmreich argues, governmental agencies were only partly informed of decisions taken by business and the military.[28] Collaborations between European countries in uranium prospecting programs, or of European countries with the US, have also been explored. For example, in a study by Matthew Adamson, Lino Camprubí, and Simone Turchetti, France, Spain, and Italy are depicted as trying to challenge US dominance in atomic energy production by planning strategic mineral surveying on their own territories. In devising such tactics, the three countries could count on the action of transnational figures such as scientist-diplomats, engineers, and prospectors.[29]

Exploring postcolonial development of uranium exploitation in Africa, Hecht's *Being Nuclear* investigates the problem of the status of nuclear resources, i.e. the contingent nature of their very 'nuclearity,' which varied according to time, space, and technopolitical regime. In her monograph, Hecht reveals how Western powers secured a steady and cheap uranium supply for their nuclear programs, while striving to prevent their use by politically undesirable nations.[30] In my fifth chapter, I will show how a similar argument was at the root of a NATO confrontation between the British and American delegations regarding the 'strategic' nature of the steel pipes to be used in a large pipeline system that the Soviet government wished to build.

Pipelines as political devices have been the subject of a monograph by Andrew Barry on the Baku-Tbilisi-Ceyhan oil pipeline from the Caspian Sea to the Mediterranean, built in the second half of the 2000s but debated throughout the entire previous decade.[31] Affirming the active role of material artifacts, Barry's book analyzes the critical part that material objects play in political life, and investigates how political conflicts developed around objects entangled in increasing amounts of information. From a different perspective than Barry, political scientist Timothy Mitchell has also highlighted the importance of pipelines as loci of intense political struggle, as well as the criticality of control over points of passage such as railway connections and, indeed, pipelines, for the effective flow of materials. Mitchell can arguably be said to have pioneered oil technopolitics. In a 2002 paper, he introduced an innovative device for analyzing the interplay between resources and geopolitics. "The politics of oil," he argued, "is usually explained in terms of the desire of the United States to protect the global supply. But that is not the problem. The real problem [...] is to protect the system of scarcity." In his more recent publications, he has developed this concept of scarcity production within oil-based political systems, or 'carbon democracies.'[32]

According to Mitchell, the emergence of oil as the main energy currency, gradually replacing coal, created new problems for production companies. Since oil was easy to transport over long distances, major companies—transnational, vertically integrated companies with activities in several areas of the globe—were vulnerable to cheaper oil coming from other worldwide sources.[33] In order to protect themselves, they devised new mechanisms to limit oil production and distribution, which emerged before World War II in consortium agreements that restricted the development of new oil discoveries in the Middle East, and in cartel arrangements to control worldwide distribution and marketing. After the war, in order to continue producing scarcity, the majors stimulated European oil consumption through the Marshall Plan, which funded oil-related activities, and designed the apparatus of national security as a strategy for defending corporate interests.[34]

In this work I will contend that, while Mitchell's argument on the production of scarcity seems to hold throughout the 1940s and 1950s, it begins to lose its explanatory power by the early 1960s, when the oil market came to be characterized by overproduction, mainly caused by the Soviet Union's renewed role as an oil exporter and by a large number of discoveries by independent oil companies in Africa. In looking at national security as a polite form for vested economic interest, Mitchell undoubtedly makes an important point. Yet one should not underrate another equally important observation by Jervis concerning superpower relations during the Cold War, namely that "much of international politics [was] ultimately driven by fear," and that appealing to national security, especially when potential military dangers were involved, did not merely amount to a defense of capitalist interests.[35]

Cold War fear—specifically, fear of the impact of Soviet clout on Europe's energy security—is also the basis of Per Högselius' work on the history of the origins of European energy dependence on the Soviet Union and, later, Russia. By adopting a transnational perspective similar to the one I rely on in this book, Högselius's is the first comprehensive study of the flow of gas between the USSR and Europe. It demonstrates how and why governments, as well as industrial and technoscientific administrators, sought to foster or oppose the establishment of an East–West natural gas regime that threatened to capsize prevalent Cold War logics.[36]

Returning to Mitchell's argument, while producing scarcity may be seen as a useful analytical tool as far as the policies of the major companies are concerned, it does not appear to be applicable to French and Italian national companies. The needs of firms such as the Italian public holding company, the National Hydrocarbon Authority (*Ente nazionale idrocarburi*, ENI); the French public holding company, the Bureau of Petroleum Research (*Bureau de recherches de pétrole*, BRP); and to a lesser extent the mixed-economy French Oil Company (*Compagnie française des pétroles*, CFP), were different from those of the majors. For France, especially after the discovery of oil and gas in Algeria and Central Africa by CFP's and BRP's affiliates in the mid-1950s, it became a 'national security duty' to protect those resources from the penetration of non-French companies, in particular British and American firms, and to increase production as rapidly as possible, in order to achieve the energy autonomy that French administrations had sought since the end of the war. Together with the development of a nuclear program, autonomy was seen as the principal way of repositioning France among the great powers.

Italy's technopolitics was first articulated in the protection of the gas-rich region of the Po Valley from foreign exploration, and in its preservation as ENI's private hunting ground from the mid-1940s onward. A grand scheme of oil trade, exploration, and production agreements with Middle Eastern and North African countries was developed in the following decade. When limited results from ENI's prospecting activities threatened Italy's security through a shortage of energy, the country's strategy and technopolitics changed radically: the oil that Italy had failed to find in sufficient quantities was to be purchased from the Soviet Bloc or obtained through innovative accords with Middle Eastern oil producers.

Geophysical Surveillance for National Security

In his formulation of the security dilemma, Jervis has argued that it took the form of an expansion of military and nuclear capabilities. However, he has paid less attention to surveillance and intelligence-gathering activities as a way of gaining greater knowledge of the earth's resources. In fact, however, resources became key to national security, as some countries sought to safeguard their own security—notably British and American companies trying to control oil in Italy and France—and, in so doing, undermined that of other countries. The very process leading to the maturity of geophysical sciences was intimately linked to national security. In order to fulfill the 'surveillance imperative'—that is, to build a strategic information-collecting apparatus capable of penetrating the secrets of the earth and, in so doing, of monitoring enemies and allies—states had to develop costly research programs. Knowing the ground (both above and below the surface) meant knowing one's enemy, as I will argue through analyses of transnational debates on Algerian and Soviet resources.[37]

Links between surveillance and geophysics had already been made explicit during the war. In 1942, the US Engineering, Science, and Management War Training Program sponsored a 12-week course in geophysics at the Colorado School of Mines, the first half of which covered applications of interest to the military sector, such as: locating hostile guns by sound and flash ranging; detecting airplanes by acoustic, optical, and radio methods; harbor surveillance, marine communication and signaling, radio acoustic position finding, and marine echo sounding.[38] Writing about the history of the Committee on the Geophysical Sciences, which was part of the Research and Development Board of the US Department of Defense, historian John Cloud has observed that the Committee's 1948 report could be used to interpret the transformation of the earth sciences that was about to follow:

> The Committee's members recognized that the geophysical sciences required support for basic research, for funding to address 'unsolved problems ... of a fundamental nature.' Yet they also confidently assumed that every single discipline [...] could and would contribute to specific Cold War military objectives.[39]

In fact, from the 1948 report we can frame a picture of the applications of geophysics to warfare: for example seismology, soon to become the dominant method in oil-prospecting geophysics, could be employed in studies on shock protection for surface and subsurface installations, and on hurricane detection. Its importance was not so much revealed by the funds allocated by the 1957–1958 International Geophysical Year (IGY)—funds for seismology amounting to only 2 percent of US IGY total funds, much less than other geophysical sciences—as by the constitution of the Panel on Seismic Improvement in 1959, when James Killian, US President Dwight Eisenhower's Special Assistant for Science and Technology, appointed a committee chaired by Berkner to draft a plan relating to new seismic tools for controlling and detecting nuclear tests. Finally, terrestrial magnetism and electricity, also used in oil prospecting, could be applied in mine detection, submarine detection, guidance systems for missiles, and for reducing or eliminating unwanted magnetic fields.[40]

Seismology's instrumental role as a method of intelligence-gathering during the Test Ban Treaty negotiations of 1957–1963 has also been noted: the negotiations overlapped with the establishment and development of a British–American collaboration to promote intelligence-sharing on the Soviet nuclear program. Applications of this geophysical sub-discipline to nuclear and earthquake detection and prediction have been extensively studied. Bruce Bolt and Kai-Henrik Barth analyzed how this field expanded from a small academic discipline to a large military–industrial enterprise during the 1960s.[41] Countering Paul Forman and Stuart Leslie's famous argument about the military stripping academia of its control over science and redirecting it toward their aims, Barth argues that in the case of seismology, which came under the Department of Defense's patronage in the 1960s as a consequence of the nuclear test detection mission, research trends did not substantially change. After the 1963 Limited Nuclear Test Ban Treaty was ratified, the importance of this discipline to Western security only increased.[42]

Geophysics, however, was only part of a larger network of surveillance systems that emerged from the field of earth sciences. In surveillance, systems such as satellites and video cameras, or sonar and radar, immediately spring to mind. Technologies developed within the earth sciences also facilitated other kinds of monitoring, however, such as the study of ocean currents to develop anti-submarine warfare measures, and geo-engineering and climate models to control and influence weather. These technologies may not be included among the 'flashy flagships' of Cold War, such as nuclear weapons and space exploration, but were nevertheless pillars of surveillance.[43]

From the picture outlined here, it comes as no surprise that "[t]he objectives, funding and equipment [of geophysics] were often secret, involving some of the highest levels of secrecy in history." It was indeed this aspect of secrecy which was the source of the expression 'science in black' coined by Doel to define a science based on the "large, unexplored continent of interconnections, maintained in secrecy, between scientists and public officials mutually interested in adopting science to serve U.S. interests and the national security state."[44] In this work, I show that the geoscientific information associated with oil is 'in grey,' rather than in black: in most cases, the links between geoscientists and oil companies were overt, but the handling of the intelligence they produced was secret. For example, French authorities were aware that, when they employed American geophysical firms, there might be a risk of sensitive knowledge being passed indirectly to US diplomats: the core issue was rather about how to regulate, minimize, and inform the flow of intelligence while still accessing American technologies, or about what to ask in exchange.

Investigations of geophysics' connections with military security have led to studies on the multiple aspects of the scientist's activity; however, much less attention has been dedicated to fields where the connection with the military or with weaponry is more tenuous. Yet, as Matthias Heymann and Janet Martin-Nielsen remind us, Cold War science was also conducted by actors outside the military sector and with less direct connections to Cold Warfare, namely civilian authorities, and the industrial and academic spheres. In the case of oil exploration, even the actors most directly involved, namely petroleum technicians and engineers, have rarely been the focus of scholarly attention.[45]

Yet there are many aspects of potential interest for a historian. As mentioned, the secrecy that characterizes the military–geophysical relations is also found in exploration geophysics, and on some occasions extends beyond the confidentiality of quantitative data regarding minerals, to include prospecting and processing techniques. In the oil sector, therefore, we are confronted not only with the secrecy specific to national security issues, but also with commercial secrecy: that is, the kind of information that could be the target of industrial espionage. Secrecy had its setbacks: for example, in 1947 John Jakosky, the President of the American Society of Exploration Geophysicists, underlined how the national security apparatus ended up being detrimental to the advancement of science, and lamented that:

> [M]any new applications in nearly all fields of engineering, are being retarded now due to a policy of secrecy forced upon many industrial and research organizations during the past five years. [...] Such a policy greatly retards our national progress by inhibiting the dissemination of fundamental information. It also fosters unnecessary rivalry between scientists and laboratories, with the resultant duplication of much fundamental research and studies [...].[46]

This secrecy found a powerful rationale in the aforementioned application of geophysical knowledge and equipment to matters that could greatly affect a nation's security, of which uranium prospecting is perhaps the best-known example. A further characteristic of historical studies on geophysics is that they have largely focused on the United States, thus missing the contested interests found in other continental contexts.[47] In fact, the analytical power and epistemic complexity of these studies would be significantly enhanced by focusing on other contexts and by taking into account narratives of postwar technoscience in Europe: these relate to a number of spheres, including scientific and industrial reconstruction and modernization, national science and technology policies, international competitiveness, sovereignty and identity, contexts of decolonization, among others.

By focusing on the establishment of governmental agencies for oil exploration in France and Italy, I show the modes through which most of these factors were implicated. Intelligence and governmental agencies devoted considerable attention to oil prospecting conducted both by their own country and by other states. This raised concerns about the circulation of knowledge beyond borders, as shown by the case of Algeria, where French, American, and Italian technical personnel operated during the 1954–1962 War of Independence.

On the Neglect of Oil Exploration Geosciences

Despite the fact that the study of technoscience in international relations has been a substantial subdomain of the history of science and technology since the early 2000s, out of the thirteen papers that constitute a 2006 issue of the *Osiris* review on science, technology, and international affairs, the words 'oil' or 'petroleum' are mentioned in only one. In an earlier collection dedicated to earth sciences in the Cold War by the *Social Studies of Sciences* journal in 2003, oil is mentioned only once, in relation to a technique used in nuclear detection. Conversely, when the focus of academic research has been oil, as was the case of the 2012 special issue of the *Journal of American Studies* on 'Oil Cultures,' technoscientific aspects were completely bypassed. Although only a rough index with limited value, this simple analysis reveals a gap in the literature.[48]

Why such neglect of exploration geophysics? I can see three reasons. First, to paraphrase Hecht's remark about uranium, it would appear that the technology involved in exploration geophysics is considered so conventional as to be uninteresting, especially in comparison with parts of the oil industry in which malfunctions have more immediate consequences on supplies, such as pipelines.[49] Second, oil, drilling, and geophysical companies carry out most oil exploration, and company archives may at times be harder to access than those of public bodies.[50] Third, the prominence of nuclear culture in the Cold War, and of narratives of apocalyptic warfare: put simply, oil does not fuel weapons of mass destruction, although it does fuel the planes carrying them.[51]

Charles Bates, Thomas Gaskell, and Robert Rice have tried to compensate for this neglect with their work on the technical and economic history of the development of geophysics.[52] While they delved extensively into the technology used in geophysical exploration, their focus is, again, mainly on the US. This choice is partly justified since, as I mentioned, American companies were historically, if not always pioneers, at least the main developers and users of most geophysical techniques. However, the absence of historical analysis and human agency are important limitations of this work. Doel, too, has reflected on how the earth sciences were influenced by factors outside geophysics proper, and identified one such factor in the demands from the oil and mining industries. The successes achieved by seismic prospecting, and especially seismic reflection—Doel maintains—facilitated a boom in the oil industry, and prompted several American universities to create courses in exploration geophysics.[53]

But while the politics of Cold War geophysics in the US has received attention from historians of technoscience, the very few works available on the history of French and Italian exploration geophysics have mainly been authored by people directly involved in geophysical research, such as former company employees, or have been published with celebratory intent by the companies themselves. These works mostly oscillate between markedly internalist narratives and epic tones, depicting the heroism of oil prospectors in domesticating a hostile nature in Equatorial swamps, African deserts, or North Sea storms.[54]

On a completely different level of accuracy and insight is work by historian Geoffrey Bowker. In his account of industrial dynamics at the French geophysics company, Schlumberger, from 1920 to 1940, inspired by Bruno Latour's and Michel Callon's actor-network theory, Bowker shows how the company's early developers established their own position on the industrial market, by imposing their method for the electrical testing of potential oil fields. They did so by propagating a 'mythological' narrative, which secured the company a position that enabled it to coin a new definition of technology, adapted to its needs.[55] What is important about Bowker's account is that nature, politics, science, and society are demonstrated to be part of the same activity. This intimate connection is also highlighted throughout this book, in particular in the definition of 'strategic pipes' during the NATO debate on the Soviet pipeline system.

There appears to have been greater interest in the history of geophysics in Italy than in France. However, even in the Italian case, early attempts to reconstruct this history are characterized by a chronological rather than an analytical perspective.[56] It is only in studies conducted in the last decade that this picture has begun to change, and the importance of the accumulation of technoscientific competences in AGIP/ENI's development has been brought to the attention of Italian scholarship. Business historian Daniele Pozzi started this trend. Pozzi's 2009 volume and his previous studies on technology, knowledge, and organization at the Italian oil company are the foundational references for my chapter on Italian oil history. In Pozzi's works the societal and human agency factors are emphasized, and geologists and geophysicists eventually acquire a role as agents of technological development.[57]

Relying heavily on ENI archival documents, Pozzi has been able to compellingly explain the limits of and reasons for the Italian company's place in history. While ENI's first President, Enrico Mattei, plays a central role in his account, the figure of the Italian entrepreneur is stripped of certain mythological features that characterize most journalistic works on ENI's history and Mattei (see below). While Pozzi made extensive use of Italian archives, however, the detailed focus of his work did not allow him to explore the international aspects of the company's activities to a similar degree of accuracy. In conclusion, there appear to be no historical accounts available of the role played by Italian or French oil prospecting within the broader geopolitical context of the Cold War. In my work, I try partially to fill this gap.

The Historiography of Oil Industry and Diplomacy

In October 2013, the US recovered its position as the leading oil and gas producing country in the world. As it held that position for most of the last century, it is not unexpected that, like American geophysics, the American oil economy has also received by far the most scholarly attention around the world.[58] While most works focus on specific periods or topics, no current reference gives a broader overview than Daniel Yergin's monumental world history of oil, *The Prize*, which is particularly relevant to my work for the broad international political and economic perspective it provides and the emphasis on the linkage between national strategies and global power politics.

Again, scholarly interest in the French and Italian cases has been of a different degree. Given the importance of energy issues in the reconstruction of postwar France, the major role of a few French individuals in managing the country's energy recovery, and the weight given by French administrations to energy autonomy, it is somewhat surprising that so little attention has been dedicated to the oil sector. Not unlike its Italian counterpart, French literature on oil and international relations has produced factual narratives rather than analyses. Also, while agency is frequently attributed to companies as unitary entities, information on the people who contributed through their practical activities is extremely scarce: the personification of large corporations is common, as is the absence of human agency, even in cases where geoscientific technologies and technical difficulties encountered by French companies in geological and geophysical exploration are described in detail.[59]

On the contrary, while the rare company histories available may highlight the role of the technicians, the geopolitical context or the importance of surveillance for national security are not analyzed.[60] Journalist Pierre Fontaine's contemporary works on France's role in Cold War oil diplomacy aim to demonstrate how British and American majors threatened French oil interests around the world. While inadequate by scholarly standards, Fontaine's works do at least shed light on one important aspect of my work, namely the ambiguous nature of Western alliances.[61]

As for the human protagonists of French public oil agencies, only one monograph is available, on Pierre Guillaumat, the BRP's first President, and the most prominent character in French energy institutions from the postwar years into the late 1970s. This volume was the outcome of a symposium on the French technocrat, so the tone is conversational, and the work lacks references and a bibliography.[62] This publication does, however, give a picture of the network of agencies surrounding Guillaumat, of his life and personality, and especially his capabilities in gathering intelligence (he was a former secret agent), an aspect that will also be emphasized in this book. The importance of networking among French cadres is a fundamental aspect of the history of national oil agencies, and is also stressed by Eric Kocher-Marbœuf, who has exposed the scale of the interconnection between executives of the French oil companies and governmental administrators. He and Douglas Yates have highlighted the role of French élite education and of the corps of high public officials, and particularly emphasized the function of the *Ecole Polytechnique* and the *Corps des Mines*, to which most administrators of French oil belonged.[63]

Diplomats are eventually brought into the picture in David Styan's history of French–Iraqi oil and weapons deals, in which he explores relations between France and the Middle Eastern country, especially in the second half of the 1960s. His most important insight for my work regards the importance Styan assigns to access to oil in French energy security. He analyzes how, from the late 1950s, French President Charles de Gaulle endeavored to carve a role of prominence for France in the Middle East, a region rapidly undergoing the transformation from an arena of confrontation between imperial powers to one of confrontation between superpowers.[64] I explored the issue of access to energy sources in greater depth through a number of documents issued by the French foreign counter-espionage agency (Service de documentation extérieure et de contre-espionnage, SDECE), which I was allowed to consult following an FOI request, and which enabled me to highlight the surveillance activities deployed by French authorities on allied countries.

The limited number of French sources on oil history is counterbalanced by a plethora on the Italian side which, given the smaller size of the Italian oil company, ENI, in comparison with CFP or BRP, does not seem to make sense. The reason for this imbalance can be summarized in a single name: Enrico Mattei, the man who became the symbol of Italian entrepreneurship and success while at the head of AGIP/ENI, directly or indirectly, almost without interruption from 1948 to 1962. Mattei's renown stems not only from his death in a controversial plane crash, which undoubtedly contributed to the construction of his legend, but also from the results *his* enterprise accomplished during his lifetime, results in which he played an undeniably primary role. From 1953 onward, in particular, Mattei guided ENI through an aggressive international expansion, taking bellicose stances, at various times, against American, British, and French interests, as well as against Italian private industrialists. As Guillaumat did in France, Mattei perfectly encapsulated Thomas Hughes's figure of the system builder: someone able to reconfigure an entire sector by creating new sources of capital, actively lobbying for his company's interests, and creating possibilities for expansion.[65]

The bibliography on Mattei is as abundant as his biographies: in many cases, the focus is not on the activities of AGIP or ENI per se, but rather on the man himself. This is the exact reverse of the French situation: there, humans are absent; here, there is only one.[66] The quality of these works, mainly produced by journalists, former ENI employees, and executives, varies greatly, as does their originality. Episodes described in early works are often repeated in later ones, without regard for the accuracy of sources, which in most cases are not even mentioned. This iterative phenomenon strengthened the narrative framework, which came to acquire a truth value by virtue of repetition alone: a 'meme,' in the terminology of biologist Richard Dawkins. In short, it created not just a founding myth, but an entire mythology, based on a simplistic David–Goliath dichotomy, with Mattei, a man of flesh and blood at the head of a small company in an impoverished, defeated country, pitted against the overwhelming, faceless and transnational might of British and American majors.[67]

Among these non-scholarly works, Marcello Colitti's 1979 publication is an exception in being one of the few non-recent ENI histories to make use of some archival sources. This enabled Colitti to avoid falling into most mythological traps, and to present the reader with a 'grayscale view' of events, rather than a black-and-white narrative. ENI activities have also been the subject of economic studies which, while avoiding the standard account through the examination of quantitative data on the Italian company, tend to be data-dense chronologies, where the little analytical insight offered is often drowned in financial figures and company names.[68]

For as much as these publications may provide snippets of valuable information, their quality is incomparably different from that of a set of historical works, whose publication began timidly in the 1990s, to take full shape in the 2000s. A decisive causative factor in this new trend may have been the establishment of ENI document collections in the mid-1990s, and the opening of a central corporate archive in 2006. Most of these studies center on ENI's international relations and its oil diplomacy. Even here, however, a distinction has to be made between publications based on company archives and those that are not (while still being based on other archival sources). The latter still exhibit a pronounced Mattei-centric, David–Goliath-like narrative, and do not significantly move away from the general orthodoxy reported in journalistic sources. One could argue they can be characterized by a statement that historian Warren Kimball made about post-revisionist history: "orthodoxy, plus archives."[69]

All of the sources on ENI that I have reviewed so far focus almost exclusively on the history of the company during Mattei's time. Works examining shorter periods of time, or focusing on a single geographical area, and based on ENI archives, started to appear in the early 2000s: works by Alberto Tonini, for example, center on ENI's activities in the Middle East, but Mattei still monopolizes the narratives, leaving almost no room for other company personnel.[70] The three monographs produced by international relations scholar Bruna Bagnato, on ENI's relations with the Soviet Union, Morocco, and Algeria, are strikingly different in quality: here, at last, ENI takes the place of Mattei, yet without slipping into French-style company essentialization. Bagnato's expertise on Italy's relations with France, North African countries, and the Soviet Union was particularly useful for my investigation, and in two of my chapters I attempt to develop the lines of research she traced. By framing ENI's policy in the 1950s and early 1960s within the larger context of Italian aspirations to assume a mediation role in the Mediterranean, Bagnato underlines how Mattei's entrepreneurship was indeed supported by a series of central political figures, all of whom shared foreign policy aspirations with the Italian tycoon.[71]

In her works on Italian–Moroccan and Italian–Algerian relations, moreover, she stresses the diplomatic difficulties faced by Italy and ENI when confronted with the declining, but still visible influence of France in North Africa, where the Italian oil company was endeavoring to expand its interests. In her volume on Italian 'Ostpolitik,' ENI's Soviet dealings are discussed within the wider framework of an Italian strategy of rapprochement with the USSR, via an extensive industrial strategy including many of Italy's leading manufacturers. Here, too, Bagnato emphasizes Italy's self-assigned role as a mediator, this time between East and West, and the support given by Italian political and diplomatic institutions to the intensification of commercial relations between ENI and the Soviets.[72] In my fifth chapter, I expand on Bagnato's work by focusing more specifically on the European Economic Community's (EEC) and NATO's reactions to the impending Soviet oil plans for distributing their oil to Europe.

Focusing on ENI's expansion into Iran, Ilaria Tremolada has described how this was paralleled, and indeed preceded, by a number of other Italian companies in the 1950s. Tremolada's work has the merit of acknowledging the important role played by Italian diplomatic officials in Middle Eastern countries where ENI operated. Even more importantly for my study, she highlights the part played by AGIP's geoscientific personnel as a beachhead for ENI's penetration into the Middle East. In this book, I explore this point further, and demonstrate both the dual role of ENI geoscientists in securing oil resources both nationally and internationally, and in improving the company's geophysical knowledge thanks to the cultivation of formal and informal contacts with foreign concerns.[73] The concept of technological transfer is also at the core of Elisabetta Bini's monograph on ENI's appropriation of the American concept of mass consumption as an engine of economic development. Bini shows how ENI, in its relations with oil producing countries, became not only a vehicle for the Italian model of development, but a veritable tool of cultural diplomacy in developing countries, as well as a source of economic aid. Her analysis is beneficial to my work in highlighting the diplomatic strategies and leverage of ENI's activities, particularly in the Middle East.

Overview of the Chapters

This book has a geopolitically 'telescopic' structure, with the main terms broadly identified from a national, international, and transnational perspective. In the first chapter, the geographical bases of my narratives are more or less national: while stressing the influence of international pressures, the focus is mainly on Italy, also because of the predominantly domestic focus of Italian oil exploration activities. In the second chapter, which is centered on French postwar reconstruction, the geographical base expands to include the Middle East and the French Union (i.e. former French African colonies), the main locus of the narrative remaining, however, France's European heartland—the *Métropole.*

In these two chapters, I discuss strategies developed in response to the urgency of rebuilding French and Italian oil infrastructures, as well as to the outcome of Cold War conditions. I first examine political developments in the two countries, the means through which they undertook the reconstruction of their oil industries and resumed exploration activities. In the first chapter I argue that, while the strong influence of Anglo-American oil interests in the peninsula is undeniable, materializing—among other things—in constant pressure on the Italian body politic for prospecting rights and a more favorable mining law, these were supported by the equally vocal interests of major industrialists within the Italian government, in an example of the co-production of hegemony conceptualized by John Krige.[74] However, the profound instability of postwar Italian administrations, together with the use of dilatory tactics, made the formulation of a new mining law an extremely lengthy process. In the early 1950s, the increasing influence within the governmental majority party of a political faction favorable to policies of state control also contributed to delaying privatization processes, and eventually favored the establishment of a national oil company able to withstand foreign pressures.

Paralleling my first chapter, my second investigates the reconstruction of the French oil sector within the broader context of a strong policy of modernization and re-industrialization. On the domestic side, French administrations set up a legislative apparatus that would allow them to moderate Anglo-American influence in mainland France without clashing directly with the oil majors, and incidentally supporting French commercial interests. Internationally, I show that, after CFP had barely managed to recover its position in the Middle Eastern oil arena through a legal struggle with its British and American partners in the Iraq Petroleum Company (IPC), French authorities deemed it safer for national energy security to move their core interests to territories under French rule in Africa.

That shift was accelerated by Middle Eastern political turmoil, by the growing superpower tensions in the area, and by France's declining prestige following the Suez expedition of 1956. This transition required the establishment of a series of new oil agencies charged with the exploration of the former French Empire and with the education of a class of petroleum technicians and engineers. The mobilization of a critical mass of geophysicists to Africa made it possible for France to develop extensive technoscientific knowledge, allowing a national geophysical industry to flourish. The shift to Africa soon prompted a debate on whether Algeria should be kept as an exclusively French hunting ground, or opened up to foreign exploration companies. Up to the mid-1950s, support for an all-French strategy prevailed; however, this would be dramatically challenged by the rise of nationalist movements in Northern Africa, and in particular by the outbreak of the Algerian War in 1954.

In my third chapter I extend my analysis to colonial interests during the Cold War, and expand my narrative to embrace multiple national actors, decolonization, official, and unofficial diplomacies. I demonstrate how North Africa acquired major geopolitical significance from the 1950s, especially after intense geophysical prospecting driven by the introduction of novel techniques and the reassessment of older ones, had led to important oil and gas discoveries. The new Saharan riches, together with the formulation and approval of more permissive prospecting legislation, in response to French difficulties in financing exploration in the entire Sahara, led initially to the arrival of independent American companies, and subsequently the US majors.

None of the sources I reviewed examines in depth the role played by US institutions in surveillance operations over Algerian hydrocarbon exploration. I argue that geoscientific intelligence acquired through secret surveillance operations by the US Consulate in Algiers, and then leaked to national companies, did much to arouse American oil interests, minimizing concerns over the war. At the same time, US companies were only allowed into Algeria on a number of conditions, which included the obligation to pass all the results of their geophysical surveys to French authorities. French geoscientists and oil administrators constantly monitored, either overtly or covertly, the operations of foreign companies.

I then show how the Algerian geostrategic scenario was further complicated by ENI's attempts to become involved in oil activities in the region. These took the form of the establishment of close relations between Italy and the Algerian nationalists of the National Liberation Front (*Front de libération nationale*, FLN). That generated serious tensions between Italian and French diplomacies. I claim that by tightening diplomatic relations with countries such as the US and Italy, Algerian nationalists could count on multilateral aid for anti-French purposes. In particular, I demonstrate that ENI supported the FLN not only financially but, more significantly, by leaking geoscientific and organizational intelligence, thus enabling Algerian representatives to substantiate some of their claims at peace negotiations with the French in 1961–1962.

In my fourth chapter, the geopolitical perspective is further enlarged, to become fully transnational. I first investigate how considerable geophysical endeavors throughout the 1950s resulted in a series of important discoveries and, ultimately, were the most direct cause of oil overproduction. Concomitantly, the new conditions of oil abundance prompted a decline in global geophysical activity. While the successful French prospecting effort led to the Algerian and Central African oil discoveries, turning the country into an oil exporter, results achieved by ENI both in Italy and the Middle East were more modest. ENI was therefore driven to look elsewhere for its oil supplies. The Soviet strategy of exporting oil to foreign countries dovetailed nicely with Italian needs: it was instrumental in directing ENI eastwards, and in laying the foundations of bilateral, Italian–Soviet oil agreements. While the details of the agreement have been thoroughly discussed in journalistic and academic publications, the repercussions on intra-ally relations, which were manifested in particular in debates within transnational organizations, have been relatively neglected.[75]

With the Italian–Soviet oil-for-technology barter agreement of 1960, I bring the USSR onto the scene. Tensions between the two superpowers, somewhat implicit during the Algerian War, since they were mediated by third countries, became explicit. The target of Soviet plans for oil exports was the whole Western economy. I claim that the new availability of oil for Italy and France caused a similar shift of interests in the two Mediterranean countries, from exploration to the transportation sector. I call this the 'midstream shift,' and explain how it culminated in fierce competition for pipeline construction, leading to the rapid 'pipelinization' of Western and Central Europe.

Finally, in my fifth chapter, I further expand my geopolitical framework to include supranational institutions: NATO and the EEC. I show how differing national strategies conflicted and were composed in transnational settings, and how national developments affected discussions. In particular, I analyze the question of Soviet oil exports, which was discussed by both organizations. I show how the outcomes of the plans devised to stem oil imports differed, and why this was so. In the case of NATO, I also examine in depth the question of technology transfers between the Soviet Union and some West European countries. Within the NATO setting, I discuss how concerns over the planned Soviet pipeline system led to the US delegation proposing an embargo on the export of large-diameter pipes and pipeline technology to the Soviet Union. The opposition between economic security and military security rationales developed through confrontations over technical expertise and negotiations around the notion of 'strategic' materials.

I chose 1962 as a temporal end for my work: this choice was motivated by the almost simultaneous occurrence of four events that represented breaking points either in global Cold War history or in the national histories of the two countries under study. In March of that year, Algeria acquired its independence from France. In October, Mattei's death in a plane crash marked the inception of less aggressive expansion plans for ENI. In the very same days, the Cuban missile crisis threatened to trigger a global nuclear conflict, an event that in retrospect would mark a climax in tensions between the superpowers, and prompt a switch in US military strategy from 'massive retaliation'—a full-scale response through weapons of mass destruction even in the case of a minor conventional attack—to the more nuanced 'flexible response,' entailing mutual deterrence at strategic, tactical, and conventional levels. Finally, in November 1962, NATO controversially approved the pipe embargo.

Moving gradually from the national to the transnational, therefore, we are slowly led to broaden our geopolitical focus, so that as the historical lens pans out, we are able to see oil flowing through increasingly larger landscapes, crossing states and continental borders, ultimately to encompass most regions of the world. In the Conclusion, I return to a number of core themes from the book, including geoscientific diplomacy, energy security, and the material politics of technological artifacts.

Notes

1 Angelique Chrisafis, Julian Borger, Justin McCurry and Terry Macalister, "Algeria hostage crisis: the full story of the kidnapping in the desert," *The Guardian*, Feb. 25, 2013 (https://www.theguardian.com/world/2013/jan/25/in-amenas-timeline-siege-algeria).
2 "Algeria details the deaths at In Amenas siege," *Euronews*, Jan. 21, 2013 (http://www.euronews.com/2013/01/21/algeria-details-the-deaths-at-in-amenas-siege).
3 Sheila Pulham, Eric Hilaire, Chris Fenn, and *Guardian* research department, "BP oil spill: an interactive timeline," *The Guardian*, Sep. 28, 2010 (http://www.theguardian.com/environment/interactive/2010/jul/08/bp-oil-spill-timeline-interactive).
4 Quoted from: Melvyn P. Leffler, "National Security," *Journal of American History* 77, no. 1 (1990): 143; Ronald E. Doel, "Scientists as Policymakers, Advisors, and Intelligence Agents: Linking Contemporary Diplomatic History with the History of Contemporary Science," in *The Historiography of Contemporary Science and Technology*, ed. Thomas Söderqvist (Amsterdam: Harwood Academic, 1997), 219. A number of studies carried out on US national security since the 1960s are reported in Doel, "Scientists," 232, note 20.
5 Doel, "Scientists"; Ronald E. Doel, "Constituting the Postwar Earth Sciences: The Military's Influence on the Environmental Sciences in the USA after 1945," *Social Studies of Science* 33, no. 5 (2003): 635–66; Ronald E. Doel and Allan A. Needell, "Science, Scientists, and the CIA: Balancing International Ideals, National Needs, and Professional Opportunities," *Intelligence and National Security* 12, no. 1 (1997): 59–81.
6 Kai-Henrik Barth, "The Politics of Seismology: Nuclear Testing, Arms Control, and the Transformation of a Discipline," *Social Studies of Science* 33, no. 5 (2003): 743–81; Barton C. Hacker, "Military Patronage and the Geophysical Sciences in the United States: An Introduction," *Historical Studies in the Physical and Biological Sciences* 30, no. 2 (2000): 309–13, and articles in the same issue; Simone Turchetti, "In God We Trust. All Others We Monitor: Seismology, Intelligence and the Test Ban Negotiations, 1957–1963," in

The Surveillance Imperative. The Rise of the Geosciences during the Cold War, ed. Simone Turchetti and Peder Roberts (London/New York: Palgrave, 2014), 85–102.

7 This is, for example, the case for: Daniel Yergin, *The Prize: The Epic Quest for Oil, Money, and Power*, 2nd edition (New York: Simon & Schuster, 2009. 1st edition: 1991); André Nouschi, *La France et le pétrole: de 1924 à nos jours* (Paris: Picard, 2001); Jean Prouvost, ed., *La recherche pétrolière française* (Paris: Éditions du CTHS, 1994). Yergin's *The Prize* has been followed in 2011 by his *The Quest: Energy, Security, and the Remaking of the Modern World* (London: Penguin, 2011), where narration begins in the late 1980s.

8 Robert Jervis, "Cooperation Under the Security Dilemma," *World Politics* 30, no. 2 (1978): 169. See also: Robert Jervis, "Was the Cold War a Security Dilemma?" *Journal of Cold War Studies* 3 (2001): 36–60.

9 Naomi Oreskes and Ronald E. Doel, "Physics and Chemistry of the Earth," in *The Cambridge History of Science*, vol. V: *Modern Physical and Mathematical Sciences*, ed. Mary Jo Nye (Cambridge: Cambridge University Press, 2002), 544; Theodore M. Porter, *Trust in Numbers. The Pursuit of Objectivity in Science and Public Life* (Princeton, NJ: Princeton University Press, 1995).

10 Ibid., 552; the quote is from 547.

11 Paul L. Lyons, "The Future of Geophysics," *Geophysics* 20, no. 3 (1955): 508.

12 David Thelen, "The Nation and Beyond: Transnational Perspectives on United States History," *Journal of American History* 86, no. 3 (1999): 965–75; Akira Iriye, "Transnational History," *Contemporary European History* 13, no. 2 (2005): 211–22; Patricia Clavin, "Introduction: Defining Transnationalism," *Contemporary European History* 14, no. 4 (2005): 421–40; Erik van der Vleuten, "Toward a Transnational History of Technology Meanings, Promises, Pitfalls," *Technology and Culture* 49, no. 4 (2008): 974–94.

13 Quoted from: Pierre-Yves Saunier, "Going Transnational? News from Down Under," *Historical Social Research* 31, no. 2 (2006): 119. See also: Pierre-Yves Saunier, "Learning by Doing: Notes about the Making of the Palgrave Dictionary of Transnational History," *Journal of Modern European History* 6, no. 2 (2008): 159–79.

14 Van der Vleuten, "Toward a Transnational History," has enumerated the various meanings and drawbacks of this concept in recent literature. The question of whether the history of science has ever been transnational is discussed in a special issue of the *British Journal for the History of Science*. Simone Turchetti, Néstor Herran, and Soraya Boudia, "Introduction: Have We Ever Been 'Transnational'? Towards a History of Science Across and Beyond Borders." In "Transnational History of Science," ed. Simone Turchetti, Néstor Herran and Soraya Boudia, special issue, *British Journal for the History of Science* 45, no. 3 (2012): 1–18. In the same issue, see also: Mark Walker, "The 'National' in International and Transnational Science," 359–76.

15 Turchetti, Herran and Boudia, "Have We Even Been Transnational?" 330. The phrase 'hybrid knowledge' is from: John Krige, "Hybrid Knowledge: The Transnational Co-production of the Gas Centrifuge for Uranium Enrichment in the 1960s," in "Transnational History of Science," ed. Turchetti, Herran and Boudia, special issue, *British Journal for the History of Science* 45, no. 3 (2012): 337–57.

16 Allan A. Needell, *Science, Cold War and the American State: Lloyd V. Berkner and the Balance of Professional Ideals* (Amsterdam: Harwood Academic, 2000); Vannevar Bush, *Science—The Endless Frontier. A report to the President by Vannevar Bush, Director of the Office of Scientific Research and Development, July 1945*. (Washington: United States Government Printing Office, 1945).

17 John Krige, *American Hegemony and the Postwar Reconstruction of Science in Europe* (Cambridge, MA/London: MIT Press, 2006), 11.
18 Ibid., 16.
19 Needell, *Science, Cold War*; Krige, *American Hegemony*, 35. L. V. Berkner to R. G. Arneson, Apr. 18, 1950; tab. 5; and R. G. Arneson to L. V. Berkner and J. W. Joyce, Feb. 2, 1950; tab. 6; box 64; Lot file 57 D 688; General Records of the Department of State; Record Group (RG, henceforth) 59; National Archives and Records Administration, College Park, Maryland (NARA). Archive sources as reported in Ronald E. Doel, "Does Scientific Intelligence Matter?," *Centaurus* 52, no. 4 (2010): 315.
20 Doel, "Scientists"; Needell, *Science, Cold War.*
21 The definitions of 'technopolitic' and 'technopolitical regime' are quoted from: *The Radiance of France: Nuclear Power and National Identity after World War II*, 2nd edition (Cambridge, MA/London: MIT Press, 2009. 1st edition: 1998), 15 and 56 respectively. See also: Gabrielle Hecht, "Technology, Politics, and National Identity in France," in *Technologies of Power. Essays in Honor of Thomas Parke Hughes and Agatha Chipley Hughes*, ed. Michael Thad Allen and Gabrielle Hecht (Cambridge, MA/London: MIT Press, 2001), 253–94.
22 Hecht, *Radiance*, 56.
23 Gabrielle Hecht, "Introduction," in *Entangled Geographies: Empire and Technopolitics in the Global Cold War*, ed. Gabrielle Hecht (Cambridge, MA/London: MIT Press, 2011), 2; Matthias Heymann and Janet Martin-Nielsen, "Introduction: Perspectives on Cold War Science in Small European States," *Centaurus* 55, no. 3 (2013): 226.
24 Barbara Curli, *Il progetto nucleare italiano (1952–1964). Conversazioni con Felice Ippolito* (Soveria Mannelli: Rubbettino, 2000); Simone Turchetti, *The Pontecorvo Affair. A Cold War Defection and Nuclear Physics* (Chicago: University of Chicago Press, 2012).
25 Emanuele Cassano, ed., "La Storia dei Gruppi Geofisici dell'AGIP" (Working Paper, Associazione Pionieri e Veterani ENI, San Donato Milanese, 2008), 125 (http://www.eageseg.org/download.php?f=0a3303d95dea6d87326ea2508b766c20).
26 On resource diplomacy, see: Massimiliano Guderzo and Matteo Luigi Napolitano, eds., *Diplomazia delle risorse: le materie prime e il sistema internazionale nel Novecento* (Firenze: Polistampa, 2001); Daniel R. Headrick, *Power over Peoples: Technology, Environments and Western Imperialism: 1400 to the Present* (Princeton, NJ: Princeton University Press, 2010); Gabrielle Hecht, *Being Nuclear: Africans and the Global Uranium Trade* (Cambridge, MA/London: MIT Press, 2012); Matthew Adamson, "Les *liaisons dangereuses*: Resource Surveillance, Uranium Diplomacy and Secret French–American collaboration in 1950s Morocco," *The British Journal for the History of Science* 49, no. 1 (2016): 79–105; Lino Camprubí, "Resource Geopolitics: Cold War Technologies, Global Fertilizers, and the Fate of Western Sahara," *Technology and Culture* 56, no. 3 (2015): 676–703; Turchetti, Herran and Boudia, "Introduction: Have We Ever Been 'Transnational'? Towards a History of Science Across and Beyond Borders," special issue, *The British Journal for the History of Science* 45 (2012): 319–36; Simone Turchetti and Peder Roberts, "Introduction: Knowing the Enemy, Knowing the Earth," in *The Surveillance Imperative: Geosciences During the Cold War and Beyond*, ed. Simone Turchetti and Peder Roberts (London: Palgrave Macmillan, 2014), 1–19. On oil economics and politics, see: Edith T. Penrose, *The Large International Firm in Developing Countries. The International Petroleum Industry* (London: George Allen and Unwin, 1968); Alberto Clô, *Oil Economics and Policy* (Boston/London: Kluwer, 2000); Francisco Parra, *Oil Politics. A Modern History of Petroleum* (New York: I. B. Tauris & Co, 2010).

27 Lino Camprubí, "Resource Geopolitics: Cold War Technologies, Global Fertilizers, and the Fate of Western Sahara," *Technology and Culture* 56, no. 3 (2015): 676–703; Roberto Cantoni and Leucha Veneer, "Underwater and Underground: Gatekeeping Oil Exploration During the Cold War," in *The Surveillance Imperative*, ed. Turchetti and Roberts, 45–66.
28 Jonathan E. Helmreich, *Gathering Rare Ores, The Diplomacy of Uranium Acquisition, 1943–1945* (Princeton, NJ: Princeton University Press, 1986).
29 Matthew Adamson, Lino Camprubí and Simone Turchetti, "From the Ground Up: Uranium Prospecting and Atomic Energy in Western Europe, 1945–1964," in *The Surveillance Imperative*, ed. Turchetti and Roberts, 23–44.
30 Hecht, *Being Nuclear*; Gabrielle Hecht, "Rupture-Talk in the Nuclear Age: Conjugating Colonial Power in Africa," *Social Studies of Science* 32, no. 5/6 (2002): 691–727; Gabrielle Hecht, "Nuclear Ontologies," *Constellations* 13, no. 3 (2006): 320–31; Gabriele Hecht, "A Cosmogram for Nuclear Things," *Isis* 98, no. 1 (2007): 100–8; Gabrielle Hecht, "The Power of Nuclear Things," *Technology and Culture* 51, no. 1 (2010): 1–30. On nuclear technopolitics and decolonization in India, see: Itty Abraham, "Rare Earths: The Cold War in the Annals of Travancore," in *Entangled Geographies*, ed. Hecht, 105–22.
31 Andrew Barry, *Material Politics: Disputes Along the Pipeline* (Chichester: Wiley-Blackwell, 2013).
32 Quoted from: Timothy Mitchell, "McJihad: Islam in the US Global Order," *Social Text* 20, no. 4 (2002): 5. See also: Timothy Mitchell, "Carbon Democracy," *Economy and Society* 38, no. 3 (2009): 399–432; Timothy Mitchell, *Carbon Democracy: Political Power in the Age of Oil* (New York: Verso, 2011).
33 Up to the early 1960s, the list of the 'oil majors' included the British Anglo-Iranian Oil Company, the Anglo-Dutch Royal Dutch Shell, the American Standard Oil of New Jersey, Standard Oil of New York, Gulf Oil, Standard Oil of California, and Texaco.
34 Mitchell, "Carbon Democracy," 409.
35 Quoted from: Jervis, "Was the Cold War a Security Dilemma?," 36. For a bibliography of US-Soviet mistrust, see notes 1 and 2 therein.
36 Per Högselius, *Red Gas. Russia and the Origins of Europe's Energy Dependence* (New York: Palgrave Macmillan, 2013).
37 The phrase 'surveillance imperative' is taken from Turchetti and Roberts, eds., *The Surveillance Imperative.*
38 R. Maurice Tripp, "'Geophysics in National Defense': An ESMWT Course Conducted at the Colorado School of Mines," *Geophysics* 10, no. 3 (1945): 432–3. The second half of the course dealt with the possibilities and results obtained by geophysical exploration for strategic minerals.
39 Quoted from: John Cloud, "Introduction: Special Guest-Edited Issue on the Earth Sciences in the Cold War," in "Earth Sciences in the Cold War," ed. John Cloud and Judith Reppy, special issue, *Social Studies of Science* 33, no. 5 (2003): 629–30.
40 Turchetti, "In God We Trust"; Ronald E. Doel, "The Earth Sciences and Geophysics," in *Companion to Science in the 20th Century*, ed. John Krige and Dominique Pestre (London: Routledge, 2003), 391–417; Charles C. Bates, Thomas F. Gaskell and Robert B. Rice, *Geophysics in the Affairs of Man* (Oxford: Pergamon Press, 1982), 131; Needell, *Science, Cold War*, 357; Barth, "The Politics of Seismology," 748.
41 Turchetti, "In God We Trust"; Barth, "The Politics of Seismology"; Bruce A. Bolt, *Nuclear Explosions and Earthquakes. The Parted Veil* (San Francisco: Freeman and Company, 1976). See also: James H. McBride, *The Test Ban Treaty: Military, Technological and Political Implications* (Chicago: Henry Regnery Company, 1967).

42 Paul Forman, "Behind Quantum Electronics: National Security as Basis for Physical Research in the United States, 1940–1960," *Historical Studies in the Physical and Biological Sciences* 18, no. 1 (1987): 149–229; Stuart W. Leslie, *The Cold War and American Science: The Military–Industrial–Academic Complex at MIT and Stanford* (New York: Columbia University Press, 1993).

43 Charles A. Ziegler and David Jacobson, *Spying without Spies: Origins of America's Nuclear Surveillance System* (Westport, CT: Praeger, 1995); Jacob Darwin Hamblin, *Oceanographers and the Cold War: Disciples of Marine Science* (Seattle: University of Washington Press, 2005); James R. Fleming, *Fixing the Sky. The Checkered History of Weather and Climate Control* (New York: Columbia University Press, 2010); Sebastian V. Grevsmühl, *La Terre vue d'en haut. L'invention de l'environnement global* (Paris: Seuil, 2014). See also articles in: Turchetti and Roberts, eds., *The Surveillance Imperative*. 'Flashy flagships' is a reference to Hecht's phrasing in *Entangled Geographies*, 2.

44 The first quote is from: Cloud, "Introduction," 630. Aspects of secrecy throughout the history of US policymaking are also treated in: Peter Galison, "Secrecy in Three Acts," *Social Research* 77, no. 3 (2010): 941–74. The second quote is from: Doel, "Scientists," 216.

45 Bates, Gaskell, and Rice, *Geophysics*; Barth, "The Politics of Seismology"; Doel, "Constituting the Postwar Earth Sciences"; Turchetti, "In God We Trust"; Hacker, "Military Patronage"; Heymann and Martin-Nielsen, "Introduction," 222. An example of a work on petroleum engineers, centered on the Texas petroleum engineers' fraternity, is: Edward W. Constant, "Science in Society: Petroleum Engineers and the Oil Fraternity in Texas, 1925–1965," *Social Studies of Science* 19, no. 3 (1989): 439–72. However, it is circumscribed to an area of the United States, and outside the Cold War context.

46 John J. Jakosky, "Whither Exploration," *Geophysics* 12, no. 3 (1947): 366.

47 Among others: Doel, "Scientists"; Doel, "Constituting the Postwar Earth Sciences"; Doel and Needell, "Science, Scientists and the CIA"; Joseph Manzione, "'Amusing and Amazing and Practical and Military': The Legacy of Scientific Internationalism in American Foreign Policy, 1945–1963," *Diplomatic History* 24 (2000): 21–55; Margaret Vining and Barton C. Hacker, eds., *Science in Uniform, Uniforms in Science. Historical Studies of American Military and Scientific Interactions* (Plymouth: Scarecrow Press, 2007); Fleming, *Fixing the Sky*; Oreskes and Doel, "Physics and Chemistry of the Earth."

48 The collection is: John Krige and Kai-Henrik Barth, eds., "Global Power Knowledge. Science and Technology in International Affairs," special issue, *Osiris* 21, no. 1 (2006). Oil is mentioned in: Stuart W. Leslie, and Robert Kargon, "Exporting MIT: Science, Technology, and Nation-Building in India and Iran," in "Global Power Knowledge," ed. Krige and Barth, 125. In the *Social Studies of Science* collection, oil is mentioned in: Barth, "The Politics of Seismology," 761. Ross Barrett and Daniel Worden, eds., "Oil Culture: Guest Editors' Introduction," special issue, *Journal of American Studies* 46, no. 2 (2012): 269–72, and articles included in the issue.

49 Hecht, "Rupture-Talk in the Nuclear Age," 693.

50 Only after a lengthy exchange of emails with the staff of the document center at the French *Compagnie générale de géophysique*'s (today, CGG Veritas) was I allowed to look at a very few brochures and photos. Unfortunately, these turned out not to be significantly relevant to my research.

51 A national example of the attention dedicated to nuclear narratives is a recent BJHS issue: Jonathan Hogg and Christoph Laucht, eds., "British Nuclear Culture," special issue, *British Journal for the History of Science* 45, no. 4 (2012): 479–669.

52 Bates, Gaskell and Rice, *Geophysics.*
53 Doel, "The Earth Sciences and Geophysics," 401.
54 This is the case with Louis Allaud and Maurice Martin's monograph on the history of Schlumberger's well-logging technique, but also, as is to be expected, of publications produced by the corporations themselves. See: Louis A. Allaud and Maurice H. Martin, *Schlumberger. The History of a Technique* (Hoboken: John Wiley & Sons, 1977); Compagnie Générale de Géophysique, *CGG 1931–2006: 75 ans de passion* (Paris: Hachette Livre, 2006).
55 Geoffrey C. Bowker, *Science on the Run. Information Management and Industrial Geophysics at Schlumberger, 1920–1940* (Cambridge, MA/London: MIT Press, 1994); Bruno Latour, *Science in Action: How to Follow Scientists and Engineers through Society* (Cambridge, MA: Harvard University Press, 1987); Michel Callon, "Eléments pour une sociologie de la traduction. La domestication des coquilles Saintjacques et des marins-pêcheurs dans la baie de Saint-Brieuc," *L'année sociologique* 36 (1986): 169–208.
56 Federico Squarzina, *Le ricerche di petrolio in Italia. Cenni storici dal 1860 e cronache dell'ultimo decennio* (Roma: Jandi Sapi, 1958); Manlio Magini, *L'Italia e il petrolio tra storia e cronologia* (Mondadori: Milano, 1976); Matteo Pizzigallo, *Alle origini della politica petrolifera italiana (1920–1925)* (Milano: Giuffrè, 1981); Matteo Pizzigallo, *L'AGIP degli anni ruggenti (1926–1932)* (Milano: Giuffrè, 1984); Matteo Pizzigallo, *La politica estera dell'AGIP (1933–1940)* (Milano: Giuffrè. 1992).
57 Daniele Pozzi, "Tra New York e Fornovo Taro: l'occasione mancata della Società petrolifera italiana (1945–1953)," *Imprese e Storia* 24 (2001): 361–408; Daniele Pozzi, "L'introduzione della sismica a riflessione in Italia," in *Energia per il territorio: Enrico Mattei e l'industria del metano in Italia*, ed. Andrea Giuntini and Daniele Pozzi (Lodi: Giona, 2003), 125–59; Daniele Pozzi, "L'industria degli idrocarburi in Italia: gli operatori privati e il problema dell'integrazione," in *Energia per il territorio*, ed. Giuntini and Pozzi, 37–57; Daniele Pozzi, "Techno-Managerial Competences in Enrico Mattei's AGIP: A Prolonged Accumulation Process in an International Network (1935–1965)," *Business and Economy History* 1 (2003): 1–32; Daniele Pozzi, "Mattei e la 'vecchia' AGIP: tra ipotesi di continuità e rilancio strategico (1945–1948)," *Imprese e Storia* 27 (2003): 67–95; Daniele Pozzi, ed., *La leggenda del pioniere. Diario Mazzini Garibaldi Pissard. Documenti dell'Archivio Storico*, vol. 2 (Roma: ENI, 2008); Daniele Pozzi, *Dai gatti selvaggi al cane a sei zampe. Tecnologia, conoscenza e organizzazione nell'AGIP e nell'ENI di Enrico Mattei* (Padova: Marsilio, 2009); Daniele Pozzi, "The Natural Gas Industry in Italy Since Autarky until ENI's Hegemony: 1935–1965," in *A Comparative History of National Oil Companies*, ed. Alain Beltran (Brussels: Peter Lang, 2010), 233–64; Daniele Pozzi, "Entrepreneurship and Capabilities in a 'Beginner' Oil Multinational: The Case of ENI," *Business History Review* 84 (2010): 253–74.
58 Suzanne Goldenberg, "US surpasses Russia as world's top oil and natural gas producer," *The Guardian*, Oct. 4, 2013 (https://www.theguardian.com/business/2013/ oct/04/us-oil-natural-gas-production-russia-saudi-arabia). To mention a few works on American oil economy: Gerald D. Nash, *United States Oil Policy. 1890–1964* (Pittsburgh: University of Pittsburgh Press, 1968); Anthony Sampson, *The Seven Sisters. The Great Oil Companies and the World They Made* (London: Hodder and Stoughton, 1975); Irvine H. Anderson, *ARAMCO. The United States and Saudi Arabia. A Study of the Dynamics of Foreign Oil Policy, 1933–1950* (Princeton, NJ: Princeton University Press, 1981); Michael B. Stoff, *Oil, War, and American Security:*

The Search for a National Policy on Foreign Oil, 1941–1947 (New Haven: Yale University Press, 1982); Richard H. K. Vietor, *Energy Policy in America Since 1945. A Study of Business–Government Relations* (Cambridge: Cambridge University Press, 1984); David S. Painter, *Oil and the American Century: The Political Economy of U.S. Foreign Oil Policy, 1941–1954* (Baltimore: Johns Hopkins University Press, 1986); David S. Painter, "Oil, Resources, and the Cold War, 1945–1962," in *The Cambridge History of the Cold War*, ed. Melvyn P. Leffler and Odd Arne Westad (Cambridge: Cambridge University Press, 2010), 486–507.

59 André Nouschi, *Luttes pétrolières au Proche-Orient* (Paris: Flammarion, 1970); André Nouschi, *Pétrole et relations internationales de 1945 à nos jours* (Paris: Armand Colin, 1999); André Nouschi, *La France*; Eric D. K. Melby, *Oil and the International System. The Case of France, 1918–1969* (New York: Arno Press, 1981); André Morange, Alain Perrodon and Francis Héritier, *Les grandes heures de l'exploration pétrolière du groupe ELF Aquitaine* (Boussens: Elf Aquitaine Éditions, 1992); Prouvost, *La recherche pétrolière française*; Sylvie Chauveau and Alain Beltran, *ELF Aquitaine. Des origines à 1989* (Paris: Fayard, 1998). François Roche's work on the oil major Total-Fina-ELF is instead focused on the merger of the French public and private companies Total and ELF with the Belgian Petrofina in 1999, and is therefore of little use for the period under study. François Roche, *TotalFinaElf: The French Major* (Paris: Le Cherche Midi, 2003).

60 Jean Rondot, *La Compagnie Française des Pétroles. Du franc-or au pétrole-franc* (Paris: Plon, 1962); Emmanuel Catta, *Victor De Metz. De la CFP au Groupe Total* (Paris: Total Edition Presse, 1990).

61 Pierre Fontaine, *La guerre froide du pétrole* (Paris: SCEL, 1956); Pierre Fontaine, *La nouvelle course au pétrole* (Paris: Les Sept Couleurs, 1957); Pierre Fontaine, *La mort étrange de Conrad Kilian, inventeur du pétrole saharien* (Paris: Les Sept Couleurs, 1959).

62 Georges-Henri Soutou and Alain Beltran, eds., *Pierre Gullaumat, la passion des grands projets industriels* (Paris: Institut d'Histoire de l'Industrie et Editions Rive Droite, 1995). A monograph entitled to CFP President, Victor de Metz, is also available, but it is essentially a company history, providing little information on de Metz (Catta, *Victor De Metz*).

63 Éric Kocher-Marbœuf, *Le Patricien et le Général. Jean-Marcel Jeanneney et Charles de Gaulle 1958–1969*, vol. I (Paris: Comité pour l'histoire économique et financière de la France, 2003), 243–95; Beltran, *A Comparative History of National Oil Companies*. The study I refer to is Yates, "Life Stories," within the volume.

64 David Styan, *France and Iraq. Oil, Arms and French Policy Making in the Middle East* (London/New York: I. B. Tauris & Co, 2006). On Iraqi oil, see also: Edith Penrose and Ernest F. Penrose, *Iraq: International Relations and National Development* (London: Ernest Benn, 1978).

65 Thomas P. Hughes, *Networks of Power: Electrification in Western Society, 1880–1930* (Baltimore: John Hopkins University Press, 1983).

66 According to Giuseppe Accorinti, the Mattei Foundation had counted around 150 works on Mattei by the end of 2005. Giuseppe Accorinti, *Quando Mattei era l'impresa energetica: io c'ero* (Matelica: Halley, 2006), 7. Works on Mattei also include a film by director Francesco Rosi (*Il caso Mattei*, 1972) and a comic: Francesco Niccolini and Simone Cortesi, *Enrico Mattei. Vita, disavventure e morte di un cavaliere solitario* (Padova: BeccoGiallo, 2012).

67 Richard Dawkins, *The Selfish Gene* (New York/Oxford: Oxford University Press, 1976). Just to mention a few works on Mattei: Dow Votaw, *The Six-legged Dog. Mattei and ENI—A Study in Power* (Berkeley/Los Angeles: University of

California Press, 1964); Paul H. Frankel, *Mattei. Oil and Power Politics* (London: Faber and Faber, 1966); Fulvio Bellini and Alessandro Previdi, *L'assassinio di Enrico Mattei* (Milano: FLAN, 1970); Riccardo De Sanctis, *Delitto al potere* (Roma: Samonà e Savelli, 1972); Giorgio Galli, *La sfida perduta. Biografia politica di Enrico Mattei* (Milano: Bompiani, 1976); Luigi Bazzoli and Riccardo Renzi, Il miracolo Mattei (Milano: Rizzoli, 1984); Italo Pietra, *Mattei: la pecora nera* (Roma: La Repubblica, 2002. First edition: Milano: Sugarco, 1987); Giorgio Galli, *La regia occulta. Dal caso Mattei a Piazza Fontana* (Milano: Marco Tropea, 1995); Carlo Maria Lomartire, *Mattei. Storia dell'italiano che sfidò i signori del petrolio* (Milano: Mondadori, 2004); Giorgio Galli, *Enrico Mattei: petrolio e complotto italiano* (Milano: Baldini Castoldi Dalai, 2005); Accorinti, *Quando Mattei era l'impresa energetica*; Marcello Colitti, *ENI. Cronache dall'interno di un'azienda* (Milano: Egea, 2008).

68 Marcello Colitti, *Energia e sviluppo in Italia. La vicenda di Enrico Mattei* (Bari: De Donato, 1979); Magini, *Italia*; Giulio Sapelli and Francesca Carnevali, *Uno sviluppo tra politica e strategia. ENI (1953–1985)* (Milano: Franco Angeli, 1992); Gastone Cottino, Angela Pressenda and Marcella Sarale, *Ricerca sulle Partecipazioni statali. 2. L'ENI da Mattei a Cefis. La politica del petrolio tra mito e realtà* (Torino: Einaudi, 1978).

69 This is the case of works such as: Nico Perrone, *Mattei il nemico italiano: vita e morte del presidente dell'ENI attraverso i documenti segreti* (Milano: Leonardo Mondadori, 1989); Leonardo Maugeri, *L'arma del petrolio. Questione petrolifera globale, guerra fredda e politica italiana nella vicenda di Enrico Mattei* (Firenze: Loggia De' Lanzi, 1994); Nico Perrone, *Obiettivo Mattei. Petrolio, Stati Uniti e politica dell'ENI* (Gamberetti: Roma, 1995); Benito Li Vigni, *La grande sfida. Mattei, il petrolio e la politica* (Milano: Mondadori, 1996); Nico Perrone, *Enrico Mattei* (Bologna: Il Mulino, 2001); Giovanni Buccianti, *Enrico Mattei. Assalto al potere petrolifero mondiale* (Milano: Giuffrè, 2005); Nico Perrone, *Perché uccisero Enrico Mattei. Petrolio e guerra fredda nel primo grande delitto italiano* (Roma: Nuova Iniziativa Editoriale, 2006). The quote is from: Lloyd C. Gardner, "Responses to John Lewis Gaddis, 'The Emerging Post-Revisionist Synthesis on the Origins of the Cold War,'" *Diplomatic History* 7, no. 3 (1983): 198.

70 Alberto Tonini, *Il sogno proibito. Mattei, il petrolio arabo e le "sette sorelle"* (Firenze: Polistampa, 2003). See also: Alberto Tonini, "L'ENI alla ricerca di un partner arabo: Egitto e Iraq, 1955–62," in *Diplomazia delle risorse*, ed. Guderzo and Napolitano, 205–24.

71 Bruna Bagnato, *Prove di Ostpolitik. Politica ed economia nella strategia italiana verso l'Unione Sovietica, 1958–1963* (Firenze: Olschki, 2003); Bruna Bagnato, *Petrolio e politica. Mattei in Marocco* (Firenze: Polistampa, 2004); Bruna Bagnto, *L'Italia e la guerra d'Algeria (1954–1962)* (Soveria Mannelli: Rubbettino, 2012).

72 Bagnato, *Prove di Ostpolitik*, 377–97, 507–20. An interesting account of Italy's 'Soviet diplomacy' of the time is also given in: Manlio Brosio and Federico Bacchetti, ed., *Diari di Mosca: 1947–1951* (Bologna: Il Mulino, 1986).

73 Ilaria Tremolada, *La via italiana al petrolio. L'ENI di Enrico Mattei e l'Iran (1945–1962)* (Milano: L'Ornitorinco, 2011). On ENI in Iran, see also: Massimo Bucarelli, "All'origine della politica energetica dell'ENI in Iran: Enrico Mattei e i negoziati per gli accordi petroliferi del 1957," *Nuova rivista storica* XCIV, no. 2 (2010): 465–99. Also Rosario Milano has worked on ENI in Iran, in the decade following the demise of Mattei. In terms of archive source use, his work resembles those by Perrone, in that it exclusively draws on foreign and Italian archives but not ENI's. Rosario Milano, *L'ENI in Iran (1962–1970)* (Napoli: Giannini, 2013).

74 Krige, *American Hegemony.*
75 James T. Duce, "The Changing Oil Industry," *Foreign Affairs* 40 (1961–1962): 627–34; D. L. Spencer, "The Role of Oil in Soviet Foreign Economic Policy," *American Journal of Economy and Society* 25, no. 1 (1966): 91–107; Robert E. Ebel, *Communist Trade in Oil and Gas* (New York/Washington/London: Praeger, 1970); John A. Berry, "Oil and Soviet Policy in the Middle East," *Middle East Journal* 26, no. 2 (1972): 149–60; Marshal I. Goldman, "The Soviet Union," in "The Oil Crisis: In Perspective," special issue, *Daedalus* 104, no. 4 (1975): 129–43; Jonathan Stern, *Soviet Oil and Gas Exports to the West: Commercial Transactions or Security Threat?* (Aldershot: Gower, 1987); Halford L. Hoskins and Leon M. Herman, *Soviet Oil in the Cold War.* U.S. Senate. Committee on the Judiciary (Washington: United States Government Printing Office, 1961); Halford L. Hoskins, *Problems Raised by the Soviet Oil Offensive.* U.S. Senate. Committee on the Judiciary (Washington: United States Government Printing Office, 1962).

1 The Allied Shadow

International Pressures and the Italian Oil Industry

> The Italian Government's right to enter directly into the oil business of course is recognized, but you should point out the disadvantages of that course particularly in the situation that will prevail in Italy after the war.
>
> —Joseph Grew to Alexander Kirk, 22 March 1945[1]

> I believe we have every right to attempt openly to influence legislation where American interests are at stake [...].
>
> —John Jones to Elbridge Durbrow, 16 September 1954[2]

In tatters. No other expression could better define the state of Italian industry by the end of the war. The oil sector was no exception. British and American properties confiscated by the Fascist regime and handed over to the Italian public oil agency, the General Italian Oil Company (*Azienda generale italiana petroli*, AGIP), had been damaged to varying degrees or completely destroyed, as had most of AGIP's plants. The majority of reservoirs were out of use, as were most fuel pumps. The vessels constituting the small tanker fleet had been lost or confiscated. Railroad tankers and exploration materials in the center and south of the country were lost, as the Allies had occupied these areas. AGIP's assets in Romania and Italy's African colonies had been requisitioned by the Nazis during the war, or by the Allies afterwards.[3] On top of all this, the company's exploration personnel had been halved, drilling equipment had been abandoned in Greece, Hungary, and Croatia—where spot exploration had been carried out during wartime—and only in northern Italy could geological, geophysical, and drilling operations be carried out.[4]

Commenting on Italy's postwar situation to the State Department in 1945, Alcide De Gasperi, the Italian Foreign Minister, and at a later stage Alberto Tarchiani, the Italian Ambassador in Washington, wrote in dramatic tones: "We have millions of people without shelter and clothing; entire towns destroyed; the greater part of our industries paralyzed by the lack of raw materials and fuel; the transportation system completely disorganized."[5]

By February 1945, over half the peninsula was under Allied control. The rest of the country was under Nazi occupation and the authority of the newly established Italian Social Republic (*Repubblica Sociale Italiana*), a puppet state led by former Italian Prime Minister, Benito Mussolini. With the aim of reconquering the remaining parts of the country, the Allied command devised a long-term strategy for oil matters. The instructions given by US Acting Secretary of State, Joseph Grew, to the US Ambassador in Rome, Alexander Kirk, and quoted at the beginning of this chapter, referred to aspects of a more extended plan, intended both to establish a US-like economic system in Italy dedicated to the free market economy, and to take control of potential resources hidden in the subsurface, in the name of Western security. Such a strategy would allow British and American oil companies to re-establish their dominant position in the Italian oil market, as had been the case until the advent of Fascism.

In this chapter I demonstrate that, while claiming to be assisting Italy on the path to recovery, Allied officials were effectively establishing a scheme to gain control of the Italian oil market. I will show that geoscientific intelligence played a key role in the struggle for control of oil, and that major players in this game of knowledge production sought to appropriate, distribute, conceal, and manage this information according to conflicting agendas, causing tensions of different degrees between Italian and Anglo-American agencies and officers. I then discuss the role of AGIP technicians and executives—especially that of the company's Vice-President, Enrico Mattei (Figure 1.1)—and Italian policymakers in responding to the Allied plan by challenging US influence, promoting a change of technopolitical regime in the administration of the oil business, and empowering the exploration sector with a greater degree of autonomy. In developing my argument, I emphasize the importance of gaining access to restricted geoscientific information, as well as securing land concessions to prospect.

Italian Oil Interests and Exploration Before and During the War

With the Allied occupation of southern and central Italy, industrial plants that had belonged to AGIP came under Anglo-American control. This was more a restitution than a requisition, as a number of these facilities had belonged to British and American concerns before being nationalized by the Fascist state. Early postwar management of requisitioned plants was carried out by a new structure, established by Allied Command in the spring of 1944: the Italian Petroleum Committee (*Comitato Italiano Petroli*, CIP). The Committee was administered by representatives of the newly constituted Italian Southern Kingdom, of the Allied occupying government, and of oil companies. These included Italian bodies such as AGIP, the National Agency for Fuel Hydrogenation (*Azienda nazionale*

Figure 1.1 Enrico Mattei (1906–1962).
Source: Courtesy of ENI's Historical Archive, Pomezia.

idrogenazione combustibili, ANIC)—a subsidiary of the private chemical company, Montecatini—and the Petrolea company run by the car manufacturer, FIAT. Also included, however, were the international oil majors active in Italy: in order of importance, American Standard Oil of New Jersey (SONJ), Anglo-Dutch Royal Dutch Shell, and American Standard Oil of New York-Vacuum Oil (SOCONY).

The CIP was initially to supply oil for Allied civil and military operations. The Committee's headquarters took over AGIP's offices and staff in Rome, since AGIP's headquarters had been temporarily moved to Milan.[6] Throughout its existence, the Committee was to be dominated by officials of the Allied governments and the two largest global oil companies, with AGIP enjoying very little decision-making power. The CIP soon extended its activities beyond its original functions, to the point of exerting almost absolute control over oil and gas distribution in the country until 1948.[7]

An intended effect of these circumstances was to prevent AGIP from autonomously planning the recovery of Italy's oil production, especially since the agency's wartime initiatives had striven to limit the influence of the oil majors. Allied dominance over the CIP was intended to ensure that this would not happen again. Indeed, although Allied plans indicated that the CIP would treat all the companies operating in Italy equally, the Committee actually laid the groundwork—as affirmed by US State Secretary, James Byrnes, to Kirk in August 1945—for "a fair share of the total business" to be reserved for American interests. The Committee would be dissolved when Anglo-American domination of the Italian market was restored, thus taking the national oil market back to the situation that had existed prior to Fascism.[8]

Before the constitution of AGIP, foreign oil companies had ruled the Italian oil market. Founded in 1926 by a consortium largely controlled by public administrators, AGIP was established to minimize the influence of British and American oil firms, in order to avoid threats to national oil security—embargoes or boycotts—in the event of war. At the time of AGIP's foundation, most crude oil imported by Italy came from the Italian-American Oil Company (*Società italo-americana pel petrolio*, SIAP), a SONJ affiliate, and from the Nafta Public Limited Company (*Società anonima Nafta)*, a Shell affiliate. The former owned numerous oil and lubricant companies, as well as refineries and a solid distribution network, while the latter controlled a refinery, oil, and lubricant factories. SOCONY also owned a refinery, and operated in lubricant transportation and sale.[9]

Among these large companies only SONJ was involved in oil exploration in Italy, through another affiliate, the Italian Petroleum Company (*Società petrolifera d'Italia*, SPI), active in the Po Valley in northern Italy (Figure 1.2). The creation of AGIP as a consequence of the Fascist regime's autarchic policies, intended to ensure Italy's economic self-sufficiency, challenged foreign interests, and resulted in a system of regulations for protecting national enterprises. However, in terms of exploration results, these policies did not live up to expectations.[10]

Exploration methods based on physical measurement of the earth's properties had been introduced in the very first years of AGIP's existence. Gravimetry—the measurement of anomalies in the terrestrial gravitational field with respect to an area's average—had first been employed, with encouraging results, in the Po Valley. But the scarcity of resources available to the Italian company, and the difficulties in finding adequately trained staff, had limited its operations considerably. Gravimetry, as business historian Daniele Pozzi has noted, soon revealed its inadequacy for a thorough exploration of the Po Valley. The reservoirs that would later turn out to be the most favorable were invisible to this technique, which was unable to differentiate them from the surrounding geological layers.[11]

The introduction at AGIP of German instruments for seismic prospecting, a technique for estimating the properties of the earth's subsurface from reflected and refracted seismic waves, together with AGIP's manufacture of its own equipment based on German models, prompted the company to focus on seismology.[12] Initially experimented during World War I by the French, British and Germans to locate enemy artillery,

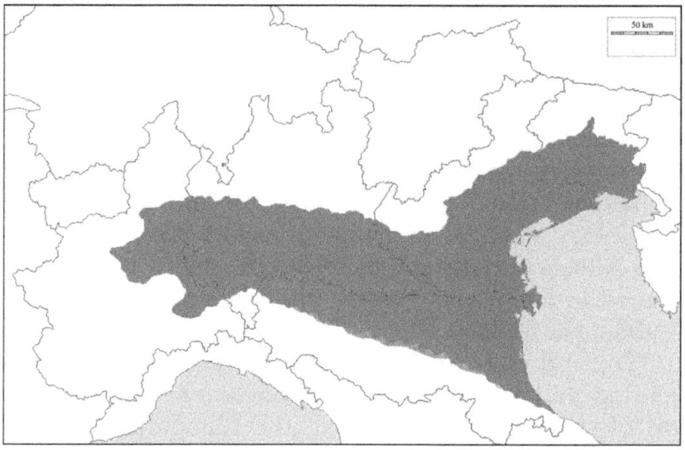

Figure 1.2 The Po Valley (shadowed).
Source: Wikimedia Commons.

seismology expanded over the following decade into seismic exploration for hydrocarbons. Blasts produced by dynamite charges buried in the ground emitted seismic waves that interacted with geological layers. Reflected or refracted waves were then recorded by seismographs, arranged in log charts and interpreted, thus giving information on the underlying geological structures.

However, while the Germans were still experimenting with this new procedure in the mid-1930s, the American geophysical industry appeared to be at a more mature stage of development. In 1936, AGIP geophysicist Tiziano Rocco had already urged his company to acquire US technology, and in the same year the Italian-American geophysicist and conservative political activist, Henry Salvatori, founder and president of the US-based Western Geophysical Company (WGC), visited AGIP's headquarters. In 1938, during an AGIP mission to the US, Rocco and his fellow geologist, Tiziano Vercelli, managed to acquire seismic reflection instrumentation created by WGC, as well as to hire one of WGC's crews. The crew was sent to Italy in mid-1940.[13]

Once in Italy, WGC carried out an exploration survey in the area of Lodi, near Milan, and began outlining some promising geological structures in the summer of 1940. However, the team had to abandon Italy in October, as war broke out, leaving AGIP all its seismic equipment. Thanks to the training received by WGC technicians during the survey, AGIP geophysicists were able to use their 'tacit knowledge' and equipment in an intense wartime exploration program. As a result, by the end of hostilities, Italian technicians were aware of the potential of the Po Valley for oil and gas, and their prolonged activity there in comparison with WGC enabled them to collect more detailed information than that possessed by American geophysicists.[14] Yet these key gas fields were yet to be revealed.

In 1944, AGIP made a further gas discovery in the Po Valley at Caviaga, but the gas field was not put into operation to avoid the Nazis taking control of it. Marcello Colitti, a former executive of the National Hydrocarbon Authority (*Ente nazionale idocarburi*, ENI)—successor to AGIP—has argued that data on the Caviaga gas field were probably disseminated widely. It is likely that besides WGC, SPI—whose director had been in close contact with an AGIP executive—as well as military intelligence, Italian partisan fighters, and Allied officials, had informed the Allied commission in Italy and the American intelligence center—the Swiss-based Office of Strategic Services—about the findings.[15]

In the 1930s and early 1940s, AGIP had then extended its activities to the refining and hydrocarbon transportation sectors, through the acquisition of a refinery near Venice, the foundation of ANIC, with Montecatini, to obtain oil substitutes by hydrogenating coal—consistent with Fascist autarchy plans—and the subsequent construction of two refineries for ANIC's use. In order to manage the construction of an Italian gas pipeline network, a dedicated company, the National Company for Methane pipelines (*Società nazionale metanodotti*, SNAM), had also been established. From this picture, we can see that, although the power of Italian industry in the country's oil sector was not comparable to its Anglo-American counterpart, it had been steadily, albeit slowly, increasing.[16]

AGIP pursued a fairly lively policy of exploration during its first two decades of existence. As well as a geophysical program including extensive gravimetric and seismic surveys in both large- and mid-scale reconnaissance, and a systematic series of geological surveys covering several of Italy's regions, the company had drilled 372 wells, half of which were exploratory. This effort demonstrates the importance AGIP attributed to the search for new, potentially oil-rich, geological structures. Prospecting had also been done outside Italy, mainly in Italian colonies in the Horn of Africa, in Libya and Albania, and more intermittently in Romania, Greece, Hungary, and northern Yugoslavia. Exploration in both Italy and its colonies had already attracted foreign interests during the conflict. The political situation in the early postwar years in Italy, and the new global geopolitics, soon gave the victorious Western powers an opportunity to try to assert their influence over Italian resources.[17]

A Grand Scheme of Action

Italy's political and infrastructural reconstruction coincided with the early years of the Cold War. From 1947, Europe's political scene was to be modeled to a significant extent by both the postwar status quo and by the autonomous or heteronomous decisions of governments about their alignment within the Western or Eastern spheres of influence. In this context, the pro-American stance of Italian, Christian Democrat-led (*Democrazia Cristiana*, DC) administrations left no room for doubt: Italy would be aligned with the United States.

Beside commercial interests, political and geostrategic factors connected with American security also had much to do with Allied interest in Italy. The American government particularly feared the widespread sympathy for the Communist Party (*Partito comunista italiano*, PCI) in the Italian population. The PCI's strong anti-American and pro-Soviet ideology threatened to jeopardize the actions of the country's government, and consequently its alignment with the Western world.

Such concerns were fully exploited by successive Christian Democrat administrations in negotiations with the American authorities. The continuing rationale behind Italian political pressure on the American government was that, without Washington's help, Italy would fall to Moscow. It was this 'tyrannical weakness' that enabled Italy at various times to obtain from the American administrations more than the latter would initially be disposed to concede.[18] Such were American anxieties before the most polarized elections in Italian history took place in April 1948, that the National Security Council (NSC) kept itself busy figuring out likely political scenarios after a victory of the People's Democratic Front, essentially a coalition of the Italian Communists and Socialists, and devising measures to prevent such an outcome. Actively supporting DC-led administrations was therefore an entirely logical decision for US President Harry Truman's government. The US administration and American concerns certainly took considerable advantage of their position as occupying powers and of Italy's poor economy: for example, they supplied covert party funding, and disseminated both propaganda and qualified financial aid. They managed to influence Italy's postwar administrations in this way, but it should be emphasized that the latter general *already* looked favorably on Allied anti-Communist initiatives.[19]

Besides its delicate political situation, there was a further reason why controlling Italy was important to the Anglo-Americans. From a geostrategic point of view, Italy—because of its position in the middle of the Mediterranean—dominated oil supply lines from the Middle East, where the US and British majors had significant assets (see Chapter 2). In addition, due to its geographical proximity to the Balkans, it was also vital both in the surveillance of Mediterranean traffic and as a possible departure point for military air actions directed eastwards. Finally, there was also an economic rationale, again connected to oil: the peninsula was an almost-obligatory point of passage between Arabian oilfields and the fast recovering, oil-thirsty Central European markets: hence the importance, as I will explain later, of installing a substantial network of refining plants here. Italy's geostrategic and commercial role was at the root of US Rear Admiral Ellery Stone's conviction, expressed in June 1945, that it was essential to make Italy the chief US ally in the Mediterranean.[20]

America's State, War and Navy Department Coordinating Committee seemed to concur with Stone's opinion, and in 1949 these geostrategic concerns informed the US government's decision to push for Italy's inclusion in NATO. While Italy would be a US ally, however, its status as a country in need of protection meant that its contribution to any proactive strategy was limited. It entered the organization as a lesser power, and only after prolonged hesitation on the part of all the instituting members of the 1948 Treaty of Brussels (Belgium, France, Luxembourg, the Netherlands, and the UK). Five years later, the instrumental role of Italy's refineries within US military plans were laid bare in a top secret memorandum by the US Joint Chiefs of Staff, which instructed that once Italian oil refining facilities returned to full operation, they should fulfill not only the needs of the Italian armed forces, but also those of other NATO countries.[21]

Finally, in the Allied stance vis-à-vis Italy there were aspects related to the hoarding of concessions and potential resources. After the war, AGIP was still dismembered and weak. Prior to the Caviaga discovery, the company's headquarters had been moved to Milan, with only a subsidiary office remaining in Rome. After Italy's partition and the formation of the Italian Social Republic and the Southern Kingdom, communications between the north and the south of the country had been interrupted.[22] In these circumstances, AGIP could hardly do any harm to American interests in Italy, so British and American companies, flanked by large Italian private companies such as Montecatini, attempted to take advantage of this situation to expand their activities at the expense of the public authority.

The Anglo-American course of action outlined by Grew in March 1945 had in fact been initiated somewhat earlier: in February, Grew had written to Kirk about an initiative devised in cooperation with the British government, concerning the liquidation of some of AGIP's properties and, in compensation for war damages, the transfer of their ownership to Anglo-American concerns. The constitution of the CIP was indeed part of the larger framework of American postwar foreign oil policy, revealed at the Chicago Council on Foreign Relations in December 1944 by the US Interior Secretary and head of the Petroleum Administration for War, Harold Ickes. The substance of its main tenets was: to assert influence in foreign governments' management of their own oil resources, and to ensure that access to international primary sources be embedded in a free market economic system.[23]

The stress on the free market is not surprising, since such a system would benefit those companies that could wield the greatest power and economic assets at international level, that is, American and British companies in the case of oil. The underlying view was that world resources could be exploited for US energy needs, and that recovery programs in US-allied countries would be more pliable to those needs, as the European Recovery Plan (ERP, also known as the Marshall Plan) was to demonstrate (see below). It was in this context that, from 1944, AGIP's board of directors started cooperating with the CIP in matters of war damages and the restitution of confiscated properties.[24]

Diplomatic initiatives, however, were accompanied by more stealthy intelligence work. In February 1945, an American petroleum adviser called West, secretly operating in Italy, informed the US Embassy in Rome that the country's authorities had not abandoned their intention to establish a strongly state-controlled oil policy. Consequently, Grew wrote to Kirk in March that there would be grounds for "considerable concern" should the Italian government contemplate pursuing a prewar oil policy in the new postwar context. Grew instructed Kirk to talk to Italian Prime Minister, Ivanoe Bonomi, in order to ensure that the Italian government aligned itself with the oil policy the Allies intended to pursue, and suggested that the Foreign Office take the same initiative. In fact, the idea of deploying a joint Anglo-American diplomatic effort in this sense had already been formulated in January 1945.[25]

It is important to remember that postwar Anglo–Italian relations were characterized by tensions. Winston Churchill's government held a much harsher attitude towards Italy than its American counterpart. Before the end of the war, as a 1945 report by the Office of Strategic Studies revealed, the British services (in particular the intelligence officer, Francis Rennel Rodd), together with Italian Army General, Giuseppe Castellano, and with the help of families belonging to the Sicilian mafia, devised a plan to bring about the secession of Sicily from Italy by funding the island's separatist movement. The UK had strong interests in the Sicilian sulfur industry, and its government planned to transform the complex of Sicily and the smaller island of Pantelleria, halfway between Sicily and Tunisia, into a new Malta, thus creating a strategic triangle in the Mediterranean.[26]

As far as Italian colonies in Northern and Eastern Africa were concerned, Anthony Eden, Churchill's Foreign Secretary, explained that Italy's return to the Red Sea area should be prevented because of British strategic interests. In addition, only control over the Cyrenaica and Tripoliania regions in northern Libya would allow the UK to build military bases, thus securing Mediterranean routes for its national economic and commercial interests.[27] We hardly need to recall the value of the Suez Canal and the Red Sea to British maritime transportation—especially oil tankers—to understand the importance to the UK of acquiring influence over former Italian colonies.

This explains why, even up to 1948, Italian pleas to the Foreign Office for concessions regarding former colonies were rejected "almost with contempt" by His Majesty's Government.[28] British plans for Italian colonies, however, clashed with American intentions of exerting their own influence on the Mediterranean Sea. While the British and American authorities were divided over this issue, they agreed that the role Italy's indigenous energy sector should play in the reconstruction of the Italian oil industry ought to be reduced.

The Allies' clear intention in the oil sector notwithstanding, the Italian government was not convinced that this was the fairest route to follow. The Italian Foreign Minister, De Gasperi, declared that it was one thing to repay the damages suffered by British and American companies as soon as possible, but that dismantling the public oil agency was a completely different matter. Compensation, he maintained, would be effected in money, not by ceding public assets to private interests. The Italian government had apparently no intention of bailing out and liberalizing the entire oil industry. Oil distribution apparatus and industrial plants were the only means available to Italy to stimulate cooperation with Allied concerns, and thus create, within certain limits, a competitive regime in the country.[29] Obviously, US officials were not merely putting requests to the Italian authorities, but also applying pressure directly on AGIP.

Back in April 1945, DC Senator, Arnaldo Petretti, a former vice-president of AGIP, had been appointed to the company's presidency. In his first address to the board of directors, he acknowledged that a resumption of AGIP's normal business was subject to the decisions of the Allied authorities, and that the Italian company would have to defer for the time being all exploration employing state funding, with the exception of a few ongoing activities that showed a significant or real chance of success. As Colitti has commented: "It is not clear whether this was 'elastic' defense by the enterprise, or a genuine decision in favor of the dismantling of the exploration sector."[30]

As for commercial operations, all power was in the hands of the CIP. In May, two Allied colonels, one from the Allied Military Government and a second from the Allied Headquarters' Petroleum Section, informed the Italian authorities of their decision that oil products imported by the Allies be exclusively distributed through Italy by the CIP. In the face of Anglo-American pressures, both in terms of the colonels' messages and the joint diplomatic campaign, Petretti reassured the American Embassy that no policy of exclusivity or monopoly would be adopted in AGIP's favor.[31] The CIP did, however, adopt a policy of preferential treatment in favor of foreign concerns. When the Committee started rebuilding refining plants with its own funds or in collaboration with oil companies, it reserved its priority aid for refineries owned by majors.[32] In fact, the Anglo-Americans were particularly concerned about Italy's refining capacity, for the geostrategic and economic reasons I previously explained. Their intention was to turn Italy into Europe's refinery.

The importance of Italian oil for American commercial interests was described in a 1943 Intelligence Memorandum. The document recorded forty-four American enterprises that had each directly invested over $30,000 in Italy. Overall, such enterprises had invested over $73 million. SONJ alone had contributed ca. $25 million, equivalent to 33.9 percent of all US investments in Italy. SOCONY ranked third (ca. $9 million) in the list, and Texaco eighth (ca. $2 million). The oil industry, the memorandum underlined, represented by far the largest investment category for American concerns, amounting to almost 49 percent of the total.[33] As for British oil interests in Italy, I have already mentioned the considerable assets Shell owned in the country in the refining and distribution sectors (in the jargon of oil, these two sectors are usually described as the 'downstream', by contrast with exploration and drilling operations—the 'upstream'—and oil transport and the wholesale market—the 'midstream'). Anglo-American oil interests had therefore to be protected, either openly or secretly, as demonstrated by the attempt to get hold of geophysical data in the hands of AGIP.

'Old' AGIP's Early Victory

On 30 April 1945, Enrico Mattei, at the age of thirty-nine, was appointed extraordinary commissioner of AGIP by the National Liberation Commission for Northern Italy. In June his role was acknowledged by the Allied command.[34] Born in 1906 into a middle-class family in central Italy, by 1931 Mattei had gone into the chemicals industry in Milan, where he developed links with the local *haute bourgeoisie* of the socialistic Catholic milieu from which Christian Democrat cadres would later emerge. In July 1943, members of this intelligentsia, who would later form the party's left-wing faction, had already established the guidelines for postwar DC policy. In economics, these consisted of advocacy of state intervention combined with acceptance of the free market; in politics, marked sympathies for developing countries. These ideas deeply influenced Mattei's conception of the state as the prime mover in economic matters.[35] Following the armistice of September 1943, Mattei had joined the Resistance movement, and in 1944 he represented the DC faction among the partisans. When he was called to AGIP, his duty was to supervise its workforce and assets during the transition from a divided to a unified company.[36] It is in these circumstances that the role of geoscientific intelligence came to the fore.

Facing the possibility of a purge of Fascist collaborators, AGIP's geologists and geophysicists, who had moved to the north of the country under the Social Republic's regime, and had collected critical geoscientific data, approached Mattei directly. It may well have been in these circumstances that the latter met geologist Carlo Zanmatti for the first time. Zanmatti had worked at AGIP during the Fascist era, and had subsequently been laid off in May 1945. After Mattei's appointment, he and other company geologists started sending the vice-president technical notes. One of these criticized the current prospecting operations being carried out by AGIP, and dismissed the majority of prewar exploration activities as fruitless. The rest of the document was dedicated to the Lodi area near Milan, where the Caviaga field was located. Its authors suggested this was an oilfield that had not yet been brought to light, and that further discoveries in the Po Valley were possible.[37] AGIP, the technicians claimed, was the only enterprise with sufficient resources and experience to develop an extensive geophysical program. Works should start at a rapid pace, as information about the reservoir had been leaked to SONJ.[38]

According to Daniele Pozzi, the tone of the note was probably exaggerated, but this was deliberate, as AGIP's geologists attempted to convince Mattei, who was not a technician, to revitalize prospecting works by presenting him with a "functioning 'black box'"—a treasure chest waiting to be opened.[39] These tactics highlight the influence of AGIP technical personnel in decision-making processes. Without the expertise and persuasiveness shown by its geoscientists, AGIP might well have remained a predominantly commercial company. This factor is very often underrated by those accounts that attribute the continuation of exploration operations exclusively to Mattei. In the summer of 1945, following meetings with company geoscientists, Mattei authorized the drilling of a second well at Caviaga.

However, expanding operations would need adequate financial backing, and that would not come smoothly. In November 1944, AGIP counselor and head of the General Directorate of Mines, Luigi Gerbella, asked the Treasury Minister and Liberal Party member, Marcello Soleri, to allocate public funds to AGIP's 1944–1945 prospecting program. However Soleri, a staunch supporter of the free market, stated his unwillingness to use public funds for exploration, and instead suggested that the old AGIP sites should be wound up (though not explicitly mentioning Caviaga, which had been surveyed using AGIP's own funds).[40]

According to political historian Giorgio Galli, representatives of the major oil companies, who arrived in Rome in the summer of 1944, put Soleri under pressure. Among them were Richard King Mellon of Gulf, an expert in Italian oil matters, and the eminent geologist and oil economist, John Elmer Thomas, who had close links with the US Ambassador in Italy, Kirk. Thomas had already surveyed the geology of Italy in the early 1930s. In August 1944, he was also allowed to view documents discovered by the Allies both at the Ministry of Agriculture and in AGIP's offices, and may have realized that the country's potential was even greater than he had previously imagined. This case proves that confidential information about Italy's underground reserves had already started to be leaked to Allied officers. In order to prevent further disclosure to foreign interests, as Mattei wished, Soleri's friendly approach to the Anglo-Americans would have to be reversed. This reversal was assisted by one instance of what would become a distinctive trait of Italy's postwar period, namely cabinet crises. Indeed, on meeting Mattei, the Industry Minister, Giovanni Gronchi, suggested he should stall, as one such crisis would soon oust Soleri from the government.[41]

In this way, while acquiescing to Soleri's guidelines, AGIP's board deferred any final decision about public-funded activities until relations could be reestablished between the Milanese and Roman company offices. A technical commission was established by the headquarters in Rome, under Gerbella's supervision, to make decisions on which sites to keep running. In October 1945, AGIP's board was reunified and brought back to Rome. Mattei was appointed as one of its two vice-presidents.[42]

At this point a conflict ensued, pitting the 'new' AGIP against the 'old': the former, younger faction advocated a rapid transformation of the enterprise's structure, and greater autonomy for the exploration branch; the latter, older faction supported a focus on commercial strategy, the recovery of financial stability and, in short, continuity with the prewar organization. As this characterization shows, besides being a generational dispute, it was also a quintessentially technopolitical one: the 'new' AGIP would bet heavily on enhancing the technological potential of the enterprise, while the 'old' AGIP would rather keep it to a minimum. Petretti, the most influential representative of the 'old' AGIP, would not take any significant independent initiative until a plan had been devised with the central political authorities.[43]

Before the end of the year, Gerbella's report was presented to the board of directors. It recommended terminating exploration activities in southern and central Italy and focusing efforts on the Po Valley. As a consequence of this report, Petretti announced that studies carried out by AGIP in areas slated for withdrawal would be made available to technicians working for other firms, so that private companies would take up the baton.[44] Such disclosures went against the advice of Mattei and the AGIP geoscientists. They not only meant capitulating to foreign interests but, more importantly, handing over an impressive amount of sensitive data about Italy's subsurface to companies possessing far more advanced exploratory apparatus. This might allow them to extract more valuable information from AGIP's data than the Italian company itself held, thus compromising AGIP's (and Italy's) future energy security. It would give an additional weapon to the oil majors already backed by the diplomatic might of their respective countries. For the majors, Petretti's decision was a considerable bonus, allowing them to acquire data based on years of work and considerable expense. This was AGIP's most valuable asset since, as Kirk's oil economy adviser, Elmer Thomas, noted, success in oil exploration consisted of "90% data, 9% technical capabilities, 1% luck."[45]

However, it appeared to be too late to contest Petretti's decision, as he had already informed representatives of SONJ and Shell of his willingness to facilitate their participation in the country's exploration.[46] When Petretti informed the board of contacts made with Shell representatives, he was probably referring to a request he received from CIP's President, and the local manager of Shell's Italian affiliate Nafta, Alberto De Graan, to carry out exploration studies in Italy. The AGIP board approved Petretti's 'oily deal' and provided information to a Shell geologist named Taverne, who visited the company's sites in the Po Valley in early 1946. Although Petretti's authorization excluded the Caviaga area, it appears that Taverne had already visited the area in January 1945. SPI's geologist, Carl Wiedenmayer, was also allowed to see AGIP's technical reports, and visited Lodi on 15 February. Later on, Leutzinger, a Gulf geologist, also obtained data from the Lodi office.[47]

In March 1946, a further commission was formed to evaluate sites to be abandoned in southern and central Italy. For this purpose, contact was established with Ralph Bolton, SONJ's Manager for European operations, as well as with Wiedenmayer, Taverne, and with the MacMillan Company, Gulf's affiliate for exploration. WGC also brought forward a proposal for funding AGIP's studies in the most promising area of the Po Valley, but the board rejected this.[48] A year later, the trend initiated by Petretti was still ongoing. The American company Sinclair Oil was authorized to look over geological studies carried out in East Africa by AGIP, in exchange for copies of future reports drawn up by its geoscientists, and a lump sum payment of $25,000 if commercially viable oil discoveries were made. Through the former provision, AGIP at least attempted to obtain new data on Italy's former African colonies.[49]

In the summer of 1946 the Treasury Minister, Epicarmo Corbino, recommended that AGIP should be wound up. Petretti disagreed, explaining to Corbino that AGIP's activities were in a recovery phase, that the conflicts with the CIP on compensation for war damages were about to be resolved, and financial stability had been restored, thus implying there would be no grounds for liquidation. Petretti then gave notice that talks were in progress for AGIP to bring in foreign capital in order to revitalize the refining sector. Gaining support from a major could neutralize the risk of liquidation and diplomatic pressure from the Anglo-Americans. Negotiations were ongoing with Britain's Anglo-Iranian Oil Company (AIOC, later British Petroleum).[50]

While disagreeing about liquidation, Petretti believed that a reorganization of the enterprise should be undertaken. It was precisely with this rationale in mind that Mattei presented his plan to the board. The picture Mattei presented, however, was very different from Petretti's. Mattei saw relations with British and American companies as problematic. Until the issue of war reparations was settled, the Italian company could not properly adjust its balance sheets. But Allied companies refused to take back their equipment and personnel until the latter were first dismissed, so that they could then be rehired with no length-of-service benefits.[51] Obviously this situation favored the status quo, with the result that AGIP remained paralyzed while SONJ, SOCONY and Shell resumed their own marketing activities.

In April 1947, negotiations with AIOC eventually reached a successful conclusion. The British company would supply AGIP with crude oil and refined products from its Venice refinery for ten years. Moreover a company, with AGIP as majority stockholder, would be constituted to manage the refinery and its supplies. While AGIP secured itself a friendly collaboration with the British major, the situation was sensitive for Italian oil security, as AIOC would supply fuel to planes in Italian airports and ships moored in Italian harbors, including military aircraft and vessels.[52]

The April meeting was the last that Mattei attended as vice-president. In November 1946, Gerbella's appointment as general manager of AGIP was an unmistakable signal that the board of directors was seeking continuity with the past, that the 'old' AGIP had won, and that the more dynamic exploration and restructuring program proposed by Mattei had been rejected.[53] However, Mattei maintained his position as a director on the board, and helped to stimulate further exploration activities in the Po Valley. By the end of the year, AGIP's board had devised a program of geophysical surveys that involved the employment of a second WGC seismic crew. At this time AGIP also negotiated with the French company Schlumberger for a crew to be dispatched to Italy to execute electrical well logging. This procedure, pioneered by the French firm, provided a detailed record of the more superficial geologic layers, prior to the drilling of an actual well. Given the high costs of drilling, the technique would bring significant savings if oil was eventually found. Contacts with Schlumberger strengthened over time, and AGIP technicians periodically took part in training courses at the company's offices in Paris.[54]

While awarding its surveys mainly to foreign contractors, AGIP was also attentive to international advances in geophysics. Beside the more conventional techniques, the Italian company was open to experimentation with technical novelties, for example closely following developments with radioactive logging in the US. Radioactive logging was especially designed for prospecting inside cased wells—where electrical logging was of no use—to survey the amount of hydrogen-containing substances in rock. This indicated the location of porous and potentially oil-bearing rocks. The method had been the subject of a study by a geophysicist from the Geological Office of the Italian Mining Service, and it had been proposed that AGIP should experiment with it. The board had approved both the expense and the execution of the experiments.[55] The board also asked the eminent Italian physicist, Bruno Pontecorvo, who had developed neutron well logging, to collaborate with AGIP. Yet, contends Pozzi, following Rocco's departure from the company early in 1948 due to a decrease in prospecting activities, and the handing over of the geophysical sector to Camillo Contini, interest in theoretical studies prevailed over applications of geophysics for the location of suitable geological structures.[56]

However, further developments in exploration activities seem to qualify the view that the 'old' AGIP adopted a totally passive attitude in this sector. In April 1948, AGIP engineer Cesare Gavotti presented a program of activities to the reconstituted Consultancy Committee for Exploration to be carried out from 1948 to 1950, which included geological, gravimetric and seismic works, and which had been commissioned by Petretti. The program also included areas that had not previously been explored using seismic techniques.[57] Ultimately, therefore, it can be argued that while CIP's efforts to control the management of oil activities in Italy had been partly successful in acquiring geoscientific knowledge, with regard to the allocation of permits it had effectively been countered by AGIP's delaying tactics and revival of prospecting activities. Prospecting activities were to undergo rapid development in the following years, after the 'new' AGIP took control.

'New' AGIP Takes Over and Reorganizes Exploration

Having resigned from the vice-presidency of AGIP, Mattei did not remain idle. His growing engagement in political activity presented him with the chance to return to AGIP in a stronger position, when the board was revamped in the spring of 1948. In order to understand how he achieved this, we need to turn to the broader national and international context. In April 1948, the first postwar political elections took place in Italy. A DC-led government then replaced the tricky collaboration between parties with different political allegiances that had characterized the years following the Liberation. The formulation of the Truman Doctrine now produced a marked opposition between the Socialists and Communists on one side, and the Christian Democrats on the other.[58] Mattei was a DC candidate, while he also campaigned against the Communists for De Gasperi, in exchange for the latter's concession of extensive decision-making power in the management of oil affairs.

These elections represented a fundamental turning point in Italian history. They marked the defeat of the Left, with the Socialist and Communist parties together achieving 31.0 percent of the votes, and the DC obtaining 48.5 percent. The Christian Democrat victory was strongly supported by American initiatives. In November 1947, for example, the NSC had advised the US government that due to "security interests of primary importance," it was necessary to support De Gasperi's cabinet. This entailed economic aid through the Marshall Plan, further loans for reconstruction, the maintenance of grain shipments, improving the capabilities of internal security forces, and winning the propaganda war.[59]

Furthermore, the NSC suggested, Italy's main foreign policy objectives, such as the revision of the Peace Treaty, United Nations membership and border claims against Yugoslavia (known as 'the Trieste question'), might also have to be supported. Significantly, the NSC ruled out the use of American armed forces if a civil war should occur.[60] In the same month, the newly established Central Intelligence Agency (CIA) was asked by Army Chief of Staff Dwight Eisenhower, to shortlist a number of Italian agents for possible covert operations in Italy. A military plan was also laid out, to strengthen Italian internal security through an increased supply program.[61]

In January 1948, the US Ambassador in Rome, James Dunn, warned Washington of the rising strength of the Left; a Communist coup—he wrote—might happen in the near future. These revelations prompted the NSC to abandon its anything-but-the-military stance.[62] A list of further pre-emptive measures was devised, including declarations by key US congressmen and the State Secretary, George Marshall, that the American economic assistance Italy had so far been receiving would be discontinued in the event of a Communist victory. In addition, the US would press for Italy's immediate inclusion in negotiations for the Western Union, and for Italian participation in allied consideration of economic matters in Germany.[63]

During the period preceding the elections, the Italian government did not put a stop to overt and covert American operations. On the contrary, De Gasperi supported and even solicited them: an attitude which, at least in the case of Italy, seems to confirm historian Geir Lundestad's claim that the US became an empire 'by invitation'. In the electoral campaign, Mattei was the main architect of a fracture between Communist and non-Communist (mainly, Catholic) partisans. Their first congress in Milan in February brought about a split in the partisan association that had already taken place in parliament when, in May 1947, De Gasperi, appointed Prime Minister in December 1945, excluded Communist and Socialist ministers from his cabinet. As I will show in the next chapter, during this period the French government had made an analogous move. The recent changes had presumably been favored by the Truman Doctrine, which allowed for the sale of modern US weapons to French and Italian armies at symbolic prices, in exchange for measures to limit Communist influence.[64]

Drawing on the links he had developed with the DC establishment, when DC won the elections in April, Mattei used this success, De Gasperi's support, and the support of the new Minister of Finances, Ezio Vanoni, to make a bid for power at AGIP. In June, a new board of directors was elected, and Marcello Boldrini, a renowned professor of statistics in Milan, who was also Mattei's friend and mentor, was appointed to the presidency, with Mattei becoming one of the two vice-presidents. The 'new' AGIP finally had the upper hand on the 'old'. The technopolitical conflict between the two had thus been won outside the company itself.

During the final period of Petretti's presidency, the prospecting sector had restored its balance sheets thanks to the revenues from Caviaga's methane gas, which had started feeding a pipeline in Milan's industrial district.[65] The creation in July 1948 of the Technical Committee for Exploration and Production (*Comitato tecnico ricerche e produzioni*, CTRP), including Mattei, geologists Ramiro Fabiani and (albeit unofficially) Carlo Zanmatti, was intended to provide a strong decision-making structure for future AGIP exploration and technical activity. Its dynamism took the form of a five-year plan for the exploration of the Po Valley, which included the completion of geophysical prospecting works within the first three years, together with the execution of over two hundred surveys and the start of production activities in at least two other gas fields.[66] Such intense expansion was undoubtedly supported—as I will show in the next section—by the discovery of oil and gas at Cortemaggiore in the Po Valley, announced to the press in June 1949.

The following year, the establishment of a Mining Directorate in Milan significantly increased the freedom of action of the company's exploration branch. The Directorate propelled the expansion and modernization of geophysical equipment, the purchase of new drilling materials, and new contracts with specialized US companies for work and personnel training. For geophysics, this meant WGC, and in turn entailed the resumption of a more formal collaboration with the geologist Rocco, who had been working for the American company after leaving AGIP, and was rehired in 1951. Rocco's transnational experience was transferred to AGIP and was instrumental in fostering more frequent connections with WGC. In the same year, Zanmatti returned to the helm of the mining section to supervise the expansion of the oil-prospecting sector.[67]Attending regular meetings that began to take place between AGIP's staff and its foreign and Italian contractors, he discussed the problems facing exploration, in what represented the embodiment of AGIP's joint production of geoscientific knowledge. From 1949, AGIP also offered scholarships to young university graduates, who could then be hired and trained in the field.[68]

Even before his return, Rocco had coordinated AGIP's seismic works within a committee formed by Italian and American geophysicists. In addition, all newly appointed AGIP geophysicists were being sent for a training period to WGC's central offices in the United States, as there was no adequate university course in applied geophysics available in Italy at that time. Only the Lerici Foundation at Milan Polytechnic owned sufficient experimental equipment to execute its own oil geophysical studies. Italian technological dependence in geophysics not only on the US, but also on France, was due first and foremost to structural reasons, as the institutions that would have had to take on the training of exploration geophysicists were practically non-existent.[69]

There was, for instance, no Italian equivalent of the French Association of Oil Technicians (*Association française des techniciens du pétrole*, AFTP), which since 1930 had brought together French technical oil experts. An Italian Petroleum Institute on the model of the French Petroleum Institute (*Institut français du pétrole*, IFP) (see Chapter 2), which could lead research and training activity in the oil sector as promulgated by AGIP geologist, Oreste Jacobini, in 1948, was never established. While an Italian Geophysical Association was constituted in 1942, unlike the American Society of Exploration Geophysicists it covered all kinds of geophysical research, and was not essentially concerned with exploration for natural resources.[70]

Essentially, as science historian Roberto Maiocchi has reasoned, while importing US technologies was an inescapable condition for a country in Italy's financial condition, which wanted to acquire know-how rapidly, it would have been necessary—in order not to compromise the long-term evolution of Italian technoscience—"to support the import of machineries and patents with autonomous industrial research."[71] This was not done in general—and for oil exploration in particular—and Italian applied research took a substantial step backwards with respect to prewar conditions.

Besides the Lerici Foundation, the other Italian contractor with which AGIP collaborated was the Italian Geological Service, from which the company hired a further seismic crew in 1952. The team was to include members from both AGIP and the Geological Service, and its recruitment followed an agreement between the Ministry of Industry and the oil company. This crew had access to a new kind of seismic recorder for its surveys, which it had received 'as a tribute' from SONJ. Actually, it had not been AGIP's choice to resort to the Italian Geological Service. Instead, it had been somewhat obliged to employ this crew, as Zanmatti confided to his CTRP colleagues: the company could have the benefit of the new seismic recorder, in exchange for training three geophysicists recommended by the ministry. Since parliament was then discussing a law that threatened to concede AGIP exclusive rights over the Po Valley, the recorder was a self-interested gift from the US major.[72] SONJ must have realized that its plans for getting hold of promising permits in the Po Valley were in jeopardy, and therefore hoped to raise its bid through a persuasive offer or 'gift'.

In 1951, at the peak of AGIP's activities, eight of the twelve seismic crews that carried out surveys for AGIP were provided by contractors. Five of these were from WGC, two from Italian institutions, and one from a British subsidiary of the US-based Seismograph Service Corporation. As for non-seismic operations, beside its own gravimetric crew and electrical logging by Schlumberger, AGIP had hired another French contractor, in fact France's geophysical flagship, the General Geophysical Company (*Compagnie générale de géophysique*, CGG), whose crews had already been working for smaller Italian companies since the late 1940s on a particular kind of electrical survey outside the Po Valley. The French company was tasked with studies employing the French-patented telluric current method, which exploited the earth's natural electric currents to determine differences in the apparent resistivity of deep down geological formations.[73]

This dependency on other foreign contractors enabled AGIP to reduce WGC's influence on its affairs by exploiting the rivalry with some of its competitors. This influence began to wane from 1952, when AGIP started a process of internalizing competences, ceasing to renew most of the contracts with WGC once AGIP's personnel had been trained. Yet this did not reduce collaboration with the Americans in terms of equipment or personnel exchanges. The excessive commitment to WGC, Pozzi argues, created a sort of path-dependence that would last until the late 1960s, when Rocco left AGIP.[74]

This collaboration enabled AGIP to exploit the most advanced technologies available without having to dedicate part of its resources to personnel training, as that burden was left to WGC. However, it had a negative effect on AGIP's innovation capabilities, as the collaboration gave the Italian company no incentive to develop its own technologies.[75] In addition, there was always the chance that the American contractor might leak geoscientific intelligence acquired in work for AGIP to its diplomatic authorities: as I will show in Chapter 3 in the case of Algeria, this was actually standard protocol for US geophysical contractors operating abroad. In any case,

AGIP did also send its own people into the international arena to acquire information on novel methods, a process that increased significantly after the foundation of ENI and the internationalization of the company in the mid-1950s.[76] In 1952, following the appointment of Antonio Selem as director of the Geophysical Section, the latter was restructured into four sections: seismology, experimental radioactive logging, geophysical laboratory, and gravimetric and magnetic laboratory.[77]

By 1953, all AGIP technicians had been trained by WGC, and all four of AGIP's teams were using WGC equipment. Between 1948 and 1953, the year of ENI's foundation, AGIP's geophysical sector expanded considerably: seismic crews increased from two to nine (peaking at twelve in 1951), corresponding to a rise of sixty-five crew months of activity. The company's only gravimetric team also expanded. Crews adopting magnetic, electrical and telluric techniques were hired for specific operations.[78] By the end of 1953, the entire Po Valley had been studied through seismic methods, several gas fields were in operation, gas production was over two billion cubic meters, and both methane gas sales and the gas pipeline network were expanding to the whole of northern Italy.[79] Such an unprecedented expansion had been unimaginable when Mattei rejoined AGIP in 1948: the company's technical capabilities were disparaged by large Italian industrialists and the oil majors, the main underlying criticism being that AGIP's limited financial means would never enable it to explore the country fully.

Beside its function as a geophysical provider, in the course of the 1950s WGC also performed strategic tasks for ENI. For example, when in 1954 the Italian company wanted to extend its permits in Sicily, it attempted to do so through secret agreements with WGC, in order to elude the regional law that prevented overly large permits being assigned to a single company. The American contractor also acted as middleman in 1958 when the Pan American Oil Company, an affiliate of Standard of Indiana and closely linked to WGC, contacted the Italians to exchange data and devise a common strategy on some Iranian permits bordering those obtained by ENI.[80]

As I have mentioned, the considerable expansion of AGIP's exploratory activities just described would hardly be thinkable without a major breakthrough in Italian oil history, and the credit the national agency would take from it. This major breakthrough was the Cortemaggiore discovery of 1949: analyzing the political pathway leading to it will help to clarify the scale of the development of AGIP's technical expertise. For this we need to backtrack to 1948, and focus on the reorganization of the Italian oil sector that was taking shape.

Premises and Consequences of the Cortemaggiore Discovery

The CIP was dissolved in December 1948. However, this formal act did not substantially affect the Italian oil scene since, following the Committee's dissolution, the main commercial operators joined forces under the

Oil Union (*Unione Petrolifera*), presided over by SONJ's general manager in Italy, Guido Ringler. When the issue of war reparations for nationalized foreign companies was resolved at the end of the year, AGIP once again found itself dominated by the majors, not least because its oil imports were only authorized within the Marshall Plan set up by the Truman administration in 1948.[81] In fact, one could argue that the dissolution of the CIP was prompted by the launch of the Plan, which would maintain a similar degree of control over Italian oil security as did the Petroleum Committee.

In the first years of the Boldrini presidency, AGIP did try to develop agreements with the majors in order to achieve a compromise. What the company's board suggested was a return to prewar market quotas, which would give AGIP-SONJ-Shell 80 percent control of the market. Fearing AGIP's more assertive stance, however, SONJ refused a market repartition, maintaining that US antitrust laws prevented the formation of cartels. This seems a farcical argument, especially in light of the far larger, global cartel SONJ had formed and jointly managed with Shell and AIOC—later joined by other majors—since the Achnacarry Agreement of 1928.[82] Meanwhile, SONJ's increased Middle Eastern production had started to flow into Europe, and the American company intended to place part of it on the Italian market, starting a dumping process that seriously hit AGIP's profits.[83]

On top of this, between 1947 and 1948 the US became a net oil importer for the first time in its history, prompting the US government to modify its oil policy. From now on, American oil would be kept for the domestic market—it had the further advantage of being far from Soviet reach—while Middle Eastern oil would fuel Europe.[84] At this point, discovering new oil became a 'make or break' move for AGIP. Either oil would be found, or the company would be crushed by its competitors.

Less than a year after Boldrini's appointment, the Cortemaggiore oil discovery made the headlines in every Italian newspaper. Much has been written on this episode, which with hindsight has largely been described as a bluff.[85] Although very little oil would be extracted at Cortemaggiore, this would be offset by the discovery of considerable amounts of natural gas. In addition, it marked a psychological victory for the public enterprise, which would market its own fuel under the slogan "Supercortemaggiore: the powerful Italian petrol," despite most of the fuel actually distributed coming from AIOC's Middle Eastern oilfields, not Italy.[86] The media hype over the discovery outweighed the rather deceptive data about real oil output. What mattered was the perception that the national company had proved its ability to find oil in Italy, and Mattei could now claim it would damage the Italian economy to spoil such a colossal achievement by conceding rights over the Po Valley to foreign companies. Italy should have autonomy to manage its energy use, and so should AGIP.

It is interesting to examine the reactions the announcement provoked among oil companies. In November, in the long wake of the discovery, SONJ executive Ralph Bolton made a speech at the American Chamber of

Commerce in Italy, stating that his company was fully determined to take part in the exploration of the Po Valley.[87] This was anathema to AGIP. Presumably, Bolton felt emboldened in his demands, having reached a partial settlement with AGIP. The previous April, ANIC had concluded an agreement with SONJ for the joint management of a new refining company. The new company, however, distributed its products only to SONJ's network. The British Ambassador in Rome, Victor Mallet, promptly informed the Foreign Office of the establishment of the new company, presumably afraid that the new Italian–American agreement would weaken the British position in the Italian refining market, and threaten Anglo–Italian cooperation between AGIP and AIOC within the Venice refinery.[88]

Bolton's 1947 speech was not the first attempt by SONJ to get involved in exploration of the Po Valley. The US major's intention to prospect in the Valley had been paralleled throughout the early postwar years by similar claims from other companies, both Italian and international. These had been dealt with in a wide variety of ways, often determined less by a pre-ordained general scheme devised by the Christian Democrats than by the political ideas of the individual industry ministers. In 1946 Giovanni Gronchi, the then Industry Minister, expressed his willingness to facilitate all possible options.[89] Given Gronchi's favorable attitude to AGIP and to Mattei, it would seem that he must have employed delaying tactics. In fact, Gronchi did not push hard for a solution to the requests by SONJ—which had applied for an exploration permit over the whole Po Valley—and other companies to issue licenses more promptly. As a consequence, AGIP could explore the Po Valley unchallenged: in 1947, its exploration rights in the Valley were confirmed.[90] In the same year, however, following Gronchi's formal opening up to private companies, the Ministry of Industry was flooded with over four hundred applications for permits and concessions.[91]

In addition, Confindustria, the influential federation of Italian employers, put pressure on the government to open the Valley to private initiatives. In August, it was announced that SONJ's affiliate, SPI, had struck oil near Ferrara, in one of the areas of the valley previously abandoned by AGIP. Although the rumors were quickly denied, they served to focus Italian and international interest on the prospecting that had been proceeding for some time in the valley under SONJ's auspices. To substantiate its request for exclusive rights over the valley, and to liaise with the Italian political community, SONJ could also count on the influence of SPI's Managing Director, Edward Borrego, former Petroleum Attaché at the US Embassy in Rome.[92]

Borrego took advantage of the media coverage of the Ferrara 'non-discovery' to argue that, in order to pursue SPI's program with good prospects of success, his company would require more extensive concessions. In the meantime, he said, seismic research was being conducted by SPI in the small portion of the valley where it operated, by a contractor only too familiar with the area, namely WGC, the same contractor that been providing AGIP with services for years.[93] So, notwithstanding confidentiality obligations with regard to third parties, at least part of the intelligence gathered by the American geophysicists while working in AGIP's area was probably transferred to SONJ's affiliate. Crucial pieces of scientific information on reservoirs, and the encrypted knowledge they contained, were therefore again at the heart of the struggle to acquire control of Italy's hydrocarbons.

In November 1947, the new DC Minister of Industry, Giuseppe Togni, submitted a request for views about the Po Valley concession to the Higher Council of Mines, which in turn tasked an ad hoc committee with examining the thorny issue. The committee presented a report the following May, which recommended splitting the valley into a few large concessions to be allotted to public and private concerns, thus leading to the liberalization of the exploration market. The report also suggested criteria for the reform of the old mining law dating from 1927, and the Council of Mines agreed to formulate a proposal for a new law. The proposal put forward by the Council of Mines allocated over two million hectares to a few private companies, and one million to AGIP. The plan was that SPI should be granted a license for 43.5 percent of the first area (slightly under a million hectares), a surface area more than twenty-four times larger than the maximum size allowed in the US to an individual license-holder. Former ENI cadre, Manlio Magini, sarcastically remarked that the provision "could not have been less favorable to the collectivity and more profitable to the private sector had it been drawn up by [SONJ]."[94]

However, despite repeated solicitations from foreign oil companies, the government came up with no legislative proposals for more than a year. In April 1949, therefore, it was the Industry Minister, the DC conservative Ivan Matteo Lombardo, who decided to present the parliament with his own legislative proposal, based on the Council of Mines recommendations, but with some amendments.[95] It still favored private oil companies. For instance, the most significant provision obliged the concessionaire to pay an 8 percent royalty to the state on any oil extracted, but *only after* a period of ten years from the enactment of the law. This would encourage private companies to exploit the concession intensively, possibly exhausting the fields before any royalty could be applied. However, Pozzi comments, a series of factors remained that allowed AGIP to operate without competition, such as ambiguity about the procedures through which the minister would evaluate applications. The outcome of an application effectively depended on the minister's arbitrary judgment.[96]

At that point, the internecine clash of economic philosophies within the Christian Democrats became apparent. The Minister of Finance, Ezio Vanoni, who unlike Lombardo favored state intervention in the economy, besides being personally connected to Mattei, managed to get parliamentary examination of the bill postponed until an Interministerial Commission for Reconstruction had presented its own advice. This triggered protest from Montecatini executive Carlo Faina, who was also President of the Italian Mining Association (*Assomineraria*), which in turn was part of the Italian employers' federation, Confindustria. While waiting for the Commission's ruling, examination of concession requests was again suspended. This once again worked in favor of AGIP.[97]

In the course of the struggle between advocates of economic liberalism and statism, Mattei managed to win over De Gasperi and Vanoni, thus clearing the ground for the achievement of a project that would completely transform the public oil company. The Cortemaggiore discovery delayed Lombardo's initiative for over a year. In July 1950, Togni, during his second mandate as Minister of Industry, in answer to a parliamentary enquiry in the Senate, confirmed that the cabinet was working on the creation of a national agency for hydrocarbons, which would enjoy rights of exclusivity over the Po Valley.[98]

In the meantime, to sweeten the pill for private companies and foreign diplomats pushing for the release of licenses, over a million hectares were assigned between 1951 and 1953 to private firms, Montecatini in particular. As if AGIP's monopoly over the Po Valley were not enough to trigger complaints from the private sector, the public company's entry into the gas market in 1951 only exacerbated the situation. Even before this, the Italian gas market was crowded, and private gas companies received the news of AGIP's entry with disquiet. Their concern was not unfounded, as the public company was to adopt dumping as its main course of action, enabling it to achieve a dominant position.[99]

The liberalization promoted by the DC's conservative wing was attributable in particular to the pressure placed on the Italian government by Ralph Bolton of SONJ. After a meeting with De Gasperi on 30 January 1951, Bolton complained that—while applications presented by SONJ's affiliate were still outstanding—AGIP's permits in the Po Valley had been extended. Such a course of action, he claimed, constituted preferential treatment, and infringed the US-Italian Treaty of Friendship, Commerce and Navigation of 1949, a free trade agreement that among other things provided for Italian and US companies to be treated on equal footing in the two countries. SONJ threatened to appeal to Washington for support.[100]

In order to make his point clearer, in the autumn of 1951 Bolton issued an 'ultimatum' to De Gasperi: unless new exploration permits were issued, giving private interests some kind of protection, hundreds of workers at the affiliate SIAP (which changed its business name that year to ESSO Standard Italiana) would lose their jobs. No new concessions were granted, and 357 workers were dismissed.[101] Gulf Oil also applied pressure on De Gasperi. In December 1949, under Ambassador Dunn's auspices, company geologist Chester Baird paid a visit to De Gasperi to state Gulf's wish to carry out prospecting operations in Italy. In 1950 two Gulf officials were allowed to confer with the President of the Republic, Luigi Einaudi, but no concessions were granted.[102]

Togni's 1950 bill was ultimately rejected, but at the same time an alternative proposal materialized, put forward by Vanoni, formally assigning control over most areas in the Po Valley to AGIP. The Vanoni bill facilitated the transformation of AGIP into a new authority, the National Hydrocarbon

Authority—ENI—while postponing the setting of regulations concerning exploration outside the Valley. In June 1951, the bill establishing ENI was presented to the Council of Ministers, but was only passed in January 1953, after a bitter political battle in the Senate.[103] The new agency was structured as a holding company, constituted of four sectorial corporations covering exploration and production, hydrocarbon transport, commercial activities, and petrochemicals. In March, Mattei resigned from his seat as deputy and was appointed president of ENI. The establishment of a vertically integrated company modeled on the majors was a clear indication from the Italian authorities that, from now on, national interests in the peninsula would be expanding, and the influence of foreign companies would be challenged.

ENI's defiance would be directed primarily at American companies, and only secondarily at British firms. Indeed, while American companies were still increasing their activities in Italy by the time ENI was founded, British companies' shares of inland trade had dropped to 30 percent (from 40 percent in 1950), and their supplies of oil to Italy had fallen to 20 percent of the total (compared with 40 percent in 1950). The Petroleum Division of the British Ministry of Fuel and Power argued that the shares of American companies had increased proportionally. The Americans had eaten alarmingly into British interests. This was not only true in Italy, but more worryingly also in the Middle East, the main source of British oil. Here, British oil security was endangered by political events in Iran, where in 1951, Prime Minister Mohammad Mosaddegh had made the decision to nationalize AIOC.[104]

Italian shipping companies—and to a lesser extent Japanese, German, US and Turkish firms—began a massive trade in nationalized Persian oil, alarming and angering the British government. While AGIP was not directly involved, the scale and frequency of the imports, and the fact that some of this oil would be delivered to the Soviet Bloc, triggered a long conflict between British and Italian authorities, which would only be resolved in the courts. Although the Italian Ministry of Foreign Trade, the Christian Democrat Ugo La Malfa, suggested Mattei take an active part in the trade, he declined in order not to jeopardize AGIP's relations with AIOC.[105] This was a wise decision, the issue having already enraged the British Prime Minister Churchill who, commenting on the Italian role in Persian oil traffic, told Eden that the Italians had demonstrated what "paltry friends and allies" they were.[106] The process leading to the approval of a new mining law appeared to confirm that Italian policymakers' desire to put ENI in the driving seat in oil exploration matters was stronger than their willingness to acquiesce to Anglo-American plans for Italian oil.

Still a Long Way to a New Mining Law

The complaints by US officials to high-level Italian politicians were stark proof that their national companies were increasingly afraid of losing to AGIP in Italy. The collection of geoscientific data and diplomatic pressure had not been enough to obtain the desired permits, but there was still one weapon left in their armory. Rather than acting on individual permits, the new US Republican government, led by Dwight Eisenhower, sought to influence Italian legislation directly, attempting to shape it to its interests, and correspondingly to oppose Vanoni's pro-ENI approach. As far as the mining law was concerned, private oil companies and politicians of the DC Right also supported the US State Department. In 1954, with the law still under discussion, staff at the US Embassy deemed it worth trying to convince Vanoni of the merits of private enterprise by giving him a "short and effective course in American institutions." The US Ambassador in Rome, Claire Boothe Luce, also suggested that her husband, Henry Luce, one of the US's most powerful magazine magnates, assist the State Department in its indoctrination attempt.[107]

Regarding oil, the message was extremely explicit. The State Department's Desk for Western European Affairs made it known to the US Embassy in Rome that the Americans had "every right to attempt openly to influence legislation where American interests [were] at stake." US experts—commented the British Ambassador in Rome, Ashley Clarke, to Eden—appeared to believe that under extensive oil reservoirs existed the methane reservoirs, and SONJ was annoyed by the current deadlock on concessions, as the current mining law prevented their exploitation.[108]

However, negotiations over a comprehensive mining law would drag on for a few years longer, and a new law would eventually be approved only in 1957, after further international pressure.[109] The tone of the exchanges between American diplomats suggests that the State Department took a patronizing view of Italian politicians. This attitude prevented US officials from understanding the ideological tenets of Vanoni's plan, and led them to underestimate the socialistic trends present not only in the Italian Left parties, but also among Christian Democrats. Vanoni would not be swayed into adopting an entire economic ideology because 'it worked' in the United States. As far as exploration was concerned, up to 1957 AGIP continued to prospect and exploit the Po Valley unchallenged.

However, this success was counterbalanced by its defeat in Sicily. One of the four Italian territories that enjoyed a higher degree of autonomy under special legislation, Sicily used its regional powers to pass its own mining law in 1950. The Sicilian law extended ownership of land below the surface, whereas Italian law held that everything found below ground was state property. Pressure from Gulf Oil resulted in a concession for the whole southeast area of Ragusa, while the large Italian private chemical company, Edison, and its affiliates, were allocated over 300,000 hectares.[110]

Private companies blocked by AGIP's policy of obstruction in the Po Valley could take advantage of the greater degree of liberalization granted by Sicilian authorities, and by 1953 had taken almost all the concessions on the island (750,000 hectares, against a mere 4,600 allotted to AGIP).

The prime locations were given to a Gulf–Montecatini joint venture, to Edison, to a local SONJ affiliate, to D'Arcy Exploration Company—an AIOC affiliate—and to WGC.[111] For AGIP the Sicilian episode was a humiliating defeat, opening up the island to its competitors, and this bitterness was only exacerbated by Gulf's oil discovery at Ragusa in January 1954. The decision to favor private companies at the expense of AGIP led to a replication in Sicily of a situation common in other parts of the world. From 1950 to 1952 no wells were drilled by any private concern; in the following two years, Gulf was the only company to drill—a total of four wells—and only twenty-two more were planned from 1955 to 1958, despite private geologists asserting the area could justify at least a thousand.[112]

Paraphrasing one of historian Timothy Mitchell's positions, it could be argued that scarcity had begun to be produced in Sicily.[113] In fact, to Anglo–American companies, the need to find new oil mattered only to a limited extent, as they were already producing enough oil elsewhere to fulfill their demands. Their objective was to establish a position of power in at least one part of the country to use as a lever to gain further concessions. An equally valid reason to gain control over potentially exploitable areas—without actually fully exploiting them—was to prevent AGIP from further strengthening its position. So, the primary goal of acquiring new concessions was not to explore and produce, but to regulate and impede production if necessary.[114]

AGIP's disappointment over the Ragusa oil discovery was not only caused by American success. What undoubtedly displeased the company technicians was that the Americans were allowed free access to intelligence about Italian subsoil. Besides obtaining control of promising areas and minimizing their exploration efforts, the majors' strategy of preventing AGIP from acquiring a degree of energy autonomy while retaining influence over the Italian market, was also implemented through other means, primarily financial. In the next section I will show how the provisions enacted in the oil sector through the Marshall Plan contributed to this.

Italian Oil in the Marshall Plan

European dependence on the US was reinforced through the Marshall Plan. Evaluations of the Plan, as well as its global necessity and benefits for Europe, have kept historians busy over the last few decades. Most agree that besides binding Western European countries within the US sphere of influence, and helping the US industrial apparatus place their surplus goods on European markets, funding did play a significant role in boosting the European economy. Historian Elena Aga Rossi and other authors have comprehensively analyzed the Plan, its benefits, and its limitations.[115] So while a general discussion of the Plan is not an objective of this work, its provisions in the oil sector are worth a closer look, especially because it permitted the development of oil-intensive lifestyles in Western Europe, which subsidized the construction of refineries and oil-based heating systems, road construction, and car manufacturing.[116]

In 1947, American companies supplied nearly half of Western Europe's oil, which had to be paid for in dollars. Oil, maintains historian David Painter, "was the largest single item in the dollar budget of most Western European countries."[117] However, its high price was rapidly exhausting those countries' dollar reserves, so the Marshall Plan was instrumental in allotting European countries enough dollars to manage their oil purchases. From April 1948 to December 1951, the Plan allocated West European countries more than $1.2 billion for the purchase of crude oil and oil products.

This point was further clarified at the time by Walter Levy, a former SONJ executive, now at the head of the Oil Division of the Economic Cooperation Administration (ECA), the agency that administered the distribution of Marshall aid. In March 1949, in a speech at the Conference of the Petroleum Industry in New York, he declared that total dollar oil imports from American companies would amount to $550 million in the fiscal year 1950. Together with payments for tanker transportation and oil equipment, the total grew to between $800 and $900 million, representing over 20 percent of the total deficit estimated for 1950 by the ECA. Oil alone accounted for 10 percent of total Marshall aid, more than any other single product.[118]

At first sight, one may wonder how a policy intended to aid the recovery of European industry could gel with the characteristics of the oil market. Indeed, it would appear that US public intervention threatened to upset the cartel-like balance established by international oil majors through the Achnacarry Agreement. There was indeed widespread concern among oil majors that aid provided through the Marshall Plan, which would allow European countries to be supplied with artificially low-priced oil, would destabilize the oil market and reduce their profits.[119] Painter has emphasized how, in effect, the 'sales' funded by the ECA were not exactly that, but rather transfers between the companies' respective corporate affiliates, because of the vertical integration of the industry.[120] So although the prices imposed by the ECA may have been lower than comparable US prices, they in any case did not reflect market forces. Even after ECA's reductions, the prices offered by the cartel were still much higher than their production costs in the Middle East, and this discrepancy enabled the companies to accumulate profits.[121]

All in all, the Plan was aligned with the interests of the British and American oil industry. According to economist Alberto Clô, it even helped US companies to penetrate European countries that were keen to protect their own national oil firms, such as France and Italy. For though the primary task assigned to Anglo–American companies by their governments may have been to manage the supply of oil to Western countries as economically as possible, they were nonetheless instruments of American and

British foreign policy, and were expected first and foremost to protect national interests.[122]

Over 56 percent of the oil supplied to West European countries by American companies between mid-1948 and late 1951 was funded by ECA and its successor, the Mutual Security Agency. The prices imposed by US agencies also helped to retain markets for American companies at a time when their potential customers would otherwise not have been able to afford to buy oil. The Plan may therefore be seen as a way of creating dependence on the majors, even if profits were lower than in ordinary conditions. Historian Philippe Tristani has described it as a veritable 'Trojan horse' for the conquest of European markets by the American majors. Significantly, over 70 percent of oil purchased by European countries through ERP funds came from SONJ (48.8 percent), Caltex (14.0 percent) and SOCONY (9.2 percent).[123]

Through the Marshall Plan, Italy received $1.2 billion between 1948 and 1951, making it the fourth-largest beneficiary in Europe after the UK, France, and West Germany. Part of these funds was used to rebuild the Italian oil industry. However, the benefits for AGIP were extremely limited. After the war, the Italian company was seeking to raise considerable quantities of capital, mainly to restore its distribution network. Resorting to Marshall funds was considered to be a viable way of rejuvenating the sector. In this context, however, according to the account given by some authors, AGIP was deliberately excluded from ERP funds for political reasons.[124]

It is fair to assume that the Italian oil industry, with the partial exception of refineries, was not at the top of ECA's list of priorities as far as reconstruction was concerned. Other industrial sectors that would rely heavily on US oil were earmarked significant sums, such as iron and steel mills, as well as small concerns in the chemical, rubber, electro-mechanical, and metallurgical industries. Further funds had also been assigned to other private enterprises such as FIAT, Montecatini chemical and mining industries, Pirelli cable and rubber manufacturers, and to four leading shipyards. The trend inaugurated by the Export-Import Bank—the US's official export credit agency—was pursued in subsequent aid programs.[125]

Although AGIP was not among the main beneficiaries of the Marshall Plan, it was allocated some ERP funds—one million pounds sterling—in 1949–50 for the Venice refinery. However, this was because the Italian company shared the plant with AIOC. By contrast, it was denied the smaller sums—a third of the above amount—it had demanded for the independent modernization of its distribution network.[126] As for drilling materials, necessary for potentiating the old drills in use in AGIP's operating fields, four of the ten requests for ERP funding presented by the company's Technical Committee were accepted.[127] However, as the procedures to obtain them dragged on, eventually coming to a standstill, the Committee decided to acquire the drills through other means. No geophysical equipment was obtained by AGIP with ERP funds.

What might look like a neglectful approach to the Italian oil industry was actually a deliberate tactic. As I have previously shown in this chapter, assisting the reconstruction of the European refining industry was instrumental to American military and economic security. However, when the Organization for European Economic Cooperation—founded in 1948 to help administer the Plan in Europe—and its oil committee in particular, presented Levy with estimates of the oil equipment needed in Europe, the chief of ECA's Oil Division replied that these were unrealistic and incomplete. As a consequence, ECA would not finance any expansion program for the time being.[128]

Levy implemented this policy by ruling that no authorization be given for petroleum equipment. It was one thing to help the Europeans reconstruct their refineries to the benefit of American corporate and strategic interests, but supporting the expansion of their national oil industries would go against the will of the majors, by giving European companies greater autonomy from them. This might trigger a chain reaction: more European autonomy could encourage greater efforts by national companies to look for indigenous oil and gas fields. And if oil and gas were found, that would prompt a decrease in oil shipments to Europe from concessions held by US companies in the Middle East. In turn, this would bring political repercussions that could even culminate in the expulsion of US interests from that area, which—Levy maintained—could endanger US energy security.[129] Of course, many of these concerns related to unlikely and extreme events, and concealed a very specific agenda. In the end, the ECA financed very few refinery projects, and allotted only $24 million to the expansion of refineries in Europe.

In the wake of the 1949 Cortemaggiore discovery, and with the mining law under discussion in parliament, rumors began to circulate of a reduction in oil supplies to Italy. A Rome correspondent of the *New York Times* claimed that, according to some ECA officials, the US government was considering diminishing exports to Italy in retaliation for the possible decision to create a state monopoly for the Po Valley.[130] This had presumably been the effect of Bolton's machinations. The SONJ representative had important connections in ECA's Oil Division. In addition, he was a close friend of David Zellerbach, head of ECA's Mission in Italy. He devised a similar strategy a few years later, outside the framework of the Plan and to the same ends. On both occasions, the US authorities did not endorse Bolton's suggestions.[131] In any case, the late start to aid distribution in Italy, together with the slowness of the country's aid allocation procedures, greatly limited AGIP's access even to the small funds available. Only after some 'bureaucratic bottlenecks' were eliminated in 1950, was AGIP able to begin borrowing ERP funds in 1951 through the mediation of the Italian Institute for Industrial Credit (*Istituto mobiliare italiano*), the body tasked with the distribution of funds nationwide.[132]

Conclusion

In this chapter, I have formulated two arguments: the first concerns the role of Anglo–American governmental and corporate interests in the Italian oil sector in the early postwar years, which I have argued was not just very real, but considerably affected the development of the sector at least until the establishment of ENI. My second argument concerns the part played in the interactions between Italian and international companies by processes of creation, distribution, and appropriation of geoscientific knowledge. This aspect has been largely neglected by existing literature on the development of Italian oil exploration activities, with a few exceptions: in particular, its international aspects had not previously been analyzed within the broader historical and political Cold War framework. I have shown that this geoscientific knowledge was not only instrumental in devising exploration policies, but also fostered links between Italian, French, and American technicians and companies, both allowing Italian agencies to acquire know-how that could be employed in further surveys, and enabling foreign companies to collect intelligence on Italian resources.

Regarding my first argument, I have demonstrated that the aim of British and American agencies was to reestablish the prewar repartition of the Italian market, under the pretext of giving Allied companies a 'fair share'. Given that the Italian public company possessed incomparably lesser resources than the Anglo–American majors, these actions would in effect neutralize AGIP, and restore SONJ and Shell to their former dominance. In this respect, while the Marshall Plan did not significantly benefit AGIP, it was not an effective political weapon for SONJ either, though it did help to consolidate the interests of American (and British, contextually) companies in the country.

The general compliance to US pressure that characterized the attitudes of Italy's Christian Democrat cabinets in the immediate post-war period began to wane in the late 1940s, due to the growing influence of the DC Left, which favored a strong public role for the state in the country's economy. Some politicians from this current understood that Italian national security depended on acquiring a degree of control over oil reserves, and if that was going to happen, AGIP should be granted some autonomy. It was this that enabled Mattei to implement his dynamic program at AGIP. His familiarity with the most influential players on the DC Left was fundamental to the change in AGIP's technopolitical regime, prompting the switch from a class of public administrators that prioritized the company's financial stability, to one that favored an expansion of the exploration sector.

The key asset in this battle for economic influence and energy security was geophysical data and knowledge, as my second argument maintains. On obtaining his second mandate as vice-president, Mattei reorganized the management of prospecting activities by establishing new structures endowed with greater decision-making powers. To pursue exploration activities, he initially employed contractors with the aim of maximizing the pace of surveys, using the most technologically advanced techniques available. Thanks to WGC's training, AGIP technicians were subsequently able to form their own crews, which from 1952 quickly became the majority.

Lasting relations formed with WGC and a few other contractors enabled AGIP to increase its geophysical capacity, while creating strong dependence on American equipment. For its part, by working side-by-side with AGIP, WGC was able to gather intelligence it could use when working for SONJ's affiliate. The transfer of geoscientific data from AGIP to foreign enterprises was also favored by the Italian company's early postwar policy, which made it easy for the majors to acquire the information it had collected. This situation radically changed under Mattei's presidency.

Mattei asserted his influence by getting politicians on his side, but also by making sure that AGIP came first in the competition to prospect for oil and gas fields, thus coupling political influence with material control. Acquiring and using geophysical data, skills, and instruments was as vital to Italy's oil security as the political game. The Italian entrepreneur also succeeded because his political allies used delaying tactics when devising new mining regulations, as well as because of the frequent cabinet reshuffles and crises that came to characterize Italian politics. The long debate about the mining law is a case in point of the influence of private interests in the Italian oil sector. The political-bureaucratic procedure that finally culminated in the new law lasted eight years, and caused frequent logjams in the license allocation procedures.

While a new national mining law would only be passed in the late 1950s, the establishment of ENI in 1953 was an important step for the advocates of public intervention in Italian oil. The restructuring of the public company, and especially the greater autonomy granted to its prospecting sector, would in subsequent years endow the country with a powerful weapon in the struggle to withstand external pressure, develop an independent geopolitical strategy, and protect the country's energy security. The general lines of this developmental path were not unique to Italy. On the other side of the Alps, the French oil industry was undergoing a similar yet different kind of restructuring, as I will now go on to show.

Notes

1 Joseph Grew, Acting Secretary of State, to Alexander Kirk, Ambassador in Italy, Mar. 22, 1945 (Grew to Kirk); Foreign Relations of the United States (FRUS), 1945, IV, Europe (Washington: United States Government Printing Office, 1968), 1309.

2 John Jones, Director of the Office of Western European Affairs, to Elbridge Durbrow, Counselor of Embassy in Italy, Sep. 16, 1954, top secret, official-informal; FRUS, 1952–1954, VI, pt. 2, Western Europe and Canada (Washington: United States Government Printing Office, 1986), 1701.

3 Daniele Pozzi, *Dai gatti selvaggi al cane a sei zampe. Tecnologia, conoscenza e organizzazione nell'Agip e nell'Eni di Enrico Mattei* (Padova: Marsilio, 2009), 136.

4 AGIP's geophysical equipment in Italy, however, had been saved from Nazi requisition: in particular a valuable seismic recorder obtained from the American Western Geophysical Company (WGC) had been disassembled and hidden in safer places. *Memoriale di Virgilio Asso.* The entire document is reported in Daniele Pozzi, "L'introduzione della sismica a riflessione in Italia," in *Energia per il territorio: Enrico Mattei e l'industria del metano in Italia*, ed. Andrea Giuntini and Daniele Pozzi (Lodi: Giona, 2003), 125–59. A description of the consequences of the war on AGIP properties can be found in: Relazione del Presidente Gestione Commissariale e sulla situazione attuale dell'Azienda, Attachment to the Minutes of Nov. 22, 1944; Verbali Consiglio di Amministrazione AGIP (C.d.A. AGIP), pp. 130–65; Organi deliberativi (OD); folder (fd.) 19 (9/8/1946–28/10/1947); box (b.) 2; Fondo AGIP; Archivio Storico ENI (ASENI).

5 Alexander C. Kirk, Ambassador in Italy, to Edward Stettinius, Secretary of State, Aug. 20, 1945; FRUS, 1945, IV, Europe, 1229. Alberto Tarchiani, Italian Ambassador, to William Phillips, Special Assistant to the Secretary of State, May 28, 1945; FRUS, 1945, IV, Europe, 1257. Kirk was reporting a memorandum Stettinius had received from De Gasperi.

6 Manlio Magini, *L'Italia e il petrolio tra storia e cronologia* (Mondadori: Milano, 1976), 89. Matteo Pizzigallo, *La politica estera dell'AGIP (1933–1940)* (Milano: Giuffrè. 1992), 136, note 38. Attachment A to the minutes of the meeting of Mar. 8, 1946; C.d.A. AGIP, p. 156; OD; fd. 18 (17/2/1945–9/8/1946); b. 2; Fondo AGIP; ASENI. *Petrolea* had been founded by the Soviet Fuel Syndicate in 1927, but had then been ceded to the Italian car company FIAT. ANIC was shared between Montecatini (50 percent), AGIP (25 percent) and *Azienda italiana petroli d'Albania* (25 percent), the latter controlled by AGIP. In 1953, AGIP bought Montecatini's share.

7 Pozzi, *Gatti selvaggi*, 142.

8 James F. Byrnes, Secretary of State, Alexander C. Kirk, Ambassador in Italy, Aug. 20, 1945; FRUS, 1945, IV, Europe, 1314–5. This and the following quotes are from p. 1315.

9 On AGIP's early history, see: Matteo Pizzigallo, *Alle origini della politica petrolifera italiana (1920–1925)* (Milano: Giuffrè, 1981); Matteo Pizzigallo, *L'AGIP degli anni ruggenti (1926–1932)* (Milano: Giuffrè, 1984); Pizzigallo, *Politica estera.* Royal Decree-Law n° 556 of 3 April 1926, published in the Official Gazette of 12 April 1926 (in Pizzigallo, *AGIP*, 7); Magini, *Italia*, 49 and 64.

10 Tiziano Rocco, *I giacimenti gassiferi dell'Europa occidentale*, vol. II (Roma: Accademia Nazionale dei Lincei, 1959), 30.

11 Pozzi, "Introduzione della sismica," 126–7.

12 Ibid.

13 The crew was led by the Italian-American, Michael Boccalery. Daniele Pozzi, ed., *La leggenda del pioniere. Diario Mazzini Garibaldi Pissard. Documenti dell'Archivio Storico,* vol. 2 (Roma: ENI), 12; Magini, *Italia*, 74.

14 Meeting of Sep. 14, 1938; C.d.A. AGIP, pp. 133–4; OD; fd. 14 (16/10/1935–6/3/1940); b. 1; Fondo AGIP; ASENI. Daniele Pozzi, "Techno-Managerial Competences in Enrico Mattei's AGIP: A Prolonged Accumulation Process in an International Network (1935–1965)," *Business and Economy History* 1 (2003): 13. 'Tacit knowledge' is characterized as a non-coded knowledge, not included in texts or manuals, but springing from education, skills, and

work experience. On this concept, see: Michael Polanyi, *The Tacit Dimension* (London: Routledge & Kegan Paul, 1967). Economic historian, Pier Angelo Toninelli, writes of "intangible assets." Pier Angelo Toninelli, "Energy supply and economic development in Italy: the role of the state-owned companies" (Working Paper 146, University of Milano-Bicocca, Department of Economics, 2008), 8–9.

15 Marcello Colitti, *Energia e sviluppo in Italia. La vicenda di Enrico Mattei* (Bari: De Donato, 1979), 61–2.

16 ANIC was shared among AGIP, together with the Italian Enterprise for Albanian oil and the chemical industry Montecatini, which was the majority shareholder.

17 *Enciclopedia del petrolio*, entry 'ENI', IV, 172 (in Magini, *Italia*, 74); Magini, *Italia*, 75; Pizzigallo, *AGIP*; Pizzigallo, *Politica estera*.

18 British Prime Minister Winston Churchill and US President Dwight D. Eisenhower used this phrase to refer to the attitude held by the French Assembly during the discussion of the European Defence Community in 1954. See: Prime Minister Churchill to President Eisenhower, Dec. 7, 1954, top secret, personal and private; FRUS, 1952–1954, VI, pt. 1, Western Europe and Canada (Washington: United States Government Printing Office, 1986) 1057, and Eisenhower's reply on Dec. 14 on p. 1060.

19 James E. Miller, "Taking Off the Gloves: The United States and the Italian Elections of 1948," *Diplomatic History* 7, no. 1 (1983): 53.

20 By 1953, Italy's refining capacity would attain a stunning 21 million tons (Mt), compared to 9.7 Mt planned by the Organisation for European Economic Co-operation. In: Magini, *Italia*, 96. Angelo Pressenda and Marcella Sarale, *Ricerca sulle Partecipazioni statali. II. L'ENI da Mattei a Cefis. La politica del petrolio tra mito e realtà* (Torino: Einaudi, 1978), 44; Rosaria Quartararo, *Italia e Stati Uniti: gli anni difficili, 1945–1952* (Napoli: Edizioni Scientifiche Italiane, 1986), 17.

21 Report on Military, Naval, and Air Clauses of the Treaty of Peace With Italy by an Ad Hoc Committee of the State-War-Navy Coordinating Committee. Enclosure to SWNCC 155/1, Sep. 6, 1945; FRUS, 1945, IV, Europe, 1038. Alessandro Brogi, *L'Italia e l'egemonia americana nel Mediterraneo. 1945–1958* (Scandicci: La Nuova Italia, 1996), 344. See also Alessandro Brogi, *A Question of Self-Esteem: the United States and the Cold War Choices in France and Italy, 1944–1958* (Westport, CT: Praeger, 2002); Memorandum by Arthur Radford, Chairman of the Joint Chiefs of Staff, to Charles Erwin Wilson, Secretary of Defense, Subject: NSC 5411-U.S. Policy Toward Italy, Mar. 23, 1954, top secret; FRUS, 1952–1954, VI, pt. 2, Western Europe and Canada, 1665–6.

22 Meeting of Feb. 17, 1945; C.d.A. AGIP; OD; b. 2, fd. 18; Fondo AGIP; ASENI.

23 Joseph Grew, Acting Secretary of State, to Alexander C. Kirk, Ambassador in Italy, Feb. 10, 1945; FRUS, 1945, IV, Europe, 1307. Addresses—Ickes, Harold L., "An Oil Policy for the United States," Dec. 8, 1944; Chicago Council on Foreign Relations Records, Special Collections; fd. 96; b. 3; University of Illinois at Chicago. Mr. Ickes Discusses An Oil Policy For the United States, Nov. 10, 1944; file (f.) 12; b. Foreign Office (FO) 371/50378, code 76; The National Archives, Kew (TNA): source as reported in Leonardo Maugeri, *L'arma del petrolio. Questione petrolifera globale, guerra fredda e politica italiana nella vicenda di Enrico Mattei* (Firenze: Loggia De' Lanzi, 1994), 20; Stephen J. Randall, "Harold Ickes and United States Foreign Petroleum Policy Planning, 1939–1945," *Business History Review* 57, no. 3 (1983): 367–87.

24 John A. Loftus, "Oil in United States Foreign Policy," *Vital Speeches of the Day* 12, no. 24 (1946): 755. On US foreign oil policy, see also: Stephen J. Randall, *United States Foreign Oil Policy Since World War I: For Profits and Security*, 2nd edition (Montreal/London: McGill-Queen's University Press, 2005). The alternative name for the ERP comes from the name of US Secretary of State, George Marshall, who launched the Plan. Before the establishment of ERP, Italy and other countries involved in the war had been given assistance by the United Nations Relief and Rehabilitation Administration, an international relief agency largely dominated by the United States.

25 Grew to Kirk, Mar. 22, 1945; FRUS, 1945, IV, Europe, 1309. Edward Stettinius, Secretary of State, to Alexander C. Kirk, Ambassador in Italy, Jan. 19, 1945; FRUS, 1945, IV, Europe, 1304–5. It was impossible to trace West's first name from documents.

26 Record Group (RG) 226 (Records of the Office of Strategic Services), s. 108B, b. 51, fd. 436; National Archives and Records Administration, College Park, MD (NARA): source as reported in Mario J. Cereghino and Giovanni Fasanella, *Il golpe inglese. Da Matteotti a Moro: le prove della guerra segreta per il controllo del petrolio e dell'Italia* (Milano: Chiarelettere, 2011), 88–93.

27 Anthony Eden, FO, to Winston Churchill, Prime Minister, "Policy towards Italy and Italian Government," Sept. 25, 1945; b. Prime Minister's Office Files (PREM) 3/243/8; TNA.

28 Quoted from: Antonio Varsori, "Italy's European Policy" (UNISCI Discussion Papers 25, Universidad Complutense de Madrid, January 2011), 45 (http://revistas.ucm.es/ index.php/ UNIS/article/download/UNIS1111130041A/26855).

29 Alexander C. Kirk, Ambassador in Italy, to Edward Stettinius, Secretary of State, Jun. 24, 1945; FRUS, 1945, IV, Europe, 1311–2. Kirk to Stettinius, Sep. 27, 1945; FRUS, 1945, IV, Europe, 1318.

30 Meeting of Apr. 10, 1945, Report attached to the minutes; C.d.A. AGIP, p. 34; OD; fd. 18; b. 2; Fondo AGIP; ASENI. The quote is from: Colitti, *Energia e sviluppo*, 68 (my translation).

31 Carte Merzagora; b. 34; Archivi dell'Istituto di storia del movimento di liberazione, Milano: source as reported in Colitti, *Energia e sviluppo*, 68. The mentioned exchange is dated May 18, 1945. The first colonel was Harry Hershenson; as for the second one, King, I could not retrieve his first name in my sources. Dean Acheson, Acting Secretary of State, to Alexander C. Kirk, Ambassador in Italy (Kirk), Sep. 14, 1945; FRUS, 1945, IV, Europe, 1316–7. Attachment to the minutes of the meeting held on Aug. 9, 1946: Memorandum # 1, Precedenti situazione e riassetto dell'A.G.I.P.; C.d.A. AGIP; OD; fd. 19 (9/8/1946–28/10/1947); b. 2; Fondo AGIP; ASENI.

32 Meeting of Dec. 19, 1945, Allegato A: Relazione al Consiglio di Amministrazione sulla situazione finanziaria; C.d.A. AGIP, p. 119–24; OD; fd. 18; b. 2; Fondo AGIP; ASENI. Giorgio E. Kovacs, *Storia delle raffinerie di petrolio in Italia* (Roma: Colombo, 1994), 150.

33 Interests of US Business Firms in Allied Italian Organizations, Intelligence Memorandum, Ocl-3526.10, Jul. 17, 1946; Office of Intelligence Coordination and Liaison (OCL); Department of State; NARA: source as reported in Nico Perrone, *Obiettivo Mattei. Petrolio, Stati Uniti e politica dell'ENI* (Gamberetti: Roma, 1995), 34–5. Data are referred to 31 May 1943, but according to Perrone they can be considered almost unvaried after the Liberation.

34 Minutes of the Decisions of the Extraordinary Commissioner on Apr. 30, 1945, C.d.A. AGIP, p. 1; OD, fd. 18; b. 2; Fondo AGIP; ASENI.

35 Franco Amatori, "Entrepreneurial Typologies in the History of Industrial Italy (1880–1960): A Review Article," *Business History Review* 54, no. 3 (1980): 380.
36 Pozzi, *Gatti selvaggi*, 155. Split into two during the war, AGIP's offices in Rome and Milan were now to be reunified.
37 Situazione delle ricerche petrolifere nell'Italia Settentrionale, Sep. 11, 1945; Presidenza Mattei; sub-fd. 4; fd. 40; b. 1; Fondo ENI; ASENI.
38 Ibid.
39 Quoted from: Pozzi, *Gatti selvaggi*, 158 (my translation).
40 Permessi e Concessioni; sub-fd. 11; fd. 6; b. 314; Direzione Generale delle Miniere; Ministero Industria Commercio e Artigianato; Archivio Centrale di Stato, Roma (ACS): source as reported in Daniele Pozzi, "Mattei e la 'vecchia' AGIP: tra ipotesi di continuità e rilancio strategico (1945–1948)," *Imprese e Storia* 27 (2003): 72, note 17. The exchange between Gerbella and Soleri occurred via the Minister of Industry, Giovanni Gronchi.
41 Fulvio Bellini and Alessandro Previdi, *L'assassinio di Enrico Mattei* (Milano: FLAN, 1970), 30–2.
42 Meeting of Dec. 19, 1945; C.d.A. AGIP, p. 114; OD; fd. 18; b. 2; Fondo AGIP; ASENI. Minutes of decisions of the Extraordinary Commissioner on Oct. 20, 1945; C.d.A. AGIP, pp. 20–2; OD; fd. 17 (Commissario Enrico Mattei, 30/4/1945–20/10/1945); b. 2; Fondo AGIP; ASENI.
43 In Pozzi, *Mattei*, Pozzi calls 'old AGIP' the former Roman branch of the company.
44 Meeting of Dec. 19, 1945; C.d.A. AGIP, p. 114; OD; fd. 18; b. 2; Fondo AGIP; ASENI.
45 Quoted from: Nicolò Pignatelli Aragona, "Petrolio ed iniziativa privata. L'esempio siciliano," in *Petrolio di Ragusa*, ed. Gulf Italia (Gulf Italia, 1958), 13: source as reported in Perrone, *Obiettivo Mattei*, 37.
46 Luigi Bruni and Marcello Colitti, *La politica petrolifera italiana* (Roma: Giuffrè, 1967), 52; Colitti, *Energia e sviluppo*, 87.
47 Colitti, *Energia e sviluppo*, 87; Pozzi, *Gatti selvaggi*, 165. Leutzinger's and Taverne's first names could not be retrieved in ENI archives or in secondary sources. Taverne's visits are documented in: Meeting of Dec. 1, 1945; Verbali Comitato esecutivo AGIP; p. 12; OD; fd. 3B (29/10/1945–24/9/1949); b. 16; Fondo AGIP; ASENI. Meeting of Jan. 4, 1946; Verbali Comitato esecutivo AGIP, p. 23; OD; fd. 3B; b. 16; Fondo AGIP; ASENI. Direzione Mineraria; Ricerche e produzione; f. 16375; fd. 2FF; b. 201; Fondo AGIP; ASENI.
48 Meeting of Mar. 5, 1946; Verbali Comitato esecutivo AGIP, pp. 69–71; OD; fd. 3B; b. 16; Fondo AGIP; ASENI.
49 Meeting of Apr. 24, 1947; C.d.A. AGIP, pp. 160–1; OD; fd. 19; b. 2. Fondo AGIP; ASENI.
50 Meeting of Aug. 9, 1946; C.d.A. AGIP, p. 1; OD; fd. 19; b. 2; Fondo AGIP; ASENI. Attachment A (dated Dec. 6, 1946) to the minutes of the meeting of Feb. 5, 1947; C.d.A. AGIP; OD; fd. 19; b. 2; Fondo AGIP; ASENI.
51 Meeting of Aug. 9, 1946; C.d.A. AGIP, pp. 9ff.; OD; f. 19; b. 2; Fondo AGIP; ASENI. Report and proposals by Vice-President Mattei for an urgent reorganization of the Enterprise; Attachment A to the minutes of the meeting held on Aug. 9, 1946; C.d.A. AGIP, pp. 21–4; OD; fd. 19; b. 2; Fondo AGIP; ASENI.
52 Meeting of Feb. 26, 1947; C.d.A. AGIP; Attachment B to the minutes of the Meeting of Apr. 24, 1947; C.d.A. AGIP, pp. 170, 172; Meeting of May 24, 1947; C.d.A. AGIP. These three documents are in found in OD; fd. 19; b. 2; Fondo AGIP; ASENI. See also files contained in b. FO 371/67785; TNA.

53 Meeting of Nov. 2, 1946; C.d.A. AGIP, pp. 170, 172; OD; fd. 19; b. 2; Fondo AGIP; ASENI.

54 Meeting of Jun. 12, 1947; C.d.A. AGIP, pp. 227–8; Meeting of Jul. 24, 1947; C.d.A. AGIP, pp. 268–9; Meeting of Aug. 30, 1947; C.d.A. AGIP, pp. 289–91. These three documents are found in OD; fd. 19; b. 2; Fondo AGIP; ASENI. Meeting of Dec. 18, 1947; C.d.A. AGIP, pp. 34–5; OD; fd. 1A (28/10/1947–27/5/1950); b. 3; Fondo AGIP; ASENI.

55 Serge A. Sherbatskoy Well Logging by Measurement of Radioactivity. US patent 2,219,273, filed Jun. 19, 1939, and issued Oct. 22, 1940 [assigned to WSI, Tulsa, Oklahoma]: source as reported in Simone Turchetti, *The Pontecorvo Affair. A Cold War Defection and Nuclear Physics* (Chicago: University of Chicago Press, 2012), 277. Bruno Pontecorvo, "Neutron Well Logging," *Oil and Gas Journal* 40 (1941): 32–3. Meeting of Dec. 18, 1947; C.d.A. AGIP, pp. 34–5; OD; fd. 1A; b. 3; Fondo AGIP; ASENI. CEDI, *Archivio storico. Verbali Comitato tecnico ricerche e produzioni (1950)* (San Donato Milanese: Centro stampa AGIP, 1992), 65, 89–90.

56 Pozzi, *Gatti selvaggi*, 217.

57 Attachment A to the minutes of the Meeting of Apr. 12, 1948; C.d.A. AGIP, pp. 94–6; OD; fd. 1A; b. 3; Fondo AGIP; ASENI. CEDI, *Archivio storico. Verbali Comitato tecnico ricerche e produzioni (1948–1949)* (San Donato Milanese: Centro stampa AGIP, 1991), 19–22.

58 On this point, see Paul Ginsborg, *Storia d'Italia dal dopoguerra a oggi* (Milano: Einaudi Scuola, 1996), 77–8. According to the Truman Doctrine, formulated in March 1947, the US was to support countries that resisted 'outside pressures' (that is, from the Soviet Union). Many historians see the enunciation of the Truman Doctrine as marking the beginning of the Cold War.

59 Quoted from: Report by the National Security Council, NSC 1/1, *The Position of the United States With Respect to Italy*, Nov. 14, 1947, top secret; FRUS, 1948, III, Western Europe (Washington: United States Government Printing Office, 1973), 724.

60 Ibid. The 'Trieste question' regarded certain territories in northeastern Italy and northwestern Yugoslavia, including the city of Trieste, whose sovereignty was disputed between the two countries.

61 Miller, "Taking Off the Gloves," 43; Memorandum by Samuel Reber, Acting Director of the Office of European Affairs, to Robert A. Lovett, Acting Secretary of State, *Present Italian Situation; Implementation of NSC 1/1 "The Position of the United States With Respect to Italy,"* Nov. 28, 1947, top secret; FRUS, 1948, III, Western Europe, 727–9. James C. Dunn, Ambassador in Italy, to George Marshall, Secretary of State, Dec. 7, 1947, top secret, urgent; FRUS, 1948, III, Western Europe, 738–9.

62 Dunn to Marshall, Jan. 21, 1948, confidential; FRUS, 1948, III, Western Europe, 819–22. Dunn to Marshall, Jan. 29, 1948, top secret, urgent; FRUS, 1948, III, Western Europe, 824. Report by the National Security Council, NSC 1/2, The Position of the United States With Respect to Italy, Feb. 10, 1948, top secret; FRUS, 1948, III, Western Europe, 767. E. Timothy Smith, "The Fear of Subversion: The United States and the Inclusion of Italy in the North Atlantic Treaty," *Diplomatic History* 7, no. 2 (1983): 139–56.

63 Further measures were: speeches by government officials and private individuals in Italy, France and the UK, including labor leaders; and a letter-writing campaign by private citizens, regarding political issues in Italy. With a view to the elections, the Catholic Church also took a strong anti-Communist stance and maintained that those who voted Communist would be excommunicated. See also: Miller, "Taking Off the Gloves," 35–56; David W. Ellwood,

"The Propaganda of the Marshall Plan in Italy in a Cold War Context," in *The Cultural Cold War in Western Europe, 1945–1960*, ed. Giles Scott-Smith and Hans Krabbendam (London/Portland, OR: Frank Cass, 2003), 224–36; Kaeten Mistry, "The Case for Political Warfare: Strategy, Organization and US Involvement in the 1948 Italian Election," *Cold War History* 6, no. 3 (2006): 301–29; Ginsborg, *Storia d'Italia*, 90. Dunn to Marshall, Feb. 21, 1948, secret; FRUS, 1948, III, Western Europe, 835. Report by the National Security Council, NSC 1/3, *Position of the United States With Respect to Italy in the Light of the Possibility of Communist Participation in the Government by Legal Means*, Mar. 8, 1948, top secret; FRUS, 1948, III, Western Europe, 778.

64 Geir Lundestad coined the phrase 'empire by invitation'. Geir Lundestad, "Empire by Invitation? The United States and Western Europe, 1945–1952," *Journal of Peace Research* 23, no. 3 (1986): 263–77. For an updated version, see: Geir Lundestad, *The Rise and Decline of the American "Empire": Power and its Limits in Comparative Perspective* (Oxford/New York, NY: Oxford University Press, 2012). See also, for alternative views: Robert O. Keohane, "The United States and the Postwar Order: Empire or Hegemony?" *Journal of Peace Research* 28, no. 4 (1991): 436–7; John Krige, *American Hegemony and the Postwar Reconstruction of Science in Europe* (Cambridge, MA/London: MIT Press, 2006), 4–9; Ginsborg, *Storia d'Italia*, 86.

65 Meeting of Oct. 28, 1947; C.d.A. AGIP; OD; fd. 1A; b. 3; Fondo AGIP; ASENI.

66 Meeting of Jul. 27, 1948; C.d.A. AGIP, pp. 137–8; Meeting of Aug. 3, 1949, C.d.A. AGIP. Both documents are found in OD; fd. 1A; b. 3; Fondo AGIP; ASENI.

67 Meeting of Feb. 3, 1950; C.d.A. AGIP, pp. 251–2; Meeting of Mar. 24, 1950; C.d.A. AGIP, p. 266. Both documents are found in OD; fd. 1A; b. 3; Fondo AGIP; ASENI. CEDI, *Archivio Storico (1950)*, 177.

68 CEDI, *Archivio storico (1948–1949)*, 152–3, 245–6, 286–7, 293–5; CEDI, *Verbali Comitato tecnico ricerche e produzioni (1952)* (San Donato Milanese: Centro stampa AGIP, 1992), 58. Segreteria societaria; fd. 2BC3; b. 162; and fd. 2DBE; b. 163; Fondo ENI; ASENI.

69 Luigi Solaini, "Lo stato della geofisica applicata in Italia"; Opening discourse of the Academic Year; Yearbook of the Higher School for Hydrocarbon Studies, 1963–1964, p. 12–22; Archivio della Scuola Superiore di Studi sugli Idrocarburi (currently ENI Corporate University), San Donato Milanese.

70 Oreste Jacobini, "La questione petrolifera mondiale e quella italiana, III parte, nota VI: La questione petrolifera italiana" (Roma, 1948), in *La questione petrolifera italiana. Studi di Oreste Jacobini tra primo e secondo dopoguerra. Documenti dell'Archivio storico*, vol. 1, ed. Pier Angelo Toninelli (Roma: ENI, 2006), 45, 173–4.

71 Quoted from: Roberto Maiocchi, "Il ruolo delle scienze nello sviluppo industriale italiano," in *Storia d'Italia. Annali 3. Scienza e tecnica nella cultura e nella società dal Rinascimento a oggi*, ed. Gianni Micheli (Torino: Einaudi, 1980), 962 (my translation). See also Giorgio Roverato, *Nuovo Pignone. Le sfide della maturità* (Bologna: Il mulino, 1991), 42.

72 CEDI, *Archivio storico* (1952), 58. The argument about SONJ's self-interested gift is maintained in Emanuele Cassano, ed., "La Storia dei Gruppi Geofisici dell'AGIP" (Working Paper, Associazione Pionieri e Veterani ENI, San Donato Milanese, 2008), 57 (http://www.eageseg.org/download.php?f=0a3303d95dea6d87326ea2508b766c20).

73 CEDI, *Archivio storico (1950)*, 36–7, 124–5; Charles C. Bates, Thomas F. Gaskell, T. F., and Robert B. Rice, *Geophysics in the Affairs of Man*

(Oxford: Pergamon Press, 1982), 330–3; Federico Squarzina, *Le ricerche di petrolio in Italia. Cenni storici dal 1860 e cronache dell'ultimo decennio* (Roma: Jandi Sapi, 1958), 75–6, 87.

74 Pozzi, *Gatti selvaggi*, 248. The close collaboration between AGIP and WGC is shown along the life of CTRP. See: CEDI, *Archivio storico (1948–1949); Archivio storico (1950); Archivio storico (1952)*. CEDI, *Archivio storico. Verbali Comitato tecnico ricerche e produzioni (1951)* (San Donato Milanese: Centro stampa AGIP, 1992); CEDI, *Archivio storico. Verbali Comitato tecnico ricerche e produzioni (1953)* (San Donato Milanese: Centro stampa AGIP, 1993).

75 This de facto monopoly, according to ENI geophysicist Francesco Guidi, had negative ramifications in terms of the company's technological innovation, as the lack of competitors gave AGIP no incentive to develop its own instruments. Francesco Guidi's interview with the Author, San Donato Milanese, February 4, 2013.

76 In 1952, for example, Edoardo Merlini, chief of the Technical Service in AGIP's Geophysical Section, was sent on a mission to Germany and the UK to collect information on state of the art technologies being developed or utilized by local firms in seismic recording devices and laboratory set-ups. "Relazione sui dispositivi di registrazione sismica, laboratori e loro organizzazione, altri reparti, notati durante il viaggio in Germania e Inghilterra effettuato dal 29/9 and 15/10/1952. Ing. Edoardo Merlini," Oct. 27, 1952; AGIP Sezione Geofisica Lodi; Presidenza Mattei; fd. 3E0; b. 48; Fondo ENI; ASENI.

77 Cassano, "Storia dei Gruppi," 20.

78 CEDI, Archivio storico (1950), passim. Direzione relazioni col personale; fd. Schede personali dirigenti AGIP Mineraria; b. 951 (1138a); Fondo ENI; ASENI: source as reported in Pozzi, "Techno-Managerial Competences," 20. ENI—Direzione Studi, Servizio IV—Attività geofisica; Presidenza Mattei; fd. 47F; b. 70; Fondo ENI; ASENI.

79 AGIP Mineraria, *Relazione sulla attività svolta nell'anno 1953* (Milano: AGIP, 1954), 68ff.

80 AGIP Mineraria—Comitato esecutivo; fd. 8; b. 29; Presidenza Mattei; Fondo ENI; ASENI: source as reported in Pozzi, *Gatti selvaggi*, 328. Mario Ferraris to Enrico Mattei, Feb. 28, 1958; Assistente del Presidente per l'estero; fd. 8B2; b. 10; Estero; Fondo ENI; ASENI.

81 Meeting of Jun. 15, 1948; C.d.A. AGIP, p. 120; OD; fd. 1A; b. 3; Fondo AGIP; ASENI.

82 Meeting of Jul. 27, 1948; C.d.A. AGIP, pp. 134–5; OD; fd 1A; b. 3; Fondo AGIP; ASENI. Both the British and the Americans reacted unfavorably to AGIP's quotas, as since June 1946 their overall quota was only 5% larger. [Illegible], Ministry of Fuel and Power, Petroleum Division, to D. Pemberton-Pigott, FO, Jan. 28, 1949; f. Z 22/1531/400; b. FO 371/79500; TNA. Daniel Yergin, *The Prize: The Epic Quest for Oil, Money, and Power*, 2nd edition (New York: Simon & Schuster, 2009. 1st edition: 1991), 246–51; James H. Bamberg, *The History of the British Petroleum Company*, vol. 2: *The Anglo-Iranian Years, 1928–1954*. (Cambridge: Cambridge University Press, 1994), 528–34. Through the Achnacarry Agreement, signed in Scotland in August 1928, the global oil market was split, according to predetermined quotas, between SONJ, Shell and the British Anglo-Persian Oil Company.

83 Meeting of Mar. 4, 1949; C.d.A. AGIP, pp. 134–5; OD; fd. 1A; b. 3; Fondo AGIP; ASENI.

84 Pozzi, *Gatti selvaggi*, 190–1.

85 Indro Montanelli, "In mano di Mattei le chiavi di una grande cassaforte dell'Italia," *Corriere della Sera*, Jul. 13, 1962. Giovanni Galli, *La sfida perduta. Biografia politica di Enrico Mattei* (Milano: Bompiani, 1976), 116, writes of "fictional oil" (my own translation); Pressenda and Sarale, *Ricerca*, 34; Carlo M. Lomartire, *Mattei. Storia dell'italiano che sfidò i signori del petrolio* (Milano: Mondadori, 2004), 157–8; Toninelli, "Energy Supply," 10. But see Pozzi, *Gatti selvaggi*, 199.
86 Paul H. Frankel, *Mattei. Oil and Power Politics* (London: Faber and Faber, 1966), 52.
87 Fondo Segreteria Particolare Presidenza del Consiglio; fd. 207; b. 27; ACS: source as reported in Colitti, *Energia e sviluppo*, 145.
88 Victor Mallet, British Embassy (Britemb) Rome, to Ernest Bevin, State Secretary, FO, Nov. 7, 1947; TNA: source as reported in Luigi Bazzoli and Riccardo Renzi, *Il miracolo Mattei* (Milano: Rizzoli, 1984), 110–11.
89 *Financial Times*, Nov. 1, 1954: source as reported in Magini, *Italia*, 101.
90 Magini, *Italia*, 101.
91 "Competition for oil concessions: Pressure on Italy to admit foreign firms," *The Manchester Guardian*, Dec. 18, 1954.
92 Ashley Clarke, Britemb Rome, to Ernest Bevin, State Secretary, FO, Sep. 10, 1947; f. Z 22/88/8061; b. FO 371/79503; TNA.
93 Ibid.
94 Quoted from: Magini, *Italia*, 108 (my translation).
95 Pressenda and Sarale, *Ricerca*, 32.
96 Pozzi, *Gatti selvaggi*, 289.
97 Provvedimenti rinviati sospesi ritirati; sub-fd. 12; fd. Industria e Commercio; b. 26; Presidenza del consiglio, Atti (1948–1949); ACS. Verbali consiglio ministri, Apr. 22, 1949; b. 27; Presidenza del consiglio; ACS: both sources as reported in Pozzi, *Gatti selvaggi*, 290. Bellini and Previdi, *Assassinio*, 55–6.
98 CDLXXV Meeting of Jul. 4, 1950; Resoconti delle sedute plenarie (vol XV), p. 18495; Senato della Repubblica, 1948–1950; Atti Parlamentari: source as reported in Pozzi, *Gatti selvaggi*, 295.
99 Magini, *Italia*, 110. *Documenti di vita italiana*, a cura del Centro di Documentazione della Presidenza del Consiglio dei Ministri (Roma, November 1952): source as reported in Pressenda and Sarale, *Ricerca*, 35.
100 Ralph Bolton, SONJ, to Giuseppe Togni, Minister of Industry, May 5, 1951; Presidenza del Consiglio dei Ministri, 1951–1954; fd. 208; b. 27; ACS: source as reported in Perrone, *Obiettivo Mattei*, 50.
101 Ralph Bolton, SONJ, to Alcide De Gasperi, Prime Minister, May 5, 1951; Presidenza del Consiglio dei Ministri, 1951–1954; fd. 207; b. 27; ACS: source as reported in Perrone, *Obiettivo Mattei*, 51. Giovanni Guatelli, Secretary General of the Trade Union of Parma and its Province, Italian Trade Unions Confederation, to Alcide De Gasperi, Prime Minister, May 23, 1950; Presidenza del Consiglio dei Ministri, 1951–1954; fd. 210; b. 27; ACS. Bolton to De Gasperi, Dec. 15, 1950, which confirms the audience with the Prime Minister held on Apr. 29; Presidenza del Consiglio dei Ministri, 1951–1954; fd. 210; b. 27; ACS: both sources as reported in Perrone, *Obiettivo Mattei*, 52.
102 [Unsigned] Pro-memoria, Jun. 7, 1950; Presidenza del Consiglio dei Ministri, 1951–1954; fd. 208; b. 27; ACS: source as reported in Perrone, *Obiettivo Mattei*, 50.
103 The constitutive law was published in the Official Gazette on Mar. 23, 1953, n. 136, but a substantial parliamentary agreement had already been reached a year earlier. Meeting of Mar. 29, 1952; C.d.A. AGIP, p. 126; OD; fd. 1B (27/5/1950–25/2/1954); b. 3; Fondo AGIP; ASENI.

104 J. H. Brook, Ministry of Fuel and Power, Petroleum Division, to A. K. Potter, H. M. Treasury, Nov. 8, 1952; f. UES 15327; b. FO 371/99194; TNA. Winston Churchill, British Prime Minister, to President Franklin D. Roosevelt, Feb. 20, 1944, FRUS, 1944, III, The British Commonwealth and Europe (Washington: United States Government Printing Office, 1965), 100–1. On the Iranian coup, see: Mark J. Gasiorowski and Malcolm Byrne, eds., *Mohammad Mosaddeq and the 1953 Coup in Iran* (Syracuse, NY: Syracuse University Press, 2004); Francis J. Gavin, "Politics, Power, and U.S. Policy in Iran, 1950–1953," *Journal of Cold War Studies* 1, no. 1 (1999): 56–89.

105 On Italian companies' dealing in Persian oil, see: Ilaria Tremolada, *La via italiana al petrolio. L'ENI di Enrico Mattei e l'Iran (1945–1962)* (Milano: L'Ornitorinco, 2011). A considerable amount of data on this matter, most of which relates to 1953, is also found in bxs. FO 371/104606, 371/104616, 371/104617, 371/104619 to 371/104630, 371/113126, b. PREM 11/501; TNA. Licenses and compensation deals, Apr. 15, 1953; f. EP1533/166; b. FO 371/104621; TNA: source as reported in Tremolada, *Via italiana*, 97 note 66.

106 Quoted from: Winston Churchill, Prime Minister, to Anthony Eden, Secretary of State, Mar. 27, 1953; Representations to the Italian Government against attempts to import Persian oil; b. PREM 11/501; TNA.

107 Quoted from: Elbridge Durbrow, Counselor of Embassy in Italy, to Livingstone T. Merchant, Assistant Secretary of State for European Affairs, Sep. 2, 1954, confidential, official-informal; FRUS, 1952–1954, VI, pt. 2, Western Europe and Canada, 1698. See also p. 1699–700 of the same document.

108 J. W. Jones, Director of the Office of Western European Affairs, to Durbrow, Counselor of Embassy in Italy, Sep. 16, 1954, top secret, official-informal; FRUS, 1952–1954, VI, pt. 2, Western Europe and Canada, 1701. See also: Stanley B. Wolff, US Embassy (Amemb) Rome, *An Evaluation of the Scelba Government's Accomplishments in the Economic Field*, Sep. 22, 1954, confidential, pp. 2, 5–6; Classified General Records, 1946–1964; b. 89; RG 84, Records of Foreign Service Posts of the Department of State, Italy, US Embassy, Rome; NARA. Ashley Clarke, Britemb Rome, to Anthony Eden, Secretary of State, Dec. 4, 1954, confidential; f. WT 1531/5; b. FO 371/113125; TNA. Interestingly, in 1955 ENI did try to interest SONJ in prospecting parts of the Po Valley which would be too expensive for the Italian company on its own, but the American major declined the offer, invoking Italy's unfavorable mining law as their reason. Carroll E. Cook, SONJ, to Tiziano Rocco, AGIP Mineraria, Apr. 14, 1955; Ricerche e produzione; fd. 36B; b. 263; Direzione Mineraria; Fondo AGIP; ASENI.

109 On British concerns over the mid-1950s developments of the mining law, see: b. POWE 33/229; TNA.

110 Clarke, Britemb Rome, to Western and Southern Department, FO, Feb. 20, 1954, restricted; f. WT 1531/3; b. FO 371/113125; TNA.

111 Magini, *Italia*, 108–9.

112 Leo Solari, *La polemica sugli idrocarburi* (Bologna: Il mulino, 1955), 500.

113 Timothy Mitchell, *Carbon Democracy: Political Power in the Age of Oil* (New York: Verso, 2011).

114 Ricerche e produzione; fd. 7DA; b. 7; Direzione Mineraria; Fondo AGIP; ASENI.

115 For global analyses of the plan with very different theoretical perspectives, see Alan S. Milward, *The Reconstruction of Western Europe, 1945–1951* (Berkeley: The University of California Press, 1984); Michael J. Hogan, *The Marshall Plan: America, Britain, and the Reconstruction of Western Europe, 1947–1952* (Cambridge: Cambridge University Press: 1987); Martin Schain,

ed., *The Marshall Plan: Fifty Years After* (New York: Palgrave, 2001); David W. Ellwood, "Was the Marshall Plan Necessary?" in *Alan S. Milward and a Century of European Change*, ed. Fernando Guirao, Frances M. B. Lynch, and Sigfrido M. Ramírez Pérez (New York: Routledge, 2012), 179–98. On the Plan in Italy, see: Elena Aga Rossi, ed., *Il Piano Marshall e l'Europa* (Roma: Istituto dell'Enciclopedia Italiana, 1983); Chiarella Esposito, *America's Feeble Weapon: Finding the Marshall Plan in France and Italy, 1948–1950* (Westport, CT/London: Greenwood Press, 1994); Carlo Spagnolo, *La stabilizzazione incompiuta. Il Piano Marshall in Italia* (Roma: Carocci, 2001). On oil in the Plan, see: David S. Painter, "Oil and the Marshall Plan," *Business History Review* 58, no. 3 (1984): 359–83; Davis S. Painter, *Oil and the American Century: The Political Economy of U.S. Foreign Oil Policy, 1941–1954* (Baltimore: Johns Hopkins University Press, 1986), ch. 7; David S. Painter, "Oil, Resources, and the Cold War, 1945–1962," in *The Cambridge History of the Cold War*, ed. Melvyn P. Leffler and Odd Arne Westad (Cambridge: Cambridge University Press, 2010), 497–8.

116 Timothy Mitchell, "Carbon Democracy," *Economy and Society* 38, no. 3 (2009): 409.

117 Painter, "Oil Resources," 497.

118 Walter Levy, *Petroleum under the ECA Program*, p. 3; Subject Files 1947–1950; b. 1, Petroleum; Mission to Trieste: Office of the Director; Mission to Trieste, Entry 1394; RG 469; NARA. Toninelli, *La questione petrolifera*, 8. Also in Yergin, *The Prize*, 406, and sources reported at p. 818, note 12. Painter, "Oil, Resources," 363.

119 Walter Levy, *Petroleum under the ECA Program*, p. 2; Subject Files 1947–1950; b. 1, Petroleum; Mission to Trieste: Office of the Director; Mission to Trieste, Entry 1394; RG 469; NARA.

120 Painter, "Oil and the Marshall Plan," 363.

121 Toninelli, *La questione petrolifera*, 10–11; Yergin, *The Prize*, ch. 21.

122 Alberto Clô, *Oil Economics and Policy* (Boston, MA/London: Kluwer, 2000), 39.

123 Philippe Tristani, "L'Iraq Petroleum Company, les États-Unis et la lutte pour le leadership pétrolier au Moyen-Orient de 1945 à 1973," *Histoire, économie & sociéte* 29 (2010): 91.

124 Schain, *Marshal Plan*, 1–3. The UK received $3.30 million, France 2.30 million, and West Germany 1.4 million. On AGIP's exclusion, see: Benito Li Vigni, *La grande sfida. Mattei, il petrolio e la politica* (Milano: Mondadori, 1996), 36; Bazzoli and Renzi, *Miracolo Mattei*, 106–7; Italo Pietra, *Mattei: la pecora nera* (Roma: La Repubblica, 2002. 1st edition: Milano: Sugarco, 1987), 93; Lomartire, *Mattei*, 128, share a similar view.

125 Hebert E. Gaston, Acting Chairman of the Export-Import Bank, to George Marshall, Secretary of State, Oct. 24, 1947; FRUS, 1947, III, The British Commonwealth and Europe (Washington: United States Government Printing Office, 1972), 997–8, plus enclosure: *Press Release Issued by the Export-Import Bank*, Oct. 23, 1947.

126 Finanziamenti ERP, fd. 955 IROM-Roma and fd. 957 AGIP-Roma; Direzione generale produzione industrial; Ministero industria e commercio; ACS: source as reported in Pozzi, *Gatti selvaggi*, 232, note 27.

127 On AGIP's ERP requests, see: CEDI, *Archivio storico (1948–1949)*, 134–5, 148–50, 159, 183, 190, 279 and 318; Meetings of: Mar. 24, 1950, pp. 257–9; Jul. 11, 1950, pp. 6–8; Dec. 13, 1951, p. 115; C.d.A. AGIP; OD; fd. 1A; b. 3; Fondo AGIP; ASENI.

128 Painter, "Oil and the Marshall Plan," 372–3.
129 Ibid., 373–4.
130 *The New York Times*, Jun. 16, 1949: source as reported in Nico Perrone, *Enrico Mattei* (Bologna: Il Mulino, 2001), 73.
131 "Oil Firms Charged With Delaying Italian Aid," *The Evening Independent*, Sep. 16, 1949, p. 14. Memorandum of conversation with Mr. Bolton, Mr. Collado, *Problems faced by the Standard Oil Company of New Jersey in Italy*, Nov. 16, 1954; Lot files 58D357, b. 19; RG 59; NARA: source as reported in Tremolada, *Via italiana*, 176.
132 Meeting of Apr. 24, 1952; C.d.A. AGIP, p. 153ff.; OD; fd. 1B; b. 3; Fondo AGIP; ASENI.

2 From Iraq to Africa

The Quest for French Energy

> Persian oil [...] is yours. We share the oil of Iraq and Kuwait. As for Saudi Arabian oil, it's ours.
>
> —Franklin Roosevelt to Edward Lindley, February 1944[1]

> The Americans came over here and they only received the information we gave them. They haven't got more information on our territories than we have got on theirs.
>
> —Pierre Guillaumat, 19 June 1947[2]

By 1939, the French oil industry had become the largest in Europe. Five years later, however, most of it was gone. The ravages of war in terms of material damages can be described in stark figures: from an estimated total prewar valuation of the industry of $10.5 million, $6.7 million had been destroyed. Of the materials available in 1939—"600 barges, 8,000 tankers, 5,000 tanker lorries, several pipelines, thousands of pumps, tens of thousands of petrol cans and metal drums, refineries, reservoirs,"—little was left. Two-thirds of the fleet had been sunk, refining capacity had decreased from 8 million tons (Mt) in 1938 to 1.5 in 1944, and the only two working pipelines had been built by the Americans, with priority of use assigned to the Allied army.[3] The Schlumberger Company, the flagship of early French geophysics, had moved its headquarters to Houston, Texas. In five years, France had lost most of what it had managed to build in the previous fifteen.

To a much larger extent than its Italian counterpart, the French oil industry was characterized by strong international links from its very inception. In the French *Métropole* (that is, the European part of France, excluding French overseas possessions), the Anglo–American majors established their activities far earlier than did any indigenous company. Abroad, following the foundation of the French Oil Company (*Compagnie française des pétroles*, CFP) in 1924 as a mixed-economy enterprise, France gained access to a substantial share of the British-dominated Middle Eastern consortium, Turkish Petroleum Company, thus aligning both the company and the country with the interests of the majors.

In this chapter I shall discuss some aspects of the particular strategies employed by French administrations and companies to gain control over the sources of its supply, in particular vis-à-vis their British and American counterparts. These strategies included maneuvers such as stockpiling, encouraging diversification of supply and, when the opportunity arose, controlling access to resources on home soil and abroad. This control required the mobilization of state and commercial geological surveying to obtain 'geostrategic intelligence', that is, to gather information on what oil and gas reserves could be found underground, on what others (whether enemies or allies, co-producers or business rivals) already knew about these reserves, and what acquisition strategies they had put in place.

This chapter focuses in particular on a traditional European imperial power because the postwar international order forced it into a position of less influence than before, with the result that its commercial and diplomatic footprint became also contracted. For this reason, its oil security circumstances appear unique (and similar only in some respects to those characterizing the UK). Here I show how these energy security imperatives prompted French geoscientific personnel to start exploring Algeria at the end of World War II, a grand exploration strategy that would, however, be challenged and derailed by the outbreak of the Algerian War of Independence.[4]

My narrative is set against a background of French reconstruction, part of a longer historical process known as the *Trente Glorieuses* ('Glorious Thirty')—the years from 1946 to 1975—that would facilitate the transformation of France from a "rural, empire-oriented, Catholic country to a fully industrialized, decolonized, and urban one." I begin with a bird's eye view of the establishment and expansion of British and American firms in France, and then broaden my narrative first to the Middle East, and later to Northern Africa. In the former area, I investigate the clash of interests between CFP and its Anglo-American partners over Turkish Petroleum's successor, the Iraq Petroleum Company (IPC), which characterized the early postwar years, and clearly revealed in its dynamics the new world balance of power in oil exploration and production.[5]

I then argue that, once the problems in the Middle East had made French public authorities aware that having CFP as the sole supplier of oil to the country was a risky strategy, issues of national security drove them to create wholly public institutions to provide financial and technical support for exploration and production activities in the French Union (as the former French Empire was called after 1946).[6] In this context, I examine the penetration of non-French companies into North African exploration endeavors, and emphasize the role played by the possession of confidential geoscientific information and surveillance activities in relations with other countries. I also highlight the role of the geoscientific training of French technicians by US companies as a *sine qua non* for the French administration to allow these companies to acquire permits in mainland France.

The Middle East and Beyond: Early Expansion of French Oil Interests

The first step taken by French authorities toward establishing a national oil industry had been the creation of CFP in 1924, at the behest of the then President of the Republic, Raymond Poincaré. This was in response to a very practical issue: through the San Remo Agreements of 1920 between the UK and France, which had divided the former Ottoman territories between the two imperial powers after World War I, France had taken a 25 percent share in the Turkish Petroleum Company, a consortium that now incorporated British and French interests, as well as those of the Turkish-born Armenian businessman, Calouste Gulbenkian. Poincaré gave CFP the mandate to develop French-controlled oil production through its participation in Turkish Petroleum. The French state held a quarter of CFP's shares, later increased to 35 percent.[7]

Following Turkish Petroleum's discovery of an extensive oilfield at the Iraqi site of Baba Gurgur in 1927, the US government and major oil companies successfully pressurized Britain to admit a consortium of five American companies to Turkish Petroleum. The Near East Development Corporation (NEDC), as the US consortium was called, included SONJ and SOCONY, each with a 25 percent holding, plus Pan American Petroleum, Gulf Oil and Atlantic Petroleum, with 16.67 percent each. Through the 1928 Group Agreement, also known as the *Red Line Agreement*, Turkish Petroleum's partners established that they would only operate jointly within a delimited territory—demarcated by a red line drawn on a map (in black in Figure 2.1)—which included most of the former Ottoman Empire.[8]

Under this arrangement, company shares were equally divided between the Anglo-Persian Oil Company, Shell, CFP, and NEDC, with Gulbenkian maintaining his original 5 percent. A year later, the company was renamed the Iraq Petroleum Company, or IPC. CFP's history is intimately linked to that of IPC, as revealed by the amount of time the French company's board of directors spent discussing topics related to the Iraqi consortium. Indeed, to a large extent, the French company's foreign production until the mid-1950s amounted to its share within IPC and its affiliates. After the war, however, it became apparent that British and American shareholders of IPC would try to force the French into a minority position.

This made CFP managers even more eager to reinforce their prospecting sector, which was by then already well developed. CFP also conducted prospecting operations outside the consortium, in mainland France, African areas of the French Union, Colombia and Russia.[9] Recovering oil and finding new technologies to assist in prospecting was thus critical to its future. In 1927, recognizing the need to fill a gap of knowledge and expertise in its exploration geophysics sector, CFP acquired a majority share in a company specialized in the use of gravimetry. Ten years later this company merged with two other geophysics firms, one specializing in electrical, the other in

Figure 2.1 The area included in the *Red Line Agreement.*
Source: Courtesy of The National Archives, Kew.[10]

seismic and magnetic prospecting, to form the General Geophysical Company (*Compagnie générale de geóphysique*, CGG).[11]

The first of the two companies CGG absorbed was none other than the renowned Electrical Prospecting Company (*Société de prospection électrique*), founded and managed by the prominent French geophysicists Conrad and Marcel Schlumberger. This company had pioneered electrical logging prospecting techniques in France and abroad, and had also created an American affiliate, the Schlumberger Well Surveying Corporation. Following the triple merger, CGG acquired from the three companies not only their staff, prospecting equipment and vehicles, but even more importantly their geophysical documentation, expertise, studies, patents and licenses, commercial organization, and funds.[12]

Once this critical mass of knowledge and resources had been put together, CGG, thanks to the initiative of its general manager, the geophysicist Raymond Maillet, and his staff, started designing its own equipment. It could also rely on the reputable theoretical works of geophysicist Vladimir Baranov, who had been working for Schlumberger before the merger.

As mentioned in Chapter 1, by 1938 CGG had experimented with, and patented, a new electrical prospecting technique, the telluric method, which—unlike the usual electrical technique employing artificial currents—used the earth's natural currents to study the electrical resistance of rocks. By the time the telluric method was invented, the company's crews had already been operating in a large number of regions around the world.[13]

The consequence of improvements in hydrocarbon prospecting methods was the discovery of a natural gas field at Saint-Marcet in southwestern France. A new public organization was set up, the Autonomous Public Company for Oil (*Régie autonome des pétroles*, RAP), to exploit the field's gas, which was distributed from 1943. By then, however, France had been defeated a few months after entering World War II, and had been under German control for over two years, either through direct occupation, mainly in the country's north, or indirectly through the collaborationist Vichy Regime, led by Marshal Philippe Pétain, in the south and center. However, the war did not bring prospecting to a halt.

In late 1941, the Vichy government founded the National Oil Company of Aquitaine (*Société nationale des pétroles d'Aquitaine*, SNPA) to supervise exploration activities in the French southwest. Two years later, the government transformed an existing public agency, responsible for controlling the import, refining, and distribution of oil products in France, into the Fuels Directorate (*Direction des carburants*, DICA).[14] The new agency was to centralize and assert tighter control over the management of funds for the hydrocarbons industry and data gathered in recent surveys, in order to draft decrees for the allocation of exploration permits in France and the French Union.

Similarly to the situation in Italy, the expanding national oil industry faced powerful rivals in the oil majors. The Vacuum Company (later to join SOCONY), SONJ, and later Texaco, had been establishing and expanding their commercial activities in the Métropole through their affiliates. SONJ's investments in France had quadrupled through the 1920s thanks to support from the Bank of Paris and the Netherlands (*Banque de Paris et des Pays-Bas*). Shell was also present, as part of a joint venture with a group of industrialists and businessmen linked to a number of important Parisian banks. The Anglo-Iranian Oil Company (AIOC) had also founded its own French affiliate, investing an initial sum four times larger than CFP's starting capital.[15]

Aside from extending prospecting activities in the French Empire and elsewhere through CGG and other, smaller prospecting companies, in order to find energy resources to bolster their own security, French authorities had attempted to limit the expansion of foreign interests. A number of laws passed from 1925 onwards were intended to regulate imports, refining activities and the commercialization of oil products on the national market. French governments had opted for a system that was equidistant from an American-like free market and a Soviet-like state monopoly. The state allowed private refining companies to obtain market share in order to guarantee the survival and development of the French refining industry.

At the same time, protection measures were approved to shield the newborn industry from foreign competition. In particular, a law passed in 1928 placed imports of crude oil and derivatives under the state's authority. It was not, as in the case of Fascist Italy, autarchy, but a revamping of protectionism. The 1928 law established import regulation: French authorities could now assign long-term authorizations for both the import of oil for refining and of products to market. The new provisions stabilized the presence of companies on the French territory, and favored long-term programs such as the construction of refineries. On the other hand, the majors benefited particularly from the establishment of import authorizations, as they made off with most of the quotas, thus consolidating their already strong positions. A further clause included in the new law provided for a preferential outlet on the national market for CFP's Iraqi oil.[16]

Such measures resulted in an unprecedented expansion of refining capacity in the country. By 1938 fifteen refineries were operating in France, most of which belonged to British and American concerns. The CFP-managed French Refining Company (*Compagnie française de raffinage*, CFR), which had been established with the aim of kick-starting the French refining industry, operated with two refineries in the country.[17] However, in the face of opposition from the majors, it was only authorized to refine up to 25 percent of the distributing companies' needs. Following the foundation of CFP, its growing Iraqi production gradually lead to a shift in the source of crude oil refined in French plants: while in 1929, they processed only American oil, by 1938 the plants were handling 55 percent American and 45 percent Middle Eastern oil.[18] The administrators who took charge of French oil agencies in the postwar period would further challenge the predominance of Anglo-American authority in France's oil affairs, with a view to restoring the grandeur of the French oil industry.

Pierre Guillaumat and the State of National Oil Technology

In the early postwar years, France's financial situation was particularly dire. Public debt was rising as steeply as inflation. Requisitions operated by the Nazis and the separation of the country into two zones affected everyday life. Means of transportation were scarce. After the fall of the Vichy regime in June 1944, the Provisional Government of the French Republic (*Gouvernement provisoire de la République française*, GPRF) was established to administer the country. Led by General Charles de Gaulle, its chief goal was to employ all available means to reconstruct France's economy and industry. Above all, France needed energy sources, if possible domestic, but definitely in large quantities.[19]

Although coal played a fundamental role in GPRF's strategy (hence French demands for authorization to exploit the German Saarland mines), the importance of oil had not to be underestimated. If the French were to reclaim their seat among the great powers, they needed to have energy autonomy. Indeed, notes historian Gabrielle Hecht, the way out of energy dependence became the main instrument through which the government envisioned the regeneration of French identity.[20] While Hecht's argument focuses on the role of nuclear energy, in the immediate aftermath of the war this objective had to be achieved first and foremost by restructuring the French oil exploration industry.

Against this background, in late 1944, with most of France liberated from the Nazis and their local allies, de Gaulle appointed 35-year-old Pierre Guillaumat (Figure 2.2) as Fuels Director. He would go on to dominate the French oil scene for the next two decades as head of a number of essential energy institutions, substantiating the common definition of him as the 'father of French oil.'[21] Son of a French army general, and a close family friend of de Gaulle, with similar political convictions, Guillaumat had been educated at France's most prestigious engineering school, the *École Polytechnique*, and had then entered the *Corps des Mines*, the most prominent of the French State's technical Grand Corps, formed by the State Engineers of Mines. This educational path, *Polytechnique* plus *Mines* (commonly referred to as *X-Mines* from the Polytechnique's shorthand notation, 'X'), soon came to embody *the* route to follow for French public high officials aspiring to prestige positions in the administration of energy institutions. The oil industry, in particular, would soon fall under the domination of *polytechniciens* and *corpsards*.[22]

Figure 2.2 Pierre Guillaumat (1909–1991).

Source: Courtesy of the Archive Services of the Commissariat à l'Energie Atomique, Fontenay-aux-Roses.[23]

As we have seen in the case of Italy, the organization of the oil industry entails first and foremost the ability to collect and use restricted information on potentially oil-rich areas, a process that favored an alliance of prospectors and intelligence agents. That Guillaumat had experience of both made him particularly suited to the tasks de Gaulle assigned him. After a few years as chief of the French mining services in Indochina from 1934 to 1939, Guillaumat had become an agent of the French intelligence services in Tunis, and later rejoined the Gaullist secret services in Algiers during the war.[24]

Although he has at times been described as a Mattei-like energy czar, the similarities do not seem to extend to personality traits: in contrast with the ENI president, the Frenchman favored a low profile and secretiveness, eschewing all sorts of media popularity. Like Mattei, however, he shared a desire to reduce the majors' influence in his country. "His tendency to secrecy and his instinctual authority"—comments historian Matthew Adamson—"became part of his system-building method." "[O]ne can affirm with no exaggeration that [Guillaumat] has been the most dynamic and the most secret inspirer [of French oil policy]," adds historian André Nouschi.[25]

While working in Tunisia and Algeria, Guillaumat had collaborated with André Rauscher, an engineer who worked for Shell Tunisia, on a mission to gather intelligence on the Italian army in Libya during the war.[26] According to journalist Pierre Péan, Rauscher created an intelligence network with Guillaumat and other former *polytechniciens*: this also included Pierre Taranger from CGG and Léon Kaplan from Shell. Soon after the war this small coterie of experts, characterized by strong personal links, would take control of the French oil agencies. Like Guillaumat, many *corpsards* had entered the cadres of the French intelligence services during the war, and were now engaging in bringing together intelligence and geoscientific expertise.[27]

Throughout his career, Guillaumat remained in close contact with the French foreign secret services, which later developed into the Service for Foreign Documentation and Counter-espionage (SDECE). He used men from the secret services to manipulate politics in former French African colonies, and to launch military operations designed to secure French oil interests.[28] In 1946, the former secret agent and new head of DICA starkly revealed the challenges facing the French public oil sector:

> France has practically no natural oil. Its foreign supply resources are under foreign control. Its oil exploration industry is very much behind and lacks modern drilling equipment; its refining techniques no longer have a leading role. Its oil fleet is weak.[29]

The industry had to be completely rebuilt. While DICA would provide direction for French oil activities, GPRF authorities knew quite well that the agency needed support from a network of other institutions operating in oil research, exploration, and production. A fundamental step in this direction was the foundation in 1944 of the French Petroleum Institute (*Institut français du pétrole*, IFP), headed by René Navarre. Besides training engineers and workers, the institute was to carry out research on oil technology, economics, and administration, and collect documentation on scientific and technological knowledge relevant to the country's oil activities.[30] In order to secure drilling equipment at affordable prices, DICA also created the National Company of Materials for Oil Exploration and Production (*Société nationale de matériels pour la recherche et l'exploitation du pétrole*).

However, especially in the decade following the end of hostilities, France's geophysics industry, much like Italy's, found itself dependent on American technologies to a significant extent. "If we wanted to be autonomous thanks to our oil, we could not wait for the development of a French technology," recalled André Giraud, an *X-Mines* and former Fuels Director with a long career at the Ministry of Industry, as well as in oil and nuclear agencies.[31] The key priority, Giraud argued, was not so much to employ national technology, but to use the best available, regardless of its origins. And that meant American technology.

The inadequate status of French geophysics, however, was regarded as a grave problem. In January 1946, Edmond Vellinger, Director of the Toulouse section of the National Higher School for Oil (*École nationale supérieure du pétrole*), in a talk at the French association of oil technicians (*Association nationale des techniciens du pétrole*), expressed his concern about such a heavy dependence on foreign equipment and methods. France, he maintained, had an "imperious necessity to make an effort of design and research" in the exploration and production sector.[32] In the face of US supremacy, French technocrats decided that, although reliance on the Americans was inevitable in the first instance, efforts would have to be made in the education and training of French technicians and engineers in order to give the country relative technological independence.

This strategy was exemplified not only by the creation of the IFP, but also by CGG's attempts to get back on track. The French geophysical company, as CFP President, the *X-Mines* Victor de Metz, stated at a 1946 board meeting, had been excluded from technological progress, and there was a profound need to familiarize the geophysical firm with new American techniques. Chances for CGG to work with a US firm, however, were not deemed encouraging. De Metz pragmatically proposed to the board a compromise in order to facilitate relations between American and French technological contractors. CGG would surrender to Schlumberger (which, though formally an American company, maintained close bonds with France) the license for using its telluric method. In return, Schlumberger would allow CGG to benefit from its experience in the use of other geophysical methods.[33]

In restoring their geophysical industry, the French could also count on their prewar prestige in this discipline. As mentioned, the Schlumberger brothers had created and trialed one of the methods that would become a sine qua non of oil exploration, namely electrical well logging, used to test potential oil fields. Indeed as Geoffrey Bowker shows in his historical reconstruction of the early years of the Schlumberger Company, the industrial strategies and image constructed by the company made it the ultimate authority in terms of well logging, and laid the foundations of a veritable myth concerning its prowess.[34]

That myth contributed substantially to the reawakening of French geophysics in the postwar period; in combination with the efforts of the new technological agencies set up by the GPRF, French geophysicists succeeded in recapturing a prominent position in Europe within a relatively short time. By 1951, of the 710 geophysicists operating in Western Europe, 35 percent were based in France, as compared with only 6 percent in Italy.[35] While it is certainly hard to overstate the roles of Schlumberger, the IFP and CGG in the renaissance of French exploration science, the greatest boost came from the foundation of a new public institution, the Bureau of Petroleum Research (*Bureau de recherches de pétrole*, BRP), which was also intended to counter British–American assertiveness in the French oil sector. In the following paragraph, I will frame the constitution and early development of the BRP within the broader political and economic context of France's postwar reconstruction programs, and focus especially on the financial resources the BRP and French oil industry were intended to employ for their activities. For that, we have to move back in time to 1945.

Tied Aid and the Constitution of the *Bureau de Recherches de Pétrole*

Although in the postwar years France was in an internationally stronger political position than Italy, it could not afford to jeopardize Allied relations. Furthermore, in 1945 oil was still subject to a partition system conditioned by war imperatives. This was particularly true for crude oil distributed in the Mediterranean, the delivery of which depended on an inter-Allied system. After February 1945, the IPC share of oil due to CFP was directed to a Shell-owned refining plant in Haifa, Palestine, while CFP received, in exchange, oil products that it could cede to a number of clients. These, however, had to be chosen in geographical markets that complied with the repartition plans drawn up by the Allied Petroleum Division.[36] Therefore, as had happened for Italy, French policymakers were obliged to seek compromises with allies and majors rather than nationalize.

In March, US Acting State Secretary Joseph Grew, whose key role in influencing oil policy in Italy I highlighted in Chapter 1, invited the GPRF to participate in a supply arrangement with the Anglo-Americans. If the government accepted, it would have to provide the British and American governments with a list setting out French needs for crude oil and oil products, which would then be passed to the Anglo-American Allocating Board. The Board, Grew stressed, "would know at all times the amount of oil and transportation available for importing countries."[37] In addition, since every country had to obtain specific amounts, if a country imported oil from other sources, the quantity assigned by the Allocating Board would be reduced accordingly (the 'reduction clause'). Finally, all French tanker capacity and all transportation facilities would be operated within the framework of the supply arrangement.

As in the Italian case, Grew's instructions amounted to handing over to the Allies all possible information on France's oil needs, as well as—temporarily—their transportation facilities. The request was disguised as a measure for equitable distribution; in fact, it was essentially a surveillance operation, which French administrators, considering their situation of weakness, could hardly oppose. Given France's low chances of obtaining its oil from IPC concessions, the reduction clause was tantamount to an obligation to use only oil distributed by the Anglo-Americans. When the GPRF asked the State Department to give France a seat on the Allocating Board as a condition for the acceptance of the supply agreement, and by virtue of the country's large role in oil importation, transportation, and refining, it was told that a response to that request would require time, and that a decision could not be made before the supply agreement was operative.[38] Now it was the Allies that were deploying dilatory tactics.

However, Grew suggested to the US Ambassador in France, Jefferson Caffery, that if the French asked for further explanation, he should advance reasons of military security. The French capitulated and sent a list of their requirements. At the end of hostilities, the supply agreement was terminated, and the Petroleum Division lifted its opposition to CFP's crude oil imports into France. However, the Americans specified that they expected the French to restore a free-market regime, with no preferential treatment for French companies.[39]

From 1945, French contacts with the American administration had resulted in financial aid, allowing imports to regain some vitality. However, exports from France had not been as consistent; in addition, not only oil, but also coal and rubber imports, remained under the allied military authorities' responsibility, as established in the Crowley-Monnet Agreements of January 1945. This inconsistency lead to a serious deficit in the French balance of payments, which France had to compensate for by selling the Bank of France's gold stocks. Only massive foreign aid could prevent the country exhausting its remaining gold stocks to pay for the 1946 imports program that French authorities had planned.[40]

Thus, in February 1945, de Gaulle sent long-time international official Jean Monnet on a mission to the US as a representative of the French government. By the end of his mission, Monnet had succeeded in securing from the Americans, within the lend-lease framework, \$1.6 billion in primary sources and foodstuffs, as well as a \$900 million loan to start reconstituting the country's economic infrastructure. The UK also gave a contribution to boost the French economy, through a \$1 million loan.[41]

In October, the first postwar legislative elections took place in France, to elect a Constituent Assembly for seven months. The victory of the Communist Party, which became France's largest party, followed by the Christian Democrats and the Socialists, meant that Left parties held over 50 percent of the Assembly. These three parties formed the first assembly—the term *Tripartisme* was coined to designate this coalition. In May 1946, US State Secretary James Byrnes, and GPRF delegate Léon Blum, signed a further agreement with the US, allowing France to cancel almost three quarters of its debt to the US and offering an attractive loan contract for \$2.3 million to be allocated through the European Recovery Plan (ERP)—the Marshall Plan—in exchange for the opening of the French market to American products.[42]

To comply with the French master plan devised for the public oil industry, in the same month as the elections that launched *Tripartisme*, de Gaulle's government created the BRP. The purpose of this structure was to coordinate oil exploration by specifying the nature of permits and concessions, and to fund prospecting activities through budget subventions. In addition, the BRP was given the task of devising a national program of oil exploration. It was to work together with DICA and the RAP: while the latter would mainly prospect in France, the efforts of the BRP would largely be focused abroad.

Through the Bureau, the Ministry of Industry signaled a new effort by the state to improve France's position in the international oil industry. In a way, the Bureau was tacitly handed the baton of energy provision previously held by CFP.[43] The direction of the new institution was entrusted to Fuels Director, Guillaumat. At the same time, he was assigned one of the two seats reserved for government representatives on CFP's board of directors. The BRP was not allowed to participate directly in exploration so, soon after its constitution, it started taking majority shares in existing exploration syndicates, constituted earlier at the initiative of French administrations throughout the French Union. This policy of share acquisition was to be a characteristic of both the BRP and the RAP, and a strategy pursued throughout the 1950s. The Bureau's program was carried out through four five-year plans between 1946 and 1965.[44]

State planning soon became characteristic of French postwar policies: as further legislative elections in late 1946 once more underlined the strength of the Communists, who gained 29 percent of the votes, this trend was anything but slowed down.[45] The predominance of the Left and the substantial financial commitment necessary to revitalize the energy sector resulted in large-scale public intervention in the management of natural resources. From 1946, a wave of nationalizations ensued, lasting until early 1947, at which time Léon Blum's short-lived government approved a five-year plan for reconstruction, which had already been formulated by Jean Monnet in 1946.

This was the famous Modernization and Equipment Plan (*Plan de modernisation et d'équipement*, also known as the Monnet Plan): it aimed to restore French production to its 1929 levels by 1948, and to exceed them by 25 percent by 1950. Its main objective was to make France the biggest producer on the continent, in place of Germany, by powering French industry with German and American coal. Monnet's scheme was meant to achieve this objective through a threefold process: renewing and improving the country's infrastructure; supporting increased demand for consumer goods; and reconstructing destroyed buildings.[46] Under the Monnet Plan, the BRP received almost 49 percent of the funds allotted to hydrocarbon exploration. Thanks to the first two five-year plans, it was able to buy the first drilling materials in the US and fund exploration in the French Union.[47]

Then in mid-1947, a mere two months after the enunciation of the Truman Doctrine, through which the US undertook to provide political, military and economic assistance to all democratic nations under threat from authoritarian forces, the Cold War materialized in France. In May, under the pretext of Communist support for a series of strikes led by France's largest trade union, the Communist-dominated General Confederation of Labor (*Confédération générale du travail*), the Socialist Prime Minister, Paul Ramadier, excluded Communist ministers from his cabinet. This act, together with the subsequent integration of the Socialists within a new, extremely heterogeneous centrist coalition known as Third Force (*Troisième Force*), marked the beginning of a long period of instability in French governmental life.

However the 1946–1947 nationalizations, which extended to many sectors of the French economy, enabled the Left to strengthen the economy under the control and will of the state. Three important sectors underwent substantial nationalizations: energy, transportation, and banking. In the energy domain, however, a dual policy was adopted. While coal, gas, and electricity were fully nationalized, oil was not. Before clarifying why this was the case, it is worth stressing that at the time of the nationalizations, oil played a lesser role than coal: by way of indication, in the first five-year reconstruction plan it was not even listed among the six sectors believed to be fundamental to the revitalization of the French economy, namely electricity, coal, steel, concrete, railway transportation, and equipment for agriculture.

A Missed Nationalization and the Threat of Over-Rapid Reconstruction

Despite the smaller part played by oil in the Monnet Plan, French planners were perfectly aware of the significance of hydrocarbons for the country's future. France's Plan Commission (*Commissariat général du Plan*) stated in 1947 that:

> In order to remedy the deficit in its energy production, France must think first of all about oil. The recovery of its economic situation, as well as that of its domestic finances, are closely linked to the development and modernization of its oil industry.[48]

Indeed crude oil and oil products were to be given significantly more funding in the subsequent five-year plans: the third and fourth plans allocated considerable funding to prospecting and exploration, the fifth and sixth to refining and distribution.[49]

Historians Serge Berstein and Pierre Milza have explained the non-nationalization of the French affiliates of foreign oil companies by arguing that it was not strictly needed, as the state was already present in that sector through CFP and SNPA.[50] In fact, this anomaly calls for a broader analysis. First, oil was in the hands of foreign majors, supported by their governments, and of CFP. This was in contrast to coal and electricity, sectors in which French private industrialists played a major part. Now as we will see in the next paragraphs, CFP's early postwar relations with its IPC partners became strained. In such circumstances, the British and American governments would have interpreted a nationalization of the oil industry as a direct threat to their interests in France, which were especially strong in the refining and marketing sectors, and would in all probability have retaliated over CFP's interests within IPC.

That was not an unrealistic threat. Indeed, during the talks leading up to the Blum-Byrnes Agreement of 1946, American negotiators had demanded the right for their companies to expand in the French market, and the elimination of some restrictive legislative provisions. Blum had not let the US government and majors have what they wanted, but instead compromised by offering treatment on an equal footing with French companies for American companies that had suffered destruction in the war (this was not the case for British companies registered in France, which received worse treatment). Moreover, Blum assured Byrnes that no American oil company would be nationalized, precisely for fear of retaliation.[51] In addition, it was deemed that the law of 1928 gave the French oil industry sufficient protection for the time being: nationalization was not urgently needed.

The Monnet Plan and US aid were deemed instrumental by the French administrations in achieving the first objectives in the reorganization of the oil sector, namely rebuilding the refining industry and laying the foundations for an aggressive oil exploration program. In the first five-year plan, the aim was to reach annual refining capacity of 13 Mt by the end of 1950.[52] To accomplish the initial stages of the Monnet Plan, France received new funding from banks and other states, such as Canada and New Zealand, although the majority of aid came from the United States. In December 1947, the *Hexagon* (as France is also called due to its approximate shape) was assigned $284 million in interim aid. Of this, $32 million was allocated to oil.[53]

Once the Marshall Plan was put into effect in April 1948, the US administration demanded that the beneficiary countries draw up detailed plans for how the funds would be used. The Monnet Plan had been ready for two years, so the France-based American authorities established that the main amounts of American funds would be distributed through it: between 1948 and 1951, France benefited from around $2.5 billion in American aid.[54]

The increase in French oil consumption, as noted in 1948 by Walter Levy, the head of the Oil Division at ECA, was striking. Consumption in 1947 had already reached 1938 levels (5.9 Mt), and was expected to rise to 8.2 Mt in 1949. Indeed the oil sector, including crude oil, products and equipment, absorbed between a fourth and a fifth of US aid, thus ranking second after foodstuffs. Unlike AGIP, CGG benefited considerably from American aid, but only until 1948. For example, the company bought the Allies' surplus vehicles, vans and jeeps, whose sturdiness made them particularly suitable for geophysical missions, while Marshall funds were used to complete their equipment: electronic materials, drills, and advanced, multi-track seismic recorders, were all acquired from the US.[55]

Actually, French recovery was happening *too* fast, and that worried the majors. American oil companies therefore put pressure on ECA since this rapidity could harm their interests in the French market. The French import program for oil products, which ECA considered too large, was therefore reduced, officially in order to manage oil resources in the dollar area. At the end of July 1948, a meeting took place in Washington between the French Ambassador Henri Bonnet, Levy, and a representative of the fuel purchase group. Levy insisted that an excessive increase in French oil production would lead to a reduction in business volumes for US companies, especially in the French Union, and declared it necessary to leave part of the market to these companies, which had been supplying those territories for years.[56]

At a further meeting, Levy used economic support as a bargaining chip to gain influence in African affairs. He pointed out that "the activities of CFP upset American companies, especially in Africa," and implied that ECA's acceptance of the French import program for oil products in the third quarter of the year would depend on how American companies were treated. In other words, it would depend on the guarantees given them about the protection of their markets in French overseas territories. An irked Bonnet remarked in a letter to Hervé Alphand, Director of Economic Affairs at the Foreign Ministry, that Levy's request was inadmissible, and that he would not recommend passing on the American's observations to the ECA mission in France.[57]

To summarize, the ECA made the approval of the oil products import program conditional on French overseas territories being opened up to American companies. In practical terms, this resulted in a cut of $4 million in France's fuel imports program in late 1948. In addition, the French Foreign Minister, Robert Schuman, explained to Bonnet that "a sort of embargo ha[d] been placed on oil equipment exports departing from the US to the participating countries [in the Marshall Plan]." This consequence was particularly serious as much of the oil equipment needed for the maintenance and expansion of oil facilities was available only from the United States.[58] Besides being a retaliation measure against the French, these restrictions were also a consequence of ECA's unwillingness to stimulate the expansion of the European oil industry more than US companies needed. Oil consumption in Europe should be encouraged, but the continent's abilities to manage the oil sector autonomously should not.

A look at the role of ECA aid in the French refining sector reveals that British and American companies received the largest share of American aid. French affiliates of Caltex, Shell, SOCONY, and SONJ (but also the French CFR) all demanded and obtained funding of over $1 million each, mainly for petrochemical equipment. While almost $11 million of aid was assigned to refining, only $1.5 million went to oil exploration.[59] The ECA was willing to help wherever their interests were concerned, but there was no economic rationale in funding exploration operations by French governmental agencies, as that could only decrease their dependence on the majors.

Besides the financial support given by the Monnet and Marshall Plans, French oil administrators also adopted a number of measures aimed at making oil exploration more palatable to companies. Further measures promoted by the French government to stimulate exploration included the 1953 provision for oilfield reconstruction, which encouraged companies to reinvest their production profits into oil exploration in the French Union by exempting 50 percent of total profits from corporate taxation. They also included the 1954 Support Funds for Hydrocarbons (*Fonds de soutien aux hydrocarbures*). Promoted by Fuels Director and *corpsard* Jean Blancard, and fed through a tax on gasoline, this fund was intended to promote exploration in the franc zone.[60] Interestingly, it was controlled by Roger Goetze, who was at the same time budget director at the French Ministry of Finance, and president of BRP's Algerian affiliate, the National Company for Exploration and Production of Oil in Algeria (*Société nationale de recherche et d'exploitation des pétroles en Algérie,* [SN]REPAL). This double function, according to historian Eric Kocher-Marbœuf, gave him "almost unlimited power" to supply the fund that financed the BRP in those years.[61]

While the early years of BRP's activities saw no oil and gas discoveries, this was not the case for other companies based in France. At the end of 1949, the SNPA struck oil at Lacq, in the country's far southwest, using seismic reflection. This was the first discovery in mainland France, and triggered as many hopes in the country as had the simultaneous Cortemaggiore finding in Italy. The Aquitanian company made another important discovery two years later, again at Lacq, this time a gas field.[62] In fact 1951 can be considered a key year for French oil exploration for a further reason. The five-year permit in the Bordeaux area granted to the SONJ affiliate Standard française was the first permit awarded by the French administration to a foreign company.[63]

Three years after the granting of its permit, in 1954, Standard Française (renamed Esso Standard in 1952) struck oil at Parentis, some 80 km southwest of Bordeaux. The oilfield was soon to be recognized as the largest in France. A fundamental role in this discovery had been played by geophysical innovations introduced by the American company in 1952: the use of arrays of detectors arranged in specific patterns, in order to obtain a better signal-to-noise ratio and improve the quality of seismograms, thus facilitating interpretation. The permit granted to SONJ's affiliate revealed that, while the Bureau was prepared to give away some licenses, it demanded in return that the US company train French technicians, through internships and stays abroad. Finally, the company had to transfer ten percent of its shares to BRP.[64]

These provisions reflected a precise strategy. SONJ's vast interests in France meant that the French authorities could not merely dismiss its permit application. They therefore opted to reap the highest possible benefit from the major in technical terms, namely enhancing and updating the know-how of French technicians. While the majors could not avoid coming to terms with the French government as far as exploration in France was concerned, the balance of power was very different in the Middle East, where France was extracting its only production in the late 1940s.

Middle Eastern Controversies

In the late 1940s and throughout the 1950s several events in the Middle East would expose the decline of the former imperial powers, and show that the region had become the field for a new confrontation: that between Cold War superpowers. This was the place where US energy security was most at stake. Although before the war the American administration and oil firms had prioritized the control of resources in Mexico, during the conflict they gradually shifted their attention to the Middle East, prompted by advice received by the eminent geologist Everette DeGolyer, now working as US Assistant Deputy of the Petroleum Administration for War.[65]

Moreover, there was a geostrategic aspect relating to Soviet influence to be taken into account, since, while the Middle East could be used as a launch point for possible attacks on the USSR by Western powers, it was also from there the Soviets could dispute the West's supremacy over the Mediterranean.[66] In a clear manifestation of Robert Jervis's security dilemma mentioned in the introductory chapter, the expansion of US interests inevitably entailed a reduction in the security of the powers already present in the region, namely France and the UK.[67] In order to understand how this dilemma arose, we need to focus on the Iraq Petroleum Company.

With World War II and the invasion of France by German troops in June 1940, French shares in IPC were confiscated by the British, and transferred to the UK's Custodian of Enemy Property branch. The sale of oil to French ships at IPC terminals in Palestine and Syria was also blocked, as occupied France was by then an enemy country. For the same reason, all CFP's contacts with IPC were severed.[68] Following the Liberation, French diplomats contacted the IPC in London and applied pressure: in consequence, a few months later in February 1945, CFP representatives were once again able to be part of the IPC board, and the French company resumed its IPC oil deliveries.[69]

This was only to a limited extent a happy ending for the French, since even once deliveries resumed, CFP faced a serious threat to its oil supplies under the Red Line Agreement. Contending that the Red Line Agreement was curbing their aspirations in the area, SONJ and SOCONY sought to take a larger share of Saudi oil, and advocated an 'open door' policy in the Middle East. The new US government, headed by Harry Truman, fully endorsed this.[70] Anglo-Iranian and Shell were willing to appease the Americans and did nothing to stop the Arabian-American Oil Company (ARAMCO), which was not originally part of the IPC and held concessions in Saudi Arabia, from 'crossing' the Red Line. So in the spring of 1946, SONJ publicly declared that they considered the agreement to have lapsed, owing to France's wartime status as an enemy power during the period of the Vichy regime.[71] During an autumn visit to Europe, representatives of the American oil majors further bolstered the US position by maintaining that the Sherman Antitrust Act forbade them to comply with the restrictive provisions of the agreement, which would amount to cartelization.[72]

Believing that the Red Line would not be restored, and since the unanimity of all IPC directors was needed in order to modify the old agreement, the State Department and SOCONY tried to negotiate a solution with the French government and de Metz, once the removal of the substantial French interests in the area was already a *fait accompli*.[73] In the end, SONJ presented its IPC partners with an ultimatum intended to speed up a settlement. Simultaneously, the State Department secretly addressed the British to ensure they agreed. During bilateral talks organized in London in November, Clement Attlee's government accepted the American view that the preservation of competition in the international oil trade demanded the non-restoration of the Red Line Agreement.[74]

The secret deals between Americans and British, revealed to the French through press leaks, convinced the French of the need to reinforce their information-gathering activities on foreign oil agreements. At a CFP board meeting in December 1946, Director René de Montaigu confirmed press rumors that SONJ and SOCONY had acquired shares in ARAMCO, while President Victor de Metz informed the board of a new agreement between Anglo-Iranian and the two Standards. The deal reassured British and US governments about controlling oil supplies in the Middle East at the expense of French energy security. Over the next twenty years the British government-controlled AIOC would sell Jersey 160 Mt of crude, and the two companies would jointly build a pipeline linking the Persian Gulf to the Mediterranean.[75] The British would use it for their Kuwaiti crude, which they exploited on a fifty-fifty basis with Gulf Oil. Shell's neutrality was also acquired through a very favorable contract allowing the company free access to Kuwaiti oil: from May 1947, Gulf would provide 30 percent of Shell's crude oil requirements in the Eastern Hemisphere.[76]

De Metz was outraged. He considered the unilateral termination of the Red Line and the simultaneous taking of shares in ARAMCO as an "extremely serious infringement of the 1928 accords," and advised the board to take legal action against NEDC's decision in the British High Courts of Justice. Guillaumat, in his dual role as CFP government commissioner and Fuels Director, announced that DICA would retaliate against British and American interests in France. In early January 1947, the French Ambassador in Washington delivered the US Undersecretary of State for Economic Affairs, William Clayton, a letter of formal protest against the unilateral termination of the agreement. The French Ambassador in London, René Massigli, also intervened in CFP's favor.[77]

The cancellation of the Red Line Agreement would put at risk not only French oil security, but all projects intended to restore the country to the status of a great power. Without energy autonomy, France would be reduced to a client of British and American companies. The two diplomatic interventions confirmed that the French government would back the lawsuit that CFP was about to start in the British courts against the unilateral termination, which represented "an erroneous and politically inadmissible interpretation of the English legislation on commerce with the enemy," and against which "the French authorities could not fail to raise the strongest protest."[78]

On the eve of the first court hearing on this agreement in London, a Shell representative, John Boyle, offered de Metz and de Montaigu a compromise. The IPC would supply CFP as its managers wished, and a new pipeline would be built from Kirkuk to the Mediterranean Sea. The counterproposal was accepted but de Metz only agreed to postpone legal proceedings. The following February the French filed the court petition again, now hoping to force the Americans to re-open negotiations.[79]

Also in January, discussions took place at the US State Department between government officials and US companies. The company representatives put forward their view that they had a rock-solid legal defense on the invalidity of the accord. They saw the French position as an effort to extort some kind of payoff under threat of retaliation, and aimed to reach an agreement that would satisfy the French as oil consumers rather than as producers, for example by setting a favorable price with CFP for short-term crude oil contracts from Saudi production. As for CFP's participation in the ARAMCO deal, which the French has also demanded, that was out of the question. The Saudi King, Ibn Saʿūd, had insisted that the concession should be exclusively in American hands. While concurring with the companies' views, the State Department diplomatically suggested that it would not oppose the two majors' "voluntary withdrawal" from ARAMCO, although they would not impose it.[80]

According to Nouschi, France was not in a strong enough position to be able to impose its will on its IPC partners, so the government consented to the American proposal. While French weakness certainly played a role, the key issue was rather how the US administration sought to exploit it, substantially reducing French influence in oil affairs in the Middle East. France needed coal, oil, and wheat, and it was to US aid that the French government turned for these supplies, as well as to curb the inflation ravaging the country's finances.[81] Negotiations between CFP and its British–American partners continued through the spring of 1947, a settlement being eventually reached at the end of May. The *Heads of Agreement* were signed by all the major IPC partners a year later, in the autumn of 1948.[82]

The new agreement restored the Red Line arrangements with the significant exception of Saudi Arabia, where US companies would have a monopoly. Average Iraqi production would largely be increased, and IPC would build a new, large-diameter pipeline in order to handle the additional production. The new deal secured IPC's development, and gave each of its members the right to obtain the amounts of oil they needed, independently of their quotas. Furthermore, restrictive clauses were eliminated; there would now be complete freedom to acquire new interests in existing concessions (as in the case of SONJ, SOCONY, and ARAMCO).[83]

Was the agreement a pyrrhic victory for the French administration? By the end of 1953, CFP's part in IPC production amounted to over 8 Mt, a tenfold increase compared with the 806,000 tons (806 kt) the company had received in 1945.[84] In 1954, CFP also acquired a small share in an oil consortium established in Iran by British and American companies, in the aftermath of the nationalization of oil resources decided by the Iranian Prime Minister Mohammad Mosaddegh, and the subsequent British–American military coup that toppled him.[85] However, the IPC issue had demonstrated that French oil revenues in the Middle East depended on American goodwill, and the Americans received the biggest slice of the cake.

By then, the existence of an oil cartel controlling the worldwide oil market had been widely publicized. In 1952, the US Federal Trade Commission published a report, entitled *The International Petroleum Cartel*, whose main conclusion revealed to the public that the world oil industry was actually controlled by a few British–American companies. The underlying implication that government measures should be taken to change this situation went against years of open and secret talks in which the US and UK governments had successfully collaborated to the opposite effect.[86]

Not unexpectedly, once the report was published in a 'sanitized' version, in August 1952, it triggered negative reactions in oil producing countries. So much so that a few months later the NSC, and the Departments of State, Defense and the Interior, suggested to President Truman that, in order not to jeopardize national security, the grand jury indictment of the companies under criminal charges be terminated and turned into a far more harmless civil action under antitrust laws. Three days after receiving the report, President Truman, in utmost secrecy, ordered the investigations ended.[87] US security had been preserved. US law had bowed to vested interests.

On the flip side of the coin, what the Red Line dispute had shown British and American diplomats was that the French government was prepared to make use of its experts, intelligence agents, and lawyers in defense of oil security, or in order to force them to renegotiate existing agreements to increase French oil supplies in the wake of the Cold War. However, more security concerns soon arose in Paris and forced the French to reconsider their position in the Middle East consortium, with a plan to invest more in North African resources.

Prospecting and Monitoring North Africa

The new IPC deal appeared to be short-lived. The superpowers' influence in the Middle East grew quickly and dramatically, making diplomatic and oil relations more volatile. In 1946, the Soviet government had urged Iran to start up an oil exploration company, though the Iranians had later cancelled the deal and struck a military agreement with the US government, allowing them to establish a radar zone to monitor nearby Soviet activities. The US authorities signed a further agreement with Saudi Arabia, enabling the establishment of a US military base in Dhahran in 1949, which was also the seat of ARAMCO's headquarters.[88]

The oil scene was of course also affected by these developments. The Arab–Israeli war of 1948 led to the permanent closure of one of IPC's terminals. And both Iraqi and Iranian officials sought to obtain fifty-fifty contracts from the oil majors modeled on the one conceded by ARAMCO to Saudi Arabia. The new arrangements would make the two contracting parties equal partners, thus ending the exploiter–exploited relation that had characterized previous contracts. The majors' refusal to accede to this request produced tensions and contributed to destabilization in the region. The French government now decided to partly disengage from the Middle East, a decision taken as a consequence of the reorganization of oil administration at government level, and also because of the presence of British–American interests within CFP; as mentioned, only 35 percent of its shares belonged to the French state.

France's partial disengagement from the Middle East stimulated sweeping surveys in the French Union, especially in their de facto private African territory, where British–American interference could be stemmed. In addition, most French overseas territories had yet to be explored using modern geophysical methods. It was therefore a logical consequence for the French oil agencies and geoscientists to start exploring Africa, especially the Sahara desert and the Gulf of Guinea.[89] Their attitude toward *their* Union had not changed much from imperial days, the underlying idea still being that the Métropole disposed of a huge territory to exploit for its own profit.

Geological studies in the northern Sahara had been conducted since the 1920s by geologists Conrad Kilian, Nicolas Menchikoff, Maurice Lelubre and their teams. In particular, Kilian had urged the French government to prospect Algeria for hydrocarbons. His observations on the sediments of the Hoggar area in the Sahara suggested the existence of geological conditions conducive to the presence of oil. In November 1948 his report was passed on to the French *Académie des Sciences*, sealed in a box, and stayed untouched until the geologist's death three years later.[90] Kilian's hypotheses on the areas turned out to be only partially accurate, but news of his exploratory activities did open the way to a new conception of the Sahara desert as a reservoir of hydrocarbons, therefore instigating further work.[91]

From 1941 onwards, geological reconnaissance missions were dispatched to the desert under the auspices first of the Mining Research Service of Algeria (*Service de recherches minières d'Algérie*), and subsequently of REPAL from 1946. REPAL's board was the clearest expression of the power of the *Corps des Mines*: the General Inspector of Mines in Algeria, Gaston Bétier; the company general manager, Armand Colot; CGG's general manager, René Migaux; and Paul Moch, one of the company's two vice-presidents, who had been appointed president of the RAP by Guillaumat a year earlier, all belonged to the Corps. One of the missions, sent in 1948 under the leadership of geologist and *corpsard* Michel Tenaille, could also count on Willy Bruderer, a CFP geologist and member of BRP's North African Commission. The results of the survey appeared to reveal the existence of promising oil structures.

However, CFP's Study Committee had emphasized the idiosyncratic geological conditions of the region. This meant that little valuable information on its real potential would be obtained without the application of a more powerful geophysical technique. Through the estimation of physical quantities, geophysics was believed to offer a better understanding of the characteristics of putative deposits than geology. As shown by studies on the history of postwar sciences, such trust in the physical sciences was characteristic of the postwar era. This was particularly true after the building of the nuclear bomb, and the subsequent development of nuclear explosion detection technologies had shown the utility of geophysics to perceived national security needs, conferring strong institutional backing on physicists.[92] Indeed, it had been the desire to train French geoscientists in novel geophysical applications that could facilitate subsurface surveys in the colonies that had persuaded the French to accept deals with SONJ in France.

CGG was thus committed to an extended gravimetry reconnaissance campaign. However, gravimetry was slow and its interpretation in the region proved hard. Besides the slowness and high cost, some lamented that the data obtained did not distinguish gravity anomalies in the deeper subsurface from the large structural traits of the sedimentary basin, closer to the surface. The use of telluric currents did not yield any spectacular results either. Non-decisive results notwithstanding, in 1950 the geophysical campaigns prompted REPAL and CFP to submit a joint application for an exploration permit for over 300,000 km^2 of the south Saharan region.[93]

In the following months, with the permit request still pending, the two companies intensified their surveys. From 1951, reflection seismology was introduced to the area, but again, because of the unfavorable surface conditions and the problem of multiple reflections, which masked the true, less energetic reflections, the results were disappointing. And photo-geology could not be applied outside the Saharan Atlas Mountains, where the mass of Mesozoic layers hindered surface geology. Even with the introduction of techniques learned from US prospecting firms, such as multiple detectors and pattern shooting, these problems were only addressed to a limited extent.[94]

In October 1952, the permit was finally issued. It covered 248,000 km^2, which CFP and REPAL split equally, and a joint geophysical campaign was agreed upon. 1952 represented a decisive year. REPAL's chief geologist, Igor Ortynski, convinced CGG to apply a method—refraction seismology (also called seismic refraction)—that had been out of fashion for two decades but seemed more appropriate to the geological characteristics of the Sahara. Refraction seismology provided a way to estimate the properties of the Earth's subsurface from an analysis of refracted seismic waves generated by man-made explosions: by eliminating the confusing multiple reflections, which affected what was at that time the most widely-employed technique, namely seismic reflection, refraction penetrated younger geological layers characterized by high reflection coefficients (coefficients that made seismic reflection useless), thus producing a picture of deeper layers.[95]

The first application of seismic refraction led to the implantation by CFP and REPAL of an exploration well at Berriane, some 600 km south of Algiers, where oil traces had been found. The accumulation of this knowledge about local underground resources helped French geoscientists to focus their exploration on specific areas. They thus gained a refined understanding of the geology of the Saharan region, which would soon prove of capital importance in the oil discoveries that took place in the subsequent years.

With refraction seismology having proved valuable in Berriane, CFP and REPAL decided to launch a general seismic refraction survey in the northern part of the desert, resulting in the discovery of more oil traces. To manage its share in the Algerian concession, in January 1953 CFP founded its affiliate CFP (Algérie) (CFP(A)), entrusting the presidency to *corpsard* Jacques Bénézit, assistant manager of CFP and a high school companion of REPAL'S president, Roger Goetze. Once again, it is hard to ignore the *esprit de corps* that guided the choice of executives in the French oil industry, which helped *X-Mines* technocrats to perpetuate their absolute leadership. The image projected in the public sphere, however, was that of a politically neutral technoscience. Technocrats were depicted as being chosen exclusively on criteria of competence, rather than political allegiance, and were described as agents whose valuable expertise and dynamism, and detachment from political power, would enable them to direct their activities to the exclusive benefit of the nation.[96]

Partially successful they might have been, but the surveys must nevertheless have attracted some interest as, by 1952, the American government had put the oil activities in Algeria under close surveillance. At the same time, in Europe, French–American tensions increased, as a result of the French Assembly's torpedoing of a plan to form a pan-European defense force, which the US government—especially State Secretary Dean Acheson—had strongly encouraged.[97] Hydrocarbons grew steadily in importance in the thick political and economic reports that the American Consulate General in Algiers sent to the State Department. Along with these reports, the State Department also recorded the initiatives of individual American oil companies, as well as French activities not directly involving American interests. The British Government also instructed its agents abroad to find out what the French were doing, and confidentially received detailed information from its Parisian embassy about BRP's five-year plans, including some details on results and prospects.[98]

Guillaumat and his entourage soon realized that secretly acquired geophysical knowledge was not enough to ensure safe and quick oil supplies from Algeria. They needed to increase their prospecting effort even further if they wanted to find oil anytime soon. They were therefore faced with two main options: let British and American enterprises into the Sahara and gain in efficiency, financial backing, and technological knowledge; or continue their path independently at the risk of having to carry a colossal prospecting burden over many years. This second choice would be a dangerous one for a country struggling with high inflation.

The admission of foreign capital soon began to be debated within the French administration. The Commission for Fuel Modernization (*Commission de modernisation des carburants*), an agency established after the constitution of the BRP, and responsible with it for devising a prospecting program in the French Union, highlighted the need for American technology, expertise, and finance for accurate exploration of the Sahara as a rationale for the admission of foreign companies. At the same time, however, the Commission established a series of clear conditions for foreign participation. It should not exceed half the shares in the companies formed; the chairman and half their boards of directors should be French; and significantly, French technicians would be seconded to foreign exploration directors to monitor their activities and improve their own technological capacity.[99] Again, as in the case of the SONJ deal, French administrators were using the lure of potential Saharan resources to boost their geoscientific knowledge through American expertise.

As a consequence, in 1947, when Gulf proposed setting up a Franco-American company with BRP's Tunisian affiliate and asked for a majority shareholding, Ramadier's government rejected the offer. Guillaumat, however, was more inclined to accept mixed companies with a foreign majority. After funding reductions in the European Recovery Plan's oil program in late 1948, and in the face of new requests from Shell and Gulf, the possibility of foreign participation was re-examined, and foreign capital majority in mixed companies in Tunisia was accepted, provided that the foreign concerns gave certain guarantees. Shell was eventually admitted to the North African country, with a majority shareholding of 65 percent in the Tunisian Oil Company (*Compagnie des pétrole de Tunisie*), with the BRP holding the remaining shares. According to historian Gérard Bossuat, the government agreed to grant licenses as it understood that only a few British–American companies had sufficient resources to exploit Tunisian oil.[100] In fact, in the Tunisian exception, informal ties between key actors may have played a fundamental role. The fact that the President of Shell Française was Léon Kaplan, who had operated as a secret agent with Guillaumat in Tunis during the war, certainly influenced the outcome, and may well have played a part in Shell's later admission to Algeria.[101]

The disagreement between authorities in favor of, and those opposing, the opening of the Sahara to foreign operations came to a head at a crucial meeting held in June 1947. The French Director of General Affairs, Pierre Maisonneuve, organized a conference at the Under-Directorate of Algeria to discuss three foreign companies that had shown an interest in Algeria: Caltex, Gulf, and AIOC. Representatives of four ministries (including Guillaumat), members of the domestic and foreign intelligence services, executives of the oil agencies BRP and REPAL, and National Defense officials, attended the conference. Guillaumat argued that collaboration with foreign companies would be extremely profitable for the French economy, because of the shaky state of French finances.[102]

As the Fuels Director reminded those at the meeting, the French had interests in Middle Eastern oilfields. So the government could not deny equivalent rights to foreign companies wishing to work in French territories. Their exclusion would trigger retaliation. Lucien-Benjamin-Gabriel Bonneau, Director of the Foreign Ministry's African and Near Eastern Department, argued that the benefits that local populations would enjoy from oil discoveries would prompt North African nationalist movements to a détente with France, and outweigh the risks of a foreign presence.[103]

In addition, non-French companies would surely favor order and stability, i.e. the political status quo in the region and French hegemony in North Africa, where the winds of Arab nationalism were beginning to blow. The discovery of oil in regions such as Tunisia or Morocco, Bonneau explained, could not in itself be seen as a threat to French security, but only in relation to the international position of France: only France's weakness would threaten its security.[104]

But Guillaumat's proposal to develop joint ventures with British and American companies encountered resistance. The representative of the Algerian Government General, Henri Urbani, challenged Guillaumat's favorable attitude to foreign companies, expressing his serious concern over too permissive a stance.[105] What worried Urbani especially was a lack of information about what US exploration teams were doing in the region, and how much they knew about French operations. It was clear that some teams had secretly been visiting Algeria already and that, once again, decisions in boardrooms and government buildings followed prospecting activities in the field:

> First of all, every day we see Americans coming back and forth to Algeria. We don't know much about what they come to do, but what we do know is that they are interested in oil. [...] Once we give the Americans exploration permits, we will see them arriving in Algeria *en masse* and, from that moment on, what kind of actions are they going to deploy in the country?[106]

Urbani's reservations were understandable: in June 1947 France was still unstable, both financially and politically, whereas the role of the US as a superpower had been made clear by the enunciation of the Truman Doctrine only three months earlier. There was little doubt that France would be forced to give in if the Americans decided to deploy all their influence in North Africa: even more so if they opted for a major prospecting effort, something that the French could not match. Urbani's point was thus that the French ought not to make concessions if they wanted to retain the upper hand in the region.

Guillaumat, however, disagreed. He believed that few American companies could work outside the US with the same proficiency they had at home. Furthermore, he was not at all convinced that such frantic foreign activity had taken place from 1942 to 1945 in Algeria. As a former intelligence officer, and thanks to his relations with people such as Kaplan, Guillaumat had access to restricted information that Urbani simply lacked. Bonneau also downplayed the extent of American influence in North Africa but was nevertheless wary. If the Americans were determined to access North Africa, they would use their powerful transportation or radio companies—and, undoubtedly, their secret services.[107]

Although skepticism persisted within the Government General, Guillaumat apparently succeeded in convincing most of his colleagues that collaboration in Algeria would not threaten French interests in the region. Was he really aware of what the British and Americans were actually doing? While the French had been surveying Algeria's geology on the ground, the US Air Force had been busy reconnoitering it from the sky.

British and American Attempts to Enter Algeria

The surveillance of potential oil-bearing areas in Algeria was a decisive element in establishing whether or not British and American companies would enter the country. Guillaumat knew that during World War II the US Air Force had taken aerial photographs in Algeria and that the photos could provide geological clues about the presence of oilfields. After the war, the GPRF had agreed with US diplomats that photographic material should not be shared without prior French consent. On the other hand the French held no copies of these photographs either. Following Guillaumat's decision to let the American companies prospect North Africa under the control of, and in coordination with, French authorities, the possibility of allowing foreign companies to view the photo set was further explored.[108]

In the summer of 1948, SONJ asked for, and gained, access to the photographs, following an agreement between the French Embassy in Washington and the State Department. The consultation was permitted under the condition that copies be sent to five French institutions (including REPAL), and that the names of the geologists involved in the American surveys be revealed to the French authorities. The agreement also enabled the French Air Force Chiefs of Staff to obtain copies of the photos. REPAL's geologist, Tenaille, was made responsible by the Ministry of Industry for monitoring the activities of the SONJ technicians, and reporting back to DICA.[109]

Gulf, AIOC, Shell, and the American Conorada Petroleum Corporation had also shown interest in French exploratory activities in Algerian regions.[110] Should oil be found, these companies were ready to wield the power their country enjoyed as a result of the war in major exploratory campaigns. Yet as they did not have access to the photos, they could not know enough about the real potential in Algeria. So before setting foot there, they used their lawyers to sound out French reactions and to determine from these reactions if the French had found oil. In September 1947, one of Gulf's lawyers sent a letter to Yves Chataigneau, Governor General of Algeria, through the French Embassy in Washington.

After that, Gulf received useful data on Algerian geology through the French Embassy and decided to begin large-scale work, subject to the French government agreement. Gulf representatives now approached DICA and BRP officials in Paris, and met Guillaumat and BRP's chief executive, Paul Moch. Gulf was ready to carry out more than $1 million of prospecting, including surface geological and seismic work, and photo-geology.[111]

We have seen that, while Guillaumat took a favorable view of collaboration with foreign interests, he wanted to retain absolute control of geological data. Instead, however, Gulf demanded a series of guarantees, including access to documentation held by the Mines Department, REPAL, and the Hydrography Department, relating to geology and oil exploration. A conflict therefore ensued between different French government departments, and when Gulf applied for an exploration license, the Algerian Assemblies refused to grant it, angering Guillaumat, especially after DICA had conceded major valuable geological intelligence to the US.[112]

In other cases, however, the Fuels Director's plans were successful. A concrete example of French–US collaboration, based on the sharing of confidential geological information, is demonstrated by a SONJ survey. SONJ had shown an interest in Algeria in early 1947, and had obtained authorization to send a team of geologists to carry out a study, provided that a full account of the team's activities was passed to REPAL. Later in 1948, the American company used the sets of aerial photographs discussed above to support their work. The report was completed in early 1950 and forwarded to REPAL as stipulated, but its conclusions were rather disappointing. The only area deemed to have serious commercial oil possibilities was one that the Americans knew would be assigned to REPAL. In light of these results, SONJ pulled out.[113]

In a memo sent in October 1950 by Governor General of Algeria, Marcel-Edmond Naegelen, to Interior Minister Henri Queuille, however, Naegelen provided reassurance on the SONJ report. He assumed that the Americans might have downplayed their actual results, since because of the current abundance of oil on the market, the majors were unwilling to commit their capital to exploring areas characterized by uncertain results. As SONJ possessed copious reserves and had recently made substantial discoveries in Canada, it might have wanted to dissimulate the geologists' results in order to keep potential oil reserves buried underground. In the summer of 1952, Caltex attempted to have two of its geologists survey an area in the Algerian west, in the region of Tindouf, close to the Moroccan border. But because of the political sensitivity of the area, which was disputed between Morocco and Algeria, and could lead to particularly tricky problems relating to French sovereignty, the Interior Ministry refused the request.[114]

One reason for Guillaumat to encourage collaboration with foreign enterprises in Algeria was that he hoped to acquire influence in oil exploration projects in other areas of the world. In October 1951 Shell, through its affiliate Shell Française, informed the new Governor General of Algeria, Roger Léonard, of its intention to apply for an extensive exploration permit (the ship-shaped zone including Timimoun in Figure 2.3) bordering the area where the CFP-REPAL joint venture had applied. Shell's request generated a debate within the BRP.[115]

Guillaumat reckoned that room could be found for Shell in the Sahara if they accepted French participation in their exploration activities in Canada

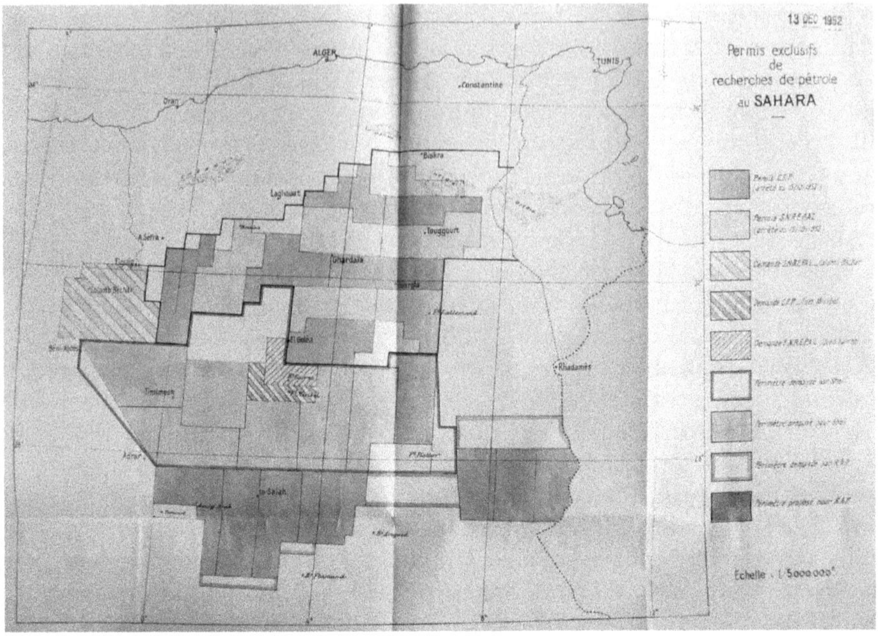

Figure 2.3 Map of oil exploration permits allocated and applied for in the Sahara by 1952.

Source: Courtesy of the Archives nationales d'outre-mer, Aix-en-Provence.[116]

and Venezuela. Representatives of the Ministry of Finances and Economic Affairs stressed the difficulties of this solution, which was ultimately shelved.[117] That Guillaumat and his collaborators were willing to facilitate relations with foreign companies did not mean all the oil executives in French companies embraced his views, especially when yielding to such firms could jeopardize their primacy in the region.

In February 1952 the President of REPAL, Roger Goetze, forwarded two letters to Moch (BRP's chief executive) urging him to consider the consequences of allocating foreign companies permits in areas bordering those requested by CFP-REPAL. Goetze stressed the existence of a clause in REPAL's permit allowing the company to prospect outside its permit zone. The French had requested their permits in August 1950, earlier than Shell, but these had not yet been awarded.[118] Furthermore, since geological knowledge about the area was less detailed at the time that REPAL had applied for its permits, Shell could now seek licenses for more promising areas. Goetze pointed out that in light of the new geological data about the Sahara basin it would be preferable to give REPAL priority over Shell or other companies in unexplored areas. In order to prevent Shell from gaining uncontrolled access to the desired area, Goetze even proposed that REPAL take a financial stake in all the companies operating in the Sahara, especially in prospecting activities, so as not to miss any opportunity that might arise. Eventually, although the applications made jointly by Shell were approved, REPAL received the Governor's support to obtain an advisory seat with no financial stake, or just a small stake (up to 5 per cent), in the companies to be formed by Shell and the RAP.[119]

The results of collaborative prospecting activities would eventually prove Guillaumat's strategy right, as they enabled the first major oil discoveries in Algeria. Until the outbreak of the Algerian War in 1954, the Algerian Sahara remained firmly in French hands and supplied France with the oil it badly needed to cope with national demands. In 1953, the reopening of Anglo–French negotiations on collaborative activity led to the constitution of two companies, the Oil Exploration and Production Company in the Sahara (*Compagnie de recherche et d'exploitation de pétrole au Sahara*, CREPS, 65 percent RAP, 35 percent Shell), and the Petroleum Company of Algeria (*Compagnie des pétroles d'Algérie*, CPA, 65 percent Shell, 35 percent RAP).[120] In 1954, the former discovered the first gas field of commercial value, and two years later, the extensive Edjeleh oilfield.

Thanks to the geophysical knowledge accumulated over the previous ten years, the French administration could thus address its energy security needs. In 1956, SN REPAL and BRP discovered Algeria's two largest oil and gas fields, Hassi Messaoud and Hassi R'Mel, and kept control of them. Since the main American concern relating to the conflict was to keep the Soviets out of North Africa, the early Cold War tensions about oil supplies between American and British oil companies and the French administration relaxed somewhat. However, this situation was complicated by events in the late 1950s, principally the conflict for Algerian independence, as we will see in the next chapter.

Conclusion

In Cold War France, oil supply was at the center of national security strategies, due to the critical role of oil in the military–industrial complex and ever-increasing domestic demand. Guided by a grand strategy directed to discovering sources of energy in their national territory and colonies that might bestow a certain degree of self-sufficiency, and finding their interests in the Middle East threatened by increasing Soviet and American influence, French administrations sought to secure control of oil reserves in Africa. They had relatively little difficulty in achieving quasi-exclusivity over exploration in Algeria, a territory over which France had complete political control.

In the late 1940s, French oil security was shattered both by ploys to evict CFP from the Middle East and by external political factors that France and CFP could not control. To re-establish oil security, the French mobilized their army of exploration geophysicists, technocrats, and intelligence agents, to learn more about what could be found in the French Union and what other countries intended to do in these regions. They shifted their focus to the French Union in an attempt to guarantee national supplies from a region that they could use as their own private domain.

The possession and management of confidential geological information shaped the beginning of the oil era in Algeria, and gave a marked advantage to French companies, which were able to exploit their effective monopoly for exploration without having to worry too much about competitors. However, foreign oil companies were also seeking to establish their presence in the Sahara and to take advantage of their international influence. Repeated demands by British and US oil firms to this end caused a long-lasting conflict between French institutional sectors, culminating in the strictly government-moderated entrance of Shell into Algeria in a joint-venture with French public agencies, or in limited concessions for the purpose of making collaborative deals in oil exploration ventures elsewhere. The rest of Algeria, however, would remain safely in French hands—at least for a few years.

Early postwar French administrations, despite their overall weakness and political instability, helped France to reclaim its prewar world ranking through strong industrialization and modernization policy. This outcome was achieved because technocrats at the head of national energy agencies survived the repeated changes of government, and formed high-level personal networks, which included people who were simultaneously elite technoscientists and government functionaries. Oil exploration and geological knowledge had become another kind of intelligence for a nation long accustomed to intelligence gathering, partially through the influence of officials such as Guillaumat, who had a background on both sides of geostrategic intelligence: information on underground resources, and the plans of those nations with an interest in them.

A key role in the technological reconstruction of France's oil sector was played by the establishment or potentiation of a number of research and exploration institutes and public agencies dedicated to hydrocarbons. The reinvigorated campaign of exploration brought the discovery of the first oil and gas fields in France. The first award of an exploration permit in France to a foreign company, in return for the provision of technical training for French technicians in new geophysical techniques, resulted in the discovery of the Parentis oilfield by SONJ in 1954.

American aid played a far greater role in the modernization of the French oil industry than it did in Italy, although here, too, initial US support for French acquisition of oil exploration equipment was soon frustrated by the ECA and pressure from oil majors. Aid to the refining sector was more significant, but a stealthy policy of discrimination was enacted, enabling British–American interests to prevail over French needs. Considering the incomparably larger role assigned by the ECA to sales of crude oil, rather than supplying the means for the reconstruction and expansion of the oil industry, the agency's oil policy seemed to be guided by the principle of acquiring more customers for British and American oil.

By the mid-1950s, France had, by and large, re-established its own role in the industry and made oil one of the pillars of its national security, especially after major discoveries were made in the mid-1950s in Central Africa and Algeria. Yet it was exactly the region that had done most to restore that role—Algeria—that would go on to place it under threat.

Notes

1 Ambassador Edward Lindley, Viscount of Halifax, British Embassy (Britemb) Washington, to Anthony Eden, Secretary of State, Feb. 19, 1944; folder (fd.) 76/34, no. 846; box (b.) Foreign Office (FO) 371/42688; The National Archives, Kew (TNA): source as reported in Daniel Yergin, *The Prize: The Epic Quest for Oil, Money, and Power*, 2nd edition (New York: Simon & Schuster, 2009. 1st edition: 1991), 383. Halifax was reporting a remark by US President Franklin Roosevelt.

2 Minutes of the Conference held on Jun. 19, 1947, at the Under-Directorate of Algeria, under the presidency of Mr. Maisonneuve, Director of General Affairs, on the subject of oil-related foreign activities in Algeria, p. 8; b. 07AH0168-6, REPAL–Correspondence; Fonds ELF-ERAP; Archives Historiques du Groupe ELF/Total, La Défense (AHTOTAL) (my translation). Pierre Guillaumat was the President of France's main public agency for oil exploration and production, the *Bureau de recherches de pétrole*.

3 André Nouschi, *La France et le pétrole: de 1924 à nos jours* (Paris: Picard, 2001), 16, 119. These economic figures are reported in francs-1938 in Nouschi's work. Throughout this chapter, they are given in dollars-1999. The quote is from: Nouschi, *France*, 119 (my translation).

4 Roberto Cantoni and Leucha Veneer, "Underground and Underwater: Gatekeeping Oil Exploration During the Cold War," in *The Surveillance Imperative: The Rise of the Geosciences During the Cold War*, ed. Simone Turchetti and Peder Roberts (London: Palgrave Macmillan, 2014), 45–66.

5 Quoted from: Kristin Ross, *Fast Cars, Clean Bodies: Decolonization and the Reordering of French Culture* (Cambridge, MA/London: MIT Press, 1995), 4. The phrase 'Trente Glorieuses' was coined by economist Jean Fourastié, in Jean Fourastié, *Les Trente Glorieuses, ou la révolution invisible de 1946 à 1975* (Paris: Fayard, 1979). On post-war reconstruction of France from a political and diplomatic point of view, see: Irwin M. Wall, *The United States and the Making of Postwar France, 1945–1954* (Cambridge: Cambridge University Press, 1991); William I. Hitchcock, *France Restored: Cold War Diplomacy and the Quest for Leadership in Europe, 1944–1954* (Chapel Hill, NC/London: University of North Carolina Press, 1998); Jean-Pierre Rioux, *The Fourth Republic, 1944–1958* (Cambridge: Cambridge University Press, 1987).

6 The change of denomination followed the abolition of forced labor and the special 'indigenous' legislative apparatus that assigned natives of French Colonies a lesser legal status than metropolitan citizens. On this subject, see: Jean-Pierre Dozon, *Frères et sujets. La France et l'Afrique en perspective* (Paris: Flammarion, 2003).

7 Meeting of Mar. 28, 1924, p. 5; Minutes of the Board of Directors (MBD); b. 92. 10/1, CFP; Fonds Total-CFP; AHTOTAL. Turkish Petroleum was a consortium operating in the area of the former Ottoman Empire, which by a few years after its creation in 1911, found itself divided between: Anglo-Iranian Oil Company's predecessor, the Anglo-Persian Oil Company, which was also the majority shareholder; the German Deutsche Bank; Shell's affiliate,

the Anglo-Saxon Company; and Gulbenkian, who held 5 percent. Yergin, *The Prize*, 169–71.

8 André Nouschi, *Luttes pétrolières au Proche-Orient* (Paris: Flammarion, 1970), 68. On pressure applied by US majors and administration, see: US Federal Trade Commission, *The International Petroleum Cartel*, Staff Report to the Federal Trade Commission, released through Subcommittee on Monopoly of Select Committee on Small Business, U.S. Senate, 83d Cong., 2nd sess (Washington, DC: US Senate, 1952).

9 Report of the Board of Directors (RBD); CFP Ordinary General Assembly (OGA) of Jun. 2, 1937, p. 3; Fonds Total-CFP; AHTOTAL. RBD; CFP OGA of Jun. 22, 1938, p. 2; Fonds Total-CFP; AHTOTAL. Jean Rondot, *La Compagnie Française des Pétroles. Du franc-or au pétrole-franc* (Paris: Plon, 1962), 65.

10 "Red Line" Agreement, Jun. 31, 1928, p. 21, Schedule B; D'Arcy Exploration Company Limited and Others, and Turkish Petroleum Company Limited; b. Ministry of Power (POWE) 33/1709, Iraq Petroleum Company: "red line" inter company agreement 31 July 1928; TNA.

11 RBD; CFP OGA of Jun. 11, 1928, p. 4; Fonds Total-CFP; AHTOTAL. RBD; CFP OGA of Jun. 2, 1937, p. 2; Fonds Total-CFP; AHTOTAL. Didier Du Castel et al., *Les aventuriers de la Terre* (Boulogne: La Sirène, 1995), 21. CFP gained complete control of the gravimetry company in 1941. RBD; CFP OGA of Jun. 30, 1942, p. 5; Fonds Total-CFP; AHTOTAL.

12 CGG only acquired Schlumberger's electrical logging sector, not the entire enterprise. On the history of Schlumberger, see: Louis A. Allaud and Maurice H. Martin, *Schlumberger. The History of a Technique* (Hoboken: John Wiley & Sons, 1977). For an analysis based on the theoretical framework of social constructivism of technology, see: Geoffrey C. Bowker, *Science on the Run. Information Management and Industrial Geophysics at Schlumberger, 1920–1940* (Cambridge, MA/London: MIT Press, 1994). b. 85. 26/5, SPG; Fonds Total-CFP; AHTOTAL.

13 Du Castel et al., *Les aventuriers*, 21. Precisely, CGG had been operating in France, Northern Africa, Gabon, Romania, the Dutch Indies, Iran, India, Venezuela, the Soviet Union, and Turkey. Meeting of Apr. 26, 1938; CGG, Minutes of the Board of Directors; b. 92. 13/8 Participations de la Compagnie française des pétroles (CFP) dans différentes sociétés: historique et vie de la société; Fonds Total-CFP; AHTOTAL.

14 Nouschi, *France*, 117. RBD;CFP OGA of Jun. 30, 1942, p. 5; Fonds Total-CFP; AHTOTAL.

15 For a complete list of majors' affiliates and participations, see: Nouschi, *France*, 39.

16 On the 1928 laws, see: André Philippon, "The French Example. The 1928s Laws. Longevity and Effectiveness of the Approach to Creating and Maintaining a National Oil Industry in a Consumer Country—Appearances and Realities," in *A Comparative History of National Oil Companies*, ed. Alain Beltran (Brussels: Peter Lang, 2010), 21–53; Julien Schvartz, *Sur les sociétés pétrolières opérant en France… Rapport de la commission d'enquête parlementaire (6 novembre 1974)* (Paris: Union Générale d'Editions, 1974), 101; Daniel Murat, *L'intervention de l'État dans le secteur pétrolier en France* (Paris: Technip, 1969), 31.

17 In particular, a large refinery at Port-Jérôme belonged to a consortium formed by SONJ's affiliate Standard Franco-Américaine, Gulf and Atlantic Refining, and was, at the time of its construction, the largest and one of the most complex oil plants in Europe. Nouschi, *France*, 95, writes of fifteen refineries. Alain Beltran writes of fourteen. Alain Beltran, "Pétrole et gaz: Nouvelles

perspectives et outils de recherché," *Bulletin de l'IHTP* 84 (2004) (http://www. ihtp. cnrs. fr/spip. phppercent3Farticle316&lang=fr. html). RBD; CFP Extraordinary General Assembly of Mar. 20, 1929, p. 2; Fonds Total-CFP; AHTOTAL. RBD;CFP OGA of Apr. 12, 1929, p. 3; Fonds Total-CFP; AHTOTAL. The refineries mentioned were located in Normandy and in Provence.

18 Murat, *Intervention*, 32; Samir Salut, "Politique nationale du pétrole, société nationales et 'pétrole franc,'" *Revue historique* 638, no. 2 (2006): 361.

19 Serge Berstein and Pierre Milza, *Histoire de la France au XXe siècle*, tome III: 1945–1958. (Paris: Éditions Complexe, 1991), 90; Nouschi, *France*, 115.

20 Gabrielle Hecht, *The Radiance of France: Nuclear Power and National Identity after World War II*, 2nd edition (Cambridge, MA/London: MIT Press, 2009. 1st edition: 1998).

21 Jean Guisnel, "Foccart, Elf et le sang noir de l'Afrique," in *Histoire secrète de la Ve République*, ed. Roger Faligot and Jean Guisnel (Paris: La Découverte), 133–43. In particular, pp. 133–6 include sparse data on Guillaumat's life and activities. On Guillaumat's biography, see also: Georges-Henri Soutou and Alain Beltran, eds., *Pierre Gullaumat, la passion des grands projets industriels* (Paris: Institut d'Histoire de l'Industrie et Editions Rive Droite, 1995).

22 Douglas A. Yates, "Life Stories and Family Histories of the French Oil Industry. The Rise and Fall of the Corps des Mines," in *A Comparative History*, ed. Beltran, 54–67.

23 Source: Visite de Monsieur le Ministre GUILLE, secrétaire d'Etat à la Présidence du Conseil chargé de l'énergie atomique (Saclay, 30 mars 1956). Courtesy of CEA.

24 Christian Stoffaës, introduction to *Pierre Guillaumat*, ed. Soutou and Beltran, xviii.

25 The first quote is from: Matthew Adamson, *Nuclear Reach* (unpublished manuscript); the second quote is from: Nouschi, *France*, 134.

26 Pierre Péan, in *Pierre Guillaumat*, ed. Soutou and Beltran, 12.

27 Péan, in *Pierre Guillaumat*, ed. Soutou and Beltran, 1–13; Pierre Péan and Jean-Pierre Séréni, *Les émirs de la République* (Paris: Seuil, 1982), 28. On Guillaumat's leadership of the French Atomic Energy Commission (*Commissariat à l'Énergie Atomique*, CEA) see: Matthew Adamson, "Les *liaisons dangereuses*: Resource Surveillance, Uranium Diplomacy and Secret French–American Collaboration in 1950s Morocco," *The British Journal for the History of Science* 49, no. 1 (2016): 92.

28 Péan, in *Pierre Guillaumat*, ed. Soutou and Beltran, 19; François-Xavier Verschave, *La Françafrique: le plus long scandale de la République* (Paris: Stock, 1998), 135ff.; François-Xavier Verschave, *Noir silence: qui arrêtera la Françafrique* (Paris: Les Arènes, 2000), 46–8.

29 Quoted from: Guillaumat speech to Comité Consultatif of DICA, Dec. 1, 1946; 130 AQ 33; Archives Nationales: source as reported in Eric D. K. Melby, *Oil and the International System. The Case of France, 1918–1969* (New York: Arno Press 1981), 226 (original in French, my translation).

30 Réalisations de 1946; Projets pour 1947 et les années suivantes; Activités de l'Institut Français du Pétrole; Institut Français du Pétrole: Fonds documentaire, Rueil Malmaison.

31 Soutou and Beltran, *Pierre Guillaumat*, 152–3.

32 Quoted from: Edmond Vellinger, "Le rôle du Physicien dans l'Industrie Extractive du Pétrole," *Bulletin de l'Association française des techniciens du pétrole* 55 (1946): 23 (my translation).

33 Meeting of Dec. 4, 1946, pp. 5–6; MBD; b. 92. 10/1, CFP; Fonds Total-CFP; AHTOTAL.

34 Bowker, *Science on the Run*.

35 Donald T. Germain-Jones, "What is our contribution?" *Geophysical Prospecting* 2, no. 3 (1954): 179. As an indication, in 1956 the number of seismic crews employed was 22 for AGIP and affiliates and 61 for BRP and affiliates (AGIP Mineraria, *Relazioni e bilancio al 31 dicembre 1956* (Roma: AGIP/CEDI, 1956), 17–18; BRP Rapport Annuel, Informations Générales, Année 1956, p. 11; b. 10AH0832-13, BRP; Fonds ELF-ERAP; AHTOTAL).

36 Emmanuel Catta, *Victor De Metz. De la CFP au Groupe Total* (Paris: Total Edition Presse, 1990), 74; Nouschi, *France*, 131.

37 Quoted from: Joseph C. Grew, Acting Secretary of State, to Jefferson Caffery, Ambassador in France, Mar. 2, 1945; Foreign Relations of the United States (FRUS), 1945, IV, Europe (Washington: United States Government Printing Office, 1968), 776.

38 Jefferson Caffery, Ambassador in France, to Edward Stettinius, Secretary of State, May 24, 1945; FRUS, 1945, IV, Europe, 778. Grew to Caffery, Jun. 7, 1945; FRUS, 1945, IV, Europe, 780.

39 Grew to Caffery, Jun. 7, 1945; FRUS, 1945, IV, Europe, 780. Caffery, Ambassador in France, to James F. Byrnes, Secretary of State, Enclosure: The American Ambassador (Caffery) to the French Minister for Foreign Affairs (Bidault), 31 October 1945; FRUS, 1945, IV, Europe, 782–3. Catta, *Victor De Metz*, 74.

40 Bossuat, Gérard Bossuat, *La France, l'aide américaine et la construction européenne, 1944–1954* (Paris: Comité pour l'histoire économique et financière de la France, 1997), 28; Gérard Bossuat, *L'Europe occidentale à l'heure américaine* (Paris: Éditions Complexe, 1992), 31. For a thorough coverage of American aids to France, see especially: Bossuat, *La France*, as well as: Irwin M. Wall, "Jean Monnet, the United States and the French Economic Plan," in *Jean Monnet: The Path to European Unity*, ed. Douglas Brinkley and Clifford Hackett (New York: Palgrave, 1991), 86–113; Chiarella Esposito, *America's Feeble Weapon: Finding the Marshall Plan in France and Italy, 1948–1950* (Westport, CT/London: Greenwood Press, 1994); Irwin M. Wall, "The Marshall Plan and French Politics," in *The Marshall Plan: Fifty Years After*, ed. Martin Schain (New York: Palgrave, 2001), 167–84; Stewart Patrick, "Embedded Liberalism in France? American Hegemony, the Monnet Plan, and Postwar Multilateralism," in *The Marshall Plan*, ed. Schain, 205–48.

41 Berstein and Milza, *Histoire de la France*, 92–3. Dollar amounts throughout this section are given in their contemporary value. For details on US aid to France, see: boxes 245 to 249; Sous-série: États-Unis; Série: Amérique 1944–1952; Archives Diplomatiques du Ministère des Affaires Etrangères, La Courneuve (ADMAE). See also: Minutes of the Twenty-second Meeting of the National Advisory Council on International Monetary and Financial Problems, Washington, Apr. 25, 1946, pp. 431–4; Minutes of the Twenty-fourth Meeting ..., May 6, 1946, pp. 440–6; Minutes of the Twenty-ninth Meeting ..., May 24, 1946, pp. 453–8; Minutes of the Thirtieth Meeting ..., May 28, 1946, pp. 459–64; FRUS, 1946, V, The British Commonwealth, Western and Central Europe (Washington: United States Government Printing Office, 1946).

42 John Krige, *American Hegemony and the Postwar Reconstruction of Science in Europe* (Cambridge, MA/London: MIT Press, 2006), 156; Ross, *Fast Cars*, 35–7.

43 Nouschi, *France*, 134–5. Nouschi argues that with BRP, the French government also intended to create a vertically integrated company. However, former Fuels Director, Jean Blancard, has claimed that no talk of distribution activities was ever made. See: Éric Kocher-Marbœuf, *Le Patricien et le Général. Jean-Marcel Jeanneney et Charles de Gaulle 1958–1969*, vol. I (Paris: Comité pour l'histoire économique et financière de la France, 2003), 244. *Extract from the ordnance creating BRP*: source as reported in Jean Devaux-Charbonnel,

L'intervention de l'Etat dans la Recherche et dans l'Exploitation des gisements de pétrole (Paris: IFP, 1951), 17.
44 For a complete list of BRP's shareholdings see André Nouschi, *Pétrole et relations internationales de 1945 à nos jours* (Paris: Armand Colin, 1999), 83; Nouschi, *France*, 135; Schvartz, *Sur les societies pétrolières*, 192–4.
45 At the October 1945 elections to elect the first Constituent Assembly, the Communists and their allies gained 27.1 percent of the Assembly seats (159 seats), the Christian Democrats 25.6 percent (150 seats), the Socialists 24.9 percent (146 seats). At the November 1946 legislative elections, the Communists and their allies gained 29.0 percent (182 seats), the Christian Democrats 27.6 percent (173 seats), the Socialists 16.3 percent (102 seats).
46 Krige, *American Hegemony*, 23–4; Berstein and Milza, *Histoire de la France*, 109.
47 Nouschi, *France*, 135. On the Monnet Plan, refer to: Gérard Bossuat, *La France, l'aide américaine et la construction européenne, 1944–1954* (Paris: Comité pour l'histoire économique et financière de la France, 1997).
48 Nouschi, *La France*, 131–2. The quote is from: Commissariat Général au Plan, Rapport sur les Carburants pour le deuxième semestre 1947 et pour l'année 1947 dans son ensemble (Paris: March 1948): source as reported in Melby, *Oil*, 227 (original in French, my translation).
49 Berstein and Milza, *Histoire de la France*, 101; Nouschi, *France*, 132.
50 Berstein and Milza, *Histoire de la France*, 101–2.
51 Second Meeting, Apr. 16, 1946; and Third Meeting, 19 April 1946; France–U.S. Financial and Economic Negotiations, Draft Agreed Minutes; b. 250, Commerce extérieur. Relations avec la France; Sous-série: États-Unis; Série: Amérique, 1944–1952; ADMAE. On the discrimination toward British companies registered in France, see: fd. 217/1525; b. FO 369/3504, War damage compensation to British and American oil interests in France; TNA; f. 2017/8, War damage claims of British oil interests in France, 1946; b. FO 950/31; TNA.
52 Bossuat, *La France*, 387; Melby, *Oil*, 227.
53 Bossuat, *La France*, 118, table 16.
54 Bossuat, *La France*, 860, table 28.
55 Walter J. Levy, "Economic Coopération [sic] Administration (E.C.A.)," *Bulletin AFTP* 73 (1949): 43; Henri Ballande, "Le Plan Marshall et le Pétrole," *Bulletin AFTP* 75 (1949): 19; Du Castel et al., *Les aventuriers*, 25.
56 CE 48, Bonnet, 30 juillet 1948, 21 h, n° 3473–78: source as reported in Bossuat, *La France*, 336. See also: Levy, "Economic Coopération," 44; Ballande, "Le Plan Marshall," 22. Note for Mr Alphand by the Directorate of Economic and Financial Affairs, "Programme d'importation de pétrole," unsigned, Aug. 11, 1948; and Télégramme à l'arrivée n. 3473 to 3478, Henri Bonnet, Fremb, to French Foreign Ministry (MAEF), Jul. 31, 1948; b. 327, DE-CE 1945–1960, Aide américaine; Sous-série: Coopération économique; Série: Affaires économiques et financières; ADMAE.
57 Télégramme à l'arrivée n. 3473 to 3478, Bonnet to MAEF, Jul. 31, 1948; b. 327, DE-CE 1945–1960, Aide américaine; Sous-série: Coopération économique; Série: Affaires économiques et financières; ADMAE. The quote is from this telegram.
58 F 60 ter 387, MAEF to Bonnet, 28 mai 1949, 26 DET: source as reported in Bossuat, *La France*, 337. Philippe Tristani, "L'Iraq Petroleum Company, les États-Unis et la lutte pour le leadership pétrolier au Moyen-Orient de 1945 à 1973," *Histoire, économie & sociéte* 29 (2010): 90–1; Horst Mendershausen, "Dollar Shortage and Oil Surplus in 1949–1950," *Essays in International Finance* 11 (1950): 8–11.

59 Bossuat, *La France*, 360, table 45, 361ff. Caltex also used Marshall funds to rebuild its destroyed refinery at Bec d'Ambès, close to Bordeaux, in order to take in new oil deliveries from Saudi Arabia (cf. Timothy Mitchell, *Carbon Democracy: Political Power in the Age of Oil* (New York: Verso, 2011), 152).

60 Sylvie Chauveau and Alain Beltran, *ELF Aquitaine. Des origines à 1989* (Paris: Fayard, 1998), 42. The franc zone included the African areas under French domination, in which the franc was employed as currency.

61 Quoted from: Kocher-Marbœuf, *Le Patricien*, 247.

62 Meeting of Oct. 3, 1950, p. 3; Minutes of the Study Committee; b. 92. 10/2, CFP; Fonds Total-CFP; AHTOTAL. Serge Lerat, "La mise en valeur du gisement de gaz de Lacq," *Annales de Géographie* 66, no. 355 (1957): 260–7; Gilbert Rutman, "Quelques éléments pour l'histoire de la Société nationale des pétroles d'Aquitaine (SNPA) de 1941 à 1976," in *La recherche pétrolière française*, ed. Jean Prouvost (Paris: Éditions du CTHS, 1994), 150. See also, in the same volume: Georges Bertrand, "Histoire des recherches pétrolières en Aquitaine. Les premiers titres d'exploration," 109–11; Francis Héritier, "Histoire de l'exploration pétrolière en France," 23.

63 Héritier, "Histoire de l'exploration," 23.

64 Dominique Michon, "Histoire de la sismique pour la recherche pétrolière," in *La recherche pétrolière française*, ed. Prouvost, 220; Bertrand, "Histoire des recherches pétrolières," 108–9.

65 DeGolyer had earlier been among the key founders of the American Association of Petroleum Geologists in 1916, as well as the founder of Geophysical Service Incorporated in 1930, an enterprise specialized in seismic reflection. Charles Bates, Thomas F. Gaskell and Robert B. Rice, *Geophysics in the Affairs of Man* (Oxford: Pergamon Press, 1982), 20, 22; Gerald D. Nash, *United States Oil Policy, 1890–1964* (Pittsburgh: University of Pittsburgh Press, 1968), 171.

66 Jean Rondot, "Les intérêts pétroliers français dans le Proche-Orient," *Politique étrangère* 17, no. 4 (1952): 288.

67 Robert Jervis, "Cooperation Under the Security Dilemma," *World Politics* 30, no. 2 (1978): 167–214; Tristani, "L'Iraq Petroleum Company," 83. For a coverage of US oil policy in the 1940s, see: Nash, *United States*, 170ff.; Michael B. Stoff, *Oil, War, and American Security: The Search for a National Policy on Foreign Oil, 1941–1947* (New Haven: Yale University Press, 1982); Robert O. Keohane, "State Power and Industry Influence: American Foreign Oil Policy," *International Organisation* 36, no. 1 (1982): 165–83; Stephen J. Randall, "Harold Ickes and United States Foreign Petroleum Policy Planning, 1939–1945," *Business History Review* 57, no. 3 (1983): 367–87; David S. Painter, *Oil and the American Century: The Political Economy of U.S. Foreign Oil Policy, 1941–1954* (Baltimore: Johns Hopkins University Press, 1986).

68 RBD; CFP OGA of Sep. 16, 1940, pp. 4, 8; Fonds Total-CFP; AHTOTAL. RBD; CFP OGA of Dec. 5, 1945, p. 4; Fonds Total-CFP; AHTOTAL.

69 Meeting of Nov. 8, 1944, p. 4; MBD; b. 92. 10/1, CFP; Fonds Total-CFP; AHTOTAL. RBD; CFP OGA of Dec. 5, 1945, p. 3; Fonds Total-CFP; AHTOTAL. RBD; CFP OGA of Jun. 26, 1946, p. 4; Fonds Total-CFP; AHTOTAL. RBD; CFP OGA of Jul. 2, 1947, p. 4; Fonds Total-CFP; AHTOTAL.

70 Memorandum by John A. Loftus, Acting Chief of the Petroleum Division, to Mr. John D. Linebaugh, Division of British Commonwealth Affairs, May 31, 1945; FRUS, 1945, VIII, The Near East and Africa (Washington: United States Government Printing Office, 1969), 52.

71 Meeting of Jun. 5, 1946, pp. 2–3; MBD; b. 92. 10/1, CFP; Fonds Total-CFP; AHTOTAL. Memorandum of Conversation, by Mr. George C. McGhee,

Special Assistant to the Under Secretary of State for Economic Affairs (William L. Clayton), Aug. 27, 1946; FRUS, 1946, VII, The Near East and Africa, 31–4.

72 Meeting of Nov. 6, 1946, p. 3; MBD; b. 92. 10/1, CFP; Fonds Total-CFP; AHTOTAL.

73 Quoted from: James F. Byrnes, Secretary of State, to Gallman, the Chargé in the United Kingdom, Nov. 29, 1946, confidential; FRUS, 1946, VII, The Near East and Africa, 40.

74 Record of Informal Anglo-American Oil Talks, Nov. 1946, undated, secret; FRUS, 1946, VII, The Near East and Africa, 44–6.

75 Meeting of Dec. 27, 1946, pp. 2–4; MBD; b. 92. 10/1, CFP; Fonds Total-CFP;AHTOTAL. Irvine H. Anderson, *ARAMCO. The United States and Saudi Arabia. A Study of the Dynamics of Foreign Oil Policy, 1933–1950* (Princeton, NJ: Princeton University Press, 1981), 153–4. See also: André Nouschi, "Un tournant de la politique pétrolière française: les Heads of Agreement de novembre 1948," *Relations Internationales* 44: 1985 [no page number reported]. The actual amount of crude oil negotiated by the three companies was 134 million tons, not 160, different from that reported in Byrnes' telegram to Gallman.

76 Rondot, *Compagnie Française*, 93–5; Stoff, *Oil, War*, 200. Acheson to Gallman, Dec. 4, 1946, secret, U.S. urgent; FRUS, 1946, VII, The Near East and Africa, 43–4. James F. Byrnes, Secretary of State, to George V. Allen, Ambassador in Iran, Jan. 8, 1947, secret, U.S. urgent; FRUS, 1946, VII, The Near East and Africa; 49–50.

77 Henri Bonnet, French Ambassador, to James F. Byrnes, Secretary of State, Jan. 4, 1947; FRUS, 1947, V, The Near East and Africa, 627–9. The quote is from: Meeting of Dec. 27, 1946, p. 3; MBD; b. 92. 10/1, CFP; Fonds Total-CFP; AHTOTAL (my translation).

78 Quoted from: Bonnet to Byrnes, Jan. 4, 1947; FRUS, 1947, V, The Near East and Africa, 628. On the French request of taking participation into ARAMCO, see: Subcommittee on Multinational Corporations, "Multinational Oil Corporation and U.S. Foreign Policy, Report Together with Individual Views, to the Committee of Foreign Relations, United States Senate, by the Subcommittee on Multinational Corporations" (Washington: United States Government Printing Office, 1975), 14–15 (http://www.mtholyoke.edu/acad/intrel/oil1.htm).

79 Catta, *Victor De Metz*, 86; Rondot, *Compagnie Française*, 97.

80 Memorandum of Conversation, by John A. Loftus, Chief of the Petroleum Division, Jan. 9, 1947; FRUS, 1947, V, The Near East and Africa, 629–31 (the quote is from p. 631). Memorandum of Conversation, by Eakens, Jan. 10, 1947; FRUS, 1947, V, The Near East and Africa, 632. Memorandum by Loy Henderson, Director of the Office of Near Eastern and African Affairs, to Dean Acheson, Under Secretary of State, Jan. 16, 1947, secret; FRUS, 1947, V, The Near East and Africa, 634–5.

81 Nouschi, *France*, 198–200; Nouschi, *Pétrole et relations internationales*, 53–4.

82 Meeting of Mar. 5, 1947, pp. 3–5, and Meeting of Jun. 4, 1947, pp. 3–5; MBD; b. 92. 10/1, CFP; Fonds Total-CFP; AHTOTAL. Memorandum of Conversation, by the Director of the Office of Near Eastern and African Affairs (Joseph C. Satterthwaite), Oct. 26, 1948, secret; FRUS, 1947, V, pt. 1, The Near East, South Asia, and Africa, 55–6. Memorandum of Conversation, by the Assistant Chief of the Petroleum Division (Edwin G. Moline), Dec. 22, 1948, confidential; FRUS, 1947, V, pt. 1, The Near East, South Asia, and Africa, 64–5. See also: Cable, Harden, and Sheets (London) to Jennings (New York), 14 May 1947, and press release, 2 June 1947, file 32929, and minutes of SONJ

executive committee meetings of May 15 and 27, 1947, file 33369, FTC Records. Sources as reported in Anderson, *ARAMCO*, 158.

83 RBD; CFP OGA of Jun. 27, 1949, p. 5; Fonds Total-CFP; AHTOTAL. Meeting of Oct. 1, 1947, p. 4, and Meeting of Nov. 3, 1948; MBD; b. 92. 10/1, CFP; Fonds Total-CFP; AHTOTAL. Memorandum of Conversation, by the Assistant Chief of the Petroleum Division (Edwin G. Moline), Dec. 22, 1948.

84 Rondot, *Compagnie Française*, 114; RDB; CFP OGA of Jun. 30, 1953, pp. 4, 10, and CFP OGA of Jun. 24, 1954, p. 4; Fonds Total-CFP; AHTOTAL.

85 On Mossadegh's attempted nationalization of Iranian oil and its outcome, see references in Chapter 1 of this volume, note 104.

86 US Federal Trade Commission, *The International Petroleum Cartel*. See esp. its chapter 4 on IPC: "Joint Control Through Common Ownership—The Iraq Petroleum Co., Ltd.," 47–112. On the involvement of the US government in the management of the Federal Trade Commission's publication, see: The development of United States policy regarding the applicability of antitrust legislation to international petroleum companies; FRUS, 1952–1954, I, pt. 2, General: economic and political matters (Washington: United States Government Printing Office, 1952–1954), 1259–378.

87 Report to the National Security Council by the Departments of State, Interior, and Justice, NSC 138/1, "National Security Problems Concerning Free World Petroleum Demands and Potential Supplies," Jan. 6, 1953, top secret; FRUS, 1952–1954, I, pt. 2, General: economic and political matters, 1317–36; Report to the National Security Council by the Departments of State, Interior, and Justice, Memorandum of discussion at the 128th Meeting of the NSC, Jan. 9, 1953, top secret; FRUS, 1952–1954, I, pt. 2, General: economic and political matters, 1338–44.

88 A second containment strategy concerned the establishment of a belt of pro-US states all around the USSR. This strategy was implemented from 1953 with the creation of a Northern Tier (Pakistan, Iran, Iraq, Turkey, US, and UK) through the Baghdad Pact. See: Alessandro Brogi, *L'Italia e l'egemonia americana nel Mediterraneo. 1945–1958* (Scandicci: La Nuova Italia, 1996), 132–4.

89 In this paragraph I focus on Algeria. As references on oil politics and exploration in French Equatorial Africa, see: Dougals A. Yates, *The Rentier State in Africa: Oil Rent Dependency and Neocolonialism in the Republic of Gabon* (Trenton/Asmara: Africa World Press, 1996); Roberto Cantoni, "Une étude de la prospection géophysique française du pétrole au Gabon entre la fin de la Seconde Guerre Mondiale et le premier choc pétrolier (1946–1973)" (Master's thesis, Université Paris 7 'Denis Diderot', 2010).

90 "Les recherches de pétrole en Algérie," undated (probably 1949); fd. Société nationale de recherches de pétrole d'Algérie; b. 81F/2068; Affaires algériennes (1873/1964); Fonds Ministériels (FM); Archives nationales d'outre-mer, Aix-en-Provence (ANOM). Alain Perrodon, "Historique des recherches pétrolières en Algérie," in *La recherche pétrolière française*, ed. Prouvost, 325. On Kilian's life and studies, see: Pierre Fontaine, *La mort étrange de Conrad Kilian, inventeur du pétrole saharien* (Paris: Les Sept Couleurs, 1959). Sedimentology studies the physical and chemical properties of sedimentary rocks and the processes involved in their formation, including transportation, deposition, and lithification of sediments.

91 In fact, notes Alain Perrodon, the surface indices mentioned by Kilian were never found later by oil companies: they were instead associated with "a sulphurous source, showing irisation due to iron oxide" by geologist Michel

Tenaille. Michel Tenaille, Note sur Conrad Kilian, Apr. 24, 1970, unpublished. Source as reported in Perrodon, "Historique des recherches pétrolières en Algérie," 326 (my translation). On Kilian's activities, see also: Cantoni and Veneer, "Underground and Underwater," 48.

92 Naomi Oreskes and Ronald E. Doel, "Physics and chemistry of the Earth," in *The Cambridge History of Science*, vol. V: *Modern Physical and Mathematical Sciences*, ed. Mary Jo Nye (Cambridge: Cambridge University Press, 2002), 539, 544; Naomi Oreskes and James R. Fleming, "Why Geophysics?" *Studies in History and Philosophy of Modern Physics* 31, no. 3 (2000): 253–7; Rondot, *Compagnie Française*, 136; Meeting of Mar. 15, 1950, p. 2; Minutes of the Study Committee; b. 92. 10/2, CFP; Fonds Total-CFP; AHTOTAL. RBD; CFP OGA of Jun. 26, 1951, p. 7; Fonds Total-CFP; AHTOTAL; "Les recherches de pétrole en Algérie," undated (probably 1949), pp. 7–8; fd. Société nationale de recherches de pétrole d'Algérie; b. 81F/2068; Affaires algériennes (1873/1964); FM; ANOM.

93 Du Castel et al., *Les aventuriers*, 28; Perrodon, *Histoire des grandes découvertes pétrolières. Un certain art de l'exploration* (Pau/Paris: Elf Aquitaine-Masson, 1995), 129; Yves Delavesne, "Développement récent des recherches de pétrole en Afrique," *Bulletin AFTP* 112 (1955): 374. RBD; CFP OGA of Jun. 28, 1950, p. 7, and CFP OGA of Jun. 26, 1951, pp. 7–8; Fonds Total-CFP; AHTOTAL.

94 Maurice Pieuchot and Henri Richard, "Some Technical Aspects of Reflection Seismic Prospecting in the Sahara," *Geophysics* 23, no. 3 (1958): 557–73. On advantages and disadvantages of multiplying seismographs, see: Andrew Gilmour, "The State of Seismic Prospecting," *Geophysics* 15, no. 3 (1950): 398; Leonard V. Lombardi, "Notes on the Use of Multiple Geophones," *Geophysics* 20, no. 2 (1955): 215–26.

95 RBD; CFP OGA of Jun. 30, 1952, p. 7, and CFP OGA of Jun. 30, 1953, p. 7; Fonds Total-CFP; AHTOTAL. Meeting of Jul. 4, 1951, p. 5; Meeting of Jul. 2, 1952, p. 7; Meeting of Nov. 5, 1952, p. 6; MBD; b. 92. 10/3, CFP; Fonds Total-CFP; AHTOTAL. C. Layat et al., "Some Technical Aspects of Refraction Seismic Prospecting in the Sahara," *Geophysics* 26, no. 4 (1961): 437–46; Chauveau and Beltran, *ELF Aquitaine*, 59; Perrodon, "Historique des recherches pétrolières en Algérie," 328. In contradiction to what has been argued in Jacques Frémeaux, *Le Sahara et la France* (Paris: SOTÉCA, 2010), 233, up to the Saharan discoveries seismic refraction was not considered a cutting-edge technology. In fact it had been almost completely abandoned in most areas of the world, and replaced by seismic reflection.

96 RBD; CFP OGA of Jun. 24, 1954, p. 7; Fonds Total-CFP; AHTOTAL; Samir Saul, "REPAL, CFP and 'Oil-Paid-in-Francs,'" in *A Comparative History*, ed. Beltran, 99–100; Kocher-Marbœuf, *Le Patricien*, 244–5.

97 The idea of a European Defense Community had been launched by French Prime Minister, René Pleven, in 1950 as an alternative to West Germany's inclusion into NATO. However, concerns about German remilitarization and about surrendering part of the control over the French armed forces to a supranational organism, caused the French Assembly to reject the ratification of the establishing treaty in 1952. For an American point of view on this issue, see: FRUS, 1952–1954, V. pt. 1, Western European Security, 571–1113 (Washington: United States Government Printing Office, 1952–1954); FRUS, 1952–1954, VI, pt. 2, Western Europe and Canada, 1139–511 (Washington: United States Government Printing Office, 1952–1954).

98 On US surveillance activities, see: American Consulate General, Algiers (Amcongen Algiers) (Leon G. Dorros), to Department of State, Washington

(DS), Monthly Economic Report—October 1952, Nov. 10, 1952; file (f.) 851S. 00/11-1052, Foreign Service Dispatch; French Africa, b. 5006; Subject Numeric Files, 1950–1954; Record Group (RG) 59; National Archives and Records Administration, College Park, MD (NARA). On British surveillance activities, see: "Observations on the Fifth Annual Report of the French Bureau of Petroleum Research (BRP) concerning oil prospecting in France and French territories overseas, "Sir Oliver Harvey, Britemb Paris, to Anthony Eden, Secretary of State, Mar. 17, 1952, confidential; file WF 1537/1; b. FO 371/101772, Observations on the Fifth Annual Report of the French Bureau of Petroleum Research (BRP) concerning oil prospecting in France and French territories overseas; TNA.

99 Georges Bidault, Minister of Foreign Affairs, to Édouard Depreux, Minister of Interior, "Memorandum sur les demandes de permis de recherche de pétrole presentées par des sociétés étrangères en Tunisie," Oct. 29, 1947, and Depreux, Minister of Interior, to Yves Chataigneau, Governor General of Algeria, Oct. 31, 1947, secret, coded telegram no. 1103–1104-1005; fd. Politique du pétrole; b. 81F/2067; Affaires algériennes (1873/1964); FN; ANOM.

100 5 A 14, MIC, Direction des Carburants, Feb. 13, 1948, DC 1125, R. Lacoste; 5 A 14, SGCEI, Apr. 6, 1948, doc. 032/A, Compte rendu séance du CEI du 5 avril 1948; 5 A 14, p. 24, Feb. 20, 1948, SG du CEI, doc. 22/B, "Observations de M. le sous-secrétaire d'État aux affaires économiques au sujet des recherches pétrolières en Tunisie." Sources as reported in Bossuat, *La France*, 242–3.

101 Kocher-Marbœuf, *Le Patricien*, 247–8.

102 Minutes of the Conference held on 19 June 1947 at the Under-Directorate of Algeria, under the presidency of Mr. Maisonneuve, Director of General Affairs, on the subject of oil-related foreign activities in Algeria, p. 5; b. 07AH0168-6, REPAL—Correspondence; Fonds ELF-ERAP; AHTOTAL.

103 Ibid., 6–7.

104 Ibid.

105 The Algerian Government General, established in July 1834, was responsible for the administration of French North African territories.

106 Minutes of the Conference held on 19 June 1947, 8.

107 Ibid., 9.

108 6th Meeting, Dec. 30, 1947, pp. 5–6; 7th Meeting, Jan. 14, 1948, p. 3; 8th Meeting, Mar. 3, 1948, p. 9; 12th Meeting, Nov. 12, 1948, p. 6; 18th Meeting, Jan. 9, 1950, p. 3; MBD; b. 07AH0168-28, REPAL; Fonds ELF-ERAP; AHTOTAL. State Secretary for Economic Affairs to Direction of General Affairs (Ministry of Interior, Jules Moch), "Cession des photographies militaires américaines du territoire algérien à une Compagnie Pétrolière Américaine," Jan. 14, 1948; Jules Moch, Ministry of Interior, to State Secretary for Economic Affairs, [same title], Jan. 30, 1948; Marcel-Edmond Naegelen, Governor General of Algeria, to René Mayer, Minister of National Defense, Air Chiefs of Staff, "Photographies aériennes prises en Algérie par l'Armée Américaine," Aug. 24, 1948; Jules Moch, Vice-President of the Council, Minister of Interior, to René Pleven, Minister of National Defense, [same title], Nov. 16, 1949; fd. Recherche pétrolière, attribution de concessions et de permis, affaires diverses, 1949–1957; b. 81F/2060; Affaires algériennes (1873/1964); FM; ANOM.

109 "Photographies aériennes prises en Algérie par l'Armée américaine," Nov. 16, 1949. Marcel-Edmond Naegelen, Governor General of Algeria, to Robert Lacoste, Minister of Industry and Commerce, and to DICA, "Politique

française du pétrole en Algérie," Apr. 17, 1948; fd. Politique du pétrole; b. 81F/2067; Affaires algériennes (1873/1964); FM; ANOM.

110 In the summer of 1949, Conorada was also authorized to access the American set of photos. Marcel-Edmond Naegelen, Governor General of Algeria, to Jules Moch, Minister of Interior, Aug. 23, 1949, secret, coded telegram no. 5939/5940; Moch to Paul Ramadier, Minister of National Defense, Air Chiefs of Staff, "Remise par les Autorités militaires américaines de photographies aériennes de l'Algérie à la Conorada Petroleum Corporation," Aug. 24, 1949, secret; fd. Recherche pétrolière, attribution de concessions et de permis, affaires diverses, 1949–1957; b. 81F/2060; Affaires algériennes (1873/1964); FM; ANOM. For the interest shown by AIOC, Caltex and Gulf, see: Yves Chataigneau, Governor General of Algeria, to Édouard Depreux, Minister of Interior, May 25, 1947, secret, coded telegram no. 5698–99; and Chataigneau to Robert Lacoste, Minister of Industry and Commerce, and to DICA, "Création d'une filiale de l'Anglo-Iranian Oil Company en Algérie," Sep. 19, 1947; fd. Politique du pétrole; b. 81F/2067; Affaires algériennes (1873/1964); FM; ANOM.

111 Letter [unsigned] dated Sep. 10, 1947, Gulf Legal Department to Yves Chataigneau, Governor General of Algeria, via French Embassy (Fremb) in Washington; b. 07AH0168-6, REPAL—Correspondence; Fonds ELF-ERAP; AHTOTAL.

112 Letter dated Apr. 9, 1948, Pierre Guillaumat, DICA, to Georges Betier, Inspector General of Mines in Algiers; b. 07AH0168-6, REPAL—Correspondence; Fonds ELF-ERAP; AHTOTAL. 7th Meeting, Jan. 14, 1948, p. 3; MBD; b. 07AH0168-28, REPAL; AHTOTAL.

113 Note dated Nov. 28, 1950, sent by Paul Moch, BRP's Delegate General, to Pierre Guillaumat, Fuels Director, DICA, "Recherches d'hydrocarbures dans le Sahara"; and Note dated Oct. 18, 1950, sent by Marcel-Edmond Naegelen, Governor General of Algeria, to Henri Queuille, Minister of Interior, and forwarded on 27 October to DICA [Guillaumat] and on 31 October to BRP's Delegate General [Moch], "Recherches d'hydrocarbures dans le Sahara"; b. 07AH0168-6, REPAL—Correspondence; Fonds ELF-ERAP; AHTOTAL.

114 Note dated Oct. 18, 1950, Naegelen to Queuille, "Recherches d'hydrocarbures dans le Sahara"; Charles Brune, Minister of Interior to, Roger Léonard, Governor General of Algeria, "Octroi de permis de recherches d'hydrocarbures dans les Territoires du Sud Algérien," Sep. 15, 1952, confidential; fd. Recherche pétrolière, attribution de concessions et de permis, affaires diverses, 1949–1957; b. 81F/2060; Affaires algériennes (1873/1964); FM; ANOM.

115 Jean-Marie Louvel, Minister of Industry and Energy, to Charles Brune, Minister of Interior, "Recherche de pétrole dans le Sahara," Jun. 23, 1952; b. 81F/2060, fd. Recherche pétrolière, correspondence, 1949–1955; Affaires algériennes (1873/1964); FM; ANOM.

116 Source: fd. Recherche pétrolière, correspondance, 1949–1955; b. 81F/2060; Affaires algériennes (1873/1964); FM; ANOM.

117 29th Meeting, Oct. 30, 1951, pp. 6–9; MBD; b. 10AH0832-26, BRP; Fonds ELF-ERAP; AHTOTAL.

118 Roger Goetze, REPAL's President, to Paul Moch, BRP's Delegate General, Feb. 27, 1952. Two undated letters from Goetze to Roger Léonard, Governor General of Algeria, were attached to this letter; b. 07AH0168-6, REPAL—Correspondence; Fonds ELF-ERAP; AHTOTAL.

119 Ibid.; Roger Goetze, REPAL's President, to Paul Moch, BRP's Delegate General, Sep. 17, 1952, and attached letter attached dated May 31, 1952 from

Roger Léonard, Governor General of Algeria, to Goetze; b. 07AH0168-6, REPAL—Correspondence; Fonds ELF-ERAP; AHTOTAL. 29th Meeting, Nov. 24, 1951, pp. 16–17; b. 07AH0168-6, REPAL—Correspondence; Fonds ELF-ERAP; AHTOTAL.

120 André Morange, Alain Perrodon and Francis Héritier, *Les grandes heures de l'exploration pétrolière du groupe ELF Aquitaine* (Boussens: Elf Aquitaine Éditions, 1992), 97; Perrodon, "Historique des recherches pétrolières en Algérie," 327. 32th Meeting, Apr. 15, 1952, pp. 7–8; MBD; b. 10AH0832-27, BRP; Fonds ELF-ERAP; AHTOTAL.

3 Oil Diplomacy in Wartime Algeria

The destiny of France lies in the Mediterranean [...]. Italy must renounce absurd rivalries.

—Charles de Gaulle, November 1944[1]

On October 22, 1956, the French Air Force, with the support of the secret services and a number of ministers from the cabinet of Prime Minister Guy Mollet, hijacked a Moroccan plane carrying four historical leaders of the Algerian pro-independence, nationalist National Liberation Front (*Front de libération nationale*, FLN). The plane was traveling from Rabat to Tunis, where the four were expected to meet the Tunisian President, Habib Bourguiba, and was under Moroccan protection. It was forced to land in Algiers, and its passengers were arrested.[2] Soon after the arrest, the French press speculated that among the documents confiscated from one of the arrested, Ahmed Ben Bella (Figure 3.1), were some which revealed that the Arabian-American Oil Company (ARAMCO), a company jointly held by US majors Standard Oil of California (SOCAL), SOCONY, Texaco and SONJ, was funding the Front in exchange for priority exploration and exploitation rights in the hydrocarbons sector if and when the country achieved independence.[3]

Between November 1954 and March 1962, French Algeria was the scene of a war for independence that has often been depicted in popular and historical literature as opposing the French settlers and armed forces to organized groups of Algerian nationalist fighters. In an oil world at that time largely dominated by the oligopoly of the majors, the ARAMCO affair made it clear that the Algerian War was not only a domestic French conflict—Algeria being then French territory—based on military confrontation, as it has long been depicted in popular and historical accounts, but was a multinational affair involving the control of hydrocarbons and the knowledge needed to find them. And this characterization holds, regardless of whether or not there was any truth in the claim of ARAMCO's involvement.

Figure 3.1 Ahmed Ben Bella in the US in 1962. On his left, US President John F. Kennedy.
Source: Wikimedia Commons.

The latter aspect is further complicated by the fact that, while the affair was developing in public, the French public oil authority, the BRP, was secretly negotiating with US oil companies to have them involved in the exploration of the Sahara desert.[4] As I will show, this apparently contradictory behavior, namely denouncing US interferences in Saharan affairs while seeking American technical help, in fact had a very precise rationale, and exemplifies well the French dilemma of asserting the stability of its power in Algeria while having to cope with the new Cold War balance of power.

France was not the only country facing a geostrategic dilemma though: Algeria, and North Africa generally, was of paramount importance to US administrations. This was not only because of the region's resources, but also because of US military facilities there (notably in Morocco). In addition, the US worried that if France, a North Atlantic Treaty Organization (NATO) member like the US, persisted in asserting its colonial influence over the area, both newly-independent countries and countries seeking independence might look for help from the Communist Bloc, thus fatally jeopardizing US—and Western—interests in the region, and extending Soviet influence to the farthest shores of the Mediterranean Sea. Fearing this, US administrations wanted France to concede some form of autonomy to the North African territories under its influence. At the same time France, as an ally of the US within the Western Bloc, served to guarantee Western influence there through its presence in North Africa. This dilemma had repercussions on French-American relations during the entire war, a fact that adds to the importance of analyzing the Algerian War from a multilateral perspective.

The Algerian War has long been a marginalized event in the history of French international relations. However, over the last twenty years, as the psychological taboo linked in particular with the French military's frequent practice of torture on Algerian prisoners has begun to fade, an increasing number of studies have been published. The war deeply influenced French national and international politics, to the point that it was the main cause of a major change in France's constitutional system in 1958. Algerian events have therefore been analyzed from many different points of view. The historiography of the Algerian War has tended to focus on political, diplomatic, military, and cultural aspects.[5]

Not unexpectedly, analyses have come mainly from the French academic milieu, and have mostly focused on French–Algerian bilateral relations. However, in the last fifteen years international aspects of the war, as well as the involvement of third parties in it, have also been investigated by works in the history of international relations. Samya El Mechat, Irwin Wall, and Matthew Connelly have produced studies on French–American–Algerian diplomatic triangulations; Martin Thomas and Christopher Goldsmith have focused on Anglo–French wartime dynamics; Jean-Paul Cahn and Klaus-Jürgen Miller have worked on West Germany's position during the War; and Bruna Bagnato has analyzed the evolution of Italy's ambiguous standpoint over the same period. The multilateral focus is not unjustified: such was the extent of international involvement in the Algerian War that Connelly went so far as to define it as a 'diplomatic revolution.'[6]

Indeed, Connelly has argued that the achievement of Algerian independence in 1962 was mainly the result of unofficial diplomatic actions carried out by the FLN around the world. The FLN, the nationalist group that gained the upper hand in Algeria from around 1958, had been weaving diplomatic ties with other countries for its anti-French purposes from even earlier. By June 1960, the French foreign secret services were aware of 177 FLN affiliates in forty states, including most Arab countries, the USSR, the US, China, and Italy.[7]

Despite the abundance of sources on the War, however, two interconnected topics have mostly been neglected: the search for energy resources, and how this objective intersected with security issues.[8] Yet the effort to prospect for and access oil and gas in the Algerian Sahara was a significant factor in the development of the conflict. This means that an analysis of the historical circumstances of Algeria's independence cannot be complete without an examination of the use of science to retrieve natural resources and the connection between science and issues of power. Oil does indeed get mentioned to varying degrees in works on the war, but how geostrategic knowledge about the subsurface was acquired and employed to achieve strategic objectives has yet to be explored: the technoscientific side of the story has largely been black-boxed.[9]

The very few works available on this dimension are purely descriptive, and lack theoretical insight. This is, for example, the case of a 1960 study by journalist Pierre Cornet, which contains extensive descriptions of geophysical operations carried out in the late 1950s by companies operating in the Algerian Sahara, significantly highlighting the interest of American prospecting and oil companies in the area, and also reviewing available training opportunities for geophysicists and geologists in France.[10]

As we will see in the case of Algeria, and has already been shown in the previous chapters, oil diplomacy was not just the job of official diplomats, but also of oil technicians and technocrats, who themselves have acted as policymakers and diplomatic agents, as noted by Ronald Doel, Allan Needell, and others.[11] In the early years of the Cold War, underground exploration in Algeria was closely linked to French national security, as the Sahara was one of the areas that France sought to develop to achieve energy autonomy from British and American majors. Indeed a number of these large international oil firms (such as SONJ, SOCONY, Texaco, the Anglo-Iranian Oil Company, and Shell) had significant activities in mainland France, where they dominated the production and distribution markets.

In this chapter, I look at the processes of political decolonization and concurrent 'oil-onization' of Algeria, focusing on the role of institutions and oil companies from France, the US, and Italy. In 1954, the discovery of the first dry gas field at Djebel Berga by the Sahara Oil Exploration and Production Company (*Compagnie de recherche et d'exploitation de pétrole au Sahara*, CREPS), a joint-venture between Shell and the French public oil exploration agency, RAP, marked the starting point in the production of Algerian hydrocarbons.[12] Major discoveries in 1956–1957 (Edjeleh and Hassi Messaoud for oil, Hassi R'Mel for gas) ignited a confrontation between several countries over control of the region's resources, placing the future of French oil security at risk. Between 1957 and 1958, US companies started negotiating with French authorities for access to new areas for exploration. From 1958, the French foreign secret services noted with concern that European and Japanese companies were following suit, often negotiating with the FLN rather than the French authorities.[13] Among these was the Italian state oil company, ENI, which will be the focus of the second half of this chapter.

Besides confirming the role of oil as a geopolitical resource, these historical events also reveal the geopolitical significance of geostrategic data. The collection of intelligence on the Algerian subsurface by US diplomats and oil technicians strengthened the role of the US in the Cold War, and helped American oil companies to enter Algeria. Meanwhile the French need for financial and technological resources to conduct a thorough exploration of the geologically complex Saharan area facilitated the involvement of foreign enterprises in Algeria. The presence of these foreign interests in turn influenced the quest for Algerian independence as French hopes of retaining control of colonial resources through geostrategic intelligence failed to materialize, while the Algerians succeeded in acquiring important information on oil reservoirs and the organizational aspects of the oil business, which allowed them to gain the upper hand in peace negotiations with the French.

I start by outlining how US interest in the Algerian subsoil was awoken after the first commercial oil and gas discoveries in the mid-1950s. I then show how major policy and legislation changes in the French hydrocarbon sector caused the American presence in the region to increase, a result both desired and feared by French administrations that longed to acquire advanced geoscientific knowledge without losing control of Algerian territory. I then show how Italy and specifically ENI also became involved in the quest for Algerian resources. I analyze how the Italian company managed its agenda of negotiating with both French authorities and Algerian nationalists, eventually taking sides with the Algerians in order to obtain favorable exploration permits in exchange for geoscientific and organizational information.

I argue that, to better understand the war in Algeria, we need to focus on the role of oil as a geopolitical device. If one leaves the corridors of power where the crisis was debated and looks at the 'oily deals' taking place in the subsurface of international politics, a new picture emerges. France's international allies could not overtly undermine its influence in North Africa. But my analysis reveals that they certainly did nothing to stop the efforts of their oil companies to unsettle France and thereby to obtain the exploration and mining concessions in conditions that French institutions had denied them for so long.

Early Findings and American Interest in Algeria

In 1953, a year before the war, four oil companies were operating on Algerian territory. The French had sole charge of CFP(A) and REPAL, while together with Shell they owned CREPS and the Petroleum Company of Algeria (*Compagnie des pétroles d'Algérie*, CPA). After the encouraging results obtained at Berriane and Djebel Berga, the prospecting efforts of the 1950s would soon bring a spectacular payoff. First, there were the southern Saharan regions: the absence or very limited extent of shallow geological layers made it possible to identify potential oil-bearing structures from photo-geological maps. In 1952, the BRP sent a French Petroleum Institute (IFP) crew on a geological mission to the Illizi basin, close to the Libyan border, where they revealed the existence of a promising geological structure (a 'salt dome,' in technical language) at Edjeleh, and found some oil traces.[14]

CREPS obtained a permit for this area in 1953, and almost three years later, integrating its geological indications with those from geophysical surveys, struck oil at Edjeleh and Tiguentourine. In the same year, CFP(A)—in association with REPAL—discovered a large oilfield at Hassi Messaoud, and a huge gas field at Hassi R'Mel, as a consequence of a massive prospecting effort launched in the late 1940s. In 1956 further oilfields were discovered by BRP's affiliates in Gabon, at Ozouri and Pointe Clairette. The description of 1956 as a French *faustus annus* is no exaggeration. In 1957, yet another oilfield was found at Zarzaitine, not far from Edjeleh.[15]

As I discussed in the previous chapter, until the first North African oil discoveries in 1956, American companies—ubiquitous in other areas of the world such as the Middle East and South America, where they had already found or were confident of finding oil reserves—were conspicuous by their absence from the Sahara region. The reasons for this were twofold: first, the restrictive provisions imposed by the French BRP, which limited foreign companies to minority shareholdings in French-dominated joint-ventures, which the US majors, accustomed to operational autonomy—unlike smaller, independent US companies—would not tolerate; and second, the difficult conditions of prospecting in the desert, which put off potential investors. The characteristics of the Saharan subsurface, the high costs of operations, and a hostile climate deterred surveyors.

Besides being a boon for French energy supplies, the 1956 discoveries of Hassi Messaoud and Hassi R'Mel were also the fruit of transnational technological advances. As mentioned in the previous chapter, these were largely the result of the reintroduction of the technique of refraction seismology by CGG. However, seismic refraction had been supplemented by a series of technical improvements in geophysical methods and equipment, such as the use of multiple detectors and shooting patterns, and of very-high-frequency radio transmission equipment, which considerably enhanced communications between field observers and shooters. The US-pioneered introduction of magnetic recording also had important consequences: it improved the interpretation and presentation of recordings, permitted the addition of seismograms from individual dynamite charges used in seismic surveys, made seismograms indefinitely reproducible and modifiable, and determined the typical signal relating to a particular marker bed.[16]

CGG's purchase in 1954 of the first American IBM analog computers for processing seismic data recordings further aided data analysis and interpretation (besides giving the US company valuable information about French geophysical progress). The deployment of small transport planes from 1955 onwards facilitated the work of prospectors, as did the introduction of portable recording equipment.[17] CGG and smaller French geophysical companies were able to start using this new equipment thanks to links they established with US manufacturers. Pierre Guillaumat's strategy of granting limited concessions to US companies on the French mainland in exchange for training and equipment was thus rewarded. Unlike the admission of US companies to Algeria, the French authorities deemed this plan less of a threat to national interests.

The discoveries of the mid-1950s, and the subsequent estimates of their magnitude, generated much optimism in France's industrial environment: at the beginning of 1957, experts reckoned that from 1959 Saharan oil would cover a quarter of France's needs, and even bring complete self-sufficiency within fifteen years. Thanks to carefully devised legislation, French capital held the lion's share of the Algerian oilfields, amounting to almost 80 percent of the total. For French administrations, revenues from the newly found hydrocarbons were also expected to contribute significantly to investments in industrial development and to poverty reduction, which had been exacerbated by the Algerian 'rebellion' of 1954.[18]

The US Consulate General in Algiers kept the State Department updated on all French surveying activities, yet initially oil seemed to remain in the background in the Department's North African reports.[19] These focused instead on conflicts between the French and the nationalist movements of Morocco and Tunisia, at that time French protectorates. The most serious problem in North Africa was deemed to be French obstinacy in keeping colonial-like links with these two countries. It made bilateral reconciliation hard, and endangered European security and the use of the North African region as a French and American base for military operations in Europe.

In August 1954, a US National Intelligence Estimate anticipated that the conflicts in North Africa were likely to prompt Soviet support for nationalist movements.[20] This made American diplomats even more anxious. Eisenhower and his State Secretary, John Foster Dulles, now faced a security dilemma. If the US helped the nationalists, it would deter collaboration between them and the Soviets, thus assuring the safety of US bases in North Africa. But this support would complicate French–American relations and compromise the use of those very bases. Conversely, assisting its NATO partner would almost certainly alienate Arab countries' support for the United States, and this would inevitably threaten its influence in the Near and Middle East to the advantage of the Soviet Union. In addition, there was a very real risk that prolonged support for the French would be condemned by the UN. The main lines of this dilemma would become a leitmotif of American policy, and lead to the US government taking a middle-of-the-road position.[21]

However, Dulles hoped that African resources could be used as a weapon of diplomacy in North Africa, prompting détente between the French, the Moroccans, and the Tunisians, as he had already suggested in 1949 to the French Foreign Minister, Robert Schuman. But for the French, these resources were expected to play a crucial role in national security, not to be the objects of diplomatic barter. As a result, in the wake of the Edjeleh discovery, Olivier Wormser, Director of Economic and Financial Affairs at the French Foreign Ministry (also referred to as the 'Quai d'Orsay'), had urged his government to hasten the development of Saharan oil. That was seen as an essential step toward the country's energy autonomy.[22]

However, in a clear manifestation of the French dilemma—keeping control of the Sahara while admitting non-French capital and technological capacity to exploit its resources adequately—this aspiration to autonomy had to be harmonized with France's desire to acquire new technological knowledge from the US. Indeed, the French authorities began explicitly to ask for US help in exploration. Resorting to US expertise was quite common, as in the case of REPAL, which approached the Independent Exploration Company of Houston, Texas, to carry out seismic work in several widely scattered areas of its concession. By 1954, the year of the outbreak of the Algerian War, geophysical activity in the Sahara was expanding at an impressive rate (Figure 3.2). Thus, the ambiguities of the late 1940s persisted.[23]

The conflict threatened this expansion. It also threatened European security. From 1956, French forces started withdrawing from the German border—where they were stationed from after World War II in accordance with war treaties—to be transferred to North Africa, with NATO's reluctant approval.[24] For State Department analysts, the Algerian war was dividing the non-Communist world between Arab, anti-colonial countries, and colonial powers. France's internal situation, as the North African conflict ensued, could cause "a most serious internal crisis [...] with unpredictable results on the future of French democracy and on France's alignment with NATO."[25] On the other hand, as Connelly reports, NATO executives were also in a quandary, since a French political and military withdrawal would remove Algeria from the NATO area, eliminate its bases there, and possibly reduce Algeria and the Maghreb to chaos. In the words of the chief of the British delegation at NATO, Sir Frank Roberts, the best solution that could be envisaged was therefore "to continue discreetly to encourage the French to come to terms with Arab nationalism while they can still count upon the help of such relatively moderate Arab leaders as the present rulers of Morocco and Tunisia."[26]

French administrations, on the other hand, did not seem to share that view; in addition, they feared that the Americans wanted to replace them in

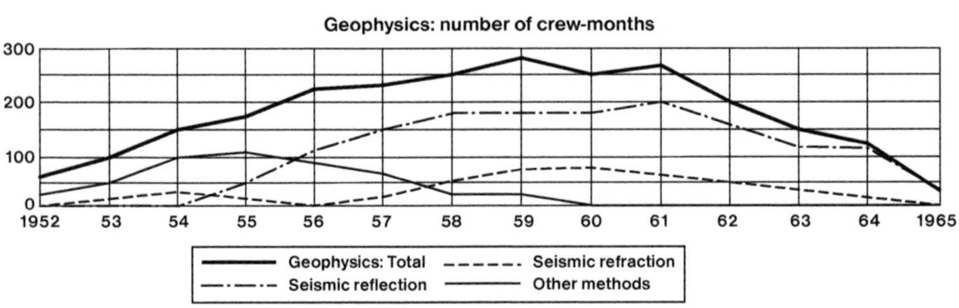

Figure 3.2 Geophysical activity in Algeria (1952–1965).

Source: Courtesy of Institut de recherches et d'études sur le monde arabe et musulman, Aix-en-Provence.[27]

North Africa, a view shared by highly-placed figures such as French Prime Minister Mollet.[28] The US Ambassador in Paris, Clarence Douglas Dillon, revealed to State Department officials that the promised delivery of a small number of helicopters to France had not been enough to stem a sharp rise in anti-Americanism in French public opinion on US policy in North Africa.[29] But while the US government continued for a long time to officially support French Algerian policy in international diplomatic contexts such as the United Nations, US majors had not remained idle. On the contrary, they had been closely monitoring French oilfield activities.

A Libyan Incident and the ARAMCO Affair

The Algerian War not only divided diplomats, it also had serious repercussions for the oil sector. While the Sahara was not particularly affected by military confrontations after 1957, it was the site of a high level of prospecting activity. Initial tensions between American companies and French administrations occurred in the first months of 1956, when the French Foreign Legion exposed illegal prospecting activities by two SONJ technicians at the border between Algeria and Libya, close to the Edjeleh oilfields, just a month after oil had been struck. SONJ had obtained a large exploration permit in Libya bordering Edjeleh, and this represented a splendid excuse to monitor CREPS's operations and results. Following this episode, Paul Moch, the French President of CREPS and RAP, called for support from the National Defense. Forty legionnaires were seconded to protect the field from prying eyes.[30]

At this point, a territorial dispute broke out between SONJ officials, Libya, and Algeria over the Libyan–Algerian borders. SONJ informed the Governor General of Algeria, Robert Lacoste, that a well drilled by CREPS in the Zarzaitine concession, was on Libyan territory, and was therefore part of the SONJ permit. Reportedly, the company's chief geologist had asked for Libyan government support on these grounds. Immediately after receiving the news, and fearing SONJ's influence over the Libyans and the diplomatic consequences of a French—Libyan dispute, Lacoste suggested that the State Secretary for Algerian Affairs, Marcel Champeix, contact the Libyans as soon as possible in order to settle the border issue to French advantage.[31]

In April, Fuels Director Jean Blancard met on two occasions with SONJ board members to discuss the Libyan affair. The American representatives reassured the French that they had not made any claim over Zarzaitine, but did not clarify their position regarding ownership of the well, which left the French worrying that the US major might make a claim at some point.[32] In any case, SONJ's monitoring made it clear to the French that the US major was very interested in entering the Algerian business, with or without French consent and, if need be, by wielding its influence over Arab countries in order to achieve its goals.

The territorial dispute was only solved in December 1956, after two months of bitter negotiations. The French managed to gain an appreciable amount of land, and retained the entire territory surrounding the Edjeleh oilfields. Significantly, during the Libyan affair, the US government, while officially supporting French policy in Algeria, did not intervene to prevent SONJ from taking a stance that could upset French interests. President Dwight Eisenhower's administration did not deem it wise to compromise its relations with Libya either, especially considering the growing interests of US oil companies there. Negotiations were also affected by two almost simultaneous events: the arrest of the four FLN chiefs described at the start of this chapter, and the Suez crisis.

The striking aspect of the October 1956 plane hijacking was that the action had not been authorized by Mollet, who judged it a terrible mistake. The arrest of the four provoked protests from Arab countries, and prompted a demarche by the FLN representative in the US, Mohamed Yazid, as well as by the Libyan government.[33] While Mollet lent weight to the rumors about ARAMCO's involvement in funding the FLN, Douglas Dillon denied the allegations, as did ARAMCO executives. Douglas Dillon also made sure the French did not publish the relevant documents. A few days later, however, Mollet's cabinet chief, Jean-Louis Biget, reassured the American Embassy: "There was virtually nothing," he claimed, "which would tend to incriminate any US individuals, private companies or labor unions."[34]

However, Mollet never retracted his claims, even when he discovered Lacoste had passed the rumors to the press without checking their likelihood. For the State Department's staff, this was a clear indication of Lacoste's influence on Mollet in Algerian affairs. Rather tellingly, in an internal memorandum, a marginal note to a sentence explaining Mollet's attitude warned that the story "must of course not be used under any condition." Indeed, Mollet's early policy of negotiation with the FLN (which he soon modified) had made him so unpopular among French settlers in Algeria that Lacoste enjoyed far more authority there.[35]

Aside from Mollet's behavior, a further point annoyed State Department officials. As mentioned, at the time the ARAMCO affair was unfolding, the French oil administrators were striving to convince American companies to become involved in the exploitation of the Sahara. A BRP official had been sent to the US expressly to persuade them. Mollet's carrot and stick approach, State Department analysts reckoned, was intended to draw the Americans into Algeria so that the US would support French policy there.[36]

The rationale behind the direct appeal to US companies can also be found in the Mollet government's awareness of the laissez-faire policy adopted by the US government vis-à-vis its national companies in North Africa. Instead of having US company officials dealing secretly with the FLN, the French Prime Minister recognized that it would be better to reach agreements with the Americans directly. This amounted to a reaffirmation of

French authority in Algeria. However, the Director of the Office of Western European Affairs, Matthew Looram, believed that if the Americans accepted those advances, French public opinion would see it as a clear sign that US oil companies, with the support of their government, were trying to corner the French in the region. If that happened, American interests would be damaged, rather than furthered.[37]

Indeed, after the arrest of the FLN leaders, there had been contact—albeit indirect—between ARAMCO and the Algerians. In November 1956, the company's Vice-President, James Duce, had received a request from King Saʿūd of Saudi Arabia to contribute to a fund for the prisoners. ARAMCO had left the issue pending, but actually kept in touch with the FLN. Rumors about ARAMCO's actions to undermine the French in Algeria continued throughout 1957.[38]

As we can see from both the Libyan incident and the ARAMCO affair, soon after the discoveries of 1956, diplomatic tension between France and the US regarding Algerian resources started to mount. As the same time, the French oil elite faced a quandary between the need to acquire technologies and capital, and the threat to its energy security caused by potential foreign access to Algeria. It therefore devised a plan to accomplish the former without triggering the latter.

Divide and Rule? An Institutional Stratagem to Keep Control of the Sahara

The FLN chiefs' arrest was near contemporaneous with another major political event, the joint British–French–Israeli expedition to intervene in the Suez Canal crisis. In October 1956, British, French and Israeli armed forces launched an attack on Egypt in response to Egyptian President Gamal Abdel Nasser's decision to nationalize the Suez Canal, a major point of passage for oil tankers from the Persian Gulf to Europe. Occurring slightly more than two weeks after the plane hijacking, the attack yielded an outcome totally different from what the aggressors had hoped. American intervention to stop the invasion by enacting a Saudi-supported oil embargo on France and the UK had turned the invaders' swift military success into a political debacle. Nasser's emerged the stronger, as did Arab nationalists in general. The outcome was the worst-case scenario for the French. Nasser was aiding the FLN, both militarily and financially, and it was in Cairo that FLN political leaders were finding refuge.[39]

For State Department officials, the Suez expedition proved that the French were dealing with the Algerian conflict in a way that endangered the world order they had in mind. The only practical result of the expedition had been the impairment of European access to Middle Eastern oil, making Western Europe more vulnerable to Soviet attack.[40] After Suez, oil provision became an even more urgent issue for Mollet's government. Due to the closing of the Suez Canal, the Arab embargo, and the sabotage of pipelines connecting Iraqi oilfields to the Mediterranean coast (France sourced a large share of its oil from Iraq through the Iraq Petroleum Company), France was forced to rely solely on its Iranian oil, shipped to the Hexagon around Africa. This oil, however, was expected to satisfy only half the country's needs. In these circumstances, the ability to fully dispose of and exploit Algerian resources became critical to French security.[41]

Believing that a solution to the oil exploration problem should be found within a broader administrative framework, the French government established such a framework to facilitate the adequate development of Saharan resources. In January 1957, the Common Organization of Saharan Territories (*Organisation commune des régions sahariennes*, OCRS) was constituted. It included the Saharan portions of Niger, Chad, Mauritania, French Sudan (now Mali), and Algeria's Saharan *départements* of Oasis and Saoura.[42] Besides the economic rationale, according to historian Pierre Boilley, the creation of OCRS had a further geostrategic value, in that controlling the Sahara would allow France to secure the possibility of intervening in the whole of North and West Africa, as well as providing a large territory for withdrawal in the event of a new occupation of mainland France (after that of World War II).[43]

In the same month, viewing this as a dangerous move to separate the Sahara from Algeria, Yazid called from New York for UN sponsorship of a new round of negotiations based on the recognition of Algeria's right to independence, before it was too late to recover Saharan hydrocarbons. Mollet immediately rejected the appeal. The Algerian question, according to the French Prime Minister, lay outside the UN's competence: it was a purely French national issue. The French supported this line through lobbying campaigns directed at almost forty ambassadors, and at the UN by having Foreign Minister, Christian Pineau, personally meet most of the heads of delegations, while SDECE agents sought to bribe a number of representatives.[44]

Soon after OCRS's establishment, and in light of the possibility that FLN actions might disrupt the operation of the oilfields, a mixed civil–military study group was set up, with representatives from a number of ministries including Fuels Director Blancard and BRP President Guillaumat.[45] The purpose of the group was to outline measures for the protection of Saharan oil and gas installations and industrial plants, as well as locations of strategic importance such as Colomb-Béchar or Reggane, where the French army was experimenting with remotely controlled missiles. This strategic function would become evident in the early 1960s, when the Algerian sites of Reggane, Hammaguir, In Ekker, and Béchar were chosen for the first French nuclear tests.[46]

The French Army collaborated in the effort by sending further regiments of parachutists and helicopters, and through the creation of a local militia, which would also protect oil transportation infrastructures. The construction of a network of military airports close to the French Union's most sensitive installations was also agreed. While defending oil facilities from possible nationalist attacks, this military escalation was also a strong indication of French determination to maintain control of the exploration sites.[47]

In June 1957, a Ministry for the Sahara was established—significantly, as distinct from the existing Ministry of Algerian Affairs—to manage the two new desert *départements* (see Figure 3.3, for a map of exploration permits in the Algerian Sahara in early 1957). According to the law establishing the new ministry, the Minister for the Sahara would also be de jure the chief executive of OCRS: however, the effect of this act was to shift the central administration of the Sahara from Algiers to Paris, which ran counter to the spirit of co-participation of the OCRS.[48]

The Socialist Minister for the Sahara, Max Lejeune, affirmed that foreign capital would not be excluded from investment in OCRS, with the proviso that the nationality and independence of French Saharan enterprises would not be up for discussion. By separating the Saharan regions from the northern Mediterranean belt, the French government believed it would be easier and less risky to make administrative concessions to an Algeria severed from her richest areas: essentially, the creation of OCRS was an early move to separate the Sahara from northern Algeria, as confirmed then by a number of high-placed French officials.[49]

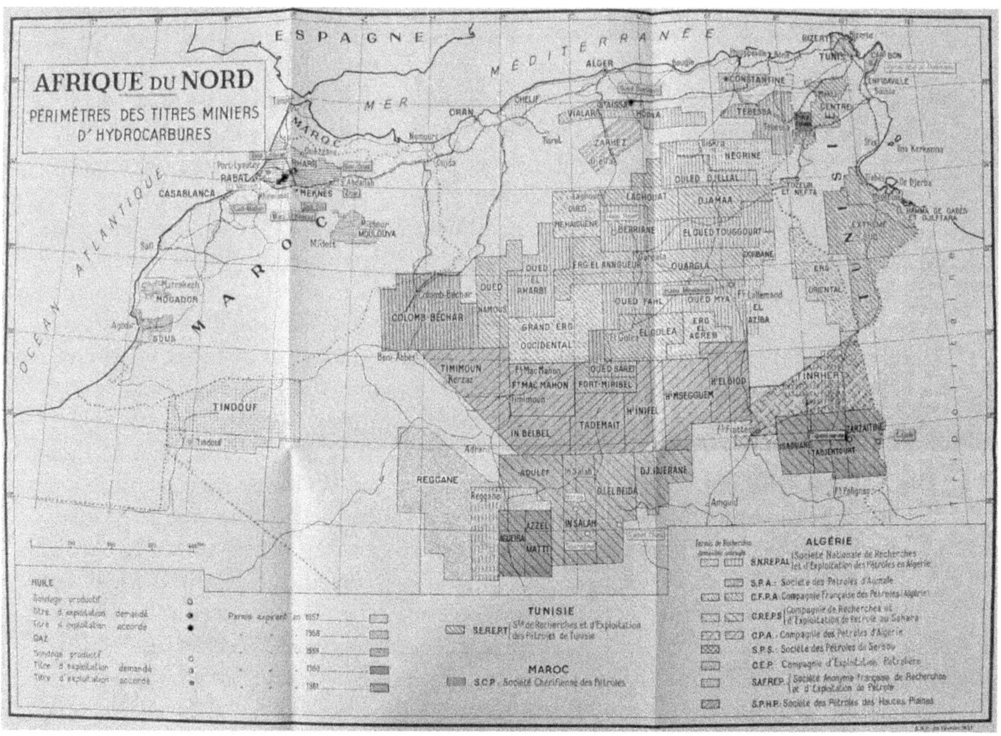

Figure 3.3 Map of exploration permits in the Algerian Sahara in early 1957.
Source: Courtesy of Archives nationales d'outre-mer, Aix-en-Provence.[50]

In March 1957, not long after the creation of OCRS, US Vice-President Richard Nixon's mission to Africa to strengthen US relations with a number of African countries also focused international political attention on North Africa. Besides fostering political connections for anti-Soviet purposes, these visits were instrumental in laying the foundations for agreements on the exploitation of natural resources. "Through his demagogic handshakes," Italian ambassador in Paris, Pietro Quaroni, caustically commented, Nixon sought to tighten US links with African countries such as Tunisia and Morocco. But that implicitly meant weakening French influence in that region. In his final confidential report to Eisenhower, Nixon explained that French prestige was rapidly decreasing in the area, and that there was a widespread conviction in North African governmental circles that the French could no longer sustain a massive military effort.[51]

Things were also moving on the British side. In May, former Minister of State for Foreign Affairs, Anthony Nutting, met a Shell executive, Denick Hirsch (whose friendly attitude toward the FLN was known to SDECE) to discuss the political and commercial scenario in the region. Hirsch's pro-FLN stance, commented the French secret services, was common among Shell executives, and was endorsed in particular by Jack Lee of Shell's commercial department. Lee had contacted the American diplomatic services in Morocco, following an endorsement by the Foreign Office, a connection that clearly revealed threateningly close relations between British political circles and the Anglo–Dutch major.[52]

British and US interests thus appeared to coincide in an anti-French strategy. As a consequence, the US government found it extremely hard to allay French fears about its duplicity. In November 1957, British and American deliveries of weapons to Tunisia, a country that was patently supporting the Algerian fighters, did nothing to consolidate French trust in its two western allies and exasperated the Quai d'Orsay.[53]

While it does not seem that the US government overtly aimed to replace the French, both the US State Department and American oil companies saw the end of French colonialism as running in the 'direction of history,' as two secret SDECE notes accurately suggested. Essentially, therefore, according to the French intelligence services, the US government would not oppose attempts by non-European French territories to achieve independence, as this would have the added advantage of permitting the US to extend its influence there. Significantly, a US plan designed by Eisenhower's Economic Advisors, part of the President's doctrine of providing economic assistance to Arab countries in order to prevent Soviet influence in the region, assumed Algerian independence. American economic penetration, therefore, went hand in hand with moves toward political independence for former colonies in Africa. However, SDECE maintained, the acquisition of such independence entailed France's "suppression as a world power."[54] One may not go so far as to support SDECE's apocalyptic conclusion, but the basic terms of its analysis seem an accurate reflection of the US Government's essential position.

While Nixon's thoughts on Algeria remained unknown to the public, this was not the case for a speech given early in July 1957 by the US Democratic Senator, John Fitzgerald Kennedy. Now openly supporting the Algerian nationalists, Kennedy pressed Eisenhower's government to adopt a definite pro-independence position, maintaining that the Algerian situation had by then become an international matter. Kennedy's speech represented a brilliant victory for the FLN in the diplomatic sphere. However, it provoked an irate reaction from Minister Pineau. The French Ambassador in Washington, Hervé Alphand, told Dulles that Kennedy's speech would inflame French public opinion and worsen Franco–American relations.[55]

The US government distanced itself from the Democrat senator's declarations, but SDECE's argument was that the speech reflected American public opinion, and according to historian Samia El Mechat, its content was in line with the State Department's analyses. Indeed, by 1958 State Department analysts considered Algerian independence as inevitable, and their preference was that it should be conceded by France rather than seized by Algeria.[56]

From 1957, changes in the French BRP's mining policy prompted American oil companies to solicit permits in the Sahara. The establishment of OCRS may not have thrilled the majors, both because of the conditions imposed by the French and the early US policy advocating no interference by US firms in regional politics. But Eisenhower's administration saw the OCRS as a way to bring together otherwise weak African states and steer them away from Communist influence. It thus favored France's exclusive approach. Contrary to the majors' apparent disinterest, the constitution of the OCRS did arouse the interest of smaller independent US companies (and later, of the majors as well).[57] This situation was also looked on favorably by Mollet's government, as we will see below.

The Suez expedition was a key point in the development of Algerian resources. The lack of oil subsequent to the ensuing Arab embargo convinced French authorities that a policy of autarky with respect to Algeria would delay thorough exploration of the territory, with possibly fatal consequences for France's energy security. Thus, when the French eventually chose to open the doors of the Sahara to the Americans, they did not do it wholeheartedly. In fact, they were forced to it by economic interests and technological imperatives. US companies were only too happy to oblige. This was particularly true of smaller, independent, American oil and service companies, which mainly provided the geoscientific expertise essential to the exploration of the Algerian subsoil.

'Half-Open Door' Policy

Unlike the majors, independent US oil companies did not possess the massive international reserves that the former had. In order to elbow a place for themselves in the oil market, they were therefore more prone to venture into financially risky opportunities, and in the event of a discovery, to commit their expertise and capital to finding and extracting as much oil as possible, in collaboration with the French authorities. There was little risk that they might try to acquire reserves simply for the purpose of keeping them in the ground—as some majors did—in order to artificially stimulate a rise in oil prices and take reserves from competitors (Timothy Mitchell's 'scarcity production'). In addition, these companies, with no activities on French domestic soil, had less power to retaliate against the French than the majors did.[58]

Independent companies seemed disposed to accept BRP's rules for access to the Sahara, namely: that no foreign group should hold a majority share in any concession; that they undertake to supply and train technicians and provide drilling equipment; that they relinquish half of their permits after five years; and finally and most importantly, that they pass all geoscientific data collected to BRP. For BRP, the last provision in particular meant obtaining intelligence at no financial cost, while the training of French specialists by the Americans would improve the quality of national geoscientific expertise. Thus, in July 1957, the US Cities Service Company informed the State Department that it was about to agree an exploration contract with REPAL for some areas close to the Libyan border.[59]

The Algerian newspaper, *Echo d'Oran*, reported two further conditions: a) that permits should not be granted to foreign companies unless they were willing to reciprocate by giving French companies concessions outside the franc zone, especially in Venezuela and Mexico, and b) that concessions would be granted only to companies that adopted a non-interference policy with respect to French–North African relations. Although the BRP denied the existence of both conditions, there seems to have been some foundation for the claim.[60]

Guillaumat declared that his agency would start an open door policy in the Sahara, and grant permits for 60,000 km^2 within the following four months. At least five companies applied for permits, two of which included American interests. According to San Harlan, Vice-President of Cities Service, the most interesting aspect of American participation was less about financial benefits than about an increase in the number of facilities and prospectors.[61] In practice, Cities Service intended to use its first permit as a bridgehead to explore the territory further, and possibly to attain other Saharan areas. A number of other US company representatives soon rushed to Paris. The US Minister Counselor in Paris, Charles Yost, talked with agents of Phillips Petroleum, Tide Water, Sun Oil, Conorada, and Continental. In the following months, more US companies applied for permits, always in joint ventures with French concerns: this was the case for Sinclair Oil, Newmont Mining, and Phillips Petroleum.[62]

By that time, American companies were not new to exploratory activities in the Sahara: the Overseas Company had explored the western region of the Sahara; the two seismic companies, Independent and Rogers, had been working for French companies in the Hassi R'Mel area and south of Reggane. In addition, between ten and twelve American technicians and engineers were working independently for French companies engaged in drilling activities, and more were expected to enter Algeria as contractors in early 1958. However, while the activities of small US companies were sponsored by the French, some could now be playing the role of double agents. The fluidity of transnational actors could therefore prove an asset for the US oil industry and administration.[63]

The sensitive information some company representatives collected in their visits was sent back to the State Department and used to enter further applications to prospect certain areas. This was typical of the scientific intelligence-gathering for national and business purposes conducted by oil companies and technology contractors. In May 1957, for example, an American representative working for a lubricant firm traveled to Hassi Messaoud to assess at first hand the likelihood of the productive potential of the wells reported by the French, subsequently downplaying the scale of the discovery. Later, an American engineer was called by CFP(A) to supervise the production of one of Hassi Messaoud's wells; meanwhile, another US citizen surveyed the Hassi R'Mel area, and reported back about its structure. In mid-1958, the American production superintendent of CFP(A) confidentially reported to the State Department that tests on one of Hassi Messaoud's wells had proved disappointing, and that reports leaked to the press about the well being a potentially huge producer had proved "extremely embarrassing for the management of the company."[64]

He then provided more realistic quantitative estimates. Once again geoscientific knowledge had proved to have unsuspected strategic qualities. "These facts," commented Consul General Frederick Lyon, "are very closely guarded secrets. No information of this type is available officially and such facts as the Consulate General had obtained come privately and principally from the source mentioned." Intelligence of this kind was fundamental for the US government to assess the Algerian Sahara's real oil potential. Thanks to the Consulate's reports, the State Department was able to transmit data to US companies. Most would consult it before engaging in negotiations with French authorities.

By June 1958, British and American geoscientific information-gathering activities had considerably increased. Fifteen geophysical crews were working in the Sahara. While six were from CGG, three were from Shell-controlled CPA; one, contracted by CGG, was from the American seismic prospecting company, MacCollum Exploration; one was from a company controlled by CFP(A). Four other American-controlled seismic reflection crews from Independent Exploration Company and Rogers Exploration Company were working at several points in the Sahara.[65]

Moreover, the Americans could count on their technological superiority in oil equipment as a lever to blackmail the French and obtain the results they desired. A secret SDECE report to the Fuels Directorate (DICA) reveals that in December 1957 British oil representatives met officers from the US's Chase

Bank (SONJ's main banker). At the meeting, the British let the latter know of their anxieties over Saharan projects developing without an adequate British presence. This concern was shared by the Americans, who declared willing to blackmail the French by blocking exports of prospecting and drilling materials if the Standard Oil group was not allowed to take part in Saharan exploration. British Petroleum (BP) was eventually admitted to exploration in the Sahara in the summer of 1958 through a minority holding in the *Société des pétroles de Valence.* Regardless of whether the technological blackmail was actually employed, this episode shows once more how technological disparity provided decisive leverage in oil diplomacy matters, as well as the connivance of the British–American majors in perpetuating their oligopoly. As for SONJ, presumably as a consequence of Chase Bank's pressure, it eventually succeeded in signing a contract for Saharan exploration by early 1959. By contrast with the BP case, the US major would be the majority shareholder.[66]

A *Major* Change: The Promulgation of the Oil Code and SONJ's Admission to the Sahara

US companies' activities in Algeria were not limited to the collection of confidential geoscientific information. Instead, as one would expect, once such information was acquired, it was used in applications for concessions. In December 1957 Arthur Proudfit, a SONJ manager, informed the State Department of his intention to travel to Paris to confer with the French 'Minister of Mines' (as no such ministry existed in France, he presumably meant the Fuels Director, Blancard). In January, he and another SONJ representative met Blancard and CFP's President, Victor de Metz, to renegotiate Algerian concessions. Proudfit candidly admitted that obtaining a concession in Algeria was not important per se, but it would enable the major to consolidate its interests on the French mainland market, and would improve relations with the government.[67]

SONJ's interest in Algeria, a secret SDECE report underlined, was the other side of the coin of ARAMCO's activities in the Middle East. Both were the results of Chase Bank's diversification policy, as the bank controlled the whole Standard galaxy. ARAMCO would leave Algeria to SONJ. As for the latter, SDECE believed its intervention had been prompted by three factors: oil had begun to flow in Algeria; its competitors had taken or were taking positions; and in some sectors there was a risk that franc oil would replace dollar oil.[68]

The negotiations continued unabated, notwithstanding the turmoil caused by the French Air Force's strike, on 8 February 1958, against the Tunisian village of Sakiet Sidi Youssef. While the French military claimed that their objective was to destroy an FLN stronghold, the attack caused over seventy civilian casualties. Not only did it definitively eradicate any US government hopes that France could solve the Algerian issue, but it also triggered a move at the UN by the Tunisian envoy, who presented the assembly with a motion of censure against France. Relations between the French and American governments were strained, especially as the Americans knew that military equipment sent to France from the US for NATO purposes had been used in the raid. In order to avoid a difficult debate at the UN Security Council, which would force the United States to take a definite position in the conflict, the American government suggested to the French and the Tunisians a joint British–American good offices mission to broker peace between the conflicting countries. The two governments accepted.[69] At the same time, the majority of UN countries agreed to back the Tunisian motion.

When, in April, the French Assembly rejected Prime Minister Félix Gaillard's request to accept the mission's conclusions, the government fell, marking a crucial step in the crumbling of the Fourth Republic. The final blow came in May, when French settlers assaulted the General Government in Algiers during a demonstration in support of French Algeria. The fear in France of a military coup on the part of the Algerian generals convinced the French government, now led by the Christian Democrat Pierre Pflimlin, to accept the only solution that would ward off this possibility. This was the return to power of the only authority the Algerian military would respect: Charles de Gaulle, who had left government in early 1946. The General accepted Pflimlin's request, and in June formed the last of the Fourth Republic's cabinets. In January 1959 he became the first President of the Fifth Republic, which replaced the parliamentary government with a semi-presidential system.[70]

While the French Republic was disintegrating before the actions of the Algerian military, the FLN took advantage of the extreme instability of the French political situation. In April, FLN's New York delegation published a report on Saharan oil, which attributed France's obstinacy in not relinquishing the region to the government's determination to exploit Algerian hydrocarbons for its own benefit.[71] The French secret services learnt that the FLN had also secretly contacted foreign oil companies and reassured them that an independent Algeria would seek their collaboration and acknowledge their legitimate interests in exchange for their help. The Front, however, clarified that only an independent Algerian government would have the right to sanction such agreements, and that Algeria would not recognize any accords or commitments made by those companies with the French.[72] French intelligence agents speculated that this was FLN's response to the ongoing negotiations between SONJ, the BRP, and the CFP. Now that the French government had decided to seek a settlement with the American major, the FLN decided to raise its bid, and offer the Americans full collaboration.

At the same time, in October 1956 the FLN announced a general offensive and the opening of a new 'Saharan front.' In November 1957 a team of CPA prospectors was attacked, and some killed. The FLN also threatened to sabotage pipelines laid by the French in Algeria, as will be described in the next chapter. Notwithstanding these episodes, by the summer of 1958 the number of American independent companies in joint ventures with

French counterparts had increased. The American Consulate in Algiers now counted twelve foreign–French partnerships involved in the development of Saharan resources.[73]

In order to promote the involvement of foreign companies in Algeria and significantly relieve a French budget burdened by the costs of both war and exploration, in November 1958 de Gaulle's government approved a fundamental, long-awaited law that would regulate oil activities in the Sahara: the Saharan Oil Code (*Code pétrolier saharien*). The Code provided companies with greater freedom to act than the previous exploration and production rules. It introduced an advantageous fiscal regime, as well as new provisions on exploration, including a prospecting permit that allowed companies to start field operations. This was a pragmatic step prior to a permit application, enabling companies to accumulate data about an area before deciding whether to make any further investment. All data, needless to say, had to be passed to the BRP, which was therefore even able to compare results from different companies in the same area, and assess the technological advances of foreign enterprises.[74]

The Code thus aligned with Guillaumat's strategy of yielding specific exploitation rights while retaining control of geoscientific knowledge. The promulgation of the Oil Code, together with a symbolic visit that De Gaulle made to an Algerian oilfield a month later, gave impetus to the Saharan oil boom (see Figure 3.4, a chart of Algerian production), which was further stimulated by the press announcement of a cooperative agreement between SONJ, CFP, and Pétropar, a government-controlled investment company. The agreement, formalized in January 1959, gave the association exploration rights over an area of 20,000 km^2 in the Eastern Dune, bordering Libya. SONJ would hold half the shares in the joint venture, the first time a foreign company had been allowed more than 49 percent control of a Saharan permit.[75]

The agreement, announced in January 1959, immediately triggered unfavorable reactions in France. Both left- and right-wing newspapers accused the government of selling off the Sahara to foreign interests. Moreover, the deal was immediately condemned by Mohamed Yazid, in his new role as Minister of Information of the FLN's government-in-exile, the Provisional Government of the Algerian Republic (*Gouvernement provisoire de la République algérienne*, GPRA), established in Cairo four months earlier. Yazid declared French–foreign agreements invalid and, to reinforce his point, continued his lobbying at the State Department and the UN, prompting vocal protests by Ambassador Alphand in Washington. As a consequence, de Gaulle urged SDECE to shadow him and Abdelkader Chanderli, the permanent FLN representative in Washington. The US government, however, did not stop the Algerian. American oil companies had been admitted to the Sahara and were developing their business presence; not least, with FLN's increasing power, frustrating Yazid's activities in the US would be counterproductive.[76]

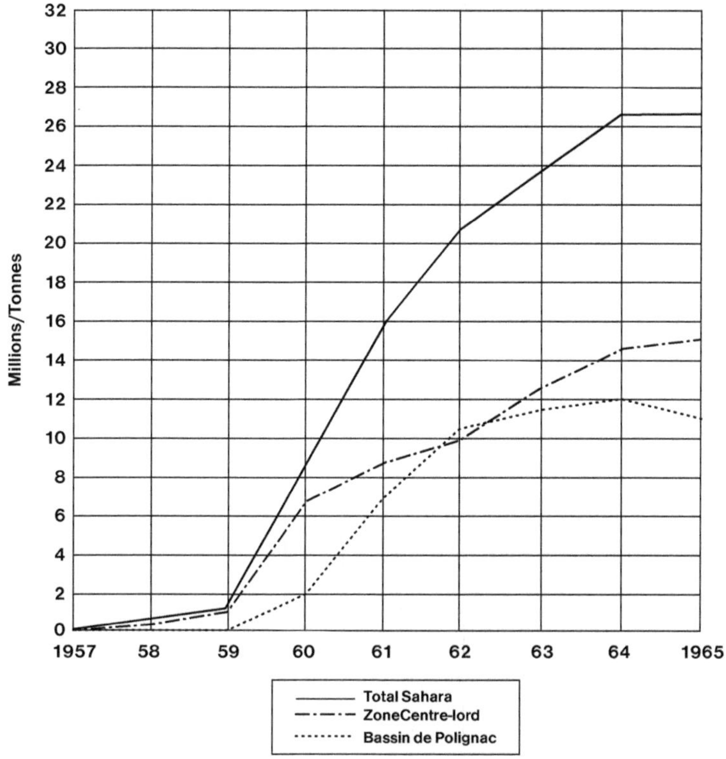

Figure 3.4 Development of Saharan oil production in million tons (1957–1965). 'Bassin de Polignac' refers to Southern Sahara; 'Zone Centre-Nord' to Central and Northern Sahara.

Source: Courtesy of Institut de recherches et d'études sur le monde arabe et musulman, Aix-en-Provence.[77]

Such incidents notwithstanding, French–American relations in North African oil gradually and steadily improved, so that by the end of 1960, out of thirty foreign companies operating in the Algerian Sahara, most were American, including the majors SOCONY Mobil, Caltex, and SONJ. Overall, they controlled 22 percent of the land, but only 7 percent of the proven reserves (Figure 3.5).[78]

The FLN and its diplomats did not confine their lobbying activities to politicians and UN representatives in the United States. They also directed their attention to European governments and oil companies, with the Italian public oil company, ENI, playing an important role in working with both the French and the FLN with a view to establishing a foothold in Saharan exploration.

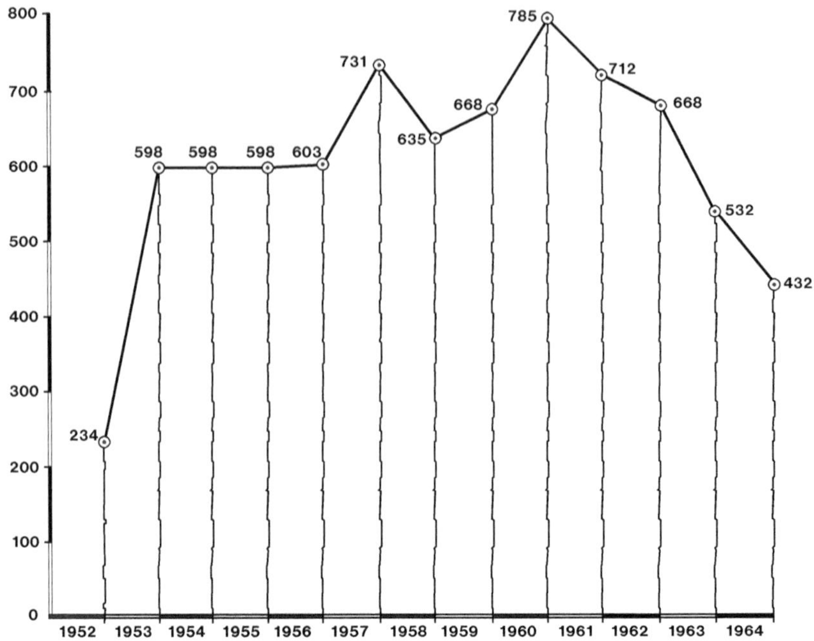

Figure 3.5 Evolution of exploration permits by surface area in the Sahara (in thousand km^2).

Source: Courtesy of Institut de recherches et d'études sur le monde arabe et musulman, Aix-en-Provence.[79]

An Italian 'Business Card' to the Sahara

In October, in a telegram sent from Pietro Quaroni, Italian Ambassador in Paris, to the Italian Minister of Foreign Affairs, Giuseppe Pella, Quaroni argued that Italy should "present [its] business card to the Sahara." Toward the end of 1957, the idea of carving out a space in Algeria by taking advantage of France's half-open door policy also began to take hold in Italian diplomatic circles. Quaroni criticized the dithering of the Italian government, which he believed was abstaining from taking the initiative in the hope more profit would come from a deal with the Algerians (assuming that they would soon be independent). This stance, Quaroni warned, could prove dramatically wrong. It seemed unlikely to Quaroni that oil concessions given to private concerns would be cancelled after the French departure.[80]

Moreover, the Ambassador noted in a later exchange, austerity measures taken by the French government had forced the Minister for the Sahara, Lejeune, to accept a budget cut, which risked jeopardizing the Saharan development program. This would soften the position of the French, who had thus far been reluctant to give permits to foreign companies. Thus Quaroni implicitly solicited ENI's intervention, especially since by late 1957 the Italian company enjoyed extremely good relations with Middle East Arab oil producers.[81] In that year, the Italian firm enacted a new approach to profit sharing that threatened the majors' oligopolistic control of oil from that area. ENI's two contracts with Iran and Egypt substantially modified the 50–50 division of profits in force at the time. To simplify an otherwise complex issue, the Italian–Iranian agreement assigned 75 percent of profits to the producer, the other 25 percent to ENI. This was an important change, as it would mean that producers could eventually become directly involved in the oil industry proper, train their technicians in Western techniques, and to some extent develop their own technical apparatus, while also gathering geoscientific data.[82]

The new contract model caused much anxiety among the majors, and it is interesting to note that from the second half of the 1950s, ENI's geophysicists played an important negotiating role in perfecting these deals. Antonio Selem, the chief geophysicist of ENI's exploration branch, AGIP Mineraria, was instrumental in this as the company's 'roving ambassador.' ENI's President, Enrico Mattei, had him secretly negotiate in countries where his own presence would have aroused suspicion, thus keeping a low profile for ENI's operations.[83] Quaroni and Mattei tacitly agreed that the French would soon be forced to leave Algeria. The Ambassador was furthermore convinced that a clearly pro-Arab policy would strengthen Italy's relations with the US. Italian support for Arab states would balance the negative effects of French actions in North Africa (but only as long as the Italians did not challenge American oil interests).[84]

Already in April 1956, ENI's newspaper *Il Giorno* had published an article on a solution to the Algerian crisis based on the acknowledgment of the FLN as a valid interlocutor—exactly what the French abhorred. Then, a year later, *Il Giorno* disputed the validity of French concessions for Saharan natural resources.[85] French diplomats were convinced that *Il Giorno*'s (and therefore Mattei's) viewpoint coincided with that of the Italian government, believing that with ENI's financial resources Mattei was able to influence parliamentary decisions. They also believed that an unfavorable attitude to France in Algeria on the part of the Italian government weakened the French position at the UN. Like the US administration, the Italian government ostensibly supported its European ally, while covertly adopting a laissez-faire policy, vis-à-vis ENI's actions in North Africa. Italy's Mediterranean aspirations, the French Ambassador in Italy, Jacques Fouques-Duparc, wrote in September 1957 to Foreign Minister Pineau, were not limited to providing the country with the most convenient energy resources, but extended to making Italy the champion of Afro–Arab nationalism.[86]

Italian attempts to replace French technical staff with Italians at the Moroccan Office for Phosphates were also viewed with apprehension. In late 1957, Pineau cautioned Italian Prime Minister, Adone Zoli, against trying to pursue these replacements.[87] ENI's Middle Eastern initiatives made the French anxious, as did a speech given by Mattei at the Center for Foreign Policy Studies in Paris in late November, in which he maintained that oil could no longer be managed in a colonial style. As a consequence of the steps taken in 1957, SDECE put Mattei under surveillance. Premiers Bourgès-Maunoury, Gaillard, de Gaulle, and later Michel Debré, were thus kept updated about his activities, trips and meetings.[88] However, the French hoped to co-opt Mattei's and ENI's interests in the Sahara. In November 1957, Italian Social-Democrat leader and former Deputy Prime Minister, Giuseppe Saragat, suggested that the new French Ambassador in Rome, Gaston Palewski, approach Mattei with a view to examining possibilities of cooperating in Saharan exploration. Palewski did not reject the suggestion outright; he wrote to Pineau to ask his opinion, leaving the possibility open.[89] Mattei, however, thought it appropriate to approach the Algerian nationalists instead.

The first contacts between him and the FLN occurred in 1958, when ENI's President met the FLN representative in Rome, Taïeb Boulahrouf. This initial introduction allowed him to meet several other FLN leaders over the following years. To find a rationale for these contacts, we need to look at what had happened on both sides of the Mediterranean. The Moroccan and Tunisian governments had welcomed de Gaulle's comeback, thus complicating their relations with the FLN. After the failure of a new Maghreb conference in June 1958 and the construction in Tunisia of a pipeline to bring Algerian oil to the coast, the crisis between Tunisian President Bourguiba and the FLN reached a peak.[90]

This departure from Maghreb unity accelerated the need for the FLN to look for interlocutors well disposed to their cause. Italy's 'Neo-Atlanticist' political doctrine—the ambition to develop a specific role for Italy in developing countries while keeping an Atlantic allegiance and protecting national interests—adopted among others by Mattei, was well tailored to the country's need for energy to fuel its growing industrial network. On the diplomatic side, it was easy for Italian administrations to support the cause of anti-colonialism, which it had opportunistically embraced after the Treaty of Paris, in February 1947, obliged Italy to renounce its colonies.[91]

Besides making contact with the Italians, the FLN (and later the GPRA) also approached other countries for help. Since the US military supported the French under the NATO banner, the Algerians requested assistance from China and the Soviet Union. The Soviets, in particular, supplied the FLN with weapons via Czechoslovakia and Egypt. In March 1961, an agreement was signed between the USSR and the GPRA, which included, among other provisions, an undertaking that Algeria would exchange half of its foreign trade with the Soviet Bloc. It would also close down French military bases within a year so as to prevent them being available to NATO.[92]

Many GPRA politicians and diplomats did not view Communist ideology particularly favorably, as it clashed with their religious beliefs. They were, however, ready to put ideological divergences aside for the sake of political objectives, whether with the Americans or the Soviets. Their priority was to get rid of the French and gain the possibility of managing their own resources. The GPRA had found the Americans uncertain, their support lukewarm. The overtures to the Soviets may also have been a move designed to convince the United States to adopt a more definite pro-Algerian stance. In the case of the Italian public oil company, by contrast, there was no ambiguity in its friendly stance toward the GPRA. It was Abdelhafid Boussouf, the GPRA Minister of Armaments and General Relations and Communications, who understood ENI executives' aspirations to carve out a prominent position for their company in the Sahara.

Early Approaches to the French and the Algerians

In July 1958, Mattei won ENI an exploration permit in southern Morocco, incidentally snatching it from under the nose of SONJ, which had shown interest in it, and taking personal revenge for a similar move by SONJ in Libya in 1957. Based on the Iranian profit-sharing template, the Moroccan–Italian agreement was a clear sign of ENI's readiness to take on the economic might of the majors. In addition, the choice of Morocco, previously almost a private French oil fiefdom, also hinted at Mattei's inclination not to accept French proposals to collaborate on joint exploitation of the Sahara. Not unexpectedly, the French protested.[93]

Boussouf also appreciated Mattei's initiative and the difference in ENI's policy on profit-sharing with producer countries, so he encouraged the ENI President in this direction by sponsoring the allotment of a concession to the Italian company in Libya, approved by the Libyan King, Idriss I, in late 1959, despite external pressures from American companies. Thankful for this support, Mattei did his best to promote the Algerian cause within the Italian political arena. Italy soon became the European country where the FLN enjoyed the greatest operational support for its own political and diplomatic aspirations.[94]

That did not mean that Mattei was absolutely bent on avoiding dealings with the French, as has generally been maintained. He carefully examined the French proposals for collaboration in Algerian oil activities (mainly in oil production), but found them unsatisfactory. According to French diplomatic sources, Mattei had approached CFP and had shown an interest in being involved in the exploitation of Hassi Messaoud. The French company had, however, rejected his proposal, while Mattei had refused CFP's counterproposal.[95] Reportedly, in early 1957 ENI executives also approached the small French Oil Production Company (*Compagnie d'exploitation pétrolière*, CEP)—which entered the Sahara that year—aiming to conduct joint exploration of CEP's Saharan permits adjacent to the Edjeleh area. From ENI sources, however, it emerges that it was CEP's President, André Demargne, who had approached AGIP Mineraria.

In any case, in January 1957, CEP was ready to sign an agreement with AGIP. The French company would be sole owner of the mining rights, and AGIP would take a stake in the partnership not exceeding 30 percent.[96] The task of discussing the proposal was delegated to ENI's Foreign Relations Department led by Franco Briatico, but in the end the French offer went unheeded. "E.N.I. did not even reply," complained the Cabinet of the French Foreign Ministry later that year.[97]

Mattei also met Guillaumat in Paris in May 1957 for the same purpose, but the talks led nowhere.[98] ENI's scant enthusiasm for dealing with the French was possibly due once again to the strictness of the conditions of partnership, especially by comparison with the opportunities offered by the 75–25 profit-sharing contracts with producers. In November 1958, during a stopover in Warsaw, the ENI President met the French Ambassador, Étienne Burin des Roziers, with a view to a possible collaboration between France, Italy, and the Arab Saharan countries. Mattei's proposal was to preserve French predominance in the Sahara, but without direct French political authority over the desert. He proposed a division of French Sahara's resources among the two European countries and the relevant Arab countries. Mixed companies would be set up, with a fixed percentage going to the European duo, and another to the Arab country concerned. If Paris agreed, Mattei would propose the establishment of such companies to the heads of state of Tunisia, Morocco, and Algeria.[99]

However, the Italian proposal presupposed de Gaulle's recognizing the GPRA as the legitimate government, which the General would not. The proposal was therefore shelved. French anxieties with respect to ENI were not limited to Algeria, but encompassed the Italian company's entire North African policy: staff at the Quai d'Orsay lamented that the Italians were "much too anxious" to play a role in Mediterranean affairs, and complained about "alleged attempts by the FLN to come to some understanding with Signor Mattei, the oil king."[100] By the end of the decade, the FLN had increased its network of contacts to include—besides the Christian Democrat mayor of Florence, Giorgio La Pira—Socialist Party Secretary Pietro Nenni, and Communist Party Secretary Palmiro Togliatti. Thanks to Mattei's mediation, and with a view to de Gaulle's visit to Italy in June 1959, the FLN representative in Rome, Boulahrouf, met with Italian President Giovanni Gronchi, describing the Algerian situation and suggesting that he sound out his French counterpart about the possibility of negotiations with the FLN.[101]

In the summer of 1960, ENI executives and Moroccan high officials laid the foundation stone of a refinery, for which ENI had been given a construction license in spite of vocal French protests. By then, ENI had also set up an Italian–Tunisian company and obtained an exploration permit in the former French protectorate. Mattei used the leverage acquired by ENI's success in Morocco to offer the French a gentleman's agreement through an unofficial ENI representative. The French ambassador in Rabat, Alexandre

Parodi, expressed his concern to Wormser about what Mattei now wished to do. ENI, he explained, intended to mediate between France, on one side, and Tunisia, Morocco, and the FLN on the other. By extending activities to Algeria's neighbors, and by forming links with the Front, a secret SDECE report revealed, ENI was seeking to open the Saharan oil and gas fields to the Italians.[102]

In June, Blancard, who after leaving DICA in 1959 had recovered the presidency of BRP, urged the French Foreign Minister, Maurice Couve de Murville, to plan countermeasures to ENI's activism, and suggested retaliating by expanding French gas interests in Italy. It was a critical moment for the French in Algeria: they had agreed to start negotiations with the FLN, and the last thing they wanted to see was an ally of the Algerian nationalists with vested interests in replacing the French, acting as mediator between them and their former North African possessions. Accepting US companies had been enough to acquire the American government's support for a French Algeria and satisfactorily 'put the desert into production': Italy, on the other hand, could not offer similar rewards. The secret battle fought between French and Italian oil agencies and diplomacies for control of Saharan resources only escalated as a result of the establishment of ENI's own diplomacy in North Africa.[103]

ENI's Underground Diplomacy and the Sahara Problem

By early 1960, the French authorities had good reason to be suspicious of ENI's maneuvers. The company had consolidated its relations with the GPRA. ENI employed journalist and former intelligence agent, Italo Pietra, as a liaison officer in Algeria. Later, in the summer of 1961, ENI set up its own quasi-diplomatic structure. Journalist Mario Pirani was sent as a covert 'ENI ambassador' to Tunis, where the GPRA had its new headquarters. Pirani was to assist the GPRA and help it plan future energy scenarios for Algeria. The French intelligence services were immediately notified of his appointment by their British counterparts.[104]

Another important player in ENI's hidden diplomacy was the Turkish citizen, Arslan Humbaraci. Connected to FLN's most radical wing, he served as an intermediary between the GPRA and ENI; yet his indirect connection to the Italian company obscured his overlapping interests with its officials. ENI's diplomatic activities were sufficiently developed for Quaroni to maintain, at a meeting at the International Affairs Institute in 1967, that: "For years, Italy's real foreign policy has been conducted by Enrico Mattei."[105]

ENI supported the Algerian fighters in various ways. At a meeting between representatives of the main Algerian trade union (*Union générale des travailleurs algériens*, closely connected to the FLN), the executives of the Italian Communist Party, and Mattei, the latter offered financial aid in exchange for their collaboration with his company.[106] According to a secret SDECE note, Mattei offered the GPRA a hundred million francs to hold out against French demands in the Sahara. Although no reliable proof of this has been provided, ENI certainly subsidized the publication of *Algeria*, a magazine by the Italian Commission for peace in Algeria, and proposed supplying fuel to FLN's armed wing. The Algerians refused, Pirani maintains, as they had already agreed a deal with SONJ and Shell.[107]

It has also been argued that ENI helped the Algerians educate their future oil industry cadres through scholarships at ENI's Higher School for Hydrocarbon Studies (*Scuola superiore di studi sugli idrocarburi*) near Milan. We know for sure that in June 1960 Krim Belkacem, GPRA's Foreign Minister, thanked Mattei "for the moral and material help" given to the FLN.[108]

We now know that ENI definitely played a significant role when the conflict came to a conclusion with peace negotiations between the French and the Algerians. In a referendum held on January 8, 1961, the Algerian population accepted a project for self-determination proposed by de Gaulle. In May, French–Algerian peace negotiations started in the French town of Évian. A month before the meeting, Bernard Tricot, one of the main authors of the Constitution of the Fifth Republic, sent the head of the French delegation and Minister for Algerian Affairs, Louis Joxe, a document outlining the government position on the Sahara. Tricot listed the following main objectives: 1) not to be expelled from the desert; 2) to retain the possibility of testing nuclear weapons there; 3) to continue paying for oil products in francs; and finally, 4) to open up Saharan extraction and transport industry outlets to French expertise and materials.[109]

As for the administration of the Saharan provinces, what the French suggested was that the effects of the self-determination referendum should be limited to Northern Algeria, while the Sahara should be internationalized (de facto leaving it under the influence of France). The legal justification for this viewpoint was that the Sahara had *already* been separated from the northern areas of Algeria through OCRS. Though this is often referred to as de Gaulle's thesis, the author was actually Guillaumat, who had easily convinced the General of its desirability. The threat of awarding independence to northern Algeria only, while keeping the Sahara French, was however a negotiating position. The very geography of the Sahara made control over it highly unlikely. An independent Algeria, in concert with Tunisia and Morocco, could well isolate the desert.[110]

Unsurprisingly, the Algerians opposed the French position, and argued that the Sahara was and ought to remain Algerian. On this and on another point regarding citizenship for French settlers in an independent country, the talks stalled, eventually being suspended in mid-June. The status of the Sahara was also one of the topics the FLN representative in the US, Abdelkader Chanderli, discussed in the same month with State Department officials. While hoping that the new Kennedy presidency would facilitate contacts with the GPRA, he said the Provisional Government was willing to resume negotiations at any time, provided France recognized Algeria's territorial integrity.[111]

French–Algerian negotiations resumed in July 1961 in Lugrin, close to the French–Swiss border. By that time, the FLN had obtained the important support of former Iraqi Economy Minister, Nadim al-Pachachi, as a petroleum adviser. The talks came to a standstill once more over the Saharan question, and were suspended after a week. Further secret negotiations took place in the autumn and winter in Switzerland and France. The French and Algerian delegations seemed to agree on future collaboration in the oil sector, but the problem of Saharan sovereignty persisted.[112] With a view to the reopening of negotiations in 1962, ENI's Studies Division covertly aided the Algerians in devising a possible treaty with France over the exploitation of Saharan resources. In practice, affirmed Pirani, all clauses regarding the future of Saharan oil were studied by ENI technicians together with the Algerians. At the peace negotiations, the delegation led by Belkacem used documentation prepared by ENI to suggest how the sector should be organized and what guarantees to demand.[113]

Covertly colluding with the Algerians, ENI also provided geoscientific intelligence on the Saharan subsoil. Mohamed Khelladi, the then Director of Communication and Research at the GPRA's Ministry of Armament and General Relations, was able to consult full ENI documentation, including the detailed content of provisions regulating the oil sector, as well as copies of contracts, concession documents, price tables and indexes, and files containing data on every single company operating in the Sahara.[114] Besides the Italians, the Algerians were also able to count on the support of BP in London, the Elwerath Company in Germany, and on the Saudi Minister of Petroleum and Mineral Resources, Abdullah Tariki. In order to collect and coordinate all this information, the GPRA set up a petroleum commission led by Claude Cixous, an aeronautical engineer who had worked on the Oil Code. The Algerians' knowledge of Saharan operational details, and their firmness on the legal framework within which the oil sector should be established, caught the French unprepared.[115]

Up to now, our knowledge about the technical support provided by ENI to the Algerians has been based on witness accounts. A tenuous trace of the existence of ENI documents used at Évian can be found in its archives, namely a folder entitled *Documents prepared for the G.P.R.A. with view to Évian*. Either the title of the folder is misleading or its contents have been removed, since it only contains documents produced after the Évian agreements had been signed. One might speculate that the extreme sensitivity of the data with respect to French–Italian relations led to their destruction after filing.[116]

Moreover, ENI's exploration personnel were in possession of the substantial report written in July 1960 by US geologist and former intelligence agent, Myron Kozáry, on prospects in the Algerian Sahara.[117] We also know that in November 1960 three geologists from AGIP Mineraria, led by Carmine Loddo, visited the Hassi Messaoud oilfield, where they had been invited by Claude de Lapparent, CFP(A)'s Exploration Director, in order to learn about the techniques and the most important results obtained by the French company. The visit had been fostered by Roberto Passega, at the same time an AGIP and CFP(A) consultant in sedimentology. The three French technicians chosen to attend the Italian delegation, Henri Vautrin, Robert Wetzel, and Willy Bruderer (whom we met in Chapter 2 as a pioneer of Algerian geological exploration), were among the most highly placed people responsible for the policies adopted by the company in oil prospecting both in France and abroad. During talks with Bruderer in Paris, where the visit had started, Loddo had the chance to go through the geological documentation on Algeria, in particular on Hassi Messaoud. The French geologists were also "very liberal" in disclosing completed and ongoing work to the Italians, but unwilling to hand over any documents such as maps, seismic sections and profiles, or electrical well logs.[118]

The Loddo report contained details about the history of oil exploration in the Sahara, geological characteristics of the Hassi Messaoud area, techniques used for prospecting, production, estimates of reserves, and details on the organization of the exploration department. A similar report was also prepared for the Hassi R'Mel gas field. The French geophysicists allowed ENI technicians to visit the oil and gas fields because of the links the Italian company had developed in the exploration sector. CGG and the Schlumberger Company, the flagships of French geophysics, had worked in Italy throughout and beyond the 1950s and CGG had on several occasions offered its services to ENI, especially in African countries. As a matter of fact, Italy was for a long time CGG's second-best customer after France.[119]

In addition, when in 1956 ENI established its School to train young graduates for the different oil sectors, its managers often invited French technicians and managers to give classes or seminars. By the end of 1961, relations between AGIP and CGG were so friendly that the general manager of CGG's Italian affiliate, Albert Roger, even sent Mineraria official Egidio Egidi a copy of an article by CGG's President, Léon Migaux, on refraction seismology in the Algerian Sahara. This was a surprising initiative in light of Italian–French diplomatic relations at the time. Even in early 1962, Mineraria had a number of its magnetic tapes processed at CGG's playback center, where Italian technicians could also assist with interpretation operations.[120]

The French government's annoyance with Mattei during the Algerian War, especially with respect to Mattei's role in passing intelligence to the Algerians during their frequent contacts with ENI managers, may also have derived from this awareness that French experts had assisted the Italians for many years. Company personnel did not refrain from using information acquired through its informal bilateral links with French geophysical and oil companies to further policies that placed French interests in jeopardy. The Italians, therefore, used the geosciences as a bargaining chip with the Algerians, in exchange for the promise that they would be allocated some exploration permits after the war.

The Évian Agreements, and Mattei's Threat Defused

Two months after the May 1961 negotiations, Mattei was invited by the BRP to be part of a pool of British, American, and French oil companies, but he declined the offer, a refusal explained by French intelligence services by his having concluded a secret agreement with the GPRA. The same explanation was used once French–Algerian peace talks resumed at Lugrin. It appeared that a contract had been signed in May between an Austrian company—serving as a cover for ENI and the Union of Swiss Banks—and the GPRA. The accord reportedly regulated prospecting and refining in an independent Algeria, and was analogous to the one signed between ENI and Morocco. French reactions took the form of diplomatic pressure on the Italian authorities to stop Mattei, and in a threat by the far-right terrorist Secret Army Organization (*Organisation de l'armée secrete*, OAS) for a French Algeria, which sent Mattei a letter in July claiming that he would be killed if he continued his "anti-French activities."[121]

The news of the supposed Algerian–Italian agreement provoked frantic diplomatic exchanges. The Italian diplomats tried to deny all allegations of GPRA-ENI contacts, but failed to convince their French counterparts. In the summer of 1961, French suspicions about the agreement became so acute they drew the attention of de Gaulle himself. However, according to the US Ambassador in Rome, George Frederick Reinhardt, "when [Mattei] gave evidence of attempting to develop special relationships with the FLN with a view to obtaining special concessions in Algeria after the liberation, the Government [...] forced him to back down."[122]

These developments coincided with a crisis in Tunisian–French relations. On July 19, 1961, serious incidents occurred near the French military base of Bizerte, in Tunisia, the evacuation of which Bourguiba had long requested. While the clash ended in a military defeat for the Tunisians, Bourguiba succeeded in reaching a settlement scheduling the withdrawal of French troops. However, the clash meant that all French hopes of internationalizing Saharan resources by involving Algeria's neighbors were now compromised. The mounting costs of the French military commitment in North Africa also affected the funding of ambitious French nuclear projects. Diplomatically isolated, with newly independent African countries ganging up against it at the UN, and confronted with waning US support, France capitulated.[123]

In September 1961, de Gaulle yielded on Algerian sovereignty over the Sahara, on condition that French interests be safeguarded. This decision was eventually sanctioned in March, through the Évian Agreements. The French government, argues historian Jacques Frémeaux, made a pragmatic decision: it calculated that the benefits accruing from Saharan oil would be relatively modest, given that its cost was higher than Middle Eastern and Libyan oil, and it was less adaptable to the characteristics of the French market. In addition, the profits going to France in the form of oil revenues were significantly lower than the investments it was making to improve the Algerian population's living standards in order to preserve its quasi-colonial power. In short, it would be much better for French finances to let Algeria go.[124]

This decision was eventually sanctioned in March, through the Évian Agreements. The Sahara was to be included in Algeria, while the Algerians committed to respecting the rights acquired by French companies and the Oil Code. The GPRA sanctioned French rights in prospecting activities over an area of 700,000 km^2, and kept Algeria within the franc zone. A French–Algerian agency was created, as suggested by ENI, to manage the hydrocarbons sector. In the military sphere, the Mers-el-Kébir base was leased to France for 15 years, and the use of Saharan facilities for nuclear tests was conceded for five years. Most importantly, French companies were to enjoy a six-year priority in distribution activities and in the allocation of exploration permits for unexplored areas, all other conditions being equal. In effect, the Évian Agreements placed a veritable *cordon sanitaire* around the hydrocarbon sector.[125]

Franco Briatico has argued that the reference to all other conditions being equal was an ingenious stratagem devised by ENI's technicians to get access to oil-rich areas in Algeria by simply proposing Iran-like contracts, which would be more advantageous to Algeria than the usual 50–50 arrangements. If that was the idea, however, it met with failure. On October 27, 1962, coinciding with the climax of the Cuban missile crisis, Mattei died in a plane crash, with speculation that it might have been caused by deliberate sabotage. In 2003, an Italian court concluded that the crash was the result of an attack carried out by a person or persons unknown. After leaving SDECE, Thyraud de Vosjoli, the intelligence service's representative in Washington, claimed that his agency's secret armed wing, known as the 'Red Hand' (*Main Rouge*), assassinated Mattei. Intelligence officials not surprisingly dismissed his claim.[126]

After Évian, Ambassador Palewski stated that frictions between France and Mattei would probably dissipate, as France would now favor foreign investments, including those by ENI. However, Palewski's hopes were soon proved misplaced. Mattei continued to oppose any idea of a partnership with the French. While maintaining an uncompromising stance on this matter, Mattei was concerned about American influence in independent Algeria. Indeed Ahmed Ben Bella, who had been freed by the French authorities and elected Prime Minister in September 1962, favored American rather than Italian participation. Before Évian he had negotiated with ARAMCO about the future exploitation of Algerian resources, an initiative that had caused a dispute within the GPRA.[127]

Also in October 1962, when ENI put a proposal to the new Algerian government to build a refinery, which triggered French protests, the US newspaper, *The Washington Post*, speculated that Ben Bella would not accept the offer, since many French technicians were already abandoning Algeria, and an agreement with ENI would accelerate the trend. In any case, we know that in early November, Mattei was due to fly to Algiers to sign an oil agreement with Ben Bella. It was probably a contract for oil extraction and transportation equipment, or for the construction of a refinery.[128]

Mattei's de facto successor at the head of ENI, Eugenio Cefis, sought—mainly for financial reasons—to follow a policy quite different from Mattei's. ENI's entry into oil prospecting activities in Algeria was temporarily removed from the company's plans, and Cefis awarded that ENI should focus on activities already in operation. Projects in an embryonic state—for instance in sub-Saharan Africa—were interrupted. Yet relations with the Algerians were never completely cut off, in spite of some ups and downs. ENI's interest shifted from oil to gas, and in the early 1970s the Italians would reach an agreement with Algeria on natural gas supplies.

Conclusion

During the Algerian War of Independence, the Sahara was not only the setting for military engagements between the French and Algerians. A secret war was fought in the hydrocarbons sector too, involving French and foreign governmental institutions, intelligence services, and oil agencies and companies. At the heart of this struggle was scientific and technological knowledge that made possible new approaches to prospecting and exploiting the Sahara. I have shown that such knowledge was critical to the development of the Algerian oil situation, and even affected the outcome of the war and Algeria's foreign relations post-independence. Data collected in confidential reports and memoranda from technicians in geoscientific contracting firms and from diplomats played a paramount role, as did the complex networks in which such data was circulated and put to political use. The critical dynamic was the tension among countries, agencies, and oil companies that were formally allied with France, but which harbored serious doubts over French war policies and had aspirations to extend their economic and strategic interests to North Africa. In this process, scientific and technical knowledge allowed the various actors to assess developments in Saharan oil prospecting and operations, utilizing such information to devise strategies appropriate to their own national interests and those of their oil companies. Such intelligence-gathering was particularly useful to the US in in the early phases of Saharan exploration, when American companies were not yet operating in the Sahara.

As pre-independence Algeria was formally French territory, foreign oil companies needed French authorization to access that area. Foreign presence in Algeria was anathema to French administrations, as the desert had just started yielding fruit after decades of exploratory efforts, providing potentially vital revenue for the French state as it still sought to recover from World War II. It is in this respect that US geophysical contractors played a major role, as their technical expertise proved crucial to French companies in surveying the Sahara. France had its own expertise, but it was not sufficient to match national ambitions, which required more exploratory crews than France had available. Without the presence of US geoscientific experts in Algeria, the State Department, let alone US majors, might never have fully understood the potential of the desert. Conversely, US technical experts, hired by French companies, gave the French government some measure of insight into the interests of US oil companies in Saharan riches, as well as into the influence these companies enjoyed in American diplomatic circles and, more broadly, into the US government's alleged interest in replacing France in North Africa.

However, in a second phase of the war starting around 1957, French institutions had to face the simple reality that if they wanted their country to achieve energy autonomy in a relatively short time and to exploit Saharan resources effectively, they would have to resort to foreign capital. This was reflected first in the establishment of the OCRS and then in the promulgation of the Oil Code. These two changes led to the admission of a number of foreign companies into oil exploration and production activities: initially independent American companies, and later international majors and Western European firms as well. At the same time, the new regulations provided the BRP with large volumes of data about the Algerian subsurface, and helped French oil technicians to improve their knowledge of prospecting methods by obliging foreign firms to train French geophysicists in the new techniques. The strategy gradually adopted by the French, mainly devised by Guillaumat and other figures at the head of the French oil industry, allowed foreign enterprises into Algeria, but under restrictive conditions which ensured that the French BRP retained control of geoscientific information and maintained a stake in the results of these operations.

The Algerians challenged French exploitation plans, forging a range of alliances characterized by a mutual interest in undermining French influence over the Sahara. A critical aspect of this were the multiple efforts made to accumulate geostrategic knowledge and use it in ways that would undermine the ability of French administrations to exercise primary control over Saharan resources. ENI was a major player in this new game. While dealing with the French authorities and trying to persuade them to set up mixed companies that would also involve North African countries, Mattei aligned with the FLN, hoping to bypass the French once Algeria became independent. ENI established a parallel diplomacy to treat with the Algerian nationalists and support them in various ways. Geoscientific and organizational knowledge transferred from ENI to the GPRA reveals the import of such knowledge in these secret negotiations, which often ran counter to official policy positions.

The links maintained by the Americans and Italians with the Algerian fighters and the GPRA helped the Algerians put together a sound case for the idea of the Sahara as an integral part of Algeria and to plan the post-independence management of oil resources. Ultimately, the interweaving of oil exploration, diplomacy, and security that I have described in this chapter adds a new dimension to our historical understanding of the use of the geosciences in geopolitics. The search for raw materials exemplified in this case illuminates the role and modes of circulation of knowledge during the Cold War and, more specifically, how the acquisition, possession, and selective distribution of geoscientific intelligence informed international power dynamics.

After Évian, Italy and France had to re-design their strategies for different reasons. As a result of the agreement with Algeria and its production from Iraq, Iran, and Central Africa, France could now rely less on prospecting as a key component of oil security. ENI, faced with the poor results from its concessions in the Middle East and North Africa, opted to obtain its energy supplies in a different way, namely by buying them abroad. In both cases, the result was a 'shift' toward other sectors of the oil industry, also relevant to national security. It is this shift that I discuss in the next chapter.

Notes

1 Charles de Gaulle, quoted in Pierre Guillen, "Le déclin de la puissance italienne à la fin de la seconde guerre mondiale," *Relations internationales* 9 (1977): 5.

2 Bruna Bagnato, *L'Italia e la guerra d'Algeria (1954–1962)* (Soveria Mannelli: Rubbettino, 2012), 155–9; Telegram From M'hammed Yazid of the National Liberation Front of Algeria to President Eisenhower, Oct. 23, 1956; Foreign Relations of the United States (FRUS), 1955–1957, XVIII, Africa, 246. The four men were: Mohamed Boudiaf, Mohamed Khider, Hocine Aït Ahmed, Ahmed Ben Bella. They were accompanied by FLN sympathiser Mostefa Lacheraf.

3 Department of State, Memorandum of Conversation between M. Jean de la Grandville, Counselor, French Embassy (Fremb) Washington, and Mr. Matthew Looram, Office of Western European Affairs, Bureau of European Affairs: "Algeria: Reports re ARAMCO Subsidizing the Algerian rebels," Apr. 18, 1956, confidential; file (f.) 851S.2553/4–1858; French Africa, box (b.) 4604; Central Decimal Files, 1955–1959; Record Group (RG) 59; NARA. Pietro Quaroni, Italian Ambassador in Paris, to Italian Foreign Ministry (MAEI) and to Italian Embassy (Itemb) London and Washington: "Presunti aiuti americani alla ribellione algerina," Feb. 5, 1957; b. 74 (Algeria '57); Ambasciata d'Italia a Parigi, 1951–1958; Archivio storico-diplomatico del Ministero degli Affari esteri, Rome (ASMAE).

4 Matthew Looram to Robert McBride, Mar. 27, 1957, official-informal, confidential; and Memorandum, Robert McBride to Matthew Looram, Feb. 25, 1957, confidential; Subject File Relating to France, 1944–1960; folder (fd.) 16 Algeria-ARAMCO; b. 2; Lot 61D30; Records of the Office of Western European Affairs; RG 59; NARA.

5 Edward A. Kolodziej, *French International Policy Under De Gaulle and Pompidou. The Politics of Grandeur* (Ithaca/London: Cornell University Press, 1974); Alistair Horne, *A Savage War of Peace: Algeria 1954–1962* (New York: Viking, 1978); John Talbott, *The War Without a Name. France in Algeria, 1954–1962* (London/Boston: Faber and Faber, 1980); Jean-Pierre Rioux and Jean-François Sirinelli, *La guerre d'Algérie et les intellectuels français* (Paris: Institut d'Histoire du Temps Présent, 1988); Patrick Eveno and Jean Planchais, *La guerre d'Algérie* (Paris: La Découverte/Le Monde, 1989);

Jean-Pierre Rioux, *La Guerre d'Algérie et les Français* (Paris: Fayard, 1990); Michael Kettle, *De Gaulle and Algeria, 1940–1960. From Mers El-Kébir to the Algiers Barracades [sic]* (London: Quartet Books, 1993); Charles-Robert Ageron, *La guerre d'Algérie et les Algériens, 1954–1962* (Paris: Armand Colin, 1995); Kristin Ross, *Fast Cars, Clean Bodies: Decolonization and the Reordering of French Culture* (Cambridge, MA/London: MIT Press, 1995); Benjamin Stora, *Histoire de la guerre d' Algérie (1954–1962)* (Paris: La Découverte, 1995); Maurice Faivre, *Les archives inédites de la politique algérienne, 1958–1962* (Paris: L'Harmattan, 2000); Pierre Vidal-Naquet, *Les Crimes de l'armée française en Algérie 1954–1962* (Paris: La Découverte, 2001); Mohammed Harbi and Benjamin Stora, *La Guerre d'Algérie. 1954–2004, la fin de l'*amnésie (Paris: Robert Laffont, 2004); Sylvie Thénault, *Histoire de la guerre d'indépendance algérienne* (Paris: Flammarion, 2005).

6 Samia El Mechat, *Les États-Unis et l'Algérie. De la méconnaissance à la reconnaissance, 1945–1962* (Paris: L'Harmattan, 1996); Martin Thomas, *The French North African Crisis. Colonial Breakdown and Anglo-French Relations, 1945–1962* (London: Macmillan, 2000), 113; Irwin M. Wall, *France, the United States and the Algerian War* (Berkeley/Los Angeles: University of California Press, 2001); Matthew Connelly, *A Diplomatic Revolution: Algeria's Fight for Independence and the Origins of the Post-Cold War Era* (Oxford: Oxford University Press, 2002); Christopher Goldsmith, "The British Embassy in Paris and the Algerian War: An Uncomfortable Partner?" In *France and the Algerian War, 1954–1962: Strategy, Operations and Diplomacy*, edited by Martin S. Alexander and J. F. V. Keiger (London/Portland: Frank Cass, 2002), 159–71; Maurice Vaïsse, *Vers la paix en Algérie. Les négociations d'Évian dans les archives diplomatiques françaises* (Bruxelles: Bruylant, 2003); Jena-Paul Cahn and Klaus-Jürgen Miller, *La RFA et la guerre d'Algérie (1954–1962)* (Paris: Félin, 2003); Bagnato, *L'Italia e la guerra d'Algeria.*

7 Note du Service de documentation extérieure et de contre-espionnage (SDECE) no. 23754/A; b. 6; Secrétariat d'État chargé des Affaires algériennes; Archives Diplomatiques du Ministère des Affaires Etrangères, La Courneuve (ADMAE): source as reported in Connelly, *Diplomatic Revolution*, 195.

8 Partial exceptions are: Faivre, *Les archives inédites*, 201–8, which includes testimonies of French geologists in Algeria during the war; Redha Malek, *L'Algérie à Évian. Histoire des négociations secrètes, 1956–1962* (Paris: Seuil, 1995); Ali Aïssaoui, *Algeria: The Political Economy of Oil and Gas* (Oxford: Oxford University Press, 2001); Belaïd Abdesselam, *Le pétrole et le gaz naturel en Algérie: comment les Algériens ont gagné la bataille de la récupération du pétrole et du gaz* (Algiers: ANEP, 2012). However, the last two books mainly cover the post-independence period.

9 Hocine Malti, *Histoire secrète du pétrole algérien* (Paris: La Découverte, 2010); Jacques Frémeaux, *Le Sahara et la France* (Paris: SOTÉCA, 2010), ch. 9 and 10. Faivre, *Les archives inédites*, 201–8, which includes testimonies of French geologists in Algeria during the war; Redha Malek, *L'Algérie à Évian. Histoire des négociations secrètes, 1956–1962* (Paris: Seuil, 1995); Ali Aïssaoui, *Algeria: The Political Economy of Oil and Gas* (Oxford: Oxford University Press, 2001); Belaïd Abdesselam, *Le pétrole et le gaz naturel en Algérie: comment les Algériens ont gagné la bataille de la récupération du pétrole et du gaz* (Algiers: ANEP, 2012). However, the last two books mainly cover the post-independence period. See also Malti's interview with Berbère Télévision: "Hocine Malti: L'histoire secrète du pétrole algérien," YouTube video, 1:02:54, from an interview given to Philippe Robichon (Berbère Télévision), posted by "abuhucem" on 14 July 2011, http://www.youtube.com/

watch?v=cGQOi9qDlRw. On oil in diplomatic studies about the war, see: Thomas, *The French North African Crisis*, 143, 206–7; Wall, *France, the United States*, 55–6, 237–8; Connelly, *Diplomatic Revolution*, 99, 203–4, 262; Berny Sèbe, "In the Shadow of the Algerian War: The United States and the Common Organisation of Saharan Regions (OCRS), 1957–62," *The Journal of Imperial and Commonwealth History* 38 (2: 2010): 303–22.

10 Pierre Cornet, *Du mirage au miracle. Pétrole saharien* (Paris: Nouvelles Editions Latines, 1960).

11 Ronald E. Doel, "Scientists as Policymakers, Advisors, and Intelligence Agents: Linking Contemporary Diplomatic History with the History of Contemporary Science," in *The Historiography of Contemporary Science and Technology*, ed. Thomas Söderqvist (Amsterdam: Harwood Academic, 1997), 215–44; Ronald E. Doel and Allan A. Needell, "Science, Scientists, and the CIA: Balancing international ideals, national needs, and professional opportunities," *Intelligence and National Security* 12 (1: 1997): 59–81; James E. Fleming, ed., "Military Patronage and the Geophysical Sciences in the United States," special issue, *Historical Studies in the Physical and Biological Sciences* 30 (2: 2000); Allan A. Needell, *Science, Cold War and the American State: Lloyd V. Berkner and the Balance of Professional Ideals* (Amsterdam: Harwood Academic, 2000); Ronald E. Doel, "Constituting the Postwar Earth Sciences: The Military's Influence on the Environmental Sciences in the USA after 1945," *Social Studies of Science* 33, no. 5 (2003): 635–66; John Krige, *American Hegemony and the Postwar Reconstruction of Science in Europe* (Cambridge, MA/London: MIT Press, 2006); John Krige and Kai-Henrik Barth, eds., "Global Power Knowledge. Science and Technology in International Affairs," special issue, *Osiris* 21, no. 1 (2006); Ronald E. Doel, "Does Scientific Intelligence Matter?," *Centaurus* 52, no. 4 (2010): 311–22.

12 However, the well found at Djebel Berga turned out not to be commercially viable. For a history of oil exploration in Algeria, see: Alain Perrodon, *Histoire des grandes découvertes pétrolières. Un certain art de l'exploration* (Pau/Paris: Elf Aquitaine-Masson, 1995), 323–40.

13 Note SDECE, "Participation des sociétés pétrolières allemandes aux projets sahariens," Jul. 24, 1957, secret; and Note SDECE, "Algérie-Japon-Italie—Accords pétroliers F.L.N.," Jan. 22, 1959, secret; and Note SDECE, "Algérie-Japon—Le Japon et les accords pétroliers F.L.N.," Mar. 10, 1959 (FOIA n° 111 382); sub-fd. Afrique 1957/77; fd. 1; b. 19900317/8; Archives Nationales, Pierrefitte-sur-Seine (AN).

14 André Combaz, "Les premières découvertes de pétrole au Sahara dans les années 1950: le témoignage d'un acteur," *Comité Français d'histoire de la géologie*, 3ème série, T.XVI (2002), [no page number in the original; p. 7 of the printed version] (http://annales.org/archives/cofrhigeo/sahara.html).

15 Douglas A.Yates, *The rentier state in Africa: oil rent dependency and neocolonialism in the Republic of Gabon* (Trenton/Asmara: Africa World Press, 1996), 57.

16 Layat, Clement, Pommier, and Buffet. "Some Technical Aspects of Refraction Seismic Prospecting in the Sahara," *Geophysics* 26, no. 4 (1961): 438–9, 442–3. A marker bed is a bed of rock strata that is readily distinguishable by reason of physical characteristics and is traceable over large horizontal distances (source: http://www.britannica.com/ EBchecked/topic/365643/marker-bed).

17 Maurice Rachline, *Geophysical Prospecting and Oil Exploration* (Paris: CGG/Editions Atlas, 1998), 16–8; Didier Du Castel et al., *Les aventuriers de la Terre* (Boulogne: La Sirène, 1995), 29; Donald T. Germain-Jones, "What is our Contribution?" *Geophysical Prospecting* 2, no. 3 (1954): 4; Henry F. Dunlap and Curtis H. Johnson, "Research and Progress in Exploration," *Geophysics* 23, no. 2 (1958): 274.

18 Frémeaux, *Le Sahara et la France*, 233–4.
19 See Chapter 2, note 98 (p. 162).
20 National Intelligence Estimate, "Probable Developments in North Africa", Aug. 31, 1954; Foreign Relations of the United States (FRUS), 1952–1954, XI, pt. 1, Africa and South Asia (Washington: United States Government Printing Office, 1952–1954), 154.
21 Connelly, *Diplomatic Revolution*, 8.
22 Ronald W. Pruessen, *John Foster Dulles: The Road to Power* (New York: Free Press, 1982), 425. Note de la Direction des Affaires Économiques et Financières (DAEF), "Suez et le pétrole," Sep. 1, 1956; N. 94. DE-CE Papiers Directeur Olivier Wormser; Sous-série: Directeur—Wormser; Série: Affaires économiques et financières; ADMAE.
23 Lewis Clark, Amcongen Algiers, to Department of State, "Indications of Petroleum Discovered in the Sahara," Jan. 27, 1956, official use only; f. 851S.2553/1-2756, Foreign Service Dispatch; French Africa, b. 4604, Central Decimal Files, 1955–1959; RG 59; NARA. The Director of the Bureau de recherches de pétrole to Monsieur Ricard, Administrateur du B.R.P., "Rapport sur les recherches de pétrole en France Métropolitaine, en Afrique du nord et dans les Territoires d'Outre-Mer au cours de l'année 1954," Feb. 19, 1955, p. IV–4; and "Rapport sur les recherches de pétrole en France Métropolitaine, en Afrique du nord et dans les Territoires d'Outre-Mer au cours de l'année 1954," Feb. 25, 1954, p. 9; fd. Untitled; b. 81F/2069; Affaires algériennes (1873/1964); FM; ANOM.
24 Bruna Bagnato, "Une solidarité ambiguë: L'OTAN, la France et la guerre d'Algérie 1954–1958," *Revue d'histoire diplomatique* 4 (2001): 329–50.
25 The quote is from: "Statement of Policy on Tunisia, Morocco, Algeria," Enclosure, Oct. 3, 1956; FRUS, 1955–1957, XVIII, Africa (Washington: United States Government Printing Office, 1955–1957), 139.
26 The quote is from: Sir Frank Roberts to A.D.M. Ross, Oct. 1, 1957; file JR 10317/59; b. Foreign Office 371/125944; Public Records Office; The National Archives, Kew: source as reported in Thomas, *The French North African Crisis*, 153–4.
27 Centre de recherches sur l'Afrique méditerraneéenne, ed., "L'Algérie et les hydrocarbures," *Annuaire de l'Afrique du Nord* 4 (1966): 99.
28 El Mechat, "Les États-Unis et la question coloniale en Afrique du Nord 1945–1962," *Outre-mers* 95, no. 358–9 (2008): 259.
29 Telegram From the Embassy in France to the Department of State, Paris, Mar. 2, 1956, top secret; FRUS, 1955–1957, XVIII, Africa, 115–6. On anti-Americanism in France, Philippe Roger wrote: "French anti-Americanism is not a short-term value. It is rooted in history, but it's very little sensitive to the conjuncture. Its basis is hundred-year-old. Its foundations are even bicentennial." Philippe Roger, *L'ennemi américain. Généalogie de l'antiaméricanisme français* (Paris: Seuil, 2002), 10 (my translation).
30 Marcel Champeix, Secretary of the Interior, Chargé of Algerian Affairs—Directorate of Algerian Affairs, to Robert Lacoste, Resident Minister in Algeria—Cabinet of the Governor General in Algiers, Feb. 17, 1956, secret, telegram to code no. 92; fd. Recherches de pétrole; b. 81F/966; Affaires algériennes (1873/1964); FM; ANOM. Robert Lacoste, Governor General of Algeria (Southern Territory), to Marcel Champeix, Secretary of the Interior, Chargé of Algerian Affairs—Directorate of Algerian Affairs, Feb. 18, 1956, secret, coded telegram no. 5218; b. 81F/966, fd. Recherches de pétrole; Affaires algériennes (1873/1964); FM; ANOM.
31 Robert Lacoste, Governor General of Algeria, to Marcel Champeix, Secretary of the Interior, Chargé of Algerian Affairs—Directorate of Algerian

Affairs, "Frontière algéro-libyenne dans la région de l'Edjele In Azaoua," Feb. 20, 1956, secret; fd. Recherches de pétrole; b. 81F/966; Affaires algériennes (1873/1964); FM; ANOM. This episode is also reported in Connelly, *Diplomatic Revolution*, 99.

32 Entretien du mercredi 26 mars à 10h, Apr. 4, 1956; b. 19900317/21, fd. 1; AN (FOIA n° 111 382). Department of State, Memorandum of Conversation, "Standard Oil Company of New Jersey Position Regarding the Algerian/Libyan Border Dispute", official use only, May 2, 1956; f. 651S.7331/5-256; France's International Politics, b. 2622; Central Decimal Files, 1955–1959; RG 59; NARA. On French activities in Fezzan preceding and following Libyan independence, see: Pierre Fontaine, *La mort étrange de Conrad Kilian, inventeur du pétrole saharien* (Paris: Les Sept Couleurs, 1959).

33 Telegram From M'hammed Yazid of the National Liberation Front of Algeria to President Eisenhower, Oct. 23, 1956.

34 Memorandum of Conversation between de la Grandville and Looram; Quaroni to MAEI and Itemb London and Washington: "Presunti aiuti americani alla ribellione algerina," Feb. 5, 1957. The quote is from: Department of State, telegram from Clarence Douglas Dillon, US Ambassador in Paris, to John Foster Dulles, Secretary of State, Nov. 7, 1956, confidential; f. 751S.00/11-756; French Africa, b. 3378; Central Decimal Files, 1955–1959; RG 59; NARA.

35 The quote is from: Memorandum, Robert McBride to Matthew Looram, Feb. 25, 1957, confidential; Subject File Relating to France, 1944–1960; fd. 16 Algeria-ARAMCO; b. 2; Lot 61D30; Records of the Office of Western European Affairs; RG 59; NARA (emphasis in the original). When Mollet visited Algiers in February 1956, a few weeks after becoming prime minister, he was pelted with rotten tomatoes by French Algerian settlers at a demonstration (Stora, *Histoire de la guerre d'Algérie*, 20).

36 Memorandum, Robert McBride to Matthew Looram, Feb. 25, 1957; Matthew Looram to Robert McBride, Mar. 27, 1957.

37 Memorandum, Robert McBride to Matthew Looram, Feb. 25, 1957; Matthew Looram to Robert McBride, Mar. 27, 1957.

38 Department of State, Memorandum of Conversation between Mr. James T. Duce, Vice President, ARAMCO, and Mr. Fraser Wilkins, Director, Division of Near Eastern Affairs: "Fund for the Algerian Rebels," Nov. 14, 1956, official use only; f. 751S.00/11-1456; French Africa, b. 3378; Central Decimal Files, 1955–1959; RG 59; NARA. Note SDECE, "Position américaine vis-à-vis de la présence française en Afrique," Jul. 9, 1957, secret; b. 19900317/8, fd. 1, sub-fd. Afrique 1957/77; AN (FOIA n° 111 382).

39 On France in Suez expedition, see: André Beaufre, *The Suez Expedition* (London: Faber, 1969); Maurice Vaïsse, "France and the Suez Crisis," in *Suez 1956*, ed. Wm. Roger Louis and Roger Owen (Oxford: Clarendon, 1989), 131–43. Irwin M. Wall, *France, the United States and the Algerian War* (Berkeley/Los Angeles: University of California Press, 2001), 33. With respect to Nasser's involvement in supporting the FLN, Jacques Soustelle, the Governor General of Algeria, had stated:

> In acting against Nasser, France is hitting the head of the octopus whose tentacles have for so many months been strangling North Africa. The duty offices from which orders for bloodshed are issued, the quays from which weapons for killing in Algeria were loaded, the camps and barracks where commandos were trained, have all come within our reach ... Everyone understands that the future of French North Africa hangs on what is happening and what will happen in Egypt.

Quoted from: Kennett Love, *Suez: The Twice-Fought War; A History* (New York: McGraw-Hill, 1969), 129, and reported in: Eric D. K. Melby, *Oil and the International System. The Case of France, 1918–1969* (New York: Arno Press 1981), 241.

40 Letter, Wm. R. Woodward to John Foster Dulles, Secretary of State, Nov. 18, 1956; French Africa, b. 3378, f. 751S.00/11-1856; Central Decimal Files, 1955–1959; RG 59; NARA. Note pour le Directeur Général Politique, Dec. 27, 1956; Action extérieure, Etats-Unis, déc. 1956–déc. 1957, Côte EU; Mission de Liaison Algérienne, vol. 23 bis (provisional number); ADMAE: source as reported in Connelly, *Diplomatic Revolution*, 101.

41 DAEF, "Note n° 1 sur le problème pétrolier français en 1957," Sep. 4, 1956; and Note DAEF, "Problème du pétrole," Nov. 27, 1956; N. 94. DE-CE Papiers Directeur Olivier Wormser; Sous-série: Directeur—Wormser; Série: Affaires économiques et financières; ADMAE.

42 Yves Jonchay, "L'infrastructure de départ du Sahara et de l'Organisation Commune des Régions Sahariennes (O.C.R.S.)," *Revue géographique* 32, no. 4 (1957): 277–92.

43 Pierre Boilley, "OCRS/Royaume Sanussi de Libye: deux tentatives pour durer?," in *L'ère des décolonisations*, ed. Charles-Robert Ageron and Marc Michel (Paris: Karthala, 1995), 364.

44 "Rapport d'activité au cours de la onzième session de l'Assemblée Générale des Nations Unies"; GPRA, b. 4, Yazid; Centre national des archives algériennes: the memo is reprinted as an annex to François Georges-Picot's report to Christian Pineau, Jan. 4, 1957, DDF, 1957, I, no. 17. "Statement by Guy Mollet, Premier on French Policy in Algeria," Jan. 9, 1957; b. 550; and "Minute" from the Secrétariat des conférences to Georges-Picot, Jan. 23, 1957; b. 549; Série: ONU; ADMAE: sources as reported in Connelly, *Diplomatic Revolution*, 124, 126. Douglas Porch, *The French Secret Services: From the Dreyfus Affair to the Gulf War* (New York: Farrar, Straus and Giroux, 1995), 366.

45 Guillaumat had taken back the leadership of the oil agency by replacing Blancard in 1955, and combined this position with that of general manager of the French CEA, which he had taken up in 1951.

46 The first French nuclear test took place at Reggane in February 1960.

47 Groupe d'études des problèmes de Défense Nationale liés à la mise en valeur du Sahara, "Compte rendu de la séance inaugurale," Mar. 21, 1957, secret; and "Compte rendu de la première séance tenue le 21 mars 1957 sous la présidence de M. l'Ambassadeur Eirik LABONNE," Apr. 12, 1957; and "Compte rendu de la séance du 30 avril 1957, sur l'étude du tracé des pipe-lines destinés à l'acheminement des richesses pétrolières en territoire algérien," May 11, 1957; and "Compte rendu de la séance du 25 juillet 1957 sur l'étude d'un programme de réalisation de l'infrastructure aérienne," Aug. 7, 1957; fd. Le FLN et le pétrole saharien; b. 81F/966; Affaires algériennes (1873/1964); FM; ANOM. The issues of the protection of oil infrastructures, and of the best layout to choose for pipelines, were extensively discussed in 1957 and 1958, and can be found in: fds: Recherches de pétrole; and Le FLN et le pétrole saharien; and Évacuation des pétroles sahariens; and Untitled; b. 81F/966; Affaires algériennes (1873/1964); FM; ANOM.

48 Sèbe, "In the Shadow," 307–8.

49 Roberto Caracciolo, Itemb Paris, to Italian Foreign Ministry (MAEI), "Conferenza stampa del Ministro Max Lejeune sullo sfruttamento del Sahara," Jul. 15, 1957; telespresso N. Ris. 1143/871; b. 74 (Algeria '57); Ambasciata d'Italia a Parigi, 1951–1958; ASMAE. Luciano Ardesi, "La politica estera della Repubblica algerina, con particolare riferimento ai rapporti con gli stati

maghrebini," in *Algeria. Il disastro e la memoria*, ed. Federico Cresti, special issue of *Oriente moderno* 22, no. 4 (2003): 10–11.

50 Rapport annuel 1956, planches; fd. Bureau de Recherches de pétrole (B-R.P.); b. 81F/2069; Affaires algériennes (1873/1964); FM; ANOM.

51 Pietro Quaroni, Itemb Paris, to MAEI, "Viaggio in Africa del Vice Presidente Nixon," Mar. 11, 1957; b. 74 (Algeria '57); Ambasciata d'Italia a Parigi, 1951–1958; ASMAE. "Report to the President on the Vice President's Visit to Africa, February 28–March 21, 1957," Apr. 5, 1957; FRUS, 1955–1957, XVIII, Africa, 57–66. On African-American agreements for natural resources, see: Gabrielle Hecht, *Being Nuclear: Africans and the Global Uranium Trade* (Cambridge, MA/London: MIT Press).

52 Note SDECE, "Au sujet de Mr Anthony Nutting et de la Shell," May 23, 1957, secret; fd. 2, Algérie 1957/64; b. 199003117/8; AN (FOIA n° 111 382).

53 Rossi Longhi, Itemb Paris, to MAEI, "La rivolta di Algeri e l'avvento del Generale De Gaulle," Jun. 13, 1958, secret; telespresso N. Ris. 0690; b. 82 (Algeria '58); Ambasciata d'Italia a Parigi, 1951–1958; ASMAE. Wall, *France, the United States*, 95 note 81.

54 Note SDECE, "Les compagnies pétrolières américaines et le Sahara français," Dec. 17, 1956, secret; fd. 2, Algérie 1957/64; b. 199003117/8; AN (FOIA n° 111 382). Note SDECE, "Position américaine vis-à-vis de la présence française en Afrique," Jul. 9, 1957; sub-fd. Algérie 1957/77; fd. 1; b. 199003117/8; (FOIA n° 111 382) (the quote is from this document; my translation). Among other things, the 1956 note reported a meeting between Arthur Flemming, Director of the US Office of Defense Mobilization, and Frederick Coqueron, member of the Chase Bank, SONJ and SOCONY's reference bank.

55 Arthur Schlesinger, *A Thousand Days: John F. Kennedy in the White House* (Boston: Houghton Mifflin, 1965), 510ff; Philippe Bourdrel, *La dernière chance de l'Algérie française. Du gouvernement socialiste au retour de De Gaulle, 1956–1958* (Paris: Albin Michel, 1996), 154; Wall, *France, the United States*, 85. Memorandum of a Conversation, Department of State, Washington, "Speech by Senator John F. Kennedy on Algeria, on Tuesday, July 2", Jul. 1, 1957, confidential; FRUS, 1955–1957, XVIII, Africa. 270–1.

56 Note SDECE, "Position américaine vis-à-vis de la présence française en Afrique," 5; El Mechat, "Les États-Unis et la question coloniale," 261; El Mechat, *Les États-Unis et l'Algérie*, 55.

57 Sèbe, "In the Shadow," 311–12.

58 Timothy Mitchell, *Carbon Democracy: Political Power in the Age of Oil* (New York: Verso, 2011).

59 Department of State, Memorandum of Conversation, "U.S. Oil Company's Concessions in the Sahara," Jul. 9, 1957; f. 851S.2553/7-957; French Africa, b. 4604; Central Decimal Files, 1955–1959; RG 59; NARA.

60 Merritt N. Cootes, Deputy Principal Officer, Algiers, to John Foster Dulles, Secretary of State; telegram no. 62, received Aug. 30, 1957, official use only; f. 851S.2553/9-957; French Africa, b. 4604; Central Decimal Files, 1955–1959; RG 59; NARA. Charles W. Yost, Minister–Counselor of the Embassy in France, to Dulles; telegram no. 1217, received Sep. 9, 1957; official use only; f. 851S.2553/9-957; French Africa, b. 4604; Central Decimal Files, 1955–1959; RG 59; NARA.

61 US Embassy (Amemb) Paris to Department of State, "Recent Development re U.S. Oil Company Interest in Sahara Exploration," Sep. 13, 1957, official use only; f. 851S.2553/9-1357; French Africa, b. 4604; Central Decimal Files, 1955–1959; RG 59; NARA.

62 Charles W. Yost, Minister–Counselor of the Embassy in France, to John Foster Dulles, Secretary of State; telegram no. 1271, received Sep. 9, 1957,

official use only; f. 851S.2553/9-957; French Africa, b. 4604; Central Decimal Files, 1955–1959; RG 59; NARA.

63 Amcongen Algiers to Department of State, "Petroleum and Mineral Development in the Sahara," Nov. 26, 1957. Amcongen Algiers to Department of State, "Minerals and Petroleum Report," Oct. 3, 1958; f. 851S.00/7-1059; French Africa, b. 4603; Central Decimal Files, 1955–1959; RG 59; NARA.

64 Amcongen Algiers to Department of State, "Petroleum and Natural Gas in the Sahara," Jun. 21, 1957, official use only, pp. 3–4; f. 851S.2553/6-2157; French Africa, b. 4604; Central Decimal Files, 1955–1959; RG 59; NARA. This quote and the next one are from: Frederick B. Lyon, Amcongen Algiers, to Department of State, "Saharan Petroleum Developments," Jun. 24, 1958, limited official use; f. 851S.2553/6-2458; French Africa, b. 4604; Central Decimal Files, 1955–1959; RG 59; NARA.

65 Lyon, Amcongen Algiers, to Department of State, "Saharan Petroleum Developments", Jun. 24, 1958.

66 Note SDECE, "Les Anglo-Saxons et le pétroles sahariens," Dec. 30, 1957, secret; fd. 2, Algérie 1957/64; b. 19900317/8; AN (FOIA n° 111 382). Frederick B. Lyon, Amcongen Alg to Department of State, "New petroleum exploration permits granted in Sahara," Sep. 15, 1958, unclassified; f. 851S.2553/9-1558; French Africa, b. 4604; Central Decimal Files, 1955–1959; RG 59; NARA. See also documents contained in: Records Relating to Algeria, 1952–1962; fd. A6 Petroleum; b. 1, entry A1 3109B; Office of Northern African Affairs; Bureau of African Affairs; African Lot; RG 59; NARA.

67 Department of State, Memorandum of Conversation, "Standard Oil's Operations in Algeria," Dec. 13, 1957, confidential; f. 851S.2553/12-1357; French Africa, b. 4604; Central Decimal Files, 1955–1959; RG 59; NARA. Outgoing telegram n. 2452 from John Foster Dulles, Secretary of State, to Amory Houghton, Amemb Paris, Jan. 4, 1958, official use only; f. 851S.2553/1-458; French Africa, b. 4604; Central Decimal Files, 1955–1959; RG 59; NARA.

68 Note SDECE, "L'attitude du Groupe Standard à l'égard du Sahara français," Feb. 1, 1958, secret, pp. 1–4; fd. 2, Algérie 1957/64; b. 19900317/8; AN (FOIA n° 111 382).

69 Bruna Bagnato, "Une solidarité ambiguë." For an analysis of the Anglo-American good offices mission, see: Geoffrey Barei, "The Sakiet Sidi Youssef Incident of 1958 in Tunisia and the Anglo-American 'Good Offices' Mission," *Journal of North African Studies* 17, no. 2 (2012): 355–71; Giampaolo Calchi Novati, "I rapporti fra FLN e Tunisia durante la Guerra di Liberazione: gli effetti del bombardamento di Sakiet Sidi Youssef," in *Algeria. Il disastro e la memoria*, ed. Federico Cresti, 23–38; Kettle, *De Gaulle and Algeria*, 482–3.

70 Martin Thomas, *The French North African Crisis. Colonial Breakdown and Anglo-French Relations, 1945–62* (London: Macmillan, 2000), 156; Bagnato, *L'Italia e la guerra d'Algeria*, 395.

71 Note SDECE, "Le F.L.N. et le pétrole du Sahara," Apr. 16, 1958, secret; b. 19900317/8, fd. 2, Algérie 1957/64, secret; AN (FOIA n° 111 382).

72 Note SDECE, "Le F.L.N. et le pétrole du Sahara," Apr. 16, 1958, secret.

73 Frémeaux, *Le Sahara et la France*, 243; Lyon, Amcongen Algiers, to Department of State, "Saharan Petroleum Developments", Jun. 24, 1958; Lyon, Amcongen Algiers, to Department of State, "New petroleum exploration permits granted in Sahara," Sep. 15, 1958.

74 Robert Fosset, "Pétrole et gaz naturel au Sahara," *Annales de Géographie* 71, no. 385 (1962): 298; Daniel Murat, *L'intervention de l'État dans le secteur pétrolier en France* (Paris: Technip, 1969), 91, 93; Madjid Benchikh, "La nouvelle loi pétrolière algérienne: direction publique et économie de

marché," *L'Année du Maghreb* II (2005–2006), points 23, 35–41, of the online version (http://anneemaghreb.revues.org/ 103). For a complete study of the Saharan Oil Code, see: Madjid Benchikh, *Les Instruments juridiques de la politique algérienne des hydrocarbures* (Paris: LGDJ, 1973); Pierre Cornet, *Du mirage au miracle. Pétrole saharien* (Paris: Nouvelles Editions Latines, 1960), 103.

75 Letter, Victor de Metz, President of CFP, to Charles de Gaulle, Prime Minister, Nov. 28, 1958; b. 1 PRES-2, Correspondence; Fonds Total-CFP; Archives Historiques du Groupe ELF/Total, La Défense (AHTOTAL). Amcongen Algiers to Department of State, "Saharan Petroleum Developments," Jan. 9, 1959, limited official use; f. 851S.2553/1-959; French Africa, b. 4604; Central Decimal Files, 1955–1959; RG 59; NARA. Amcongen Algiers to Department of State, "Annual Mineral and Petroleum Report for Algeria, 1959," May 13, 1960, unclassified; f. 851S.25/5-1360; French Africa, b. 2569; Central Decimal Files, 1960–1963; RG 59; NARA. Johnson, Amcongen Algiers to Department of State, Dec. 22, 1958, unclassified; f. 851S.2553/12-2258; French Africa, b. 4604; Central Decimal Files, 1955–1959; RG 59; NARA. W. E. Wallis and E. M. McNatt, "Selection of new regions for overseas exploration," *Geophysics* 23, no. 2 (1958): 306; Emmanuel Catta, *Victor De Metz. De la CFP au Groupe Total* (Paris: Total Edition Presse, 1990), 226; Cornet, *Du mirage au miracle*, 90. For coverage of the final phases of the Fourth Republic, and in particular on the events of May 1958, see: Jean-Pierre Rioux, *The Fourth Republic, 1944–1958* (Cambridge: Cambridge University Press, 1987), 303–8.

76 However, when in January 1959 Yazid asked the State Department to buy US weapons, this refused. Department of State, Memorandum of Conversation, "FLN Relations with U.S. Oil Companies," Feb. 6, 1959, official use only; f. 851S.2553/2-659; French Africa, b. 4604; Central Decimal Files, 1955–1959; RG 59; NARA. Department of State, Memorandum of Conversation, "U.S. Oil Company Interests in the Sahara", Feb. 19, 1959. *Free Algeria*—Front of National Liberation Delegation, News Bulletin, Press Release, "The Provisional Government of the Algerian Republic repudiates Sahara oil pacts made with France by foreign concerns," Jan. 28, 1959; Records Relating to Algeria, 1952–1962; fd. A6 Petroleum; entry A1 3109B; b. 1; Office of Northern African Affairs; Bureau of African Affairs; African Lot; RG 59; NARA. See also, in the same folder: "Interview of Mr. A. Chanderli, permanent representative of the Algerian Front of National Liberation in the United States with Mr. Bill Oatis (Associated Press)," New York, Jan. 28, 1959, 12.00 p.m. Note SDECE, "Le F.L.N. et le pétrole saharien," Feb. 24, 1959, secret; fd. 2, Algérie 1957/64; b. 199003117/8; AN (FOIA n° 111 382). See also, in the same folder: Note SDECE, "Le F.L.N. et le compagnies pétrolières américaines," Jan. 30, 1959, secret.

77 Centre de recherches sur l'Afrique méditerraneéenne, ed., "L'Algérie et les hydrocarbures," 100.

78 Wall, *France, the United States*, 167; Fosset, "Pétrole et gaz naturel," 298. J. M. Guldner to M. de Laboulaye: CISL—Cercle Ouvrier, "Pétrole et gaz sahariens," Mar. 1, 1961; fd. Politique algérienne jusque fin 1962; b. 92.26/9, Vincent Labouret; Fonds Total-CFP; AHTOTAL.

79 Centre de recherches sur l'Afrique méditerraneéenne, ed., "L'Algérie et les hydrocarbures," 98.

80 The quote is from: Pietro Quaroni to MAEI, "Ricerche petrolifere nel Sahara," Oct. 28, 1957; telespresso N. Ris. 1484/1143; b. 74 (Algeria '57); Ambasciata d'Italia a Parigi, 1951–1958; ASMAE (my translation).

81 Pietro Quaroni to MAEI, "Conseguenze dell'austerità sulla valorizzazione del Sahara," Dec. 5, 1957; telespresso N. Ris. 1663/1297; b. 74 (Algeria '57); Ambasciata d'Italia a Parigi, 1951–1958; ASMAE.

82 The model for the new contracts had been proposed by the Iranians, not Mattei as has often been maintained in the Italian literature. Ilaria Tremolada, *La via italiana al petrolio. L'ENI di Enrico Mattei e l'Iran (1945–1962)* (Milano: L'Ornitorinco, 2011), 310. For an analysis of ENI's activities in Iran in the 1950s, refer to the same volume. For American diplomacy's point of view on the Italian–Iranian agreement, see: Iran, bxs. 4973 and 4974; Central Decimal Files, 1955–1959; RG 59; NARA. See also: Leopoldo Nuti, *Gli Stati Uniti e l'apertura a sinistra. Importanza e limiti della presenza americana in Italia* (Bari: Laterza, 1999), 136–46.

83 For example, he was sent on missions to Jeddah and Cairo in early 1959. Tremolada, *Via italiana*, 350.

84 Pietro Quaroni to MAEI, "I rapporti italo-francesi," Mar. 14, 1958; telespresso N. Ris. 851; b. 81 (Algeria '58); Ambasciata d'Italia a Parigi, 1951–1958; ASMAE. Also in: Bruna Bagnato, *Petrolio e politica. Mattei in Marocco* (Firenze: Polistampa, 2004), 27; Bagnato, *L'Italia e la guerra d'Algeria*, 399. The quote is from: Pietro Quaroni to MAEI, "Limiti delle possibilità francesi nello sfruttamento del Sahara," Dec. 3, 1957; telespresso N. Ris. 1863/1297; b. 74 (Algeria '57); Ambasciata d'Italia a Parigi, 1951–1958; ASMAE (my translation).

85 ENI's ownership of Il Giorno would not be publicly disclosed until 1960. Pietro Quaroni to MAEI, "Attacco dei ribelli ad un gruppo di esperti petroliferi francesi nel Sahara—Reazioni francesi all'articolo del 'Giorno' sul Sahara," Nov. 11, 1957; telespresso n. Ris. 1539/1191; b. 43; Direzione Generale Affari Politici, Ufficio I (1947–1960); ASMAE. Note pour Monsieur de Directeur—"Compte rendu de la réunion tenue chez M. Daridant avec MM. Baudet, Sébilleau, Jordan, le 14.11.57, Articles inspirés par M. MATTEI, dans 'Il Giorno'—Conférence de MATTEI à PARIS le 22 Novembre: 'L'Italie et le pétrole,' Nov. 16, 1957; sub-fd. Italie 1955/1979; fd. 1; b. 19900317/13; AN (FOIA n° 111 382).

86 Télégramme from Jacques Fouques-Duparc to MAEF, Sep. 10, 1957; Dossier 15, Italie, Politique Extérieure; Sous-série 23; Série 21; EU 1956–1960, Italie, 297, Europe; ADMAE: source as reported in Giovanni Buccianti, *Enrico Mattei. Assalto al potere petrolifero mondiale* (Milano: Giuffrè, 2005), 61 (my translation). Pietro Quaroni to Massimo Magistrati, Direzione Generale Affari Politici, MAEI, Nov. 12, 1957; b. 74 (Algeria '57); Ambasciata d'Italia a Parigi, 1951–1958; ASMAE. For an account of arms dealings among North African, Eastern and Western Bloc countries, see: Wall, *France, the United States*, 93–5.

87 Télegramme from Jacques Fouques-Duparc à MAEF, Sep. 13, 1957; Dossier 15, Italie, Politique Extérieure; Sous-série 23; Série 21; EU 1956–1960, Italie, 297, Europe; ADMAE: source as reported in Buccianti, *Enrico Mattei*, 60. Gaston Palewski to MAEF, Oct. 26, 1957; and Palewski to Christian Pineau, Nov. 28, 1957; Italie, 300; Directorate of Political and Economic Affairs; ADMAE: source as reported in Federico Cresti and Anna Maria Gregni, "La Guerra di Liberazione algerina e l'Italia nella visione dei documenti diplomatici francesi," in *Algeria*, ed. Cresti, 55.

88 Maurice Bourgès-Maunoury was the France's Prime Minister from June to November 1957; Félix Gaillard succeeded him until May 1958.

89 Gaston Palewski, Fremb Rome, to Chrstian Pineau, Minister of Foreign Affairs, "Opinion italienne et question algérienne. Propos de M. SARAGAT," Dec. 5, 1957; sub-fd. Italie 1955/1979; fd. 1; b. 19900317/13; AN (FOIA n° 111 382).

90 Dahou O. Kablia, "Enrico Mattei e la Rivoluzione Algerina," in *Enrico Mattei e l'Algeria durante la Guerra di Liberazione Nazionale*, ed. Ambasciata d'Italia and Istituto Italiano di Cultura di Algeri (Algiers: Ambasciata d'Italia and Istituto Italiano di Cultura di Algeri, 2010), 18. An indication of the good disposition of the Italian government toward the FLN/GPRA representative was given after a failed attempt to assassinate Taïeb Boulahrouf in July 1959, presumably orchestrated by the terrorist organization *Main Rouge*, which secretly acted as SDECE's armed wing. According to Rédha Malek, after this episode the Italian Minister of Interior, Fernando Tambroni, offered the Algerian a Beretta gun and a gun license. Malek, *L'Algérie à Évian*, 75. See also: Thénault, *Histoire de la guerre*, 158.

91 Alessandro Brogi, *L'Italia e l'egemonia americana nel Mediterraneo. 1945–1958* (Scandicci: La Nuova Italia, 1996), 59, 125–6; Alessandro Brogi, *A Question of Self-Esteem: the United States and the Cold War Choices in France and Italy, 1944–1958* (Westport, CT: Praeger, 2002), 172, 193–7, 204–10; Ilaria Tremolada, *All'ombra degli arabi. Le relazioni italo-israeliane 1948–1956. Dalla fondazione dello Stato Ebraico alla crisi di Suez* (Milano: M&B, 2003), 80; Bagnato, *L'Italia e la guerra d'Algeria*, 32–4.

92 Patrick Eveno and Jean Planchais, eds., *La guerre d'Algérie* (Paris: La Découverte/Le Monde, 1989), 177. China was to be the first non-Arab country to recognize Algerian independence in 1962. "Un accord de coopération entre l'U.R.S.S. et le G.P.R.A.," Agence France-Presse, Bulletin de 12 heures, Nov. 17, 1961; b. 90.4/164, Négociations franco-GPRA et le Sahara; fd. Réactions des pays arabes aux Accords d'Évian; Fonds Total-CFP; AHTOTAL.

93 Bagnato, L'Italia e la guerra d'Algeria, 442–5 (and notes 76 and 78 therein), 470. Note DAEF, "Visite de M. Fanfani—M. Mattéi et le pétrole," Aug. 6, 1958, pp. 3–4; N. 85. DE-CE Papiers Directeur Olivier Wormser; Sous-série: Directeur—Wormser; Série: Affaires économiques et financières; ADMAE.

94 About ENI's Moroccan exploration permit, see files contained in: fd. M-12, Mattei/Moroccan Oil Concession; entry A1 3109D; b. 4; Records Relating to Morocco, 1955–1962; Office of Northern African Affairs; Bureau of African Affairs; African Lot; RG 59; NARA.

95 Note DAEF, "Visite de M. Fanfani—M. Mattéi et le pétrole," Aug. 6, 1958, pp. 3–4.

96 Jean Blancard, BRP, to MAEF, Jun. 24, 1960; N. 70; Sous-série: Couve de Murville (1958–1968); Série: Cabinet du Ministre; ADMAE. Cesare Gavotti, "Proposta di collaborazione per le ricerche di idrocarburi nel Sahara Francese,", Jan. 11, 1957; fd. A2A; b. 16; Assistente del Presidente per l'estero; Estero; Fondo ENI; Archivio Storico ENI (ASENI). Cesare Gavotti, "Notizie e prospettive Sahara," Apr. 13, 1957; fd. A3E; b. 16; Assistente del Presidente per l'estero; Estero; Fondo ENI; ASENI. PV du Comité Spécial du BRP, séance n. 64 du 22 janvier 1957, Annexe III p. 4, Jan. 22, 1957; sub-fd. Italie Mons Mattei, 1957/58; fd. 3; b. 19900317/24; AN (FOIA n° 111 382).

97 Quoted from: Note pour Monsieur de Directeur—Compte rendu de la réunion tenue chez M. Daridant avec MM. Baudet, Sébilleau, Jordan, le 14.11.57, "Articles inspirés par M. Mattei, dans 'Il Giorno'—Conférence de MATTEI à PARIS le 22 novembre: 'L'Italie et le pétrole'," Nov. 16, 1957; sub-fd. Italie Mons Mattei, 1957/58; fd. 3; b. 19900317/24; AN (FOIA n° 111 382) (my translation).

98 Roberto Caracciolo, Itemb, to MAEI, May 10, 1957, confidential; telespresso N. Ris. 785/575; b. 81 (Algeria '58); Ambasciata d'Italia a Parigi, 1951–1958; ASMAE.

99 Etienne Burin des Roziers, Fremb Warsaw, to Maurice Couve de Murville, Minister of Foreign Affairs, "Conversation avec M. Mattei au sujet du

pétrole saharien," Nov. 20, 1958; sub-fd. Italie Mons Mattei, 1957/58; fd. 3; b. 19900317/24; AN (FOIA n° 111 382). Appunto, Roma, Nov. 20, 1958; fd. 150; b. 75; Presidenza Mattei; Fondo ENI; ASENI: source as reported in Bagnato, *L'Italia e la guerra d'Algeria*, 703.

100 The quote, by Henri Langlais, is reported in: Kettle, *De Gaulle and Algeria*, 357. Bagnato, *Petrolio e politica*, 222–3; Bagnato, *L'Italia e la guerra d'Algeria*, 706.

101 Malek, *L'Algérie à Évian*, 73–4, 202. In October 1958, Giorgio La Pira organized a Mediterranean Meeting in Florence, which was funded by ENI. The meeting became an excellent political platform for FLN's representatives, causing the withdrawal of the French delegation. On the meeting, see: Bruna Bagnato, "La Pira, de Gaulle e il primo Colloquio mediterraneo di Firenze," in *Giorgio La Pira e la Francia. Temi e percorsi di ricerca. Da Maritain a de Gaulle*, ed. Pier Luigi Ballini (Firenze: Giunti, 2005), 99–134; Bruna Bagnato, "L'Italia e la guerra d'Algeria: il governo, i partiti, le forze sociali e l'ENI di Mattei," in *Enrico Mattei*, ed. Ambasciata d'Italia and Istituto Italiano di Cultura di Algeri, 33; Cresti and Gregni, "La Guerra di Liberazione," 78–84; Bagnato, *L'Italia e la guerra d'Algeria*, 414–15, 482–512. About Mattei's funding of the meeting: G. Palewski, Rome, 16 October 1958; b. 299, n. 1599/EU; Série: Italie; ADMAE: source as reported in Bagnato, *L'Italia e la guerra d'Algeria*, 502 note 192.

102 On the Tunisian–Italian agreement, see: AHTOTAL—Fonds Total-CFP, b. 97AA096, fd. 1, f. 1, ENI 1960–1961: Relazioni e bilanci delle principali società del gruppo al 31 dicembre 60, p. 42. The agreement between AGIP Mineraria and the Tunisian Government was signed on 1 June 1960. Alexandre Parodi, Fremb Rabat, to Olivier Wormser, MAEF, Aug. 22, 1960; N. 85. DE-CE Papiers Directeur Olivier Wormser; Sous-série: Directeur—Wormser; Série: Affaires économiques et financières; ADMAE. SDECE, Notice d'information—"L'activité de l'Ente nazionale idrocarburi (octobre 1959–octobre 1960)," Oct. 18, 1960, p. 3, secret; sub-fd. Italie 1955/1979; fd. 1; b. 19900317/13; AN (FOIA n° 111 382).

103 Olivier Wormser, MAEF, to Alexandre Parodi, Fremb Rabat, Sep. 20, 1960; N. 85. DE-CE Papiers Directeur Olivier Wormser; Sous-série: Directeur—Wormser; Série: Affaires économiques et financières; ADMAE. The quote is from: Jean Blancard, BRP, to Maurice Couve de Murville, MAEF, Jun. 24, 1960; N. 70; Sous-série: Couve de Murville (1958–1968); Série: Cabinet du Ministre; ADMAE (my translation).

104 Colloquio di Mario Pirani con Vincenzo Gandolfi, "Ricordi e riflessioni di un ex-ambasciatore di Metanopoli," Oct. 22, 1992; fds. 462B and 462C; b. 3; Interviste, n. 47: Mario Pirani; Fonti orali; ASENI. Buccianti, *Enrico Mattei*, 250ff; Nico Perrone, *Obiettivo Mattei. Petrolio, Stati Uniti e politica dell'ENI* (Gamberetti: Roma, 1995), 19–20; Mario Pirani, *Poteva andare peggio. Mezzo secolo di ragionevoli illusioni* (Milano: Mondadori, 2012), 292–3. Note SDECE, "Algérie-Italie—Mattei et le G.P.R.A.," Sep. 26, 1961, secret (do not communicate to Allies); fd. 2, Algérie 1957/64; b. 19900317/8; AN (FOIA n° 111 382). "Note du service de renseignement britannique," very secret, source to be protected, Sep. 23, 1961; Secrétariat d'État aux Affaires Algériennes, 1959–1967; ADMAE: source as reported in Bagnato, *Petrolio e politica*, 367.

105 Franco Briatico, *Ascesa e declino del capitale pubblico in Italia. Vicende e protagonisti* (Bologna: Il Mulino, 2004), 15. The quote is from p. 20 (my translation). See also: Pirani, *Poteva andare peggio*, 303.

106 SDECE, "Note d'information," Bureau du Premier Ministre, very secret, source to be very carefully protected, Nov. 16, 1961; Secrétariat d'État aux Affaires Algériennes, 1959–1967; ADMAE: source as reported in Bagnato, *Petrolio e politica*, 367. The *Union générale* was also part of the American Federation of Labor and Congress of Industrial Organizations AFL-CIO, directed by Irving Brown, who actively supported the Algerian cause (Malek, *L'Algérie à Évian*, 35).

107 SDECE report, unsigned, Jun. 2, 1961; b. 114—Affaires Politiques, Evian Accords; Secrétariat d'État aux Affaires Algériennes; ADMAE: source as reported in Connelly, *Diplomatic Revolution*, 343 note 58. Note d'information personnelle, "Quelques aspects des activités extérieures de M. Enrico Mattei en Afrique et en Europe," 331/II E, Jul. 7, 1961; b. 10777; Centre des archives économiques et financières, Savigy le Temple: source as reported in Bagnato, "L'Italia e la guerra," 39. Note SDECE, "Algérie-Italie, Ingérences d'Enrico Mattei," Jan. 16, 1962, secret (do not communicate to Allies); fd. 2, Algérie 1957/64; b. 19900317/8; AN. Bagnato, *L'Italia e la guerra d'Algeria*, 724; Pirani, *Poteva andare peggio*, 305; Porch, *The French Secret Services*, 372–3, 581.

108 Bagnato bases her claim on the training of French–Algerian students at the School, (Bagnato, "L'Italia e la guerra," 39) on an interview with ENI's second president, Eugenio Cefis, recorded on Apr. 17, 2003. In the School's archive, however, I could not find any document supporting this claim at least up until 1962. The quote is from: Krim Belkacem to Enrico Mattei, Cairo, Jun. 28, 1960; Fonds GPRA; Archives nationales d'Algérie, Algiers: source as reported in Bagnato, *L'Italia e la guerra d'Algeria*, 708 (my translation).

109 Bernard Tricot to Louis Joxe, "Essai de définition d'une position gouvernementale sur le Sahara," Apr. 10, 1961: source as reported in Maurice Faivre, *Les archives inédites*, 337. On Tricot's role at the first Évian negotiations, see: Malek, *L'Algérie à Évian*, 136–40.

110 Charles de Gaulle, *Memoirs of Hope: Renewal and Endeavour* (New York: Simon and Schuster, 1971), 115; Mohamed Khelladi, "Testimonianza," in *Enrico Mattei*, ed. Ambasciata d'Italia and Istituto Italiano di Cultura di Algeri, 58; Melby, *Oil and the International System*, 278.

111 Procès-verbeaux [sic] de la Conférence d'Evian, May 21–June 13, 1961, DDF, 1961, I, pp. 772–95: source as reported in: Wall, *France, the United States*, 307 note 40. Michèle Cointet, *De Gaulle et l'Algérie française* (Paris: Perrin, 1995), 202–42; John Talbott, *War Without a Name*, 223. Department of State, Memorandum of Conversation, "Algeria," Jun. 16, 1961, confidential; fd. A8 FLN—French—Self-determination Negotiations, Jan. 61; entry A1 3109B; b. 1; Records Relating to Algeria, 1952–1962; Office of Northern African Affairs; Bureau of African Affairs; African Lot; RG 59; NARA.

112 Harry F. Kern, Director of *Foreign Report*, to François de Laboulaye, CFP, Jul. 11, 1961; fd. Politique algérienne jusque fin 1962; b. 92.26/9, Vincent Labouret; Fonds Total-CFP; AHTOTAL. Malek, *L'Algérie à Évian*, 158–63.

113 Bagnato, "L'Italia e la guerra," 39; Bruna Bagnato, "L'Italia e la causa algerina: tra prudenza delle Istituzioni e solidarietà della società civile," in *Il contributo dell'Italia alla costruzione dell'Algeria indipendente*, ed. Ambasciata d'Italia and Istituto Italiano di Cultura di Algeri (Algiers: Ambasciata d'Italia and Istituto Italiano di Cultura di Algeri, 2011), 64. Colloquio di Mario Pirani con Vincenzo Gandolfi, "Ricordi e riflessioni di un ex-ambasciatore di Metanopoli," Oct. 22, 1992, pp. 13–14. Briatico, *Ascesa e declino*, 14; Italo Pietra, *Mattei: la pecora nera* (Roma: La Repubblica, 2002. First edition: Milano: Sugarco, 1987), 220.

114 Khelladi, "Testimonianza," 58; Kablia, "Enrico Mattei," 19–20. Abdelmadjid Chikhi, General Director of the National Algerian Archives, tells about the help provided by ENI to the Algerian Minister of Armaments and General Relations for the collection of data on the Algerian subsoil. Abdelmadjid Chikhi, "Gli Accordi di Evian," in *Enrico Mattei*, ed. Ambasciata d'Italia and Istituto Italiano di Cultura di Algeri, 62.

115 Kablia, *Enrico Mattei*, 197–8, 201.

116 Testimonies of ENI "ambassadors" have also been reported by other authors. See, for example, Buccianti, Enrico Mattei, 231. The folder supposedly including documents prepared by ENI for the GPRA is found in: fd. 2F2B; b. 129; Relazioni Esterne; Fondo ENI; ASENI.

117 Myron T. Kozáry, "Algeria—Prospects of the Algerian Sahara, Geological Report no. 6"; ENI U 1.018.801; Archivio Tecnico-Scientifico ENI, San Donato Milanese. C. R. DeLand, "Memorial: Myron Theodore Kozary (1918–1966)," *AAPG Bulletin* (September 1967): 1881–2.

118 Myron T. Kozáry, "Algeria—Prospects of the Algerian Sahara, Geological Report no. 6"; ENI U 1.018.801; Archivio Tecnico-Scientifico ENI, San Donato Milanese. Carmine Loddo, "Visita agli uffici, ai laboratori e al giacimento petrolifero di Hassi-Messaoud," Dec. 20, 1960; fd. 2003; b. 73; Rapporti commerciali con l'estero; Estero; Fondo ENI; ASENI. The "very liberal" quote is from the same document (my translation).

119 Loddo, "Visita agli uffici, ai laboratori e al giacimento petrolifero di Hassi-Messaoud," Dec. 20, 1960; Albert Roger, CGG, to Egidio Egidi, AGIP Mineraria, Mar. 8, 1962; and Roger to Egidi, Mar. 29, 1962; fd. 3FC; b. 355; Ricerche e produzione; Direzione Mineraria; Fondo AGIP; ASENI. "50 ans de géophysique", 1964; fd. 13, CGG's yearly reports; b. 92AA039, Rapports annuels de la CFP et de différentes filiales; Fonds Total-CFP; AHTOTAL. CEDI, *Archivio storico. Verbali Comitato tecnico ricerche e produzioni (1950)* (San Donato Milanese: Centro stampa AGIP, 1992), Meeting of Apr. 17, 1950, 124; Federico Squarzina, *Le ricerche di petrolio in Italia. Cenni storici dal 1860 e cronache dell'ultimo decennio* (Roma: Jandi Sapi, 1958), 76, 87.

120 Albert Roger, CGG, to Tiziano Rocco, AGIP Mineraria, Jan. 26, 1962; and Roger to Egidio Egidi, AGIP Mineraria, Feb. 26, 1962; fd. 36F; b. 260; Ricerche e produzione; Direzione Mineraria; Fondo AGIP; ASENI.

121 Note d'information personnelle, "Quelques aspects des activités extérieures de M. Enrico Mattei en Afrique et en Europe," 331/II E, Jul. 7, 1961: source as reported in Bagnato, *Petrolio e politica*, 348–9. See also: Bagnato, *L'Italia e la guerra d'Algeria*, 627–8, 709, 716–7. The quote is from p. 716 (my translation). On the connections between the Secret Army Organization and the Italian secret services, see: Aldo Giannuli, *La guerra fredda delle spie. L'ufficio affari riservati*, vol. I (Roma: Nuova Iniziativa Editoriale, 2005), 71–8.

122 Diari 1954–1962, XIII, Jul. 4, 1961; Fondo Manlio Brosio; Archivio Storico della Fondazione Luigi Einaudi, Torino: source as reported in Bagnato, *L'Italia e la guerra d'Algeria*, 711 note 253. Bagnato, *L'Italia e la guerra d'Algeria*, 702, 712–3. *The Observer*, Jul. 23, 1961; Rassegna stampa estera 1961, special issue Aug. 3, 1961; ASENI. For a detailed account of the diplomatic turmoil caused by what Bagnato calls the 'Mattei effect' on French activities, see Bagnato, *L'Italia e la guerra d'Algeria*, 703–33 (especially, 710–15). On Brosio's activity as Italian Ambassador in Paris with regard to Mattei, see: Manlio Brosio, and Umberto Gentoni Silveri, ed., *Diari di Parigi: 1961–1964* (Bologna: Il Mulino, 2009), 59, 132, 136, 180, 210–11. The quote is from: Memorandum of Conversation, "Mattei and ENI," Mar. 17, 1962; FRUS, 1961–1963, XIII, Western Europe and Canada (Washington: United States Government Printing Office, 1994), 830.

123 Bagnato, *L'Italia e la guerra d'Algeria*, 697. Eveno and Planchais, 318 (the authors report a document dated 1962, by Jean Lacouture, "Les étapes de la négociation"); Talbott, *War Without a Name*, 224; Thomas, *French North African Crisis*, 193.

124 Frémeaux, *Le Sahara et la France*, 268.

125 MAEI—General Direction of Economic Affairs, Bureau VI, to Ministries of Industry and Commerce, State Holdings, Foreign Trade, ENI: "Accordi di Evian—Ricerca e sfruttamento petrolio nel Sahara," Mar. 23, 1962, urgent; fd. 20D6; b. 76; Assistente del Presidente per l'estero; Estero; Fondo ENI; ASENI. See also: Rémi Kauffer, "L'or noir et la bombe: la face cachée des accords d'Évian," in *Histoire secrète de la Ve République*, ed. Roger Faligot and Jean Guisnel (Paris: La Découverte, 2006), 83–6. An official document of October 1961, listing French conditions to the acknowledgement of Sahara to Algeria and signed by de Gaulle, is: Comité des affaires algériennes, "Décisions prises le 28 octobre 1961," and it is reported in Faivre, *Les archives inédites*, 283–4. However, affirms Melby, the French amended the Oil Code a few weeks before the signature of the Évian agreements, so to limit the degree of control the Algerians could exert on French companies operating in the Sahara. Melby, *Oil and the International System*, 279, 281–2. See also: Pierre Péan and Jean-Pierre Séréni, *Les émirs de la République. L'aventure du pétrole tricolore* (Paris: Seuil, 1982), 86.

126 Briatico, *Ascesa e declino*, 31. The placing of explosives on Mattei's plane has in the past been attributed to American majors backed by the Sicilian mafia; large Italian industrialists; to Mattei's de facto successor at the presidency of ENI, Eugenio Cefis; to the Secret Army Organization; or to collaborations between these suspects. De Vosjoli's statement is reported in: Porch, *The French Secret Services*, 373 notes 28 and 29.

127 Gaston Palewski, Fremb Rome, to MAEF, Mission de Liaison avec l'Algérie, n. 590/MLA, "L'Italie, les accords d'Evian et les perspectives maghrébines," Apr. 12, 1962; N. 45; Sous-série: 1957–1966. Série: Service de liaison avec l'Algérie; ADMAE. Note SDECE, "Italie—Activités de M. Mattei," May 2, 1962, secret; N. 45; Sous-série: 1957–1966; Série: Service de liaison avec l'Algérie; ADMAE. Note SDECE, "Algérie-Italie-R.F.A.-Maroc—Le G.P.R.A. et l'exploitation des pétroles sahariens," Jan. 19, 1962, secret; fd. 2, Algérie 1957/64; b. 199003117/8; AN (FOIA n° 111 382).

128 *The Washington Post*, "Mattei's Projects in Africa," Oct. 1, 1962; Giuseppe Lo Bianco and Sandra Rizza, *Profondo Nero. Mattei, De Mauro, Pasolini. Un'unica pista all'origine delle stragi di stato* (Milano: Chiarelettere, 2009), 65–6. Note SDECE, "Italie—Activités de la Fiat et de l'ENI en Afrique du Nord," Aug. 10, 1962, secret; sub-fd. Italie 1955/1979; fd. 1; b. 199003117/13; AN (FOIA n° 111 382).

4 The Midstream Shift

> Like death itself, the ultimate decline of our complex and wonderful oil industry is already distantly in view. Any discussion on the future of geophysics as we know must contemplate the ultimate partial replacement of oil and gas as energy sources and the ultimate role of geophysics in finding ores for atomic energy.
>
> —Paul Lyons, President of the American Society of Exploration Geophysicists[1]

By the end of the 1950s, the petroleum industry was characterized by an overcapacity in production, a general trend that would continue until the oil crisis of 1973. By way of example, between 1959 and 1960, world production increased by 6.2 percent. In 1960, for the first time, three Middle Eastern countries (Saudi Arabia, Kuwait, and Iraq) all averaged over 50 Mt of oil per year, while African production more than doubled. Even more significantly, the Soviet Union overtook Venezuela as the world's second-largest producer. Consumption rates also rose considerably over the same period, but new reserves were added much faster than they were used up.[2]

The most significant causative factor in overproduction was the large volume of global oil discoveries in the 1950s. As we have seen in the case of Algeria, quantitative and qualitative improvements in prospecting, a sharp rise in geophysical activity, and the introduction of new techniques, paved the way for these discoveries. To some extent, overproduction was the consequence of the coming of age of exploration geophysics. However, I will argue that it was also the cause of the relative and temporary demise of geophysics as a geostrategic weapon in areas already subject to intense exploration.

In the cases of Italy and France, the availability in the early 1960s of cheap and abundant Soviet oil for the former, and copious production from French-controlled African oilfields for the latter, placed new demands on national security, and reduced the urgency of the need for new exploration. The fundamental phase for the national oil companies of both countries now became the transportation of oil from the oilfields to the industrialized areas where it was needed, both within and beyond national borders.

The establishment of the European Economic Community (EEC) in 1957 opened up a large new market for this oil.

Finding yet more oil therefore became less crucial to the security of both countries than reliable oil transportation. The flow of oil from oilfield to market needed to be smooth, without interruptions that could endanger the fuelling apparatus and thereby put energy security at risk. To employ a physiological metaphor, pipelines are the vessels through which the energy of a country flows. Problems in the flow impede energy supply, affecting the health of a state, in terms of its industry, military, transportation, and heating. A shift in security priorities therefore occurred in the two countries that are the subject of this study, from prospecting activities to transport and the wholesale marketing of crude; in other words, from the 'upstream' to the 'midstream' sector. I call this phase the 'midstream shift.'

The first section of this chapter looks at the causes of overproduction, detailing in particular the role of the Soviet Union as an exporter. I then show how geophysical activities declined globally from the second half of the 1950s, and look briefly at the differing development of Italian and French geophysical operations up to that point. In the remaining sections, I focus on how oil operations moved to the midstream in Italy and France. Regarding ENI, I analyze how the abundance of Soviet oil led to agreements with the Italian company, and the diplomatic issue determined by these initiatives. I then demonstrate how ENI engaged in a pipeline duel with a consortium of American and European companies with the aim of supplying the West European market.

At the same time, I show how the Italian company eventually came to terms with the American majors on the commercial side, and by the early 1960s had signed a number of substantial supply contracts with them. I also look at how the French authorities established a system of pipelines in Algeria, designing their routes on the basis of geopolitical factors. Saharan oil not only allowed France to attain a degree of energy autonomy, it also generated the problem of commercializing the new oil in mainland France, where the distribution market was mainly in the hands of foreign companies. Finally, I discuss the strategies devised by French oil agencies and governmental institutions to overcome this problem.

An Oversupplied Market

The 1950s were the age of 'elephants,' as large oilfields were known among oilmen. In 1953 that situation had already prompted Everette DeGolyer, the prominent American geophysicist, to predict one of the majors' nightmares: overproduction. Marketing oil, rather than producing it, became the main problem.[3] The striking figures Daniel Yergin reports are self-explanatory in this respect: world oil production increased from 438 million tons a year in 1948 to 2.1 billion in 1972. Unsurprisingly, this colossal production also affected world prices, which fell between 1954 and 1970 from $15 to $10 a barrel.[4] We have seen how, in the 1940s and for most of the 1950s, the strategy of scarcity production enabled a cartel of British–American companies to manage the oil market by acquiring larger numbers of concessions in oil-rich areas and imposing limits on oil production.[5] I have also explained how intelligence activity and diplomacy were employed to reduce the influence of Italian and French interests in this strategy. However, by the late 1950s, not only had the growth of national oil enterprises undermined these plans in a number of areas, but several new market factors were putting this approach at risk. One such factor was the colossal amount of oil the Soviet Union had begun to extract and sell.[6]

A further element was the appearance on the market of some aggressive independent oil companies. For example, while in 1946 only nine companies were operating in the Middle East, by 1956 there were nineteen (and eighty-one by 1970). The most significant instance of the activism of these new competitors was in Libya. Here, especially after the Algerian discovery of Edjeleh in 1956, and thanks to new legislation that welcomed foreign intervention, British, French, North American, Dutch, German, and Italian companies hastened to apply for exploration permits.

Most of the new enterprises were private and had their headquarters in the US, but a few were national companies backed by their governments, like ENI and BRP's affiliates. By 1963, crude oil production in the hands of independent companies in exporting countries, plus net exports from the Soviet Bloc, amounted to roughly 10 percent of all oil entering primary international trade. Five years later, this share had risen to 15 percent.[7] This was still low in comparison with the output of the majors, but it was increasing rapidly. Producing scarcity stopped being an effective strategy because of the frantic commercial operations of rival firms. Keeping prices high by reducing the availability of oil would not work when a throng of aggressive competitors was waiting for the slightest opportunity to capture market share. This strategy was also put in jeopardy by the Soviet Union.

Between 1955 and 1965, Soviet oil production rose spectacularly from 71 to 243 Mt: a 3.5-fold increase. This bonanza was the outcome of major prospective efforts, which bore finest fruit in the Ural–Volga region, where a number of large oilfields were discovered. Soon the crucial issue for the Soviet oil industry became the marketing of this newfound oil. They ultimately decided to export oil to Western Europe at prices significantly lower than those prevailing on the international oil market.[8] Whether these low prices were part of a deliberate political strategy to make Western Europe dependent on the USSR for its energy, or simply an economic consequence of the quantities of oil found and of the Soviets' urgent need of Western technologies in exchange, has been debated ever since the phenomenon emerged. In hindsight, energy analysts like Robert Ebel see the economic rationale as the most likely. However, an examination of the unfolding events from a historical perspective reveals a knot that is harder to unravel, which will be analyzed in greater depth in Chapter 5.[9]

Whatever the explanation for the Soviet oil export strategy, what is certain is that it massively unnerved all the most prominent players in the international oil industry, starting with the US. One of the first signs of American anxiety about the increase in Soviet oil production came from Allen Dulles, the then-Director of the Central Intelligence Agency (CIA), who in 1958 warned Eisenhower's cabinet that: "[T]he free world face[d] a quite dangerous situation in the Soviet capacity to dislocate established markets."[10] Indeed over the course of ten years, the share of total Soviet production slated for export rose from 5.2 percent to 26.4 percent, and oil exported to non-Communist countries increased from 3.8 Mt in 1955 to a stunning 35.5 Mt in 1965. The prices offered by the USSR were so low compared with the international market price that most US sources had no hesitation in talking about dumping. By way of example, in 1957 a barrel of Soviet oil sold on the international market for $2.06, compared to $2.79 for Middle Eastern oil and $2.92 for Venezuelan oil. In the coming years Soviet prices offered to West European countries decreased even further, to as little as $1 a barrel in the case of an Italian–Russian agreement signed in 1960.[11]

In order to compete, the majors opted to cut the 'posted' prices (i.e. the published prices at which companies sold oil), allowing them to share losses with producing countries rather than having to bear them alone. Between 1959 and 1960, BP, SONJ and other majors agreed cuts of between 7 and 10 percent. This was immediately condemned by producing countries. Price cuts by the majors would ultimately prompt producers, fed up with their lack of decision-making power, to club together in the Organization of Petroleum Exporting Countries (OPEC) in 1960.[12] As BP cut prices, Eisenhower's government imposed a system of mandatory quotas on foreign oil imports to the US, intended to protect American domestic production from cheap foreign oil and prevent the country becoming dependent on imported supplies.

Essentially, this system restricted imports to an amount equal to the difference between the government's estimate of domestic oil demand and its estimate of domestic oil supply. This provision shut off the world's largest market from growing Middle Eastern production. As African and Asian oil consumption was still negligible, and as the Soviet Bloc was closed to the majors, the only conceivable solution for producers was to attempt to place this oil surplus in a Western Europe that they were already supplying to a massive extent.[13] In general, nevertheless, as I showed in the Italian and French cases in the 1950s, the efforts by the majors to control European oil markets met with resistance, and were only partially successful.

Soviet oil exports were part of a larger scheme, in which barter agreements were employed as powerful economic and diplomatic weapons, enabling beneficiary countries to find outlets for their production. When trading with Egypt, the Russians bartered oil for cotton; with Cuba, they swapped oil for sugar. Technoscientific expertise was also used as a lever to convince developing countries to collaborate. This was a cornerstone of Soviet oil policy, and was successfully employed in Afghanistan, Ethiopia, Pakistan, and Egypt. The USSR provided crews of experts to assist locals in the construction of pipelines and tankers, in geological studies, and in training the executives of national oil industries. Indeed, this training was not limited to technical domains, but also included political and social engineering.[14]

The Soviet oil trade met with different international reactions. Almost all of them, however, had in common the image of Soviet oil as a major threat to West European energy, economy, and security. Indeed, in most contemporary US State Department documents, the phrase 'Soviet oil offensive' was employed to describe the Soviet oil trade, a description that soon became widespread in other Western sources. With regard to Soviet oil exports, while the US government firmly refused them access to the United States, European positions were more varied, depending on each country's trading relationship with the USSR. In terms of Soviet exports, the top three West European countries in 1957 (the United Kingdom, West Germany, and France) imported merchandise worth respectively 756, 286, and 268 million rubles. Exports to Italy amounted to 117 million rubles. However, Italy was the only one of these countries to post a negative balance of trade.[15]

In Britain, Harold Macmillan's government implemented an embargo on Soviet oil in 1959, but serious divergences remained between government departments, notably between the Board of Trade and the Ministry of Power: the latter was in favor, the former against an embargo. In France, Victor de Metz, president of the CFP, feared that Soviet trade could expand to the entire EEC, thus jeopardizing French plans to market their newly found African oil in Europe. De Metz thus hoped to counter the 'red oil flood' by an alliance between Arab producers and Western oil majors. A number of oil-producing Arab countries turned up their noses at the Soviet export strategy, but their heavy dependence on the USSR's economy and technical expertise prevented them from taking any retaliatory measures.[16]

The situation was different for Italy and West Germany, which were deeply involved in trade with the USSR. In West Germany, this applied specifically to the steel producers in the Ruhr region, who were on good terms with a number of Soviet firms. Commercial exchanges also existed between Soviet firms and many large Italian industrial enterprises, such as the car manufacturer FIAT. At the end of 1959, ENI was negotiating terms for a massive oil-for-technology contract with the Soviet Union. This came into force in 1960, causing a scandal in the Western industrial and political world, as I will show in the course of this chapter. But before analyzing this major aspect of the Italian midstream shift, I first consider how overproduction in the Soviet Union and elsewhere led to an important change in prospecting activities.

Decline in Geophysical Activity

One of the causative factors of overproduction was the number of discoveries brought about by oil prospecting in the 1950s, a "burgeoning era of geophysics," as geophysicist Charles Bates and colleagues have described it.[17] The geophysical boom was heralded as an augur of prosperity for the sector, all the more so after the launch of International Geophysical Year (IGY) 1957–1958. The IGY initiative "rapidly became the largest, most complex, and costliest of any international scientific effort ever undertaken," and was followed by the establishment in the US, after the 1958 Geneva talks on a nuclear test-ban, of the Panel on Seismic Improvement presided over by Lloyd Berkner. The objective of the panel was to promote research in seismology in the US, especially for the detection and identification of underground nuclear explosions. It showered American seismology with funds.[18]

What was perhaps more important, projects such as the Panel for Seismic Improvement, or the similarly-purposed Vela Uniform, conducted jointly by the US Department of Energy and the Advanced Research Projects Agency from 1960, also had knock-on effects on exploration geophysics: for example, Vela Uniform led to the reawakening of interest in the Earth's natural electromagnetic fields and, in consequence, to a reconsideration of the potential of telluric methods, from both the theoretical and the empirical perspectives. Historian Bruce Bolt remarks: "Soon the realization dawned that testing of nuclear weapons would force seismology to expand from a small, rather obscure discipline to one that would play a key social role." The significance attributed to seismology in the nuclear context spread to exploration geophysics as well: so much money and trust were put into this sector, that it dwarfed other branches of geophysics, to the point that general knowledge in geophysics ended up being modeled by seismology.[19]

As a consequence, innovation in geophysical prospecting—and seismology in particular—greatly improved the study of oil reservoirs and enhanced the efficiency of their exploitation. The introduction of magnetic recording (which I touched upon in Chapter 3), coupled with the advent of electronic analog computers, revolutionized the handling of data. Thanks to the new devices and more refined data analysis techniques, geophysicists could now devote more time to examining, interpreting and reinterpreting logs of new and existing oilfields. The speed and performance of computers made it possible to untangle tough problems in a timeframe that was beyond the scope of humans.[20]

Data from multiple field crews could now be processed entirely through central offices equipped with magnetic playback devices. These included tools for carrying out routine time corrections and computations on data, and for preparing time-corrected depth records. More generally, the readability of seismic sections was significantly improved. Processed records and sections were now sent to an interpretation group. Playback centers took on paramount importance in the interpretation aspects of geophysics, and it made a big difference to oil companies to have their own playback centers. Those who did not, necessarily had to rely on other companies to have their data interpreted and processed.[21] Besides the very high risk of compromise to data confidentiality, this placed a substantial financial burden on such companies.

AGIP Mineraria (ENI's exploration division), for example, employed the US Western Geophysical Company's (WGC) playback center from 1960 to 1961. In 1961, Mineraria's electronics labs were given the task of building a system capable of reading and 'cleaning' magnetic tapes produced by WGC. After company representatives visited the US to choose the best available equipment, Mineraria built its own playback center by purchasing American units and assembling them on its own, an appropriate instance of what could be termed the transnational co-production of hybrid knowledge, as defined by John Krige. The center the company opened in 1962, however, soon proved inadequate, and was only used for a couple of years. It was replaced in 1964 by an analog playback center purchased from the American firm GeoSpace.[22] The operational heart of exploration geophysics moved from the field to these new units. Data interpretation became an activity that could only be performed by personnel specifically trained in the use of the new electronic tools, and a new professional figure, the computer scientist, began to support the work of field geophysicists.[23]

After magnetic recording, a second major breakthrough in data processing came from the introduction of digital techniques. Although military restrictions imposed on the private use of digital electronic computers at the end of World War II delayed geophysical development in this domain, the problems encountered in digital recording for seismology were essentially the same as those encountered, and solved, in related fields such as telemetric data from rockets and satellites, and seismic detection of nuclear tests. In the early 1960s, some of this information on digital techniques was more freely available in the literature. From this time on, therefore, digital computers, simple programming languages such as FORTRAN, and high-speed analog-to-digital converters, allow the rapid conversion of raw seismic data without the intermediate stage of analog recording. This in turn stimulated the growth of digital methods for the processing of geophysical data. Texas Instruments produced the first integrated circuit-based computer for the US Air Force in 1961, and in 1963 commercialized its first digital computer.[24]

Besides being faster than their analog counterparts, digital methods were characterized by greater dynamic range, that is, a larger ratio between the largest and smallest possible values of a changeable quantity, by greater flexibility in signal filtering, and by less noise and distortion in compositing tracks originating from new seismic sources such as weight-droppers and vibrators. These new non-explosive seismic sources brought savings on the cost of explosives and reduced the safety risks to personnel. Computers were also better at automatic plotting and contouring, and for transferring telemetric seismic data from field to playback centers.[25] By the mid-1960s, most oil companies working with digital field recorders were themselves beginning to process the data provided by their contractors.

But although geophysics was progressing at a rapid pace, global geophysical activity started to decline. In fact, the unparalleled increase in geophysical activity for most of the 1950s caused a negative feedback loop in the exploration–discovery–production cycle. To simplify the issue, more exploration had ultimately led to more discoveries, which in turn resulted in increased production, thus reducing the impetus for further exploration, at least in areas where a great deal of exploration had already been done (e.g. not in the North Sea or Libya). This process did not slow down research on geophysical technology. Instead, the effects of forthcoming overproduction made themselves felt in the declining number of crews engaged in exploration proper.

At the same time, the need for companies to remain in the technological vanguard prompted them to invest their funds in the development of new instruments. It is worth stressing that most research and development on new instruments was done in the US whereas, with a few exceptions, European oil companies and geophysical contractors tended to borrow American equipment or use it as a model. So US companies, together with a few European companies such as the French Company for Geophysical Equipment (*Société française de matériel géophysique*, SFMG) and CGG could counterbalance the negative effects of overproduction by restructuring the geophysical prospecting sector. Their European competitors, in general, could not, so had to develop other forms of technical expertise that could be used as bargaining chips in oil agreements. This explains why, for instance, ENI sought partners in the Middle East, North Africa, and Russia, with a view to exchanging crude oil for support in typical midstream services such as pipelining.

In his 1952 report to the Society of Exploration Geophysicists, Gulf Research and Development's executive, Engelhardt Eckhardt, had described the expansion of geophysical operations in 1951 as 'unprecedented' in comparison with previous years. But the trend very soon went into reverse. US-based geophysical exploration activity peaked the following year, and then started to decline (Figure 4.1). Ten years after Eckhardt's report, the number of seismic crews operating in the United States had fallen from 710 to 283. Whereas the *Geophysics* review recorded a marked rise throughout the 1950s in 'Middle Eastern and African' activity, this was only because of the huge expansion in activities in that area.[26]

This decline was deepened once African geophysical activities also plateaued in the early 1960s. The year 1962 saw an overall fall of 32 percent in world geophysical activity, compared with the peak year of 1956 (Figures 4.2 and 4.3). In all areas of the globe, excluding a few parts of Africa and the Soviet Union, geophysical operations seemed to have faded

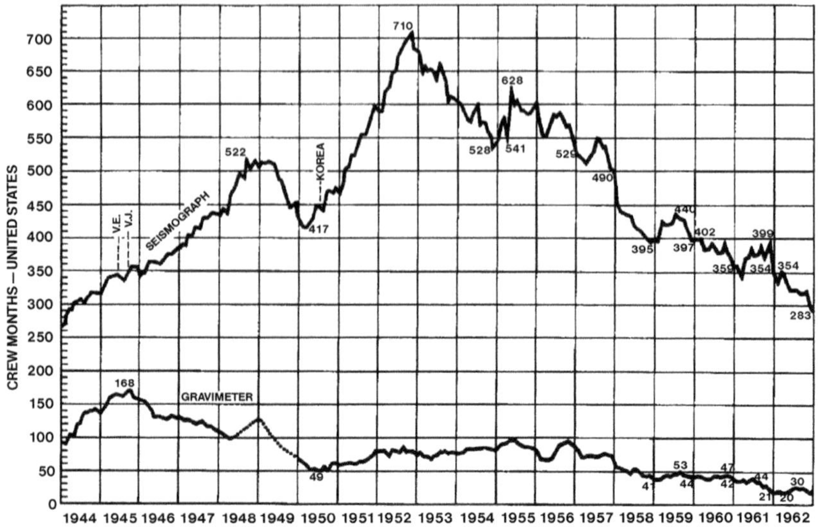

Figure 4.1 Monthly variations in seismograph and gravimeter crew-months in the US.
Source: Courtesy of *Geophysics*.[27]

into the background. By contrast with the rest of the world, however, in the 1950s the Soviet Union geophysical prospecting grew at an incredible pace. In 1958, the USSR was running 758 geophysical crews; as the trend fell in the US, the Soviets had scheduled operations for around 1,200 geophysical crews by 1965.[28]

Another factor that contributed to the general sense of 'doom and gloom' in American oil exploration geophysics was the rise of atomic energy. In 1955, when the downward trend had already started in the US, but had not yet extended to the rest of the world, Paul Lyons, the President of the Society of Exploration Geophysicists, commented: "Already to some extent our old oil finding instruments have given way to the Geiger counter and the scintillometer." He then went on to make the bleak forecast for oil exploration geophysics quoted at the beginning of this chapter.[29]

However, Lyons acknowledged that this decline had not primarily been due to atomic energy, but rather to the excessive quantities of oil recently discovered, which in turn had been caused by the "the firstest with the mostest" tactic adopted by oil companies in tackling the exploration of new areas.[30] At the beginning of the exploration era in many new territories, the companies that were the quickest to obtain concessions and employ large numbers of technologically advanced seismographs or gravimeters, had the greatest chance of prospecting for large oil-bearing structures that responded easily to geophysical measurements. This had resulted in a feverish rush to yet uncharted zones.

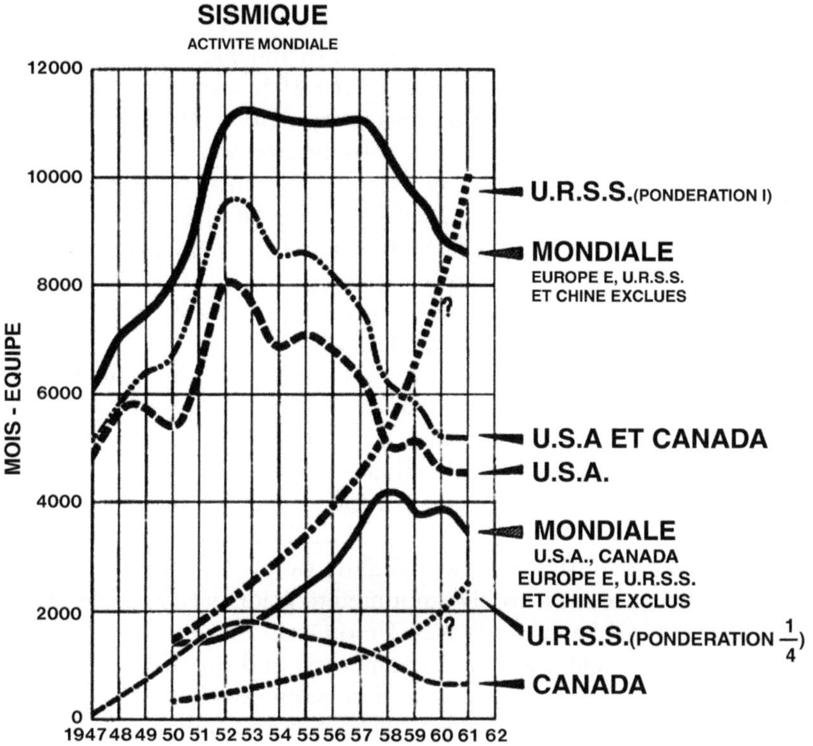

Figure 4.2 World seismic activity #1 (1947–1962).
Source: Courtesy of the European Association of Geoscientists and Engineers, EAGE.[31]

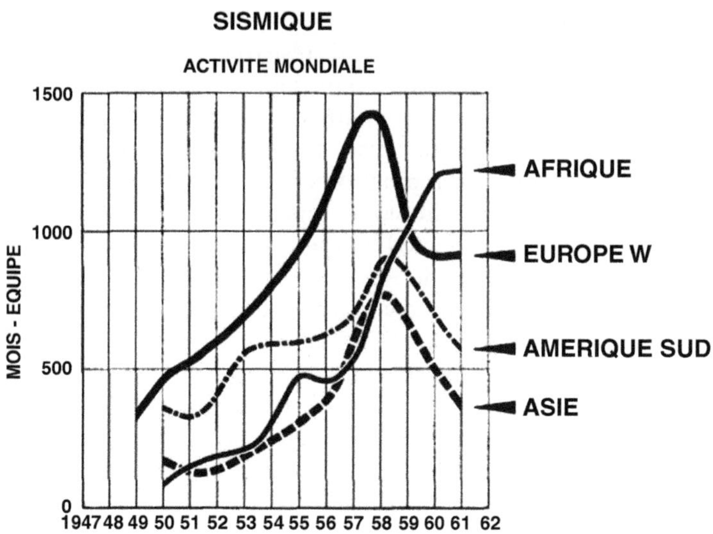

Figure 4.3 World seismic activity #2 (1949–1961).
Source: Courtesy of the European Association of Geoscientists and Engineers, EAGE.[32]

This *modus operandi*, characteristic of the United States in the early days of exploration, was now being applied by independent companies, especially in Africa. In the second half of the 1950s, in a few parts of the Sahara desert, and in Algeria and Libya in particular, exploration was taking place at a fantastically rapid rate, with hundreds of crews operating on the ground, employing advanced or even experimental prospecting instruments. Francesco Guidi, former Chief Geophysicist of ENI's Libyan affiliate, gives an idea of the massive level of technological competition between oil companies swarming into Libya: "[I]n the 1960s [Libya] had the highest concentration of world exploration outside the US. Around 40 seismic groups and 80 drilling plants operated there."[33]

Italian and French companies were no exception to the general decline. Their exploration activities dwindled as oil became increasingly available (Figures 4.4 and 4.5). In its 1958 annual report, the BRP lamented a sudden halt in the increase in geophysical activities, and a marked fall in revenues. However, the scale of the French slowdown was different to that of the Italians, as the diagrams show. At its peak, BRP's activity reached around 850 crew-months; AGIP's peak was slightly over 200.[34] By the late 1950s CGG, thanks to what essentially amounted to priority rights over geophysical prospecting in the entire French Union, had become Europe's largest geophysical firm (excluding Soviet companies) and the third largest in the world. This was unrivalled by any Italian geophysical agency. In fact, the striking contrast in the development of French and Italian geophysics can be explained by several structural circumstances.

In Chapters 1 and 2 I highlighted how important difference existed in the consideration given by both countries' elites to the development of autonomous technoscientific research. In the French case, technoscientific prowess was seen as a fundamental way of re-establishing the country's greatness, and stimulated geophysical research correspondingly.[35] The Italian Parliament, however, firmly opposed any increase in expenditure on research, seeing it as one among many factors affecting public spending, which was perceived as the main cause of inflation.[36] In general, the Italian scientific industry, while developing expertise in sectors such as mechanics, chemistry, and rubber technology, especially in the twenty years between 1950 and 1970, was affected by the limited role of innovation in the country's economic development. According to historian Renato Giannetti, Italy remained essentially a country of technology importers, imitators, and tinkerers, rather than innovators.[37]

A further difference lay in the attention paid to applied geophysics. While France was home to CGG and had strong links with US-based well-logging giant Schlumberger, Italy had no national firms of equivalent status in prospecting innovation. The Hexagon could benefit from elite technical education and professional corps such as the *École Polytechnique* and the *Corps des mines*, whose important role in the training and management of oil institutions I have already demonstrated.[38] In addition, the actions of the French Petroleum Institute (IFP) provided a strong backbone for

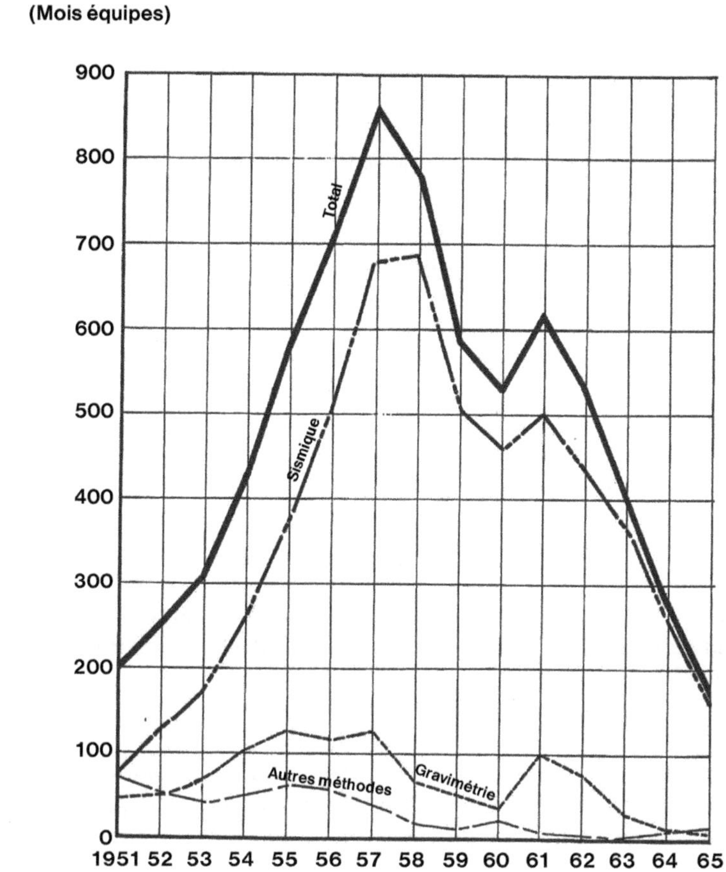

Figure 4.4 The BRP and affiliates: geophysical activity (number of crew-months) in the franc zone (1951–1965).

Source: Courtesy of Archives Historiques du Groupe ELF/Total.[39]

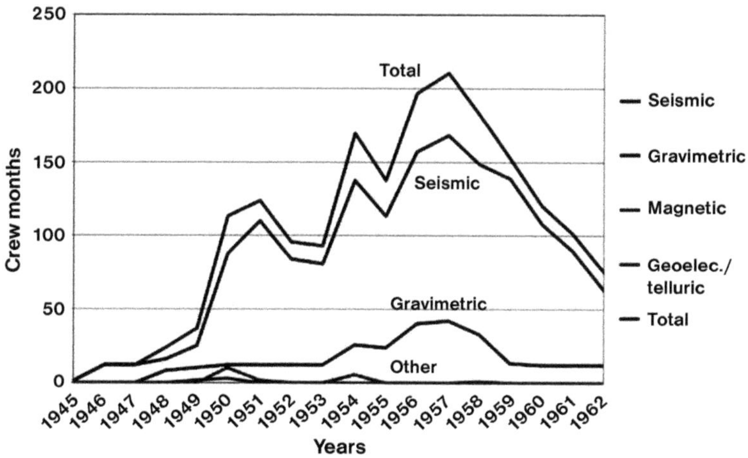

Figure 4.5 AGIP and affiliates: geophysical activity (1945–1962).[40]

oil-related research. In contrast, by the early 1960s there were only two chairs of applied geophysics in Italy—in Rome and Trieste—and, among the remaining academic institutes, only the Lerici Foundation, affiliated to Milan's Polytechnical University, carried out its own studies in oil exploration, mostly for ENI.

The poor status of applied geophysics in Italy was bitterly summed up in 1963 by Lerici's Director, Luigi Solaini, in his opening speech for the inauguration of the ENI School's academic year. So far, he argued, Italian contributions to applied geophysics had been rather modest, with a few exceptions. While in theoretical studies the position of Italian research was not too weak, this was not case in the development of geophysical equipment, which required financial resources unavailable to university institutes. Italy could not aspire to a prominent position in this sphere because of the supremacy of US constructors in the manufacture and development of exploration machineries, and because of a weak internal market.[41] However, Solaini believed that special tools could be made, existing tools studied, and modifications of some significance carried out by a well-equipped laboratory even in the absence of large financial resources. Italian scholars would have the opportunity to dedicate themselves successfully to this second kind of activity.[42]

The Lerici Director's view of Italian geophysical institutions was bleak:

> National geophysical centers are non-existent. The National Geophysical Institute does not work with applied science; the geophysical section of the Italian Geological Service has derisory resources and staff, and confines itself to performing a few surveys, but does not commit to research.[43]

That was not completely true, as the Italian Geophysical Institute did commit to research in seismology. However, it focused mainly on earthquake seismology, not oil and gas exploration, as an examination of *Annals of Geophysics*, the Institute's review, reveals.[44] Furthermore, the institute operated with limited funds, forcing it—especially in the early postwar years—to focus on surveys and the mapping of key geophysical features, casting aside specific studies on natural resources. ENI, and in particular its affiliate the Italian Public Limited Company for Drilling and Installations (*Società anonima italiana perforazioni e montaggi*, SAIPEM), founded in 1956, did contribute to technological innovation in exploration, even becoming the European leader in some specific subfields such as the construction of pipelines and marine platforms for drilling operations, but it did not deal with geophysical prospecting proper.

On the French side, CGG had developed to industrial scale by the early 1960s, expanding to a broad range of countries and mastering an extensive range of techniques. After the early years of technological dependency on US equipment, French administrations and CGG engaged in creating a French research and development sector capable of producing innovative technology. SFMG was set up by CGG in 1956 to develop French-built electronic materials, in particular magnetic recorders. It was thus able to achieve some autonomy from American manufacturers. The French geophysical industry could therefore eventually count on its own electronic instrumentation for geophysics. SFMG soon commercialized the first French-made transistorized amplifiers for reflection and refraction seismology.[45]

In the late 1950s, CGG also developed its own radio-location procedure for marine seismological studies, *Toran*. Still in marine studies, in 1966 IFP patented an innovative seismic source of its own, *Flexotir*, and equipped a number of CGG ships with it.[46] In a way then, France's diminished geophysical activity in terms of crew months and personnel was counterbalanced by the internationalization of the French prospecting industry, which started exporting its own technological products, thus fulfilling one of the functions originally planned by Charles de Gaulle and Pierre Guillaumat for the rebirth of France as a great technoscientific power.

Efforts were also deployed to establish a France-based training institute for oil technicians within IFP. In 1954, the National Higher School for Petroleum and Engines (*École nationale supérieure du pétrole et des moteurs*) was created. It maintained close links with Fuels Directorate and the Ministry of Industry, and its teachers, besides working as consultants within the Institute's central scientific department, also liaised with universities. Constant exchanges between geophysical manufacturing companies and the Institute's engineers facilitated the development and commercialization of new equipment.[47] Notwithstanding such progress in technological developments, by the early 1960s it looked as if the era of expansion in French and Italian geophysical exploration activities was over. The looming midstream shift materialized in 1960, with ENI's Soviet contracts.

The Contracts That Threatened the Western Bloc

By 1960 Egypt was the only other country where ENI was extracting oil. It provided 1.9 Mt of crude oil per year out of ENI's total production of 2.5 Mt.[48] The lack of further oil findings of the same magnitude prompted the company to reassess its supply strategy; immediate availability of oil was prioritized over long-term exploration programs. This led first to the signing of contracts between ENI and the Soviet public monopoly, *Soyuznefteexport* (SNE), and later to agreements with American majors. Everybody who has written about ENI underlines the significance of a big agreement signed in October 1960 between ENI and SNE, although Bagnato has emphasized that this was only a further step in a trade that had started much earlier. Since the end of 1958, ENI had agreed to import crude oil in exchange for goods and services. The first of these contracts bartered oil for synthetic rubber produced by the ENI affiliate, the National Agency for Fuel Hydrogenation (ANIC), under a license owned by Phillips Petroleum.[49]

In late 1958 ENI's President, Enrico Mattei, secretly met a number of government officials in Moscow, including SNE's President, Evgeniy Gurov, and consolidated the group's relations with the Soviet company. For ENI, 1958 also marked the beginning of trade relations with another important pawn on the geopolitical chessboard: Mao Zedong's China. In 1958, Mattei secretly visited the Far Eastern country, whose government had not been recognized by either the Italian government or the UN as a result of American pressure. This visit would culminate three years later in ENI's first Chinese trade agreement.[50] Transactions between Italy and the Soviet Union did not stop even when the Italian Premier, Amintore Fanfani, decided to accommodate US intermediate-range ballistic missiles on Italian territory, although the Soviets complained loudly. Historian Leopoldo Nuti has argued that the Italian government looked favorably on the deployment of US missiles in Italy, as it would give Italy "a nuclear status of some sort and would enhance its national prestige."[51] However, Fanfani's decision was a clear statement of the dependence of Italian security on American goodwill, and was not welcomed by diplomats such as Pietro Quaroni, then Italian Ambassador in West Germany, who lamented Christian Democrat passivity in the face of American diktats. According to Soviet newspaper *Sovetskaja Rossija*, he declared: "We are simply [US] satellites, and nothing else."[52]

As a result of ENI's politically risky policies, US and French diplomats (as well as their foreign intelligence services, the CIA and SDECE) kept the Italian company under surveillance, updating their governments about it in a number of secret reports. The French contended that an Italian–Soviet agreement on oil would be highly dangerous. Italy could process Soviet crude oil in its refineries, relabel its products as Italian, and export them to the Common Market, thus undermining sales of French oil from Algeria to Western Europe.[53]

Mattei's travels to Moscow prompted Fanfani's visit to the US Embassy in Rome, where Ambassador James Zellerbach cautioned him that Mattei's acts cast doubt on the Italian government's alignment with NATO objectives. Fanfani argued that although Mattei's behavior was risky, he had no means of stopping state companies from trading.[54] But if he could not do it, who else could have? Fanfani himself must have known that his explanations were not wholly convincing. His argument suggested a deliberate refusal to stop the ENI President's initiatives.

A year later, in November 1959, Giuseppe Ratti, ENI's marketing adviser, met US Embassy staff. In a conversation with the Embassy's First Secretary, Albert Nyren, he described ENI's contacts with the Soviet Bloc. Nyren stated that Ratti had "always been friendly and open to the Embassy representatives." Ratti confirmed ENI–SNE contacts, while clarifying that his company's future purchases would depend on the price offered by the Soviets and on the opportunities offered to Italian firms to sell their goods in return.[55] By the end of 1959, negotiations for the one contract that would cause a scandal in the oil world were already ongoing, and it is hard to believe that Ratti was not aware of the prospective increase in ENI's oil imports from the USSR.

However, Ratti was operating in a climate of uncertainty. Fanfani's government, disposed to an opening to the Socialists, had fallen in January 1959, and the Christian Democrat party was now controlled by its right wing. The new leadership was hostile to statism, and this threatened Fanfani's and President Giovanni Gronchi's Neo-Atlanticist project of asserting a degree of autonomy from the US in foreign policy, a project also endorsed by Mattei.[56] Without government support, ENI needed to show a favorable attitude to American diplomats, so as to avoid the consequences of Fanfani's fall and the subsequent changes in government attitude. To sum up, it may be presumed that Ratti was using his friendly relations with the US Embassy to buy time, dispel Americans' concerns, and misrepresent ENI's oily deals with the Soviets.

Although the signing of the October 1960 deal by Mattei and the Soviet Minister of Foreign Trade, Nikolai Patolichev, was not surprising, its size undoubtedly was. The Soviets undertook to sell ENI 11 Mt of crude and 1 Mt of fuel oil over four years (1961 to 1964). ENI would provide the Soviets with technological products such as synthetic rubber, steel pipes, and equipment for pipelines.[57] The overall deal was worth $100 million in each direction. While contemporary American commentators highlighted the consequences of such an agreement for the majors' oil market in Italy, historian Jaroslav Polach saw it, and more broadly the whole Soviet oil offensive, as a means to undermine the attractiveness of nuclear energy for European countries.[58] Western Europe's dependence on Soviet oil would give the USSR greater negotiating power, concomitantly reducing the influence the US had achieved thanks to its predominant position in nuclear technoscience.

In February 1961, ENI signed a further commercial protocol, which incorporated the earlier deal, and covered the period from 1962 to 1965. Italy would import 21.4 Mt of crude oil over the next five years and 700 thousand tons (kt) of fuel oil per year. The Soviets accepted that these provisions would be reviewed if increases in Italian consumption led to a corresponding rise in the amount of Soviet oil, and agreed to respect a limit of 14 percent of Italy's total imports. An interesting aspect of the new deal was the Italians' contract to build eight oil tankers for the Russians, which was the largest ever signed by the Soviet company *Sudoimport*, whether with European or non-European countries, and triggered criticism from Washington.[59]

Incidentally, two months before the Italian contract, the Soviets had also signed an important barter contract with West Germany, involving steel producers from the Ruhr region. The exchange value was double that of the 1960 ENI–SNE agreement. West German trade with the USSR rose from $196.5 million in 1959 to $401.5 million in 1962. Among German exports to the USSR were plants for chemical and extractive industries, iron and steel products, ships, and large-diameter pipes. Among its imports were crude oil and oil products.[60]

The CIA was alarmed that the Soviets' successful strategy of exporting oil had a powerful symbolic significance that could affect US national security. The Soviet system, by "beating Western private enterprise in competitive markets, would be used as an example of the Soviet system winning out over the American system."[61] But one of the reasons most frequently stated by Italian officials for buying oil from the USSR was the necessity of sourcing energy from abroad. France and Germany could count on large domestic resources of coal; Italy depended almost totally on oil. Moreover, ENI's production was not sufficient for growing national energy needs.[62] But it was exactly this reliance on Soviet imports that made the Italian–Soviet deal appear as a greater threat to Western security than the German trade agreements. It was only too logical that ENI's trading with the Soviets would soon bring the Italian company to the attention of transnational organizations. In Chapter 5, I will show how NATO and the EEC established ad hoc committees to study the impact of Soviet oil imports on Western economic and military security, and to prevent further trade.

With regard to bilateral American–Italian relations, in March 1961 Kennedy's Ambassador at Large, William Harriman, flew to Rome to meet Italian government officials and party leaders. Hoping to exert pressure on ENI's next moves, he also met Mattei, with the sole result of having to endure the tycoon's tirade on how it had been Western companies' blind, short-term profit policy that had induced ENI's Soviet deal. In the same month, work started on a pipeline that ENI intended to build, connecting Italy to Switzerland: the Central European Line (CEL). Laying this pipeline seemed to constitute the first step toward what most West European governments, NATO and the oil majors feared most, namely Soviet oil flooding the West European market via Italy.[63] ENI's midstream shift thus took a form that troubled US officials. Security concerns were no longer exclusively associated with outsourcing oil, but also with its transport and distribution. The ENI case was a clear demonstration of this, as more intelligence about the Italian company's purchases was amassed in France, the UK, and the US, and more diplomats considered how to prevent an expansion of Soviet influence in oil deals in Western Europe.

Like Italian relations with Middle Eastern and North African countries, Italy's contacts with the Soviets were part of a strategy of international expansion. By July 1960 Fanfani was back in his seat as Prime Minister, and Mattei knew he could count on him. He had a further ally in the Italian Ambassador in Moscow, Luca Pietromarchi. Fanfani and Pietromarchi were sponsoring a general commercial détente with the USSR, and ENI was not just a part of this, it was the leading edge. The entire Italian industry—ENI was not alone in this respect—felt that it was constrained by exclusively Western alliances, and was missing out on an incredible opportunity to enter an untapped market.[64] Similar expansionist aspirations had also emerged in moves by ENI and other large Italian enterprises in North Africa.

In addition, the Soviet dealings squared with Fanfani and Mattei's Neo-Atlanticist policy. Only by establishing itself as a bridge between the West and non-Western countries, be they Arab producers or the Soviet Union, could Italy aspire to an independent role in the Atlantic setting, and avoid international marginalization. Under the US's wing, it did receive protection, but at the high cost of neutralizing its own autonomy in foreign policy.[65] From the Soviet perspective, deals with the Italians were part of a plan launched by Soviet First Secretary Nikita Khrushchev in May 1958. Khrushchev sought to strengthen the Soviet chemical industry and the production of plastics with the help of foreign technicians, machinery, and capital. This is why the Soviet government approached not only Italy, but West Germany and the UK as well; it also planned collaboration with US industries.[66]

Anticipating accusations against ENI in the following months, the *New York Times* warned of the consequences of the Soviet agreement for Italy's position regarding the security of the Western world, while also raising questions about the effectiveness of Italy's contribution in the event of an international crisis.[67] The dangers arising from dependency on Soviet oil were always highlighted in the American press, as well as in NSC and State Department reports: for example, the Russians might abruptly decide to interrupt deliveries following unfavorable political decisions by Western Bloc governments. Soviet dependency on Western technology, however, was largely neglected; discontinuing exports would have deprived the Eastern giant of part of its industrial power. This reason, more than any other, made the interruption of supplies unlikely.

When French diplomats were made aware of the negotiations over the ENI–SNE agreement, they protested to Italy, but ENI responded with a short memorandum defending itself on economic grounds, and turned the accusations back on the French on technical grounds. ENI maintained that Soviet crude oil had characteristics more suited to the needs of Italian refiners and the national consumption structure, in comparison with Saharan crude. The French, the memorandum continued, were trying to politicize a justifiable technical and economic issue, so as to favor their Algerian crude.[68] But ENI's plans also endangered British interests. In early 1959 Mattei had taken initial steps toward the expansion of ENI's distribution activities in the UK, where he aimed to conquer a quarter of the distribution market using Soviet oil. However, this threatened the embargo that the British had barely managed to push through parliament. Confronted with BP and Shell's skepticism about Mattei, the British Ambassador in Rome, Ashley Clarke, reiterated his proposal that they begin talks with him. ENI and its President were not, in the Ambassador's view, "passing phenomena which [would] conveniently disappear if the British Oil Companies avoid[ed] looking at them."[69]

However, Assistant Undersecretary at the Foreign Office, Roger Jackling, replied that it was too early for companies to make life easier for ENI. If British companies came to terms with it, it would only encourage the

Italians to continue using their aggressive strategy, and escalate their demands on the majors. Moreover, ENI's growing dependency on the Russians might be a source of embarrassment for the Italian government in regard to its Western allies, and had also been very coldly received at the Second Arab Petroleum Congress held in Beirut in mid-October.[70] Things would fall into place by themselves, Jackling thought, due to ENI's overstretched and hazardous tactics.

ENI's expansionist attitude, which was already being manifested in North Africa, also worried the French Ambassador in Rome, Gaston Palewski. When in late 1959 the Italian President, Gronchi, was invited by Khrushchev to visit the USSR, Palewski was not so much anxious about an Italian–Russian political rapprochement, as he was of the fact that Gronchi could become a beachhead for ENI's plans.[71] Anxieties expressed by diplomats with respect to the Soviet oil offensive were substantiated after the signature of ENI–SNE contracts in mid-1961, when Gurov declared to a Soviet journal that the USSR meant to demolish the edifice the majors had built:

> It should be borne in mind that oil concessions represent the foundation of the entire edifice of western political influence in the [less developed] world, of all military bases and aggressive blocs. If this foundation cracks, the entire edifice may begin to totter and then come tumbling down.[72]

While US security and government authorities were trying to keep a low profile on the issue of Soviet oil, and prevent their anxieties from leaking beyond their offices, the Soviets were blatantly broadcasting's their intentions. As a consequence, in July an alarmed Harry Kern, the Director of the US review *Foreign Reports*, circulated a memorandum to top policy officials in the State Department and to the West German Chancellor, Konrad Adenauer. The document advocated an oil embargo against the USSR as a retaliation measure against its stance on the Berlin crisis, which the Soviet government had opened in June by issuing an ultimatum demanding the withdrawal of Western armed forces from West Berlin. The embargo, Kern suggested, would only end once the Soviet accepted "normal standards" in the marketing of their petroleum products.[73]

Kern further advised that Adenauer, in declaring the oil embargo, should point out that it was being put into effect not only because of the Berlin issue but also in the interests of Arab producing countries. Adenauer should therefore ask these countries to associate themselves in solidarity with the defense of Berlin. An association of some Afro—Asian countries would be essential at the UN, especially at a time when these countries were receiving no support from the West in key international disputes such as the Bizerte affair.[74] However, State Secretary Dean Rusk did not look favorably on Kern's proposal. A Soviet oil embargo was not discarded, but NATO authorities, to which the memorandum had also been forwarded, believed it was too early to declare it. Kern's proposal was a further indication of the influence of pragmatist dynamics in energy security. Economic interests were often camouflaged under a political cover, and the Berlin crisis was used as a convenient excuse to justify a long-sought embargo on Soviet oil.

American anxieties were clearly expressed in two documents produced by the US Senate in 1961 and 1962 respectively: *Soviet Oil in the Cold War* and *Problems raised by the Soviet oil offensive*. In these studies, Halford Hoskins, a senior specialist in international relations, and Leon Herman, an analyst of Soviet economics, warned that Soviet exports to foreign countries constituted "a political hand that has worn the economic glove."[75] They maintained that if the Italian attitude spread throughout Western Europe, more countries would divert part of their oil imports from the majors to the USSR, thus reducing the revenues of American, British, Dutch, and French international companies. In *Problems raised by the Soviet oil offensive*, Hoskins went further to provide various examples of a Soviet oil offensive in several countries in Asia, Africa, and Europe, and their consequences. As for Italy, he warned that ENI's policy was intended to eliminate as many foreign companies from the Italian market as possible.[76]

In 1957, Willard Thorp, the prominent American economist, had forecast: "It does not now appear that the new programs will place the Soviet Union in a position within the next few years to take over political control through economic domination."[77] Not many in Western governments seemed to believe his argument in 1962, and it is doubtful they had, even before.[78] The Soviet plan to build an extended network of pipelines from Russian oilfields to the rest of the Eastern Bloc did nothing to appease Western governments. Nor did ENI's plans to build a pipeline to connect Italy's Adriatic Sea terminal to a city 65 km away from one of the terminals on the Soviet system, Vienna. Pipelines became the new bone of contention in the administration of security matters.

Battling on Pipelines, Compromising on Their Content

In light of recent oil availability, there was little doubt about the strategy Italian and French companies should now follow. While both countries' oil administrators redirected oil exploration toward less-charted zones, building pipelines became their main objective. For CFP and the BRP, this meant connecting Algerian oilfields to the European continent. For ENI, it meant connecting Italian terminals where Italy received its Egyptian—and especially its Soviet—oil, to the industrial areas of Central Europe. But this plan was anathema to both Anglo–Dutch–American majors and French oil companies, as it would strip them of their European market. They decided therefore to counteract it by laying their own pipeline, the South European Pipeline (SEPL), to connect France to Germany.

ENI's interest in pipelines had already emerged in late 1959, during Gronchi's visit to the USSR. A comprehensive agreement between the Italian company and the Soviet authorities enabled ENI to build a pipeline connecting East Germany and the USSR. The French and US governments had promptly been informed of the news by their secret services. The pipeline was expected to pave the way for future deals with the Eastern Bloc, involving further pipeline construction and Italian offers of drilling equipment and technical assistance. The implementation of Mattei's project was depicted as a dramatic security threat to the Western Bloc, as the very possibility of having an oil terminal in East Germany might sooner or later lead to its being connected to West Germany, thus initiating a Soviet oil invasion.[79]

While publicly offering no comments on this issue, American diplomats displayed their disquiet in a confidential State Department meeting, in the presence of the Italian Ambassador in Paris, Manlio Brosio. The pipeline, US officials admonished, was one of the pillars of the Soviet Seven Year Plan, and the Italians were making a significant contribution to its fulfillment. As a consequence Brosio was instructed to apply pressure on his government, and the pipeline agreement was never finalized. ENI eventually supplied certain pumping and auxiliary equipment, while the plan to provide technical assistance toward installing the pipelines was dropped.[80]

While ENI participation in building the East German pipeline was cancelled, by 1960 the Italian company had already started working on the project for a pipeline from Genoa in northwest Italy to Aigle, in Switzerland, the previously mentioned CEL. Endowed with a final capacity of 12 Mt, CEL was scheduled to complete by the end of 1961, and intended to branch to the industrial areas of Lombardy in northern Italy. An extension was also proposed to the south German area of Bavaria at Ingolstadt, near Munich. To understand how this project developed, we need to take a step back. In May 1959, Mattei had persuaded the Bavarian State Minister for Transport and Economic Affairs, Otto Schedl, of the project's viability, with the help of Hjalmar Schacht, the former President of the Nazi *Reichsbank*, and one of Mattei's personal friends. The pipeline was to be built by an equal joint venture between ENI and a German banking consortium, including a bank run by Schacht.[81]

Possibly as a further reward for Schacht's mediation, in August 1959 Mattei had proposed to the German businessman, together with the Japanese petrochemical industrialist, Keisuke Idemitsu, the signature of a secret agreement on the exploitation of the Qum area in Iran. However, in the face of opposition from the National Iranian Oil Company, the project had been dropped.[82] It is, nevertheless, easy to imagine the diplomatic consequences of the conclusion of an Italian–German–Japanese agreement, mediated by the Nazi regime's former highest banking authority.

Aware of the disruption that SEPL would mean for ENI's plans, the company executives understood that without the support of the majors, the CEL project would be outcompeted. On the other hand, by acquiring their backing, they might stem the implementation of SEPL. Mattei therefore initially proposed that SONJ should join ENI in building the pipeline and two refineries in Switzerland and Germany, in return for purchases of refined products. He also gave his word that if the American major joined, the pipeline would not carry Russian oil, and that he would drop a lawsuit he had started against SONJ over two refineries the American major and ENI jointly managed in Italy.[83]

However, SONJ refused, as it had already given consent to CFP and other majors for SEPL. This would begin in southern France, at Lavéra, and end in Karlsruhe, Germany, in Western Europe's main industrial zone. Like ENI's project, an extension was also planned to Bavaria (Figure 4.6).[84] This second pipeline, however, and especially its Bavarian link, would inevitably deprive the port of Genoa of the traffic ENI's pipeline was designed to intercept. SONJ's refusal incensed Mattei, who threatened an all-out war on international oil companies. The risk that such a declaration might have dangerous ramifications was rather high, according to US Ambassador Zellerbach. Indeed after a period of conflict with Italian Premier Antonio Segni, who had succeeded Fanfani in February 1959, Mattei had come to terms with him, and Segni was once again supportive of ENI's plans.[85] In July 1960, on the eve of Fanfani's reappointment as premier, Brosio, commenting on the pipeline project, recorded in his personal diary that Mattei now revealed "a violent hatred" of the Americans.[86]

One considerable difficulty in implementing the CEL project was of a legal and territorial nature. The pool of majors that was planning SEPL only needed the authorization of France and West Germany to lay their pipeline. French approval was taken for granted, considering CFP's interest in the project. As for West German acquiescence, this seemed to be guaranteed by the presence of a number of small oil companies in the consortium. ENI, on the other hand, not only needed the approval of the Germans, but also of the Swiss and Austrians. Getting authorizations from these countries involved a lengthy process, especially in the case of Switzerland, where federal administrative procedures further complicated the situation. Legal disputes with the cantonal and federal governments further delayed procedures, as did the Swiss government's concern that the pipeline would carry Soviet oil, a subject on which ENI executives had maintained an ambiguous stance. Protests also arose in Austria over the risk of water pollution. German communities residing on Lake Constance blocked the project for several months.[87]

As mentioned in the last section, ENI's technical services were also planning a pipeline that would run from the Adriatic port of Trieste to Vienna. This project was a further source of anxiety not only for the oil majors but, as I will show in the next chapter, also for NATO and the EEC. The pipe might easily be linked to Bratislava, where the Soviets planned to establish the Czechoslovakian terminal of their pipeline system. Starting from the Ural–Volga oilfields, the European branch of the Soviet system was projected to branch into a northern line serving Poland and East Germany, and a southern line serving Hungary and Czechoslovakia. The short distance

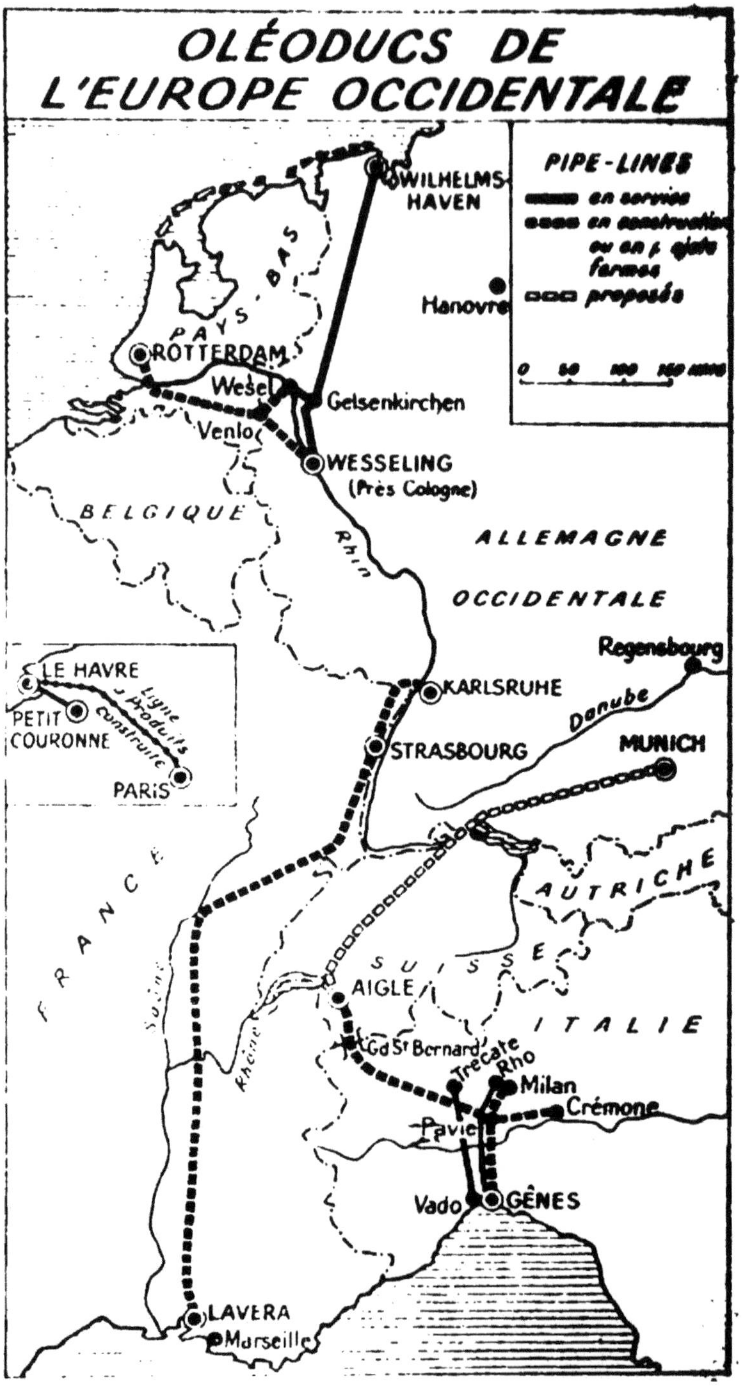

Figure 4.6 West European pipelines operating or under construction in 1960.
Source: Courtesy of *Petroleum Economist*.[88]

between Vienna and Bratislava made the project a threat for supplies of Middle Eastern oil delivered by the majors.[89]

The Swiss newspaper, *Neue Zürcher Zeitung*, argued in June 1961 that from a geographical viewpoint the Soviet project contained elements that made it more enticing than a continued commitment to the majors' Middle Eastern oil, transported through the Mediterranean. The proximity of Sweden and the Netherlands to the Baltic port of Klaipėda, where another terminal of the Soviet European pipeline was to be built, would make the Soviet pipeline a constant temptation for countries belonging to the Western Bloc, thanks to the savings its use would allow. Moreover, oil could easily be carried from the Baltic port to West Germany by rail. On top of that, by linking the Soviet pipeline to ENI's planned pipeline, Soviet oil could reach the Mediterranean though a new outlet, and thence be exported by tanker to areas already supplied by British and American majors in Southern Europe, thus increasing the quantities that were already being delivered from the Soviet Union via the Black Sea.[90]

In 1961, work started on the Genoa–Ingolstadt pipeline. Contrary to the original plan, however, in which the pipeline was scheduled to open by 1963, high costs, frequent conflicts with local and national authorities, and environmental problems, postponed the completion of CEL to 1966, with a considerable time lag on SEPL, which was instead laid at a fantastic speed, and operative from 1962–1963. As for the Trieste-Vienna pipeline, the project was approved only in 1963. The laying of the Transalpine Pipeline, as it would be called, was eventually to include a number of majors beside ENI. It was commissioned in 1967, while its extension to Vienna had to wait until 1970 to become operational.

All these initiatives are a clear indication of the prominent role that pipelines acquired at the turn of the decade in Cold War Europe. Did the majors sponsor SEPL because of the threat ENI's projects posed to them? They probably did (prompted especially by French needs to move their Algerian oil to industries in Central Europe and, through a restoration of cordial relations with the majors) recover quickly from the international diplomatic turmoil resulting from events in Algeria. ENI's projects greatly speeded up the majors' project and the 'pipelinization' of Western Europe. While ENI was leading the battle on pipelines with the oil majors, the latter were attempting to reach a compromise with the Italians regarding their massive purchases of Soviet oil. In fact, it could be argued that, if one of the aims of the ENI administrators in purchasing Soviet oil was to attract the attention of the majors and acquire ENI a place within the international oil arena, they were successful. By mid-1961, but especially from early 1962, the State Department was already persuaded that ENI and its president should be dealt with, and that firstly the American government, and then US oil companies, should reach an agreement with Mattei in order to curb his plans.

So in March 1962 some of the most important personalities in Kennedy's administration, including Undersecretary of State George Ball, and the

President's Special Assistant, Arthur Schlesinger, met to discuss the problems the Italian company and its combative president were causing. US Ambassador in Italy, George Frederick Reinhardt, reassured the other participants that in the coming years the Soviet oil share in Italy's consumption would decrease. Thus, even if ENI continued its Soviet imports, it would also diversify its supplying strategy, and be less dependent on SNE.[91] However, ENI's current line of action still went against US oil interests. The Special Assistant to Secretary of State Dean Rusk, Theodore Achilles, suggested two possible lines of action: one amounted to what can easily be interpreted as physical elimination ("[W]e could try to get rid of him"); the other, to collaboration ("or we could try to win him over.") Apparently, the second typology of suggestion prevailed.[92]

The view was therefore expressed that contacts be made with Walter Levy of SONJ (whom we met in Chapters 1 and 2 as head of the ECA Mission's Petroleum Division) in order to reach an arrangement with the Italian company. A major role in the conclusion of a settlement was played by John McCloy, who was at the same time the President of the Committee of Advisors to the US President for questions regarding disarmament, and a member of a legal practice that managed the interests of a number of oil majors. He liaised between the US government and the majors in oil affairs.[93]

Mattei was invited to negotiate at the US Embassy in Rome in May. He welcomed the change of attitude in the majors toward ENI. When asked by Ball whether he would prefer to deal with Western companies if they offered competitive prices, Mattei said he would, but did not clarify whether he would stop buying Soviet oil.[94] As a result of the State Department's repeated pressure, SONJ eventually reached an agreement with ENI. The Italian company was to purchase large amounts of SONJ's Arabian crude oil in exchange for a similar amount of ENI's Egyptian crude (the former met ENI's domestic requirements far better than the latter).[95] A further agreement with SONJ on Libyan crude followed the ENI–SNE barter model, and a third, larger agreement was signed with Gulf Oil in 1964. The second SONJ deal does not appear in any of the State Department papers, only being reported in a CIA secret report in April 1964. Perhaps SONJ wanted to conceal the agreement, to avoid giving diplomats the impression that their attitude toward ENI was too compliant.[96]

The two SONJ contracts were signed by Mattei's de facto successor, Eugenio Cefis, in the spring of 1963. When the public became aware of the agreement, speculations over Mattei's death and his actions being betrayed by his successor were rampant. However, such interpretations are contradicted by exchanges between the State Department and SONJ officials over the course of 1961 and 1962, and by the novel atmosphere of 'cold peace' between the two companies. There is little doubt, however, that both SONJ and the State Department took advantage of Mattei's demise, believing that doing business with ENI would now become easier.[97] While both British and American companies considered ENI to be the biggest danger in oil trade in the Common Market, the Italian company was certainly not the only one trying to set itself up as a powerful newcomer there. In the wake of their African oil discoveries, CFP and BRP's affiliates also strove to carve a place for French oil in Europe.

Virtues and Vices of Algerian Oil

The fruitful results of prospecting efforts in Algeria, together with Middle Eastern supplies assured by CFP, had guaranteed France a high degree of energy independence by the beginning of the 1960s. As for the former colonies in French Equatorial Africa, while the wave of independence that swept through Africa from the early 1960s on enabled them to officially break free of the colonial power, these separations were more legal than actual. Countries such as Gabon or Niger maintained strong commercial links with France, and it could be argued that the post-independence situation did not significantly alter the technical management of the energy sector.[98] For France, the main consequence of the now high availability of energy sources was the possibility of at last developing national oil autonomy. In order to accomplish this, national oil agencies and companies had to concentrate their security concerns on transport and marketing.

By January 1958, France had already become an oil exporting country, thanks to the gradual completion of a pipeline system from Hassi Messaoud in Algeria to the Mediterranean coast. At first, the oil from this field was carried to the coast at the terminal of Philippeville (today, Skikda) by a dual system involving a small-diameter pipeline and a railway. In late 1959, however, a larger pipeline was opened from Messaoud to the port of Bougie (today, Béjaïa), 250 km west of Philippeville. It was expected to transport 10 Mt per year in 1960, and 14 Mt in 1963.[99] The National Liberation Front (FLN), however, threatened to sabotage the pipeline, and in fact, in January 1959, had already led a successful attack on the small pipeline. As a consequence, an inter-ministerial committee including Prime Minister Michel Debré, members of the secret services, and Pierre Guillaumat—now Minister of Armed Forces—designed a plan to protect oil installations.[100]

As for the other major Algerian oilfield, Edjeleh, its connection to maritime outlets had generated an intra-ministerial dispute back in 1957–1958. It had originally been envisaged to connect Edjeleh to the Hassi Messaoud pipeline system, as the Minister for Algeria, Robert Lacoste, had strongly recommended. It was true, Lacoste admitted at that time, that financial arguments would lead to the Algerian solution being discarded as too expensive, but he felt that, due to crucial political considerations, a Tunisian or Libyan terminal should not be chosen.[101] He emphasized that electing to channel Edjeleh oil through non-French territory would not only be badly received by the Algerian populations, but would also surprise most mainland French citizens. Lacoste was probably alluding to the fact that the French population might see a non-Algerian outlet as a sign of military weakness; since the military were not able to secure a French infrastructure on Algerian territory, they were opting for a safer route. Should his own political considerations not be enough to convince Foreign Minister, Christian Pineau, Lacoste reminded him that National Defense authorities and the Commander-in-Chief of the French Fleet in the Mediterranean (who was also NATO Commander in the Western Mediterranean) had also underlined the inherent problems of a Tunisian or Libyan solution.[102]

Yet an all-Algerian solution, apart from being far costlier, also posed geographical problems. Edjeleh was located around 500 km southeast of Hassi Messaoud across the Grand Erg Oriental ('Great Eastern Sand Sea'). Beyond political and security considerations regarding FLN raids, this was the reason why, disregarding Lacoste's advice, Debré's government decided to link the nearby village of In Amenas to the Tunisian port of Skhira, on the Gulf of Gabès. As we have seen, Tunisian President Habib Bourguiba's undertaking to allow this solution provoked the ire of the FLN leaders, and a breakdown in the Front's friendly relations with the Tunisian leader.[103] From Cairo where he was based, Mohamed Lamine Debaghine, a member of FLN's Coordination and Execution Committee, raged at Bourguiba that any agreement to the construction of a pipeline designed to evacuate Algerian oil via Tunisian territory would be seen as a hostile act. The war that the FLN was fighting, Debaghine contended, was both military and economic, thus it was fundamental to deprive France of the resources it needed to refuel its military. In sum, the FLN viewed Bourguiba's decision as a stab in the back, especially since the Front had obtained considerable support from Tunisia in the past.[104]

The Edjeleh–Skhira pipeline was completed by September 1960, and exports started in the same year. The pipeline's initial flow of 7 Mt per year was soon increased to 12–13 Mt per year. By July 1961, however, Lacoste's warnings concerning a non-Algerian outlet for Edjeleh oil were realized. As a consequence of the Bizerte affair in July 1961, the Tunisians blocked Skhira's port; Edjeleh's Mediterranean outlet was rendered unusable. The Ministry for the Sahara had another pipeline branch hastily laid from the new oilfield of Ohanet, discovered in 1960, to the Hassi Messaoud area, which was completed by the end of 1961.[105] As Ohanet was only about 100 km from In Amenas, in the Edjeleh area, it would therefore be easy to link with CREPS's oilfields, thus connecting Edjeleh to the pipeline from Hassi Messaoud to Bougie in northern Algeria, providing an alternative outlet to Skhira. Indeed, by the end of the Algerian War, this connection had been finalized (Figure 4.7).[106] Besides the need to meet French energy demand and make the country more independent of foreign sources, from 1961 increases in Algerian oil production were also dictated by the French government's awareness that the Sahara might be lost. It thus became mandatory to try and extract as much oil as possible before the situation irreparably changed.

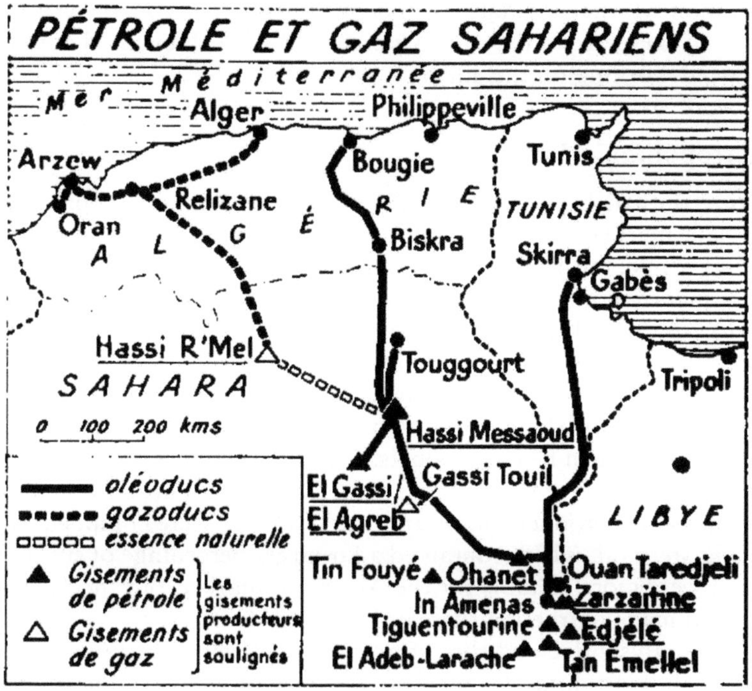

Figure 4.7 The Algerian pipeline system in 1962.
Source: Courtesy of *Petroleum Economist*.[107]

The Edjeleh and Hassi Messaoud oilfields, geographer John Clarke reported in 1960, were "of tremendous importance to France," as their combined production would exceed 20 Mt by 1963, almost meeting French annual consumption.[108] Moreover, Algerian oil would be paid for in francs, thus avoiding significant expenditure of foreign currency. Nevertheless, marketing Saharan oil was not going to be simple, despite the geographical advantage of Algerian oilfields being closer to European markets than those in the Middle East, meaning lower freight costs. The oil-bearing rocks of Algerian oilfields were less porous, which made extraction harder; oil was found at greater depths and it needed to be carried from Algeria's internal territories to the coast. These circumstances all entailed higher extraction and transportation costs. According to the US rule for assessing exploration expenses, a 'barrel in the ground' from the Middle East would cost 4 or 5¢, in Algeria 21 to 27¢.[109]

Although with Algeria being French territory, supplies were in principle less affected by political turmoil than those from the Middle East; France was in the middle of a war, so reassurances about greater security amounted to nothing. Despite all these impediments, French companies might still be able to market oil in Europe by taking advantage of the political benefits of Common Market regulations and of the fact that Algeria was part of France and therefore of the same Common Market. French oil administrators started working on this idea.

A 'Metropolitan' Market

Now that oil had been found, it was crucial for French companies to secure a safe market. The geographically most appropriate appeared to be Western Europe, but ENI's Soviet contracts risked upsetting the apple cart. In consequence, French governmental and corporate agents were firmly opposed to ENI's CEL project. Although they hid this opposition under a 'red scare' cloak, no one in the oil industry doubted for a second what the French agenda was. Another problematic issue was the quality of Saharan oil. Unlike oil from the world's western hemisphere, it was rich in light products and poor in heavy products, making it more suitable for gasoline than fuel oil. Now, not only were the French and European markets in need of heavy oil products, but European refineries were equipped to refine Middle Eastern oil, which contained a far larger percentage of sulfur. Light products were more suitable for the American market, but the 1959 quota system had made marketing there impossible.[110]

French analysts decided that exporting to Western Europe was essential. The Algerian domestic market was only just developing, and possibilities in the African franc zone were limited. As for the French market, it absorbed 23 Mt of oil in 1960, but French production would rise to 30–45 Mt by 1965. The West European market was developing very rapidly, with consumption expected to rise faster than production over the next fifteen years.[111] In the first five months of 1961, 24.3 percent of Saharan oil was sold within the Common Market. However, from 1959, discoveries in Libya made the marketing of this oil harder. Although Libyan fields were smaller and thinner than Algerian ones, they were closer to the coast and shallower, meaning lower extraction and transport costs. Soviet oil exports were the cherry on the cake. In December 1959, after ENI had made its significant Soviet oil purchases, the British newspaper *Financial Times* stated that these imports would be a tough blow to French aspirations for their Algerian oil, all the more so as the BRP and CFP had previously applied pressure on Italy to buy their oil instead.[112]

Conversely, a secret SDECE memorandum pointed out that Algerian and Libyan discoveries by British, American, and French companies would hinder the marketing of ENI oil to European and African markets. The majors disposed of large distribution chains in both markets, thus limiting ENI's scope to increase its oil sales. This was why, the intelligence services contended, Mattei was trying to set up a *cordon sanitaire* around the Sahara, Libya, and France, through his agreements with Tunisia, Morocco, and

Libya, in order to guarantee ENI the markets necessary to its expansion.[113] ENI's further, recent expansions in Sudan, Ethiopia, Ghana, and the UK, countries where the company was about to establish—or had already established—distribution chains and refineries, deeply concerned French oil authorities. As did the fact that Netherlands, being a Shell stronghold, would oppose a flow of protected Saharan oil through Western Europe. An unfavorable reaction was also expected from Germany and Belgium, which both had strong coal industries. Therefore, in order to provide outlets for Saharan oil, the French market seemed to be the only option available. It was also the most advantageous choice for France, as Saharan production could be protected under the law of 1928 (see p. 81). It was furthermore appropriately priced, and constituted an important counterweight, in terms of the trade balance between Algeria and France, to French imports and investments.[114]

Once it had been established that Algerian oil would have to be used mainly in France for the time being, another problem arose: how to market it in the Hexagon? French public companies did not own any refining and distribution networks in France: the existing downstream sector was in the hands of British and American majors, and of CFP, which demanded considerable discounts (10 to 15 percent) from the public companies to accept, refine, and distribute the light Algerian oil.[115] For the majors and CFP, being obliged to take Saharan oil was not an enticing prospect, as it would be more expensive than Middle Eastern oil, less suited to the French market, and would affect their profits, with negative consequences on the development of refining and petrochemistry in France.[116] Not to mention the influence CFP had at the Quai d'Orsay for its traditional role as unofficial diplomatic link with the Arab countries. On the other hand, BRP's affiliates could not just go on selling oil below cost to the majors, as they also wanted to make profits.

According to historian Eric Kocher-Marbœuf, the prolonged absence of serious planning for the marketing of Saharan oil, in blatant contrast with the massively structured organization of the exploration and production sector, was attributable to three general factors. First, the reassuring presence of the laws of 1928: these obliged France-based companies to accept national oil. Second, engineers and technocrats displayed a marked disinterest toward the areas of refining and distribution, presumably because of their perception of the greater technoscientific 'purity' of more geoscience-oriented sectors of the industry. Blancard himself explicitly stated his opposition to the BRP becoming engaged in marketing. Finally, the BRP had lost a great deal of control over the tactics of its larger affiliates such as REPAL. Evidence of the latter point could be seen in REPAL President Roger Goetze's attempts to independently reach a mutual agreement with his personal friend, Jacques Bénézit, President of CFP(A), and especially with CFP's de Metz, enabling REPAL to take 10 percent of the French Refining Company.[117]

As a consequence of these three factors, it was now urgent, in the eyes of Fuels Director Blancard, and RAP President Paul Moch, to set up an integrated public oil industry. A primary effect of this would be a boost to French security, as it would mark the end of any possible distribution blackmail by foreign companies in the area of highest consumption, mainland France. The French state was already involved in the upstream, the midstream and, via the IFP, in oil research. The most logical step was to expand its activities to the downstream sector, thereby impacting on the international market. Between 1959 and 1960, such a strategy led to the creation of the General Petroleum Union (*Union générale des pétroles*, UGP), a grouping formed of the RAP, REPAL, and BRP's other producing affiliates, prompted by Minister of Industry, Jean-Marcel Jeanneney, and Minister of Finances, Antoine Pinay.[118]

The establishment of UGP caused high levels of tension between the public authorities and CFP, and a long and bitter dispute between Jeanneney and de Metz ensued. The new agency eventually arranged to sell Algerian crude to private companies at a discounted world market price, and agreed deliveries until the end of 1962.[119] When UGP was created in November 1960, Moch was appointed president, while Pierre Desprairies was designated general manager. Kocher-Marbœuf claimed that the latter choice was sponsored by Guillaumat, as Desprairies had been Deputy Director of Guillaumat's Ministry of Armed Forces before becoming President of BRP's Equatorial African affiliate. Although he was not a *corpsard*, Desprairies was a member of the 'Guillaumat network,' and, in spite of Moch's higher position, held executive power in the new agency. In the autumn of 1962, Moch was replaced by an officer to whom no one in France would dare deny the seat: Pierre Guillaumat. His ideas about the French domestic market were more than clear: it had to be protected.[120] As I will show in the next chapter, this plan did not quite match EEC aspirations for a common energy policy.

As far as Algeria was concerned, although the 1962 Évian agreements had not dramatically modified the status quo, and left France with all of its producing oilfields, the French and Algerians both knew that the new situation would not last long. From 1962 on, the French accelerated their operations. As already mentioned, what mattered now was to import from the Sahara as much oil and gas as possible in the shortest time possible. The Algerians soon escalated their demands. In 1965, the Algerian government forced France to renegotiate the agreements, subsequently imposing a heavier fiscal burden on foreign companies for oil-related activities, and eventually nationalizing them between 1968 and 1971. However, French imports from Algeria doubled in the course of the 1960s, from 13.9 to 27.0 Mt.[121]

Conclusion

In this chapter, I have argued that worldwide overproduction of oil from the second half of the 1950s into the early 1960s caused a shift in the priorities of Italian and French companies from the upstream to the midstream sector: what I have termed the 'midstream shift.' The unprecedented expansion of geophysical activities that occurred during the 1950s was responsible for the high number of oil discoveries. That expansion was in turn brought about by technical developments in the instruments used for exploration. While most geophysical innovations were created in the US, they were utilized in both Italian and French exploration activities. However, the two industries developed to different degrees: while the French geophysical industry managed to achieve technological innovation in equipment and establish itself on an industrial scale, its Italian counterpart did not. The negative outcome of the massive geophysical effort deployed worldwide through the 1950s, and the consequent overproduction, was a marked decline in geophysical activity by the end of the decade.

Concomitantly, the focus of security for the two countries under study gradually shifted to the midstream sector. This by no means led to the cessation of oil exploration, as shown, for example, by the burgeoning of exploratory activities in areas such as Libya; however, it certainly meant sharpened focus on international transport and marketing activities. By analyzing the Soviet oil trade strategy, I have elucidated how it generated widespread fears both in Western diplomatic circles and the oil industry. In this respect, ENI's oil-for-technology agreements with the Soviets were a particularly acute thorn in the flesh, not only of British and American companies, but also of French aspirations to supply the West European market with oil recently extracted from Algeria. Thanks to Italian purchases of Soviet oil, and to new African oil reserves for France (plus their Middle Eastern share obtained from CFP), by the early 1960s both countries found themselves with significant quantities of crude that only needed to be sold.

I then showed how the two countries' midstream shifts were embodied in the battles for European pipelines, with a project devised by ENI countering a project developed by a consortium of majors, including CFP. In this rush to complete pipelines, CFP's proximity to the majors played a crucial role, enabling the French to count on the latter's capital and political support to curb the Italian plan. ENI did attempt to adopt a similar strategy, trying to win SONJ's favor by including it in its own project, but Mattei's multitude of outstanding issues with the US major frustrated this attempt.

Last, I examined the problematic consequences of France's new Algerian production: first, in terms of political differences between ministerial representatives, and then in terms of the security issues associated with pipeline routes in Algeria. I discussed how the characteristics of Saharan oil affected its marketing in Western Europe and France, and how, given Anglo-American predominance in the French refining and distribution market, the French public authorities decided to create an integrated system capable of using the new resources without having to kowtow to the diktats of established companies.

While laying the foundation of a French metropolitan market may have solved the problem of the commercialization of African oil in the short-term,

ENI's alliance with the USSR was seen by the French, the British and the Americans as a warning sign of what could happen if the Soviet oil offensive was supported by other West European countries. The threats deriving from Soviet exports soon became the chief bone of contention for international organizations, and led to further disputes concerning not only economic, but also military, security.

Notes

1 Paul L. Lyons, "The Future of Geophysics," *Geophysics* 20, no. 3 (1955): 506.
2 Zeb Mayhew, "A Review of Foreign Oil Production in 1960," *Journal of Petroleum Technology* 13, no. 4 (1961): 320–1; Peter R. Odell, *An Economic Geography of Oil* (London: G. Bell and Sons, 1963), 18.
3 Daniel Yergin, *The Prize: The Epic Quest for Oil, Money, and Power*, 2nd edition (New York: Simon & Schuster. 1st edition: 1991), ch. 25, 481ff. DeGolyer's thought is reported at p. 481 (source reported: DeGolyer to Wellings, Dec. 24, 1953; DeGolyer papers, 1982). The most important oilfields discovered in the decade were: Rumaila in Iraq and Pembina in Canada (1953); Ahwaz in Iran (1958); Zelten in Libya and Daquing in China (1959); the Algerian and Central African fields (1956–1960); the Ural–Volga fields in the Soviet Union (early 1950s). The world's largest oilfield, Ghawar, discovered in 1949, started its production in 1951.
4 Yergin, *The Prize*, 481–2. Figures here are given in tons per day, whereas in the original source they are given in barrels per day. Francisco Parra, *Oil Politics. A Modern History of Petroleum* (New York: I. B. Tauris & Co), 73–4.
5 Timothy Mitchell, "Carbon Democracy," *Economy and Society* 38, no. 3 (2009): 409; Timothy Mitchell, *Carbon Democracy: Political Power in the Age of Oil* (New York: Verso, 2011), 7; Lea Winter, "Fueling Oil Scarcity: Produced Scarcity and the Sociopolitical Fate of Renewable Energy," *Journal of International Affairs* 69, no. 1 (2015): 195–206.
6 Robert E. Ebel, *Communist Trade in Oil and Gas* (New York/Washington/London: Praeger), 40.
7 Yergin, *The Prize*, 497, 513; Benito Li Vigni, *La grande sfida. Mattei, il petrolio e la politica* (Milano: Mondadori, 1996), 184–5; Leonardo Maugeri, *L'arma del petrolio. Questione petrolifera globale, guerra fredda e politica italiana nella vicenda di Enrico Mattei* (Firenze: Loggia De'Lanzi, 1994), 218–20; John I. Clarke, "Economic and Political Changes in the Sahara," *Geography* 46, no. 2 (1961), 114–15; W. E. Wallis and E. M. McNatt, "Selection of New Regions for Overseas Exploration," *Geophysics* 23, no. 2 (1958): 312; Parra, *Oil Politics*, 87.
8 Soviet figures are reported in: Economist Intelligence Unit, *Quarterly Economic Review*, "USSR Annual Supplement—1971," 10: source as reported in John A. Berry, "Oil and Soviet Policy in the Middle East," *Middle East Journal* 26, no. 2 (1972): 150. Ebel, *Communist Trade*, 40; D. L. Spencer, "The Role of Oil in Soviet Foreign Economic Policy," *American Journal of Economy and Society* 25, no. 1 (1966): 98.
9 See for example: Ebel, *Communist Trade*; Halford L. Hoskins, *Problems Raised by the Soviet Oil Offensive*. U.S. Senate. Committee on the Judiciary (Washington: United States Government Printing Office, 1962); Jonathan P. Stern, *Soviet Oil and Gas Exports to the West: Commercial Transactions or Security Threat* (Aldershot: Gower, 1987).

10 The quote is from: Cabinet Minutes, Jul. 25, 1958; Cabinet Series, b. 11; Whitman Files, 1953–1961; Eisenhower Library: source as reported in Yergin, *The Prize*, 497.

11 Ebel, *Communist Trade in Oil and Gas*, 40, 44, 61. Ebel's data are sourced from various annual statistical trade handbooks issues by the Ministry of Trade of the USSR; Halford L. Hoskins and Leon M. Herman, *Soviet Oil in the Cold War.* U.S. Senate, Committee on the Judiciary (Washington: United States Government Printing Office, 1961), 5.

12 Yergin, *The Prize*, 497.

13 "Restriction obligatoire des importations américaines," *Petroleum Press Service* XXVI, no. 4 (1959): 126–30.

14 "Chronologie des accords politiques entre l'URSS et les pays arabes," Dec. 1958; Revue de presse, n. 30; b. 90.4/102, Revues de presse; Fonds Total-CFP; Archives Historiques du Groupe ELF/Total, La Défense (AHTOTAL). Leon M. Herman, "The Soviet Oil Offensive," *The Reporter*, Jun. 21, 1962, 27. Not unexpectedly, the French and Italian oil agencies also put technoscientific expertise at the service of diplomatic aims. For example, in the early 1960s, IFP helped establish the Iranian Exploration, Refining and Petrochemistry Centre in Tehran. Its technicians also ran courses for Indian engineers at the Indian Oil Institute, which the IFP had also contributed to establishing. After Algerian independence, IFP also helped to set up the Algerian Oil Institute ("Rapport d'activité 1961 et programme pour 1962"; Activités de l'Institut Français du Pétrole; Institut Français du Pétrole: Fonds documentaire, Rueil Malmaison).

15 The equivalence in 1957 was 1 ruble = 4 dollars (http://www.cbr.ru/currency_base/OldDataFiles/USD.xls), so the figures reported correspond to $3.02 billion for the UK, $1.14 billion for West Germany, $1.07 billion for France, and $468 million for Italy. Figures reported in: Bruna Bagnato, *Prove di Ostpolitik. Politica ed economia nella strategia italiana verso l'Unione Sovietica, 1958–1963* (Firenze: Olschki, 2003), 97.

16 Niklas Jensen-Eriksen, "The Cold War in Energy Markets. British Efforts to Contain Soviet Oil Exports to Non-Communist Countries, 1950–1965," in *Le pétrole et la guerre/Oil and War*, ed. Alain Beltran (Brussels: Peter Lang, 2012), 204. The embargo notwithstanding, Italian-labeled oil products made from Soviet oil were sold by ENI's British affiliate in the UK in the early 1960s (Spencer, "The Role of Oil," 100–1). Emmanuel Catta, *Victor De Metz. De la CFP au Groupe Total* (Paris: Total Edition Presse, 1990), 289. On Soviet aid to Arab countries, see: "Sub-Committee on Soviet Economic Policy—The Economic Offensive of the Sino-Soviet Bloc, Note by the Chairman," Jul. 6, 1960; Atlantic Community Committee (AC); AC/89-WP/67, confidential (later unclassified); NATO Archives, Brussels (NATOA). "Sub-Committee on Soviet Economic Policy—The Economic Offensive of the Sino-Soviet Bloc (1st July, 1960—31st December, 1960)," May 12, 1961; AC; AC/89-WP/76 (Revised 1), confidential (later unclassified); NATOA. Note Service de documentation extérieure et de contre-espionnage (SDECE), "Pénétration italienne (ENI) et soviétique dans le domaine pétrolier en Afrique," Aug. 30, 1960, secret; sub-folder (sub-fd.) Afrique 1957/77; folder (fd.) 1; box (b.) 19900317/8; Archives Nationales, Pierrefitte-sur-Seine (AN) (FOIA n° 111 382).

17 Quoted from: Charles C. Bates, Thomas F. Gaskell and Robert B. Rice, *Geophysics in the Affairs of Man* (Oxford: Pergamon Press, 1982), 101.

18 Ibid., 137–8.

19 F. A. Van Melle et al., "Geophysical research and progress in exploration," *Geophysics* 28, no. 3 (June 1963): 466, 475–6; Geoffrey C. Bowker, *Science on the Run: Information Management and Industrial Geophysics at Schlumberger, 1920–1940* (Cambridge, MA/London: MIT Press, 1994), 49; Allan A. Needell,

Science, Cold War and the American State: Lloyd V. Berkner and the Balance of Professional Ideals (Amsterdam: Harwood Academic, 2000), 356–7. The quote is from: Bruce A. Bolt, *Nuclear Explosions and Earthquakes: The Parted Veil* (San Francisco: Freeman and Company, 1976), 20.

20 L. S. Morrison and Robert Watson, "The Electronic Computer and Geophysics," *Geophysics* 26 (1): 40; "Bienfaits du calculateur électronique," *Petroleum Press Service* XXVI, no. 8 (1959): 302–3.

21 H. J. Jones, "Central Office Processing of Seismic Data," *World Petroleum* 28, no. 3 (1957): 68–70.

22 Tiziano Rocco, "Osservazioni sulla 'Proposta di costituzione di un play-back center' del Servizio Geofisico," Oct. 26, 1961; fd. 37F; b. 275; Ricerche e produzione; Direzione Mineraria; Fondo AGIP; Archivio Storico ENI (ASENI). Lucio Deluchi, (undated, TPQ 1992), "Storia dei Centri Elaborazione AGIP" (Working Paper, Associazione Pionieri e Veterani ENI, San Donato Milanese), 1 (http://www.pionierieni.it/wp/?p=915); John Krige, "Hybrid Knowledge: The Transnational Co-production of the Gas Centrifuge for Uranium Enrichment in the 1960s," in "Transnational History of Science," edited by Simone Turchetti, Néstor Herran and Soraya Boudia, special issue, *British Journal for the History of Science* 45, no. 3 (2012): 337–57.

23 The introduction of computers and mechanized data handling also led to a new subfield of support for exploration, namely operations research, supporting activities planning and decision-making by means of complex statistical analyses. Howard Cobb, "Operations Research: A Tool in Oil Exploration," *Geophysics* 25, no. 5 (1960): 1009–22.

24 Bates, Gaskell and Rice, *Geophysics*, 164–9.

25 Milton B. Dobrin and Stanley H. Ward, "Tools for Tomorrow's Geophysics," *Geophysical Prospecting* 10, no. 1 (1962): 438.

26 Engelhardt A. Eckhardt, "Geophysical Activity in 1951," *Geophysics* 17, no. 3 (1952): 441. From 1954 to 1958, the discrepancy between the Western and Eastern hemispheres' exploration effort decreased from ten-fold to two-fold. Sigmund Hammer, "Geophysical Activity in 1953," *Geophysics* 19, no. 3 (1954): 518; Homer G. Patrick, "Geophysical Activity in 1955," *Geophysics* 22, no. 1 (1957): 89–90.

27 Neal J. Smith, "Geophysical Activity in 1962," *Geophysics* 28, no. 6 (1963): 1054.

28 However, airborne magnetometry rose by 25 percent between 1961 and 1962. Unless otherwise specified, these data do not include the Sino-Soviet Bloc. Smith, "Geophysical Activity," 1049. "Les géants rivaux (USA et URSS)," *Petroleum Press Service* XXVII, no. 10 (1960): 361.

29 Quoted from: Lyons, "Future of Geophysics," 506.

30 Ibid., 507.

31 R. Desaint and H. Richard, "Évolution de l'activité géophysique de surface (pétrole)," *Geophysical Prospecting* 11, no. 2 (1963): 204.

32 Desaint and Richard, "Évolution de l'activité," 203.

33 Desaint and Richard, "Évolution de l'activité"; John M. Crawford, William E. N. Doty and Milford R. Lee, "Continuous signal seismograph," *Geophysics* 25, no. 1 (1960): 95–105. The quote is from: Francesco Guidi, "VII. A braccetto con geofisica e mitologia, fra il Lete e il giardino delle Esperidi," in *Documenti dell'Archivio storico*, vol. 3, *La memoria raccontata*, eds. ENI and APVE (Roma/San Donato Milanese: ENI/APVE, 2012), 77–8 (my translation). See also: Letter, James N. Wilson, Seismograph Service Co. of Libya, to Claudio Sommaruga, CORI, Jun. 9, 1962; fd. 37F; b. 275; Ricerche e produzione; Direzione Mineraria; Fondo AGIP; ASENI.

34 Rapport annuel 1958, Partie Géophysique, pp. 3–4; fd. 411386, BRP—Dép. Exploration; b. 07AH0008-110, BRP; Fonds ELF-ERAP; AHTOTAL. In the same folder, see also: BRP—Informations Techniques—Rapport annuel 1959, p. 98 (my translation). For data on AGIP, see note 37.

35 Gabrielle Hecht makes the case for the development of French nuclear power in the post-war context, but her argument can be easily applied also to the oil exploration industry. Gabrielle Hecht, *The Radiance of France: Nuclear Power and National Identity after World War II*, 2nd edition (Cambridge, MA/London: MIT Press, 2009. 1st edition, 1998), 2.

36 Roberto Maiocchi, "Il ruolo delle scienze nello sviluppo industriale italiano," in *Storia d'Italia. Annali 3. Scienza e tecnica nella cultura e nella società dal Rinascimento a oggi*, ed. Giuseppe Micheli (Torino: Einaudi, 1980), 961.

37 Renato Giannetti, *Tecnologia e sviluppo economico italiano, 1870–1990* (Bologna: Il Mulino, 1998), 42–5, 57, 201ff.

38 Douglas A. Yates, "Life Stories and Family Histories of the French Oil Industry. The Rise and Fall of the Corps des Mines," in *A Comparative History of National Oil Companies*, ed. Alain Beltran (Brussels: Peter Lang, 2001), 54–67.

39 Éléments Statistiques Activité Industrie du Pétrole, 1965; b. 07AH0024, DHYCA; Fonds ELF-ERAP; AHTOTAL. A.P.Z.F. stands for "Other countries of the franc zone."

40 Data for this graph were extracted from: 1) Processi Verbali Assemblee: 59/1953–1959, pp. 76–7, 115–16, 154–5, 193–5; and 5A/1959–1962, pp. 48–9, 132–3, 195–7; AGIP DI.MI.; ASENI. 2) AGIP Mineraria—Relazioni e Bilanci, 1954–1961. Roma: AGIP/CEDI; fd. 3EF; b. 348; Ricerche e produzione; Direzione Mineraria; Fondo AGIP; ASENI.

41 Anno accademico 1963–1964. pp. 12–22; Scuola Superiore di Studi sugli Idrocarburi; Archivio Scuola Superiore di Studi sugli Idrocarburi.

42 Ibid., 16.

43 Quoted from: Ibid., 20 (my translation).

44 Franco Foresta Martin and Geppi Calcara, *Per una storia della geofisica italiana: la nascita dell'Istituto Nazionale di Geofisica (1936) e la figura di Antonino Lo Surdo* (Milano: Springer, 2010). *Annals of Geophysics*' archives are found at: http://www.annalsofgeophysics.eu/index.php/annals/issue/archive).

45 Maurice Rachline, *Geophysical Prospecting and Oil Exploration* (Paris: CGG/Editions Atlas, 1998), 16–8.

46 Similar to other radio-location techniques, *Toran* determined the location of ships by triangulation through a multiplicity of geographically distributed stations, electronically connected with a central data processing station. Rachline, *Geophysical Prospecting*, 16–8; "La recherche sous-marine," *Petroleum Press Service* XXVI, no. 6 (1959): 227–30. *Flexotir* used explosives in a pierced spherical cage, the idea being to disperse the bubble to prevent oscillations. Rapport annuel 1966, p. 8; Institut Français du Pétrole: Fonds documentaire. Rachline, *Geophysical Prospecting*, 46.

47 IFP, *Institut Française du Pétrole* (booklet) (Paris: IFP, 1967); IFP, *Institut Française du Pétrole* (booklet) (Paris: IFP, 1969).

48 Daniele Pozzi, *Dai gatti selvaggi al cane a sei zampe. Tecnologia, conoscenza e organizzazione nell'Agip e nell'Eni di Enrico Mattei* (Padova: Marsilio, 2009), 431. Although ENI's first Iranian field, Bahrgan Sar, was discovered in 1960, it would only come into production two years later. The Iranian production, however, would prove quite modest (Pozzi, *Gatti selvaggi*, 439; William B. Fisher, ed., *The Cambridge History of Iran, vol. 1. The Land of Iran* (London: Cambridge University Press, 1968), 538. On the first ENI discovery in the Persian Gulf, see also: Riccardo Varvelli, "Il Campo di Bahrgan Sar (Persia,

ora Iran 1957—1961)" (Working Paper, Associazione Pionieri e Veterani ENI, San Donato Milanese, 2010) (http://www.pionierieni.it/wp/?p=2061).

49 Letter, ANIC to Rasno-import, Oct. 27, 1958; fd. 7E0; b. 2; Rapporti commerciali con l'estero; Estero; Fondo ENI; ASENI. "Nouvelles briêves," *Petroleum Press Service* XXVI, no. 1 (1959): 38. The most complete study on the political-diplomatic aspects of Italian trade with the USSR is Bagnato, *Prove di Ostpolitik*.

50 Nico Perrone, *Obiettivo Mattei. Petrolio, Stati Uniti e politica dell'ENI* (Gamberetti: Roma, 1995), 157–8.

51 Telegram n. 10280, Bounous, Italian Embassy (Itemb) Moscow, to Italian Foreign Ministry (MAEI), "Nota sovietica all'Italia sui missili," Apr. 28, 1959; and Telegram n. 10291, "Nota sovietica sui missili," Apr. 28, 1959; vol. 42 arrivo (gen-mag); Telegrammi ordinari, Russia (Ambasciata Mosca), 1959; Archivio storico-diplomatico del Ministero degli Affari esteri, Rome (ASMAE). Telegram n. 5953, Carlo Alberto Straneo, MAEI, to Itemb Moscow, "Risposta a Nota sovietica circa missili," May 8, 1959; vol. 43 partenza (gen-ago); Telegrammi ordinari, Russia (Ambasciata Mosca), 1959; ASMAE. Nuti's quote is from: Leopoldo Nuti, "Commitment to NATO and Domestic Politics: The Italian Case and Some Comparative," *Contemporary European History* 7, no. 3 (1998): 369.

52 Pietro Quaroni's quote is from: Telegram n. 13480, Luca Pietromarchi, Itemb Moscow, to MAEI, May 28, 1959, p. 3; vol. 42 arrivo (gen-mag); Telegrammi ordinari, Russia (Ambasciata Mosca), 1959; ASMAE (my translation). See also, on the issue of US missiles in Italy: Leopoldo Nuti, *La sfida nucleare: la politica estera italiana e le armi atomiche, 1945–1991* (Bologna: Il Mulino, 2007), 171–99.

53 Letter, Gaston Palewski, French Embassy (Fremb) Rome, to French Foreign Ministry (MAEF), Jan. 15, 1959; N. 288; Sous-série: Italie 1944–1970; Série: Direction d'Europe (Z-Europe); Archives Diplomatiques du Ministère des Affaires Etrangères, La Courneuve (ADMAE). John D. Jernegan, US Embassy (Amemb) Rome, to John Foster Dulles, Secretary of State, Nov. 19, 1958; James D. Zellerbach, Amemb Rome, to John Foster Dulles, Secretary of State, Dec. 11, 1958, confidential; file (f.) 456.9341/11-1958; b. 2021, Italy; Central Decimal Files, 1955–59; Record Group (RG) 59; National Archives and Records Administration, College Park, MD (NARA). Central Intelligence Bulletin, Dec. 20, 1958, top secret; CIA; CIA Records Search Tool Database (CREST); NARA. Note SDECE, "L'activité de l'Ente Nazionale Idrocarburi et de son président (novembre 1958—avril 1959)," May 11, 1959, secret, pp. 4, 7, 10–11; sub-fd. Italie 1955/1979; fd. 1; b. 19900317/13; AN (FOIA n° 111 382).

54 James D. Zellerbach, Amemb Rome, to Department of State, "Conversation with Prime Minister Fanfani," Dec. 29, 1958; f. 765.13/12-2958, Foreign Service Dispatch; b. 3617, Italy; Central Decimal Files, 1955–1959; RG 59; NARA.

55 James D. Zellerbach, Amemb Rome, to Department of State, "Impressions of ENI's Marketing Counselor of Commercial Prospects of Soviet Bloc Countries," Nov. 3, 1959; f. 865.2553/11-359, Foreign Service Dispatch; b. 4826, Italy; Central Decimal Files, 1955–1959; RG 59; NARA.

56 Rash political moves by DC Right's government would bring Fanfani back to his role of Prime Minister in July 1960. Paul Ginsborg, *Storia d'Italia dal dopoguerra a oggi* (Milano: Einaudi Scuola, 1996), 202–3.

57 According to former ENI's Vice-President, Eugenio Cefis (statement made on Jul. 18, 2002 to Bruna Bagnto (reported in Bagnato, *Prove di Ostpolitik*, 374), an important role in liaising between ENI and the Soviets was played

by Communist Party executive and Cefis' wartime friend, Giancarlo Pajetta. Telegram n. 36288, Luca Peitromarchi, Itemb Moscow, to MAEI, "Contratto ENI-FINSIDER," Oct. 3, 1960; and Telegram n. 37331, Luca Pietromarchi, Itemb Moscow, to MAEI, "Importazione petrolio," Oct. 11, 1960; vol. 59 arrivo (lug-dic); Telegrammi ordinari, Russia (Ambasciata Mosca), 1960; ASMAE. For the laborious negotiations preceding the agreement, mainly carried out by Giuseppe Ratti, and under the auspices of Italian Ambassador Luca Pietromarchi, see: fd. 482E; b. 264; Presidenza Raffaele Girotti; Fondo ENI; ASENI (the following files in particular: "Missione a Mosca," Mar. 8–17, 1960; "Missione a Mosca per affare 'Oleodotto,'" Jun. 23–28, 1960; "Missione a Mosca per 'Affare oleodotto,'" Jul. 1960; "Missione conclusiva dell''Affare Oleodotto,'" Moscow, Sep. 14–Oct. 14, 1960.

58 Jaroslav G. Polach, *EURATOM: Its Background, Issues and Economic Implications* (Dobbs Ferry: Oceana, 1964), 135.

59 "Committee of Economic Advisers, Report by the Ad Hoc Study Group on Soviet Oil Policy to the Econad," May 23; 1961, p. 38; AC; AC/127-D/68, confidential; NATOA. The Committee of Economic Advisers will hereafter be referred to as ECONAD. H. Gardner Ainsworth, Amemb Rome, to Department of State, "Petroleum—Notes of an Interview With Enrico Mattei by Time-Life Writer John M. Scott," Jul. 11, 1961, limited official use, pp. 1, 3–4; file 865.2553/7-1161, Foreign Service Dispatch; b. 2695, Italy; Central Decimal File, 1960–1963; RG 59; NARA. On Italian–Soviet negotiations on the new agreement, see: Telegram n. 898, Jan. 12, 1961; and n. 1146, Jan. 14, 1961; and n. 1395, Jan. 17, 1961; and n. 2416, Jan. 26, 1961; and n. 2889, Jan. 30, 1961; and n. 5014, Feb. 21, 1961; vol. 55 arrivo (gen-giu); Telegrammi ordinari, Russia (Ambasciata Mosca), 1961; ASMAE. "Missione a Mosca per acquisto greggio," Feb. 14–19, 1961, p. 7; fd. 482E; b. 264; Presidenza Raffaele Girotti; Fondo ENI; ASENI. On the details of this new agreement, see: Bagnato, *Prove di Ostpolitik*, 403–7. The contract was later reduced to six tankers due to Fanfani's opposition. Telegram n. 5014, Enrico Carrara, Itemb Moscow, to MAEI, "Trattative commerciali con la Russia," Feb. 21, 1961; and Telegram n. 13, Luca Pietromarchi, Itemb Moscow, to MAEI, "Stampa sovietica," Jan. 2, 1961; vol. 55 arrivo (gen-giu); Telegrammi ordinari, Russia (Ambasciata Mosca), 1961; ASMAE.

60 Pietromarchi to MAEI, "Stampa sovietica," Jan. 2, 1961; Angela Stent, *From Embargo to Ostpolitik. The Political Economy of West Germany–Soviet Relations, 1955–1980* (Cambridge: Cambridge University Press, 1981), 97.

61 Quoted from: Memorandum for Deputy Director/Intelligence, "Western Problems in Marketing Petroleum," Nov. 30, 1960, confidential; CIA; CREST; NARA.

62 Perrone, *Obiettivo Mattei*, 146–7.

63 "Editorial Note"; Foreign Relations of the United States (FRUS), 1961–1963, XIII, Western Europe and Canada (Washington: United States Government Printing Office, 1994), 799–800. Robert P. Joyce, US Consulate General, to Department of State, "Ceremony in Genoa Initiates Construction of Central European Oil Pipeline," Jul. 7, 1961, official use only, pp. 3–4; f. 865.2553/7-761, official use only, Foreign Service Dispatch; b. 2695, Italy; Central Decimal File, 1960–1963; RG 59; NARA.

64 On the important support of Italian–Soviet trade by Ambassador Pietromarchi, see: Bruna Bagnato, ed., *I diari di Luca Pietromarchi: ambasciatore italiano a Mosca, 1958–1961* (Firenze: Olschki, 2002).

65 Bagnato, *Prove di Ostpolitik*, 14.

66 Ibid., 60–2.

67 Peter J. E. Male, Foreign Office (FO), to J. Gwynn, Ministry of Power, "Italy and Russian Oil," reporting *New York Times* article, "Italy Oil Deal With Soviet Weakens Her Ties to West," Nov. 11, 1960; fd. RT 1532/17; b. FO 371/153362; The National Archives, Kew (TNA).

68 "Promemoria sulle importazioni petrolifere dall'URSS," Aug. 24, 1960; fd. CB8; b. 24; Presidenza Eugenio Cefis; Fondo ENI; ASENI.

69 Ashley Clarke, UK Embassy (Britemb) Rome, to FO, "Visit to UK by President of ENI-AGIP of Italy," Jan. 15, 1959, confidential; fd. RT 1152; b. FO 371/145054; TNA. The quote is from: Ashley Clarke, Britemb Rome, to Roger W. Jackling, FO, "Relations between Signor Mattei and the Western Oil Group," Oct. 21, 1960, secret; fd. RT 1532/10 (A); b. FO 371/153362; TNA.

70 Roger W. Jackling, FO, to Ashley Clarke, Britemb Rome, Nov. 4, 1960, secret; fd. RT 1532/10; b. FO 371/153362; TNA.

71 Bagnato, *Prove di Ostpolitik*, 176.

72 Quoted from: Leon M. Herman, "The Soviet Oil Offensive," *The Reporter*, Jun. 21, 1962, p. 27.

73 The crisis culminated with the city's de facto partition and the construction of the Berlin Wall. Letter, Harry F. Kern, Director of *Foreign Report*, to François de Laboulaye, CFP, Aug. 24, 1961; fd. Pétrole soviétique; b. 92.26/31; Fonds Total-CFP; AHTOTAL.

74 Ibid.

75 Quoted from: Hoskins and Herman, *Soviet Oil*, 4.

76 Hoskins and Herman, *Soviet Oil*, 6; Hoskins, *Problems Raised*, 11.

77 Quoted from: Willard L. Thorp, "American Policy and the Soviet Economic Offensive," *Foreign Affairs* 35 (1956–1957): 282.

78 Spencer, "The Role of Oil," 99.

79 Letter, Luca Pietromarchi, Itemb Moscow, to Enrico Mattei, ENI, Nov. 25, 1959; and Letter, Enrico Mattei, ENI, to Luca Pietromarchi, Itemb Moscow, Dec. 28, 1959; fd. 7E6; b. 2; Rapporti commerciali con l'estero; Estero; Fondo ENI; ASENI. Note SDECE, "L'activité de l'Ente Nazionale Idrocarburi (mai 1958–septembre 1959)," Oct. 23, 1959, secret, p. 5; sub-fd. Italie 1955/1979; fd. 1; b. 19900317/13; AN (FOIA n° 111 382). CIA Current Intelligence Weekly Summary, "Italian Oil Combine May Build Pipeline for USSR," Jan. 28, 1960, confidential, p. 11; CIA; CREST; NARA. Amemb Rome to Department of State, Jan. 26, 1960, confidential; file 865.2553/1-2660, Foreign Service Dispatch; b. 2694, Italy; Central Decimal File, 1960–1963; RG 59; NARA. "Les pipe-lines d'exportation de l'U.R.S.S.," *Petroleum Press Service* XXVI, no. 5 (1959): 169; Bagnato, *Prove di Ostpolitik*, 176.

80 Memorandum of Conversation, "Italian Government Guaranteed Credit for Soviet Pipeline Project," Feb. 6, 1960, confidential; file 865.2553/2-660; b. 2694, Italy; NARA—Central Decimal File, 1960–1963; RG 59; NARA. James D. Zellerbach, Amemb Rome, to Department of State, Mar. 1, 1960, limited official use; file 865.25553/3-160; b. 2694, Italy; Central Decimal File, 1960–1963; RG 59; NARA. Note SDECE, "L'activité de l'Ente Nazionale Idrocarburi (octobre 1959–octobre 1960)," Oct. 18, 1960, secret, p. 15; sub-fd. Italie 1955/1979; fd. 1; b. 19900317/13; AN (FOIA n° 111 382).

81 Mario Pirani, *Poteva andare peggio. Mezzo secolo di ragionevoli illusioni* (Milano: Mondadori, 2012), 291.

82 Pozzi, *Gatti selvaggi*, 423.

83 Outerbridge Horsey, Amemb Rome, to Dean Rusk, Secretary of State, Mar. 14, 1961, confidential; f. 865.2553/3-1461; b. 2694, Italy; Central Decimal File,

1960–1963; RG 59; NARA. Memorandum of Conversation, "Petroleum—Conversation with ESSO Official About Enrico Mattei and Soviet Petroleum," Apr. 9, 1962, confidential; file 865.2553/4-962, confidential; b. 2695, Italy; Central Decimal File, 1960–1963; RG 59; NARA.

84 "Le pipe-line Méditerranée-Strasbourg," *Petroleum Press Service* XXV, no. 9 (1958): 347; "Répercussions des pipe-lines en Europe," *Petroleum Press Service* XXVII, no. 2 (1960): 61–5; "Raffineries et oléoducs pour la Bavière," *Petroleum Press Service* XXVII, no. 3 (1960): 256–7; "Liaison par pipe-line entre la région de Marseille et la Bavière," *Petroleum Press Service* XXVII, no. 6 (1960): 226–7.

85 John H. Wardle-Smith, Britemb Rome, to Henry C. Hainworth, Atomic Energy Department (FO), "Signor Mattei's position in connection with oil. Threat of a price war in European Markets," Jul. 20, 1960, confidential; fd. RT 1532/9; b. FO 371/153362; TNA. James D. Zellerbach, Amemb Rome, to Christian Herter, Secretary of State, Jan. 19, 1960, secret; f. 865.2553/1-2960; b. 2694, Italy; Central Decimal File, 1960–1963; RG 59; NARA.

86 Quoted from: Manlio Brosio, and Umberto Gentiloni Silveri, ed., *Diari di Washington: 1955–1961* (Bologna: Il Mulino, 2008), 530 (my translation).

87 This is an interesting and often underrated aspect, in that it represents an early episode of environmental awareness in Europe. For an analysis of environmental protests against CEL, see: Miriam Gassner, "Lokale Umwelt oder transnationale Chance? ENIs Reaktion auf die Proteste gegen die CEL-Pipeline in den 1960er Jahren," *Zeitschrift für Unternehmensgeschichte* 57, no. 1 (2012): 31–46.

88 "Répercussions des pipe-lines en Europe," *Petroleum Press Service* XXVII, no. 2 (1960): 62.

89 "ECONAD, Sino-Soviet Bloc Oil on World Markets, Note by the Economic Service," Jul. 11, 1960, confidential, p. 2; AC; AC/127-WP/56 (Revised); NATOA. A. A. Jarratt, Ministry of Power, to J. T. Fearnley, FO, Jun. 17, 1960, p. 10; fd. RT 1532/6; b. FO 371/153362; TNA. *Neue Zürcher Zeitung*, Jun. 11, 1961; Rassegna stampa estera 1961, n. 39, para 370; ASENI.

90 *Neue Zürcher Zeitung*, Jun. 11, 1961; Rassegna stampa estera 1961, n. 39, para 370; ASENI.

91 Memorandum of Conversation, "Mattei and ENI," Mar. 17, 1962, secret; f. 865.2553/3-1762; b. 2695, Italy; Central Decimal File, 1960–1963; RG 59; NARA. On contacts with AMOCO, see: Amemb Rome to Department of State, "AMOCO Official Talks of Business Agreement With ENI for U.S. Market," Jun. 13, 1962; f. 523.1 Petrol, limited official use; fd. 523.1 Petroleum (Jan.–Jun.) 1962; b. 129; U.S. Embassy, Rome, Classified General Records, 1946–1964; Records of the Foreign Service Posts of the Department of State, Italy, US Embassy, Rome Classified General Records, 1946–1964; Records of the Foreign Service Posts of the Department of State, Italy; RG 84; NARA.

92 Quoted from: Memorandum of Conversation, "Mattei and ENI," Mar. 17, 1962; FRUS, 1961–1963, XIII, Western Europe and Canada, 831.

93 Leopoldo Nuti, *Gli Stati Uniti e l'apertura a sinistra. Importanza e limiti della presenza americana in Italia* (Bari: Laterza, 1999), 528–9. See also: pp. 406–9 on the Fanfani-Kennedy talks of June 1961, where the possibility of reaching an agreement on oil was discussed; and pp. 518–36 on the 'Mattei case' and on the final phases of the rapprochement. Walter Levy is mentioned at p. 521.

94 Giovanni Galli, *Enrico Mattei: petrolio e complotto italiano* (Milano: Baldini Castoldi Dalai), 251. On the May conversation, see: Memorandum of

Conversation, May 22, 1962, confidential, p. 3; f. 865.04/5-2262; b. 2684; Central Decimal File, 1960–1963; RG 59; NARA. The use of refined Soviet oil by Italy-based US Sixth Fleet had already been denied in February by a NATO spokesperson, who had nevertheless admitted that NATO terrestrial forces in Italy were using that oil. *La Tribune de Lausanne*, Mar. 1, 1962; and *Neue Zürcher Zeitung*, Mar. 3, 1962; Rassegna stampa estera 1962, n. 14, Mar. 6, 1962; ASENI.

95 On Esso's initial opposition, see: Memorandum of Conversation, "Petroleum—Conversation with SONJ Official About Enrico Mattei and Soviet Petroleum," Apr. 9, 1962, confidential; f. 865.2553/4-962; b. 2695; Central Decimal File, 1960–1963; RG 59; NARA.

On the SONJ-ENI final settlement, see: H. Gardner Ainsworth, Amemb Rome, to Department of State, "Petroleum: ESSO-ENI Agreements," Dec. 18, 1962, confidential; f. 865.2553/121862; b. 2695; Central Decimal File, 1960–1963; RG 59; NARA. Note SDECE, "Italie - États-Unis - À propos du contrat ENI - Standard Oil," Apr. 17, 1963, secret; sub-fd. Italie 1955/1979; fd. 1; b. 199003117/13; AN (FOIA n° 111 382).

96 CIA Special Report, "Recent Activities of Italy's State Petroleum Corporation," Apr. 17, 1964, secret, pp. 4–5; CIA; CREST; NARA.

97 Perrone, *Obiettivo Mattei*, 165–6. Amemb Rome to Secretary of State, "Comment on some effects of Mattei's death," Nov. 1, 1962, confidential; and George C. McGhee to Mr. Tyler, "Effects of Mr. Mattei's Death on ENI operations," Nov. 2, 1962, confidential; f. 865.2553/11.162; b. 2695; Central Decimal File, 1960–1963; RG 59; NARA. NARA. Anthony Cuomo, Amemb Rome, to Department of State, Nov. 28, 1962, confidential; and Anthony Cuomo, Amemb Rome, to Department of State, Nov. 29, 1962; fd. Petroleum; b. 1; entry 5294; Lot 67D319; Records Relating to Italy 1943–1968; Bureau of European Affairs Country Director for Italy, Austria, and Switzerland (EUR/AIS); RG 59; NARA. Amemb Rome to Department of State, "Italian Politic-Economic Relations with the Sino-Soviet Bloc, First Half of 1962," Nov. 28, 1962, confidential; f. 511.12; fd. 511.12 Export-Import; b. 128; U.S. Embassy, Rome, Classified General Records, 1946–1964; Records of the Foreign Service Posts of the Department of State, Italy; RG 84. William N. Fraleigh, Amemb Rome, to Department of State, "Italian Politico-Economic Relations with the Soviet Bloc," Dec. 24, 1962, confidential; f. 511.2 East–West Relation; fd. 511.2 East West Trade, 1962–1964; b. 128; U.S. Embassy, Rome, Classified General Records, 1946–1964; Records of the Foreign Service Posts of the Department of State, Italy; RG 84.

98 A particularly significant study on this aspect is: Douglas A. Yates, *The Rentier State in Africa: Oil Rent Dependency and Neocolonialism in the Republic of Gabon* (Trenton/Asmara: Africa World Press, 1996). See also: Guy Martin, "Uranium: A Case-Study in Franco–African Relations," *Journal of Modern African Studies* 27, no. 4 (1989): 625–40; Pierre-Claver Maganga-Moussavou, *L'aide publique de la France au développement du Gabon depuis l'indépendance (1960–1978)* (Paris: Publications de la Sorbonne, 1982).

99 John I. Clarke, "Saharan Oil," *Geography* 45, no. 1/2 (1960): 106.

100 Documentation of the exchanges between members of the staff of Saharan and metropolitan ministries on this subject is found in: fd. Examen du projet de décret par le Conseil d'État; and fd. Protection du Pipe-Line Hassi-Messaoud; b. 81F/1476; Affaires algériennes (1873/1964); Fonds Ministériels (FM); Archives nationales d'outre-mer, Aix-en-Provence (ANOM). On FLN's plans of sabotaging oil infrastructures, see: Note SDECE, "Le F.L.N. et le pétrole algérien," Jan. 7, 1958, secret; and Note SDECE, "Algérie—Projet de sabotage

à Laghouat," Apr. 28, 1958, secret; Note SDECE, "Algérie-Libye—Projet de sabotage du prochain pipe-line Edjélé-Tunisie," Jul. 23, 1958; fd. Recherches de pétrole; b. 81F/966; Affaires algériennes (1873/1964); FM; ANOM. Note SDECE, "Action F.L.N. contre le transport du pétrole," Jan. 21, 1958, secret; and Note SDECE, "Le F.L.N. et le pétrole du Sahara," Apr. 16, 1958, secret, pp. 11–12; and Note SDECE, "Le F.L.N. et le pétrole saharien," Jul. 27, 1958. fd. 2, Algérie 1957/64; b. 19900317/8; AN (FOIA n° 111 382). On the inter-ministerial meeting: Éric Kocher-Marbœuf, *Le Patricien et le Général. Jean-Marcel Jeanneney et Charles de Gaulle 1958–1969*, vol. I (Paris: Comité pour l'histoire économique et financière de la France, 2003), 253. On the January 1959 sabotage: Pierre Cornet, *Du mirage au miracle. Pétrole saharien* (Paris: Nouvelles Editions Latines, 1960), 47.

101 Robert Lacoste, Minister of Algeria, to Christian Pineau, Minister of Foreign Affairs, "Evacuation des pétroles d'Edjelé," Dec. 7, 1957, secret/confidential, p. 1; fd. Untitled; b. 81F/2064; Affaires algériennes (1873/1964); FM; ANOM.

102 Lacoste to Pineau, "Evacuation des pétroles d'Edjelé," Dec. 7, 1957, secret/confidential, p. 9. The Army General, General Delegate of the Government, Commander-in-Chief of the Forces in Algeria, Commander of the 10th Military Region, to the President of the Council, Minister of National Defense, "Evacuation du gisement d'EDJELE," undated [probably 1957]; fd. Évacuation des pétroles sahariens; b. 81F/966; Affaires algériennes (1873/1964); FM; ANOM.

103 Agence France Presse—Sahara, n. 30, "Le pipe-line d'Edjeleh aboutira-t-il en Tunisie?" Jul. 25, 1958; fd. Pipe-line Edjeleh/La Skirra (Pourpalers préliminaires + attitude du F.L.N.); b. 90.4/180); Fonds Total-CFP; AHTOTAL. On the negotiations about which layout the pipeline should follow, see: Note de la Direction des Affaires Économiques et Financières (DAEF), MAEF, "Evacuation des pétroles d'Edjélé," Oct. 25, 1957; N. 70; Sous-série: Couve du Murville (1958–1968); Série: Cabinet du Ministre; ADMAE. Note SDECE, "Tunisie-Algérie—L'évolution du différend tuniso-algérien dans l'affaire du pipe-line Edjelé-Gabès," Jul. 24, 1958, secret; fd. Le FLN et le pétrole saharien; b. 81F/966; Affaires algériennes (1873/1964); FM, ANOM.

104 Agence France Presse—Sahara", n. 30, "Un mémorandum du FLN au Président Bourguiba", 25 July 1958. fd. Pipe-line Edjeleh/La Skirra (Pourpalers préliminaires + attitude du F.L.N.); b. 90.4/180; Fonds Total-CFP; AHTOTAL.

105 Clarke, "Saharan Oil," 106; Clarke, "Economic and Political Changes," 109–10; Samir Salut, "Politique nationale du pétrole, sociétés nationales et pétrole franc," *Revue historique* 638, no. 2 (2006): 366; "Le potentel saharien s'accroît," *Petroleum Press Service* XXVII, no. 10 (1960): 364. The pipeline was scheduled to attain 14 Mt in 1963, once fully operative. "Sahara français. Les investissements commencent de se rembourser," *Petroleum Press Service* XXVIII, no. 3 (1961): 106–7; Fosset (1962), 290–1.

106 Robert Fosset, "Pétrole et gaz naturel au Sahara," *Annales de Géographie* 71, no. 385 (1962), 290–1.

107 "Le Sahara fera partie de l'Algérie," *Petroleum Press Service* XXIX, no. 4 (1962): 125.

108 Quoted from: Clarke, "Saharan Oil," 107.

109 Fosset, "Pétrole et gaz naturel," 286–7; Samir Saul, "REPAL, CFP and 'Oil-Paid-in-Francs,'" in *A Comparative History of National Oil Companies*, ed. Alain Beltran (Brussels: Peter Lang, 2010), 104.

110 Salut, "Politique nationale," 368. In general, however, lighter and low-density crude oil is easier to refine due to its low sulfur rate, which makes 'cracking' (breaking up heavy molecules) unnecessary. Unsigned, "Note pour Monsieur de Metz: Écoulement en France du brut produit dans la zone franc," Jul. 11,

1958, p. 3; fd. Études; b. 3 SG/2, Secrétariat général: archives de Vincent Labouret; Fonds Total-CFP; AHTOTAL.

111 *Pétrole-Informations*, Apr. 5, 1961: source as reported in Fosset, "Pétrole et gaz naturel," 302.

112 "La Libye est lancée dans la carrière pétrolière," *Petroleum Press Service* XXVIII, no. 12 (1961): 451–5. Clarke, "Economic and Political Changes," 114–15. "Altro petrolio sovietico per l'Italia," *Financial Times*, Dec. 11, 1959; fd. 7DA; b. 2; Rapporti commerciali con l'estero; Estero; Fondo ENI; ASENI.

113 Note SDECE, "L'activité de l'Ente Nazionale Idrocarburi (mai 1958–septembre 1959)," Oct. 23, 1959, secret, pp. 11–12; sub-fd. Italie 1955/1979; fd. 1; b. 19900317/13; AN (FOIA n° 111 382).

114 Note SDECE, L'activité de l'Ente Nazionale Idrocarburi (mai 1958–septembre 1959)," Oct. 23, 1959, secret, pp. 11–12. Jacques Bénézit, CFP(A), to François de Laboulaye, CFP, "Les entreprises pétrolières françaises et le Sahara," Mar. 21, 1962, p. 4. fd. Sahara—Politique algérienne concernant le Sahara; b. 92.26/7, Vincent Labouret; Fonds Total-CFP; AHTOTAL.

115 Salut, "Politique nationale," 369.

116 Kocher-Marbœuf, *Le Patricien*, 251.

117 Ibid., 256.

118 Laurence Badel, Stanislas Jeannesson and N. Piers Ludlow, eds., *Les administrations nationales et la construction européenne. Une approche historique (1919–1975)* (Brussels: Peter Lang, 2005), 291.

119 François de Laboulaye, CFP, to Victor de Metz, CFP, "Note pour monsieur de Metz: Conversations C.F.P.-Gouvernement relatives à l'écoulement du pétrole saharien," Sep. 10, 1959; and Unsigned, "Suggestions relatives au placement sur le marché du pétrole saharien," Sep. 14, 1959; and Unsigned, "Schéma de conversation avec M. Jeanneney," Sep. 21, 1959; and Unsigned, "Commercialisation du pétrole saharien sur les marchés métropolitains et pétrole française du Moyen-Orient," Oct. 27, 1959; fd. Écoulement du pétrole saharien; b. 92.26/7, Vincent Labouret; Fonds Total-CFP; AHTOTAL. See also documents in: fd. Commercialisation du pétrole saharien; b. 92.26/7, Vincent Labouret; Fonds Total-CFP; AHTOTAL. Letter, François de Laboulaye, CFP, to Olivier Wormser, MAEF—DAEF, "Thèse de M. de Metz sur les questions pétrolières," Nov. 25, 1959; and Olivier Wormser, MAEF—DAEF, Note, "Distribution du pétrole saharien," Dec. 1, 1959; N. 85. DE-CE Papiers Dirécteur Olivier Wormser; Sous-série: Dirécteur—Wormser; Série: Affaires économiques et financières; ADMAE. Salut, "Politique nationale," 371.

120 Kocher-Marbœuf, Le Patricien, 278. In 1969, Guillaumat is reported to have said: "If a country does not protect its national market, it is necessarily eliminated from international competition" (Eric D. K. Melby, *Oil and the International System. The Case of France, 1918–1969* (New York: Arno Press 1981), 272). Guillaumat's quote is reported from the *Expansion* magazine of Oct. 23, 1969 (my translation).

121 André Nouschi, *La France et le pétrole: de 1924 à nos jours* (Paris: Picard, 2001), 247–9.

5 Transnational Counterattack Against Soviet Oil Plans

> The Communists intend to conquer the Free World through economic means. [...] [T]hey direct their trade most carefully, with an aim to strengthen their industrial machine by the procurement from the Free World of capital goods, equipment and machines which they cannot produce. These transactions, in addition, supply the Communists with the latest Western technology and know-how.
>
> —SONJ, Statement of position on the threat of Communist trade, January 19, 1962[1]

Concern about the Soviet oil offensive was not restricted to national governments. Transnational organizations, notably the EEC and NATO, also reacted. The Russian project to build a grand pipeline system triggered debate, since the pipeline would connect the country's oilfields with the rest of the Soviet Bloc and reach the fringes of the Iron Curtain. By consequence, both the oil exports and the technologies that made the construction of the pipeline possible were placed under strict surveillance by the Atlantic Alliance and the European Community alike. But were the Soviets really attempting to flood Europe with oil to unsettle its political and military institutions? And what kinds of motivations really determined NATO and EEC members' actions?

In cases such as the one presented in this chapter, it is not easy to distinguish between the political, economic, and military motives underlying a country's policy. Often, the three different elements can be found in the same discourse, and the interpretative weight assigned to each of them by different historical actors varied according to each country's contingent political agenda. While one may want to eradicate the root of the problem by lumping economic and military motives under the heading of 'national security,' it is important to distinguish among the diverse inflections of the phrase, because the predominance of either narrative not only governs which institutional contexts will be the loci of debate, but also gives an indication of the argumentative framework that might most appropriately be employed in those loci. Timothy Mitchell invites us to read national security issues as a manifestation of power struggles within oil-dominated regimes.

In this chapter, I will show that the constant economically-oriented consultations between governments and their respective national oil companies took place in parallel with the debates at the EEC and NATO, and helped to shape them.[2]

While the full rationale of the Soviet oil export strategy might not be easy to grasp, the means chosen by the Soviet administration to bring the country's oil to Europe was straightforward: an extensive pipeline system would connect production sites to prospective markets on the western edge of the Iron Curtain, and possibly to Western Europe itself. The pipeline system, whose westernmost terminals were planned to be located in East Germany and Czechoslovakia, was also expected to reach the shores of the Caspian Sea, and as far as China on its eastern path. More branches were planned to the Baltic ports of Klaipėda and Ventspils, and to the Far East port of Nakhodka (Figures 5.1 and 5.2).[3] This project would nevertheless require specific capabilities to produce the materials needed to build the pipeline system, including a number of advanced technological artifacts such as turbines and compressors, and most particularly large-diameter steel pipes (those with a diameter larger than 40 inches). In the early 1960s, the Soviets had neither the know-how nor the industrial infrastructure to produce such pipes in the requisite quantities. It was the Soviet effort to acquire these technologies, and the different estimates of Soviet productive capabilities, which gave rise to one of the two debates at the core of this chapter.

Historians of technology have long recognized the importance of social, political, and economic factors in shaping what a technological artifact is.[4] In particular, understanding of the sizes and functions of the pipes was reflected in the measures that NATO implemented in order to face the threat of the Soviet 'oil flood'. The eighteen-month debate that followed the US NATO delegation's proposal of an embargo on large-diameter pipes and pipeline equipment was indicative of the multiple status of pipes as technological items, a point reminiscent of Hecht's argument about uranium. Like 'nuclearity' for uranium, 'pipeness'—that is the intrinsic nature of pipes—was ontologically ambiguous. It depended on the political context in which these items were embedded. Furthermore, the interpretation of a technological artifact in a transnational context is wholly dependent on views that reflect national economic and political interests. In the transnational arena, these views are subject to debate and, at times, to hybridization.[5]

The analysis of this debate also refines our understanding of the role of pipelines as the locus of political struggle, an observation emphasized by Mitchell, and more recently by geographer Andrew Barry, who have both highlighted the importance of controlling the strategic points of passage (such as sea straits or territories crossed by pipelines) in order for oil to flow smoothly. As will become clear in what follows, the availability of large-diameter pipes came to constitute an example of such points of passage. It can also be interpreted, in Thomas Hughes' terminology, as a 'reverse salient,' namely a component of a technological system, which, because of insufficient development, compromises the effective operation of the system as a whole.[6]

Finally, this chapter picks up the work of historian Per Högselius on Euro–Soviet gas trading, which focused on the period starting in the late 1960s, by extending the narrative back in time to the early 1960s, at a time when oil, not gas, was the main player in energy trade relations between the USSR and Western Europe. It also builds on Angela Stent's seminal monograph on West German–Soviet relations, which extensively covered the embargo from the West German perspective, while applying it to a more transnational framework.[7]

This chapter starts by examining the debate in the EEC about imports of Soviet oil by EEC member countries. It then moves on to the NATO debate on the possibility of stemming the Soviet oil trade by enacting a supranational regulatory framework, and placing an embargo on certain sensitive Western technologies that the Soviets might use for building their pipelines. Throughout the debates, French and Italian administrations at the EEC, and the US and UK administrations at NATO, held conflicting points of view. These reflected markedly different perceptions of the rights and wrongs of Soviet trade and were dictated by national political agendas. The EEC and NATO discussions differed not only in the nature of their results, but also in the rationales underlying those results: in the European case, the rationale was essentially economic; in the Atlantic case, it alternated between economic and strategic. At NATO in particular, the debate

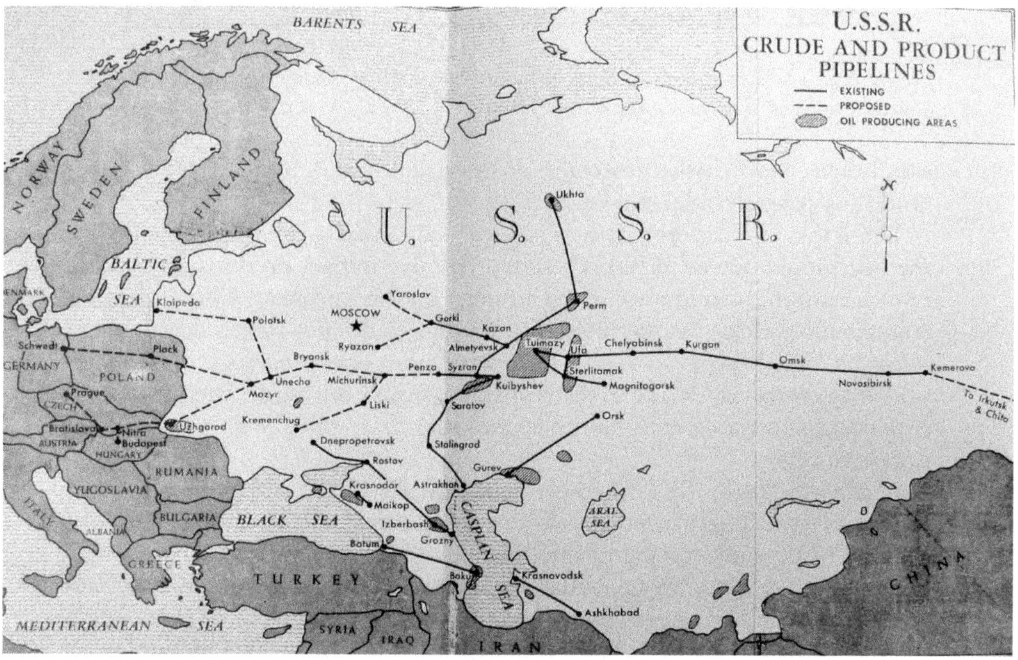

Figure 5.1 The Soviet pipeline system in late 1960.
Source: Courtesy of Archives Historiques du Groupe ELF/Total.[8]

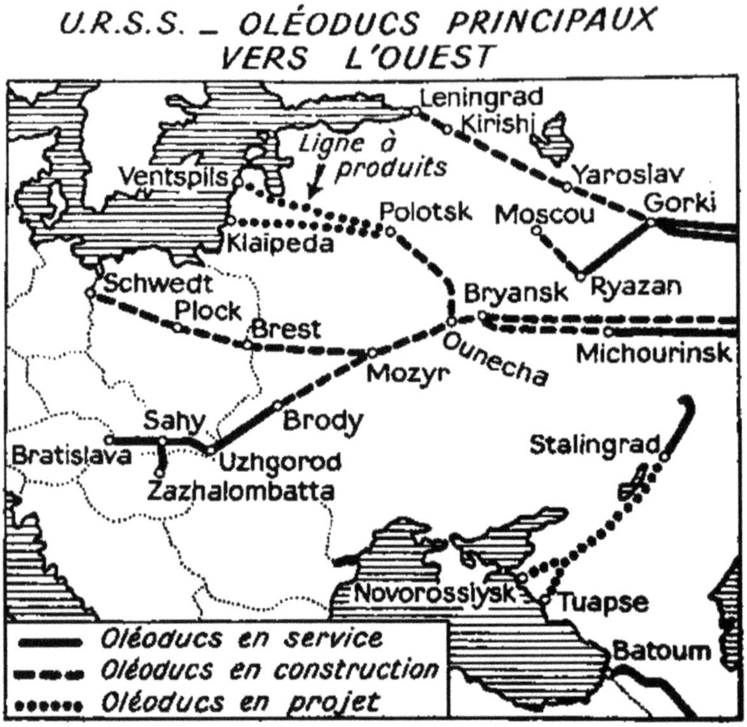

Figure 5.2 The European branch of the Soviet pipeline system (Druzhba) in 1962. Source: Courtesy of *Petroleum Economist*.[9]

was between a British, pro-trade position, and an American pro-security (and thus contra-trade) stance.

The actors also differed in their influence in the debate: whereas the US was the hegemonic power in NATO with a decisive impact on decision-making, France's attempts to impose its oil strategy on the European Community encountered obstacles, and ultimately failed. These debates clearly demonstrate, however, that both France and Italy were now operating in a new dimension that effectively marked the transition from addressing energy security issues as a matter of national policymaking, to aligning with transnational organizations.

In general, at the EEC and even more clearly in NATO, the main actors in the debates fought their battles through industrial forecasts, the mobilization of their military and intelligence agents, as well as oil companies, and through distinctions made between different kinds of pipes on the basis of their potential contents (oil or gas). During and *because of* this debate, the nature of the artifact 'pipe' changed. Its final status as a technological artifact was ultimately the result—in Hecthian terms—of this technopolitical negotiation.

Common Market Debates on Algerian and Soviet Oil

The French oil marketing system was characterized by nationalist and protectionist aspects that clashed with the appeal for the implementation of a free market within the EEC. In particular, the dispositions of the 1957 Treaty of Rome, which had established the European Community and the European nuclear energy community—Euratom—clashed with the protectionist nature of France's 1928 law. France needed to adjust its situation to the new regulations, with a gradual dissolution of the French oil monopoly into the Common Market (also called 'the Six' from the number of states constituting the Market).[10]

France opened a limited quota to oil from EEC members from 1959, but made its extension conditional on progress toward a European energy policy. French oil administrators wanted the European authorities to reassure them on a point they deemed fundamental: a common definition of the origin of products. Without that, nothing would prevent Italy from re-exporting its Soviet oil to the Common Market and thus, to France, since it would then be relabeled as Italian.[11]

In the autumn of 1959, the French government asked EEC members to adopt measures to protect the Common Market for crude oil, by creating EEC crude oil quotas that would be exempt from customs duties. Duties would be levied only on oil products obtained from imports of crude outside these quotas. Reductions in the quotas accepted by member states would correspond to future production increases from EEC sources (in particular, from Saharan oilfields), in order to make place for 'European' oil.[12] In essence, France was asking its European partners to prioritize the sale of Saharan crude within the EEC. The *Petroleum Press Service* review doubted the practicality of the French proposal. It would impose on all EEC refiners the same strict control policies that had been imposed on French refiners by the French State, by subjecting them to a surplus of regulations. Given that, in Italy alone, there were around eighteen refiners, one can picture how complex things would be.[13]

Another problem concerned prices: the higher cost of Saharan crude oil compared with Middle Eastern would oblige North African producers to grant large discounts to refiners, who would otherwise be unwilling to use Saharan oil. From a political point of view, the French system envisioned the creation of a protectionist zone within the Common Market, which might lead non-EEC governments to retaliate by discriminating against exports of EEC oil products, and levying duties on them. The Vice-President of the European Commission, Robert Marjolin, presented the French proposal at the first EEC meeting on oil issues. However, the proposal met with Dutch and German opposition, while from outside the Community the US also made representations in very energetic terms, labeling the French plan as contrary to the rules of the General Agreement on Tariffs and Trade rules and to the liberal policy that the Six planned to follow.[14]

An Italian committee at the Ministry of Industry also examined the possible prioritization of Algerian oil in December 1959. A technical adviser to the French Minister of Industry, Jean-Marcel Jeanneney, attended the meeting to explain the French project. An important presence within the Italian group was AGIP's Deputy General Manager, Nicola Melodia, representing ENI. Besides the obvious damage the implementation of the French proposal would cause to ENI's expected Soviet imports, the Italian company's efforts to curtail French profits from Algerian oil in agreement with the FLN strategy was a further reason for ENI to urge the Italian government to reject Jeanneney's plan.[15]

Confronted with the French proposal, Melodia objected that it would not be advantageous to the Italian economy and that, in addition, the British and American governments would see the discrimination against products emanating from their companies' foreign affiliates as an unfriendly act, and react accordingly. The Arab world, already against French policy in Algeria, might also respond unfavorably. From an economic point of view, limiting the free choice of crude supplies by giving priority to one source would generate an increase in prices for consumers, and this would greatly affect Italy.[16]

After talks with the leaders of US majors and the British government, the State Department urged the Quai d'Orsay to drop its project, and suggested that collaboration between French companies and British–American majors would ensure conditions that were satisfactory to France. Reporting the US counterproposal to Jeanneney, the Director of Economic Affairs at the Quai d'Orsay, Olivier Wormser, concluded that the Americans and British, and their national majors would be disposed to award French oil firms "substantial benefits." He believed that the American government would be willing to solve the problem posed by oil from Edjeleh by contributing to the acquisition of part of the 30–32 million tons of oil that would be carried by the Hassi Messaoud pipeline once it was fully operational.[17]

It would appear that, while resisting France's prioritization of Algerian oil in the Common Market, the US government was instead secretly supporting the prioritization of Libyan oil. As the discoverers of the first Libyan oilfields were US majors, the State Department was pushing the Libyan government to solicit a partnership with Italy within the Common Market. The possibility of trade links between the Six and states previously associated with them (politically or economically) was envisaged in the Treaty of Rome, and if accomplished would facilitate the marketing of Libyan oil—in which US companies had large stakes—in Italy and the EEC. Notwithstanding the willingness of the Libyan government to request a partnership, a French diplomatic source reported, they could not act freely: British influence in the country was so strong that CFP's analyst, Vincent Labouret, claimed that the domestic government only enjoyed partial sovereignty.[18] The US government was thus playing a secret game of its own: while siding against Italy's Soviet oil imports in NATO, as we will see in the next paragraphs, it spared no efforts to favor Italy at France's expense whenever American oil interests might benefit.

It is telling that US pressure was able to modify the French stance on European policies. This can only be understood if we consider the transnational challenges facing French firms in the Middle East and in France, where even in the late 1950s, respect for their oil deals always depended on American and British goodwill. In any case, by early 1960, the question of preferential treatment for Algerian oil had been mothballed. Yet French companies continued to press the Common Market to make room for their oil. In May 1961 for instance, CFP adviser François de Laboulaye showed his awareness that, if Algeria separated from France, the Algerians would only be willing to retain French legislation and the franc if it were to their advantage. This meant that they needed to be assured of a market for their product, which explained the necessity of reaching the broadest possible west European agreement in order to protect the Algerian market from crude originating in the Middle East.[19] But while French companies continued to press more or less heavily to make room for their oil, it was now the Soviet oil offensive that took central stage within the community's oil debates.

Unlike coal or nuclear energy, respectively administered through the High Authority of the European Coal and Steel Community (ECSC) and Euratom, in the late 1950s hydrocarbons were the only major form of energy resource not regulated by a Western European institution. Following the discoveries of African oil, the Soviet oil offensive, and the glut of oil on the market, it became necessary to devise a common hydrocarbon policy. Simultaneously, through Euratom, European countries formalized their determination to diversify their energy sources by developing a nuclear industry. As with hydrocarbons, Atlantic influence in European affairs was manifested in the State Department's endorsement of the new energy authority. The high level of technological expertise attained by the Americans was to be used as a further tool of foreign policy. By restricting the pool of technological options available to Euratom countries, and counting on the support of European national partners, US officials would seek to control the development of European programs.[20]

Impeding Soviet oil exports was also part of the same strategy of controlling Europe's energy. An EEC working group of high officials, chaired by Marjolin, was set up in April 1960, following a memorandum on the coordination of energy policies devised by an inter-executive group formed by representatives of the ECSC, the European Commission—the EEC's executive body—and Euratom.[21] Significantly, Italy was not represented in the group.

The battle against Soviet oil was also waged at the European Parliament, where the French Gaullist deputy, Christian de la Malène, once again highlighted the problem of Soviet oil exports and prompted the Commission to set up periodic exchanges of data on imports of oil products from all origins. In the statistics eventually provided by the Commission for the first five months of 1960, Italy's position as the largest importer of Soviet oil was striking; Italy's imports were three times larger than West Germany's and four times larger than France's.[22]

French lobbying against Soviet oil imports sanctioned the French effort to realign with the majors. But France was not alone in its anti-Soviet tactics. On 11 October 1960, the very day the ENI–SNE agreement was signed, Diego Guicciardi, the distressed president of Shell's Italian branch, declared his intention to raise the alarm with Italian representatives at the EEC, since ENI's deals threatened to nullify the very common policy of collaboration the EEC was trying to establish.[23] In November 1960, SONJ's president Monroe Rathbone also solicited the State Department to make representations to the Italian government. A few days later, ENI managers learnt that Rathbone had sent SONJ's foreign affiliates a note highlighting the deleterious impact of the ENI–SNE agreement for Western Europe. Rathbone was later joined in his protest by Gordon Reed of Texas Gulf and Arnold Hofland of Shell. Reed submitted several recommendations to the US Congress as well as to federal petroleum committees and the State Department, while Hofland intervened with the British and Dutch governments and contacted the US Embassy in Paris.[24] These protests, interventions, and confidential cables were further examples of the strong lobbying pressure applied by oil majors. By contrast with US governmental papers, however, considerations of threats to Western military security do not seem to have played a significant role in these exchanges.

The tripartite inter-executive working group eventually submitted its proposals to the general secretariat of the Council of the European Communities in January 1961. The aim of these proposals was to harmonize energy policies and safeguard supplies in case the energy market deteriorated. The harmonization measures amounted to a renunciation of the right to make decisions on energy matters before consultation with other EEC countries and the Commission itself. The second set of provisions, to be introduced over a period of three to five years, included import quotas for coal, crude and oil products, customs duties on imported coal and fuel oil, and community-funded subsidies for coal production.[25] Although Italy acknowledged the need for a common energy policy, it did not adhere to the inter-executive proposals, which it saw as dictated by the majors' vested interests. On the contrary, ENI suggested that the Italian government should object to both harmonization and safeguarding measures until the group outlined the aims of a global common energy policy and the means whereby it intended to achieve them.[26]

Aside from ENI's ostracism at the EEC, the company also pursued a nuclear policy that did nothing to reassure US industrial circles of its acquiescence to American technological hegemony. Together with other Italian public and private concerns, in 1957 ENI had entered the nuclear sector by establishing its affiliate, AGIP Nucleare. While all other national agencies had agreed to fuel their nuclear power plants with American enriched uranium, Mattei and ENI's engineers had decided to build a nuclear reactor in collaboration with the British Nuclear Power Plant Company. This would be fueled with British slightly enriched uranium, a decision that was seen as a further indication of ENI's opposition to the Americans. A few months after the 1960 oil contract with the Soviet Union, ENI had also secretly attempted to obtain Russian uranium, but the Soviets had offered only a "firm and definitive refusal."[27] ENI's 'British choice' in a very security-sensitive sector thus added up to a rejection of the EEC's oil policy.

In fact, Italian opposition perturbed not only the French, but also the Germans. Opposition to ENI's Soviet imports reappeared at the European Parliament when the German Liberal deputy, Walter Scheel, referring to ENI's Soviet agreement of 1960, asked if the Commission had been informed of the details of the contract, and then attacked its passivity.[28] The Commission's President, Scheel's fellow countryman Walter Hallstein, replied that it had been informed of the contract and of its details, but because the contract had been signed before a community policy was set, the Commission could not intervene. ENI's calculations had been correct; the timely conclusion of the 1960 deal had paid off.[29]

In April 1961, the group of EEC oil experts met in Brussels to discuss a survey they had previously submitted to member states to collect statistics on their oil regulations. A serious problem emerged regarding re-exports. Beside relabeling and re-exporting problems, a member state might have Soviet oil refined on its behalf in refineries located in another member country. The situation was further complicated by the lack of precise data on re-exports, which made it impossible to determine to what extent security of supply was at risk. In addition, Italy's commitment to Soviet oil also raised anxieties in the Common Market's industrial environment: cheap oil implied lower production costs in many Italian industrial sectors, giving Italy an advantage over its competitors in Europe.[30]

ENI Moves Faster

In view of the July 1961 meeting of oil experts, the European Commission eventually prepared a draft regulation intended to limit Soviet imports. The proposed regulation was also designed to prevent France appealing, in the case of re-exports, to article 115 of the Treaty of Rome, which would block the free circulation of products originating in the Eastern Bloc, and constitute a patent rejection of one of the pillars of the young Common Market. The Commission's proposal was based on a simple limitation of imports, taking effect retroactively from January 1961. Each country would commit to limit its annual imports from the Eastern Bloc to their 1960 level. If a member state wanted to import volumes above that threshold, it would have to consult its EEC partners and the commission three months before taking up negotiations for additional purchases.

The French Fuels Director, Maurice Leblond, objected that the flexibility given to states to increase their Soviet oil quotas was far too generous, as imports had been growing considerably since 1955.[31] This, the French agency contended, would benefit Italy, which had considerably increased its imports in 1960. The cut-off date should instead be that of the signature of the Treaty, when Soviet imports had been much smaller.[32] The most serious criticism concerned the considerable latitude given to the states that wanted to increase their Soviet oil quotas, in that nothing would oblige them to conform to the advice received from partners and the Commission. Finally, while import procedures would be applied nationally, the consequences of imports would affect the whole Community, so that Italy would once again be advantaged, given its position as the largest importer of Soviet oil, and the largest re-exporter to the Community. Leblond proposed instead that a global EEC quota be established for imports of Soviet oil into the Community, which would then be distributed between countries on the basis of their consumptions levels.[33]

Considerations of Italian advantages notwithstanding, ENI did not react favorably to the Commission's proposal either. The company speculated that, prior to its presentation to the Commission, the proposal had been secretly vetted by SONJ and Shell. First and foremost, ENI argued, international oil companies should commit to a reduction in crude prices to a level that reflected real market conditions. As a consequence of ENI's position, at a European Commission meeting in July 1961, the Italian delegation was the only one to oppose a pilot study on an agreement on the self-limitation of Soviet oil imports.[34]

Despite the opposition, Marjolin proposed that the pilot study should be presented to the Commission and submitted as a proposal to the EEC Council. The Commission reached the decision that countries should first have to consult the Council's members before concluding trade agreements with third parties. In April 1962, the Council assigned the working group the task of devising a detailed study of the energy market and the guiding principles for energy policy in the Common Market. Two months later the group submitted a *Memorandum on Energy Policy*. Among other provisions, it proposed a quota system for Soviet crude oil and petrol products across the European Community. This legitimization-with-restrictions meant that other operators were allocated shares of the available Soviet quotas, lowering the Italian share. ENI responded to this eventuality by suggesting that the Italian delegation should seek to obtain adequate quota guarantees, or reject the proposal altogether.[35]

A secret note from the French Chiefs of Staff of the National Defense warned Georges Pompidou, prime minister since April 1962, that even though the EEC appeared to be succeeding in its limitation policy, the 'Mattei threat' was anything but defused. European authorities might limit ENI's Soviet imports, but anxieties relating to its multiple and systematic activities in the former French colonies in Africa were more real than ever. The French military authorities thus believed that their government should neutralize the Italian group in those French hunting grounds.[36] Mattei knew that Italy's resistance to the quota system at the EEC could not continue forever. He thus attempted to negotiate a further agreement with the Soviets and sent ENI executive officer, Giuseppe Ratti, to Moscow in September 1962. Two days after Ratti's return to Italy, the Commission proposed the quota system and sent it to national governments for approval. ENI was skating on thin ice, but had an advantage: it was able to act much faster than the European bureaucratic machine.[37]

However, negotiations between ENI, SNE, and other Soviet companies dragged on for a year, the new agreement only being signed in November 1963. This delay was apparently a result of the uncertainty following Mattei's death, and of the political embarrassment the company's Soviet dealings were causing vis-à-vis Italy's allies. Eventually, even after the two contracts with SONJ had been agreed (see p. 192), ENI committed to buying 25 million tons of Soviet crude oil between 1965 and 1970, in return for goods the Russians would buy from the Italian holding company. While the quantities involved were still considerable, they would represent a smaller share of Italy's prospective oil needs than ENI's previous contracts.[38]

As for the EEC, in the months following June 1962, the policy devised in the inter-executive group's memorandum was reshaped, modified, and amended to accommodate each member's interests, but no agreement could be reached within a short time, especially due to Italy's obstructionism. Only in April 1964 was a protocol of agreement on energy policy approved by a special council of ministers, far too late to stop the new Italian–Soviet agreement. The first to act against the Soviet export strategy was therefore NATO. Besides oil exports, the main bone of contention in this case was the trade in Western technological artifacts for use in the Soviet pipeline system. These are the topics I will analyze in the next paragraphs.[39]

A Dangerous *Friendship*

In 1958, Soviet oil transportation was still handicapped by an overloaded railway system, which carried around 60 percent of the extracted oil, as compared with 5 percent in the US. The Soviets aimed to meet 35 percent of oil transportation requirements via a new pipeline system, whose European branch would be named *Druzhba* (Russian for 'friendship'). Druzhba would connect the new oilfields to potential commercial outlets. Aside from relieving the strain on their railway network, the system would also allow the Soviets to increase exports and reduce the demand for tankers. In addition, the pipeline could easily be connected to seaport terminals where the Soviet Navy's vessels were moored. The importance of these terminals for the Soviet military had already been pointed out by the American Frank Uhlig, a member of the US Naval Institute, in the early 1950s. He had maintained that, the bulk of the Soviet fleet being in the Baltic, the Soviets could easily prevail over the Swedish fleet and, by clearing naval opposition there, could expand their operations. As for the Black Sea fleet, its only opponent was the weak Turkish fleet: if the Dardanelles fell to the Russians, Uhlig argued, they could easily reach the Mediterranean.[40]

As a consequence Soviet oil flows, at least at a first glance, promised to upset the Western Bloc militarily and economically. More worryingly for the US, as we saw in Chapter 4, by the late 1950s individual countries that were members of Western-Bloc international organizations, such as the EEC and NATO, notably Italy and West Germany, were already engaged in negotiating agreements to import Soviet hydrocarbons, and had also agreed to sell the pipes and equipment the Soviets needed. The US administration first, and NATO afterwards, swiftly moved to block these deals. The sticking point—oil-for-technology barter deals and in particular large-diameter pipes—did not just feature as an object of political controversy; their very nature was molded in the clash between national representatives.

Because of possible military consequences, Soviet plans for Druzhba soon generated frantic debate at NATO. From 1960, the pipeline question came under scrutiny from NATO's Committee of Economic Advisers (ECONAD), operating under the authority of the North Atlantic Council (NAC). Founded in 1957, ECONAD was designated as a venue for the study of oil-related issues, including assessments of Russian oil production, exports, and reserves, NATO countries' oil imports from Communist countries, and issues relating to pipelines. ECONAD was particularly concerned with those issues that had political or defense implications, or which affected the economic health of the Atlantic Community. Envisaged as a standing committee, it was intended to complement the role performed by the Committee on Soviet Economic Policy (though the functions of the two committees sometimes overlapped).[41]

In July 1960, ECONAD met to examine the impact of Soviet oil on world markets. In the same month, it decided that NATO members should prepare statistics on their trade with the Soviet Bloc, and proposed the preparation of a common policy for Western oil-supplying countries in the face of the Soviet oil threat. An ad hoc Study Group on Soviet Oil Policy was then established. NATO's need for such an assessment became even more urgent following the creation of OPEC in September, which triggered fears that the USSR might conclude an agreement with Arab producers to the ultimate detriment of Western oil majors.[42]

ECONAD had been charting Soviet efforts to increase oil exports since the beginning of 1960, noting that these had been highly successful, especially outside Europe, and that attempts to stop them had failed. At the same time, the capacity of the Russian tanker fleet had been growing at an alarming speed, further boosting Soviet export capacity.[43] Starting in September, the Study Group debated a common policy to counter the threats. The national delegations abided by the recommendations issued by their national oil companies. Most of the knowledge passed by oil companies and intelligence services to their national governments concerned details of operations by competitors from allied countries, obtained through surveillance activities. This information enabled NATO delegates to draw on the latest data and most accurate estimates, and thereby to foresee, parry, and immediately respond to their allies' moves. In the case of Italy's oil deals, intelligence gathered by the French and American agencies was used to drive international criticism of Italian arrangements with the Soviets, and with Communist countries in general.

Not that the criticism was always unfounded. For instance, US intelligence may well have been leaked information from the French that in September 1960, ENI was asked by the Cuban Prime Minister, Fidel Castro, to take responsibility for operating British and American refineries expropriated during the Cuban Revolution. Mattei refused, but affirmed ENI's availability to supply the necessary equipment and technical assistance in return for cash payment. But ENI executives also passed strategic intelligence to the Study Group's Italian delegation, which consisted of two officials from the Ministry of Industry and was headed by the General Director of Energy Sources, Guido Giorgi. Ultimately, the company had significant input into the drafting of Italy's line at the meetings.[44]

That national enterprises collaborated with their NATO delegations within the Study Group was to be expected, and adds to the strength of the argument about a symbiosis between military and economic motivations in confronting the Soviet oil export strategy. But these contacts also reveal the network of relations between the oil industry and top-ranking figures in national administrations. US majors such as SONJ, SOCONY, and Texaco lobbied the State Department. BP and Shell also had frequent exchanges with the British Foreign Office, and as historian Niklas Jensen-Eriksen has noted, when the Joint Intelligence Bureau of the Ministry of Defence was asked to draft a memorandum on Soviet oil exports in 1958, it was Shell that the Ministry of Power consulted when collecting material. CFP worked closely with the French Foreign Ministry, to the point of plainly suggesting which tactics to pursue.[45]

The Study Group meetings soon coalesced into an attack on ENI's trade with the USSR. ENI responded with a defensive memorandum attempting to divert criticism. Competition on the international oil market and the crisis in the coal industry, the memorandum's authors claimed, had impelled the oil majors to promote international initiatives to constrain countries that drew considerable advantages from low energy prices. The problem of Western security and the weakening of the Western oil industry, the Italian diplomats commented in correspondence with ENI executive Giorgio Ruffolo, had been brought up at NATO at the initiative of the State Department, in a direct reflection of the interests of the oil majors: "The attempt to smuggle [...], under the pretext of security, the control and limitation of oil imports from the Soviet Union, seems evident."[46]

A further ENI memorandum for the Italian delegation included counter-arguments to possible accusations by the Study Group, namely the potential threats to Italian and Western security posed by Soviet oil imports, and the consequences for Western oil companies if the Soviets engaged in dumping tactics. Against these allegations it was argued that, given Italy's expanding market, Soviet oil imports would never reach a critical share of Italian supplies, and that the current abundance of oil on the world market would make replacement easy in the event of a sudden interruption of Soviet deliveries. ENI claimed that a relaxation of trade exchanges with the USSR would be beneficial to East–West relations; and that the real problem was not Soviet dumping but the majors' current inability to control crude oil prices.[47] In his correspondence with Giorgi, Ruffolo retorted that the reason why the majors were being out-competed by the Soviets was their artificially high posted prices. The Italians believed Soviet imports would make consumers less vulnerable to further crises in the Middle East. ENI's claim had more than a grain of truth in it: we have seen how the majors pursued their strategy of producing scarcity, which made the Middle East highly dependent on their commercial plans.[48]

The Italian Foreign Ministry endorsed ENI's defense strategy in the context of negotiations. Emphasis was placed on changes occurring in the international oil market, where the entry of independent producing companies had increased the availability of crude oil. Moreover, the establishment of a US quota system in 1959 had already radically altered the market price of oil prior to the appearance of Soviet oil. Another point stressed by Italian diplomats was that Italy's position became more defensible if, rather than focusing only on oil, one looked at all trade exchanges with the USSR. NATO estimates revealed that West Germany, the UK, and France exchanged a higher volume of goods than the Italians, and there was no reason why Italian oil deals alone should be on trial.[49]

The NATO Study Group, under the chairmanship of Keith Stock, Undersecretary of the Petroleum Division at the British Ministry of Power, met for the first time two months after the signing of the 1960 ENI–SNE agreement. Group members were asked to provide data on current and planned Soviet oil imports to their countries and of their exports to the USSR; on the conditions under which such trade took place; and on the destination of imported oil. The last provision, although non-specific, emphasized NATO's preoccupation with the destination of Italian transshipped Soviet-sourced oil products. In February 1961, the Group explicitly asked the Italian delegates to circulate a note on their country's re-exports.[50]

A draft report by the Study Group was ready by May 1961. It concluded that due to the substantial trade in Soviet-Bloc-sourced oil products by both NATO and non-NATO countries, restrictive measures needed to be taken and implemented by all members.[51] On the effects of Soviet exports on prices, the Study Group endorsed the majors' argument that the Soviets did not have to bear the costs borne by the transnational oil companies, such as royalties and export taxes. The majors—the Group's argument went—also faced additional costs for exploration, production, refining, and distribution, which justified their higher prices. As for Soviet Bloc exports, these had already affected traditional producers' interests in Venezuela and the Middle East, and had been one cause of the price cuts made by British and American companies in 1959–60. Middle Eastern producing countries had also been affected by the replacement of their oil on the market with Soviet oil.[52]

The report also provided figures on Soviet oil exports: these had reached 6 percent of NATO Europe's total consumption, although this figure varied across countries. Soviet oil's share of total imports was 14.8 percent for Italy, 7.1 percent for West Germany, 3.7 percent for France, and 0.3 percent for the UK. If these exports continued to grow, the Study Group warned, their level in NATO European countries would rise to 15 percent in 1965 (see Figure 5.3).[53] Of most concern was the fact that Soviet oil changed its identity through multiple transactions, making import controls inefficient. If restrictions were imposed, these would have to be applied on first entry of imports into the NATO area. It was acknowledged that these restrictions would negatively affect the economies of members in bilateral agreements with the USSR. In order to prevent this, it was suggested that, rather than cut existing quantities, future increases in imports should be avoided. As in the case of the EEC debate, this provision greatly disturbed the French (while it suited the Italian delegation quite well), since once again sticking to current levels would be prejudicial to the European marketing of Saharan oil.[54]

Country	Direct Imports from Soviet bloc (a)	Retained Imports (a)	Total Imports	Total Consumption (b)	(1) as a % of (3)	(1) as a % of (4)	(2) as a % of (4)
(0)	(1)	(2)	(3)	(4)	(5)	(6)	(7)
Belgium-Luxembourg	355.4	355.4	10,835.2	7,252.3	3.3	4.9	4.9
Denmark	90.0	90.0	5,065.0	5,262.0	1.8	1.7	1.7
France	977.6	1,179.8	26,100.0	27,300.0	3.7	3.6	4.3
Germany (FR)	2,202.6	2,142.7	31,041.0	29,651.0	7.1	7.4	7.2
Greece	568.5	568.5	2,643.5	2,497.1	21.5	22.8	22.8
Iceland	385.0	385.0	405.0	400.0	95.1	96.3	96.3
Italy (c)	4,605.2	3,265.5	31,049.5	22,383.0	14.8	20.5	14.6
Netherlands	57.5	60.7	23,946.0	10,761.0	0.2	0.5	0.6
Norway	340.4	356.8	3,951.5	3,635.5	8.6	9.4	9.8
Portugal	25.6	25.6	1,759.4	1,561.2	1.5	1.6	1.6
Turkey	-	-	1,208.5	1,395.4	-	-	-
United Kingdom	205.0	233.0	59,547.0	43,858.0	0.3	0.5	0.5
NATO unspecified	-	487.0					
TOTAL	9,812.8	9,150.0	197,556.6	155,956.5	5.0	6.3	5.9

Figure 5.3 Dependence on Soviet Bloc oil in NATO European countries in 1960.
Source: Courtesy of NATO Archives, Brussels.[55]

NATO's ambition to reform East–West oil trading was now taking oil geopolitics to a new level, making the Atlantic Alliance the transnational forum for conflicts that had hitherto unfolded through national representations. The pressure applied by the State Department in the postwar years to mold the Italian and French oil markets to the benefit of the majors now manifested directly in discussions at the Alliance's headquarters. That the conflict between Italian and French diplomats arose at the same time as Italian support for Algerian nationalists, further embittered the debate. The result of the discussion—as I will now show—was a standoff. The Study Group report was to be examined by ECONAD in November 1961, but after a draft was presented in March, the Italian delegation raised objections.

In April 1961, the Italian delegation drafted a memorandum with observations and comments on the final report. The document was largely based on ENI's paper to Giorgi in December 1960, but pruned of its bitterest invective against the international majors. According to the Italians, a coordinated NATO policy against the Soviet offensive would not be effective unless it included an in-depth technical and political study of East–West trade. The oil problem should not be separated from other strategic issues relating to the Communist threat, the Italians argued. With respect to economic matters, they criticized the report's emphasis on the dangers of Soviet oil for producers, while the advantages for non-producing countries, which needed to obtain supplies easily and cheaply, were neglected. The Study Group's draft report, the Italians concluded, seemed to focus more on prospective threats than on the real consequences deriving from the surplus created by new oil discoveries and the appearance on the market of new producers.[56]

The Group's conclusions were admittedly rather abstract, and no practical measure was implemented to diminish Soviet imports. In June 1961, a note by the UK delegation expressed the desire that more be done with such a massive study, and that a recommendation be issued to limit Soviet oil imports. The note included a latent reference to Italy: "For those countries with high levels of imports already, restraint should be especially recommended."[57] US delegates, however, voiced their security concerns far more openly. It was necessary for NATO to adopt surveillance measures and consult more about oil trade with the Soviet Bloc. The Alliance should compel its members to submit periodic reports on Soviet oil imports, and strongly advise them to consult NATO in advance on agreements that might lead to a significant increase in those imports.

Based on the results of the Study Group, the US NATO delegate, Alfred Reifman, suggested an embargo on Western-Bloc large-diameter pipes and pipeline equipment, the strategic and military advantages the USSR would derive from its exports. The embargo, comments historian Angela Stent, "more than any other single incident, highlighted the U.S.'s primary role both in the establishment of the East–West trade agenda and in the politicization of specific economic issues." It also marked a turning point in the definitional pathway that would transform pipes from freely tradable to embargoed merchandise.[58]

The American Argument: The Military Threat

Following the embargo proposal, ECONAD requested that a study be conducted before a definitive decision was reached. The new Study Group on Soviet pipelines was formed in Washington, and when its final report reached ECONAD in September, it closely reflected the American viewpoint. The report argued that Druzhba had "obvious military significance."[59] As a consequence, at a subsequent meeting of the pipeline Study Group, US General Major Francis Piggott, Assistant Chief of Staff for Intelligence at the Supreme Headquarters Allied Powers Europe (SHAPE), urged that the construction of the pipeline be delayed in order to prevent oil supplies to both the Soviet Navy and Soviet divisions in Eastern Europe. Unlike the Soviet railway, which ran north to south, pipelines would run east to west, and the flow of oil in that direction would make supplying the Soviet military machine in Eastern Europe easier.[60]

According to the report, moreover, the Soviets were not producing large-diameter pipes at over 40-inch diameter, and there seemed to be no evidence at that time that they were progressing rapidly enough to build large capacity tube mills or steel rolling mills capable of producing steel plate wide enough to enable the manufacture of single-weld 40-inch pipe. Considerations of the Soviet ability to access certain technologies led the Study Group to conclude that, although the Soviets claimed to be able to produce pipe by welding two pre-formed halves, there was no indication that they were actually doing so. Large-diameter pipes were critical to the Soviet oil export strategy, as they would make it possible to improve significantly the flow rate at which oil could be delivered to Europe. Soviet industries were also reported to be unable to build gas turbines, electric motors, and other equipment required for 40-inch lines. As for auxiliary equipment, they were in need of Western technology as corrosion was a major problem in their pipes and equipment, due to the high sulfur content of their oil. They lacked pumps, compressors, turbines, valves, pipe fittings, large electrical engines, gauges, and telemetering and short-wave control equipment. An embargo, the report's compilers concluded, would effectively delay the completion of Druzhba.[61]

By the time the report was presented at ECONAD, the significance of pipelines for the Soviet marine military apparatus was clearer than ever to NATO, and added to concerns about Russian technological progress in war vessels. Such concerns had eventually led NATO to establish an ad hoc group to produce oceanographic knowledge for anti-submarine warfare needs in late 1958. NATO military authorities were especially worried about the Soviet warships docked along the Baltic and Pacific coasts.

The Soviet railway and naval units, relieved of transporting oil, could then be used to carry logistically critical goods, such as ammunition and foodstuffs.[62]

It was not the first time the US had proposed blockades in order to hinder Soviet industrial projects. In 1946, a penicillin plant program launched by the United Nations Relief and Rehabilitation Administration to build up the capacity of the pharmaceutical industry in Eastern and Southern Europe was significantly delayed by an American embargo on extractor technologies. The State Department refused to grant export licenses for the necessary equipment to pass the Iron Curtain. Other products including radioisotopes and computer equipment were also embargoed to stifle Soviet technological progress. In October 1960, after Fidel Castro nationalized the property of US citizens and companies in Cuba, an embargo was famously enacted against the Caribbean island. It is therefore not surprising that the US delegation hoped to try another embargo, this time on western oil technologies. By enacting it, Western countries would create a bottleneck in Soviet oil flows, and cause a reverse salient in Soviet trading and military power.[63]

In hindsight, the 1962 embargo on oil pipes and pipeline technology marked a foundational decision that became a template for future USSR–US conflicts, as shown by the embargo on pipeline technologies implemented in the early 1980s by Ronald Reagan's government, which strained US relations with the UK and the European Community. In the summer of 1961, US delegates at NATO alleged that European countries' Soviet trade was imperiling the security of the entire Western Bloc: it is not easy to assess to what extent American responses reflected genuine security concerns, or were rather the disguised commercial interests of US oil majors.[64]

During the NATO debate, the latter interests were never named, but their presence lingered in the discussions and is revealed by the constant contact between the American representatives and officers of US oil companies. It would probably not be too far from the truth to argue that these two preoccupations dovetailed nicely. Indeed in 1963, the *World Petroleum* review admitted that the first demand to use NATO and US diplomatic channels to restrict trade in oil between the West and the USSR had been made in November 1960 at an annual meeting of the American Petroleum Institute, by Gulf Oil's President, Ernest Brockett, and by SONJ's President, Monroe Rathbone. Jersey recommended exactly what Reifman's proposal was designed to achieve: a NATO agreement on a list of strategic materials, the sale of which would be prohibited, including those allowing the Soviets to complete their pipeline system and refineries in Eastern Europe.[65]

Whatever the rationale of the American strategy at NATO, the Washington Group's report asserted that in order to complete their pipeline system, the Soviets would need significant foreign assistance. The USSR had already been importing large-diameter pipes from abroad for several years. NATO members had not prevented these kinds of exports since the Coordinating Committee for Multilateral Export Controls (CoCom)—an informal non-treaty organization established soon after World War II by the powers allied with the US and NATO to limit the flow of technology to the Eastern Bloc—had reduced restrictions on pipe and oil equipment exports to the Soviet Bloc in 1958. In the 1958 review of international strategic controls, however, almost all items relating to the oil industry had been deleted or downgraded to 'Watch List' status, which only required that any deliveries to the Eastern Bloc be reported to the Atlantic Alliance's authorities. Since Soviet demand for large-diameter pipes had lately been limited, these items had been deleted from the list.[66]

As a consequence of this regulatory relaxation, by the spring of 1961 the Soviets had placed, or were negotiating, new orders with West Germany, Italy, Sweden, and Japan. Soviet companies were also trying to acquire the new industrial technology required to produce the pipes. By the end of 1960, they had already been in contact with German firms to negotiate the use of a new spiral welding process, a German innovation that enabled the construction of pipes from long strips of steel plate fitted together to form helical seams, thus minimizing leaks in the pipeline.[67] It was the ease with which the Soviets could acquire foreign technology that drove the US to propose the embargo, in a clear manifestation of pipe technopolitics. The request, however, triggered a firm British reaction at the following ECONAD meetings.

The British Counterargument: The Trade Boomerang

Considering that the UK topped the list of Soviet trade partners in Europe, it may not come as a surprise that the British would object to American arguments that framed Druzbha as a military threat. However, considering the oil sector alone, British firms (Shell and BP) would achieve significant benefits from an embargo. In consequence, the position taken on the embargo by the UK reflected a domestic clash of interests. As mentioned, the British government had implemented an embargo on Soviet oil and oil products in 1959. It is possible that the inter-ministerial discrepancies that had emerged at the time of that embargo were now returning to the surface. In 1959, the opinion of the Ministry of Power had prevailed over that of the Board of Trade, which favored a continuation of trade with the Soviets.

This time, however, the opinion of the Board of Trade was supported by the Treasury, whose Joint Permanent Secretary, Frank Lee, had earlier been the Permanent Secretary of the Board of Trade. Lee was open to the possibility of British oil companies reaching an 'accommodation' with the Soviets, meaning some sort of gentlemen's agreement, but his proposal was firmly opposed by British majors. However, by early 1960 the Treasury had already come to doubt that oil would be of crucial significance to the country's balance of payments when compared with the remaining trade sectors, and its opinion tilted the scales. Many British manufacturing companies were trading with the Soviet Union, and the scale of these exchanges exceeded that of oil. So an embargo made little economic sense to the British Treasury.[68]

That was part of the argument that the British delegate at NATO sought to defend at ECONAD meetings. Not only, he asserted, would a ban pose difficulties for the exporting industries of member countries. It would also either be ineffective or postpone increases in oil exports from the Eastern Bloc until the Soviets arranged to produce the necessary equipment themselves. In fact, he argued, it would push the Russians to scale up their production installations. The British delegation replied to the American data with its own, contradicting, data. The predominantly military nature of the pipeline, asserted by the Americans, was denied by the British. The latter maintained that since the embargo would cover all large-diameter pipes and related equipment, it would have to include all possible materials and equipment useful in the construction and installation of pipelines. But these included items in general use such as valves and earth-moving equipment, which surely were not strategically sensitive technologies. An embargo would then heavily and unnecessarily hit a number of branches of European industry.[69]

When in March 1962, French representatives proposed that NATO countries accept a moral obligation to discourage their nationals from entering into new contracts for deliveries of large-diameter pipes to the Soviet Bloc during embargo discussions, the British responded by making clear that the 'special relationship' between the UK and the US would not be allowed to put Britain's Soviet trade in jeopardy. The UK delegate questioned ECONAD's competence to debate the matter, and invoked the help of the Economic Adviser to the UK Joint Intelligence Bureau, Edward Radice. Radice stressed the British preference for a technical and economic analysis over strategic and military aspects. He maintained that, in general, implementing economic measures to stem industrial efforts had proved ineffective, because economic systems were much more flexible than was generally supposed.[70]

As for the 40-inch pipes, Radice estimated that Soviet requirements for Druzhba were 400 kt, not 1.2 Mt as the American estimates seemed to imply: in fact, the latter estimates referred to the overall Soviet requirements for oil and gas pipeline systems, not to the one system that was seen as threatening to the West, namely Druzhba. Radice maintained that, considering the USSR's expected production—Soviet manufacturers had by then managed to acquire a fair command of the production process for large-diameter pipes—plus the deliveries from Germany and Italy under existing contracts, the gap would eventually be small, and the Soviets could cover it if they faced an embargo. For example, they might try and step up production of 40-inch pipes, or use smaller diameters and double the lines if necessary (although in the latter case, the production of smaller pipes would have to double, thus generating further industrial issues: a point Radice did not mention).[71]

The British argument rested on their understanding of the Soviet preference for a pipe design that favored flexible usage over economic advantage. The British had acquired information that the Soviets were planning to manufacture 40-inch oil and gas pipes with similar pressure requirements, unlike the usual European practice of designing oil pipes for higher pressure than gas pipes. The equal-pressure requirement would allow Soviet 40-inch-pipe production to be used equally for oil or gas: all manufacturers could then produce the same kind of pipes, and that would result in a single large production machinery for 40-inch pipes, instead of two differentiated, smaller productions of oil and gas pipes. It was this flexibility, the British maintained, that would make the embargo ineffective.[72]

But was Soviet economy as flexible as Radice maintained? Not for the US delegation, which retorted that the Soviets were not going to interrupt their gas expansion program, since any interruption in that plan could lead to delays in output for military purposes.[73] Thus, the Soviet gap in large-diameter pipes *would* be significant, and so would the embargo. While the special relationship between the US and the UK was deteriorating over technical estimates, it concomitantly polarized the debate at NATO, where it soon appeared that the British government was not the only one alarmed by the embargo proposal.

A Technical Distinction Gone Unheeded

Representatives of other countries involved in trade relations with the Soviets in the sphere of oil and oil industry equipment were not at all convinced that an embargo was a desirable solution. In early 1962, in order to reassure NATO allies, the US representative at ECONAD clarified that the proposal was not intended to prevent existing contracts from being honored. The clarification was welcomed by the Italians and Germans, and also earned Belgian, French, Dutch, Portuguese, and Turkish approval. As for the French government, it supported the embargo from the very beginning. Like most other NATO countries, France had no interests in the Soviet pipe trade and, as shown earlier in this chapter, had much to gain in impeding cheap Soviet oil from reaching Western Europe. A similar 'national' objection to Soviet oil came from the Netherlands, which was not eager that Shell should face competition and had no ongoing major trading activities with the USSR. Italian acquiescence to the embargo proposal was unexpected, especially in light of ENI–Soviet relations.[74]

A rationale for Italy's go-ahead can be found in the fact that, during the embargo discussion, the Italian government was already effectively torpedoing the NATO Study Group on Soviet Oil Policy, by opposing any reduction in Soviet imports. Any further opposition to the pipe embargo would be most embarrassing to the Italian authorities, especially considering that the practical consequences of the embargo would be economically less problematic for Italy than a halt to oil imports. Opposition would also be pointless, since British hostility and German hesitation were currently preventing the embargo from being implemented, as I will show below. Finally, the favorable stance the Americans took to existing contracts between the Soviets and NATO countries seemed to reassure ENI that no major diplomatic incident would occur between them and the Soviets.[75]

The German government dithered. Large sections of the German Parliament objected to the embargo, as did many of those in industrial circles, while the ruling Christian Democrat government adhered to the US position. West German firms had been selling large-diameter pipes to the USSR since 1959, taking advantage of Washington's implementation of a policy prohibiting US firms from selling the USSR this kind of pipe: the volume of pipe sold by German firms had increased from 3.2 kt in 1958 to 255.4 kt in 1962. In addition, in October 1962, three large firms from the Ruhr region, namely Mannesmann, Hoesch and Phoenix-Rheinrohr, signed a contract to supply the USSR with 163 kt of 40-inch steel pipe, in exchange for pig iron.[76]

West German firms were therefore extensively involved in steel pipe trade with the Soviets: however, because of its strict political allegiance to—and in fact, dependence on—US policy, the German government found it politically impossible to oppose the embargo. However, the Germans could make technical objections: if the pipes involved in the German–Soviet trade were categorized as gas pipes, and thus not strategically relevant to the crux of the embargo, German firms could skirt the NATO resolution and honor their agreements with the Soviets. Thus the German delegation proposed that gas pipes be exempt from the embargo, and advanced an argument to make a distinction between oil 40-inch pipes and gas 40-inch pipes.[77] At the time of the NATO debate, gas was not regarded as a strategic resource, and it was only after the late 1960s that gas purchases would gradually acquire greater importance in East–West trade. In the early 1960s, gas trade was still relatively undeveloped in Western Europe, as were gas transmission infrastructures (though with significant exceptions in regions such as the Netherlands, North Italy, or France). It is therefore not surprising that gas pipes were not seen as strategically equivalent to oil pipes.[78]

How could the two kinds of 40-inch pipes be distinguished? As mentioned earlier, while the possibility of such a distinction in Soviet pipes was unlikely because of the equal-pressure specification adopted by local manufacturers, Western pipes could in principle be distinguished by pressure characteristics. Therefore, these pressure characteristics formed the core of the debate. The American Petroleum Institute maintained that 40-inch pipes for gas pipelines (characterized by lower pressure than oil pipes) could be used for the transportation of both oil and gas, and that it would therefore be possible to transport oil in the 40-inch pipes supplied for gas pipelines.

The Germans disagreed, and challenged the US institute's viewpoint. When trading with the Soviets, German pipe manufacturers had been required to supply them with an impact factor—the ratio of a dynamic force to its static weight—for temperatures of -40 °C and +20 °C. That seemed to indicate that this pipe was going to be used for gas pipelines, since such quality requirements, which made pipes substantially more expensive, were "pointless in the case of oil pipe since only at temperatures above 15°C was oil sufficiently fluid for conveyance by pipeline."[79]

The Germans supposed that the USSR would, as most countries did, consider its pipeline projects from the standpoint of economical operation, and that seemed to rule out the use for carrying oil of pipes specifically intended for gas. However, the German experts added a final clause to their document, acquiescing to the American argument that *in theory* there was the possibility that the two types of pipe could *to some extent* be regarded as interchangeable.[80] This linguistically nuanced specification, suggesting a possibility that otherwise appeared remote in the phrasing characteristic of scientific papers, might also have incautiously opened the way to its own ultimate dismissal. As a matter of fact, in the meetings that followed the German statement, no further mention was made of it.

The Embargo Approval and Its Consequences

As no agreement could be reached at ECONAD due to the British–American conflict, the embargo proposal finally reached the North Atlantic Council (NAC) in the spring of 1962. Eventually, thirteen countries out of fifteen agreed to the Council's recommendations. But here, too, the British remained contrarians. The findings of a further study group were needed before ECONAD reached the conclusion that the Soviets would indeed be short of 40-inch pipes, and that if these shortages were not filled by further imports from the free world, the pipeline system might be delayed for a period ranging from eight months to over two years. As for pipeline equipment, lack of sufficient information ruled out any final decisions.[81]

When the experts' draft was eventually debated at ECONAD, its members agreed to submit it to the Council with the recommendation that member countries, "under their own responsibility," should "to the extent possible": stop deliveries of large diameter pipe to the Soviet Bloc under existing contracts; and prevent new contracts for such deliveries. It was decided the Council would monitor the situation. In the end, therefore, the provision applied to existing contracts: I was unable to find in archival sources any explanation for the modification of this point, nor any mention of reactions from West Germany or Italy, although it is plausible that these were vocal. What we do know is that the absence of the 'existing contracts clause' caused serious trouble for West Germany and Italy in their trade relations with the Soviets. The embargo was finally approved by the Council on 21 November 1962 in the form of a recommendation (and therefore, at least legally, less binding than an order), but its enforcement was going to be problematic.[82]

In early 1963, alleged Polish attempts to place new large-diameter pipe orders in Italy caused the German government to react by requesting that member countries take the necessary steps to prevent the execution of Soviet Bloc orders placed later than the date of the embargo's enactment. The tensions generated by the embargo within the German government itself, and especially between the government and German industrialists, as described by Angela Stent, were linked with the pressing need of the Ruhr steel industry to increase production after a long period of stagnation. Tensions visibly materialized in March, when Konrad Adenauer's government avoided a defeat on the embargo resolution by a handful of votes. Obviously, Soviet firms involved in the German contracts, and in general the Soviet government, were not happy about the cancellation of existing contracts: they saw the German about-face as an openly hostile act, an infringement of the principles of international law, and reserved the right to take retaliatory measures.[83]

The embargo, notes Stent, and its approval by the German government in particular, marked a diplomatic victory for the US. In late 1962, ongoing negotiations between France and West Germany over a friendship agreement that finally materialized early the next year, suggested to the US administration that Germany favored alignment with France, and with the European policy proposed by French President de Gaulle, who had just rejected the UK's application to join the European Community. Thus Germany's alignment with the US over the embargo issue might have been seen as a way for the German government to appease the US government at a time of political tension between the two countries.[84]

Several attempts to break or sidestep the embargo were made. As far as Italy is concerned, one of the NATO reports mentioned 181 kt of 40-inch pipes as the amount that Italian firms were to deliver to the Soviets (they were actually 180). Yet we know that the 1960 ENI–SNE agreement scheduled deliveries of 240 kt of 40-inch pipe. The missing tons were at the center of an interesting episode, which coincided with the embargo discussions. The Italian iron and steel manufacturer that had been selected to supply the Soviets with large-diameter pipes was Finsider, a public agency on good terms with ENI. With a view to fulfilling its Soviet orders, Finsider had started the construction of a plant in southern Italy, using construction materials supplied by the American firm, US Steel. When the company directors realized that the factory would be supplying the Soviets, they prohibited Finsider from using their equipment to produce pipes, and threatened to stop deliveries for the plant's equipment and spare parts. The company president, Ernesto Manuelli, immediately discussed the matter with ENI's executives, and lamented being "forced by Italian and American authorities" to cut its Soviet deliveries by 25 percent. Manuelli had suggested that the Russians purchase the remaining quantity from the German firm Phoenix-Rheinrohr, which had worked with ENI in the past. The Soviet company, however, refused to go along with this.[85]

At his meeting with ENI executives, Manuelli argued that he had already promised the Americans not to export more than 180 kt of large-diameter pipes to the USSR, and called on ENI management to mediate between Finsider and the Soviet companies. Finding a solution was of paramount importance, since a breach of part of the ENI–SNE contract by one of ENI's partners could jeopardize the whole deal. An irritated Enrico Mattei therefore replied to Manuelli that it was not worth amending the Finsider contract because of American pressure. Mattei was also disappointed that the Italian authorities seemed to support, or at least not to oppose, American pressures. Manuelli and the management of the Soviet enterprises that had commissioned the pipes, Siderexport and Promsyrioimport, eventually reached a compromise in early March. Finsider's deliveries were reduced by 60 kt, and a clause was added to the new contract to the effect that the reduction would not affect other exchanges included in the 1960 agreement. Although there was no direct repercussion on the comprehensive agreement, the whole affair did cause the Soviet First Deputy Foreign Minister, Vasili Kuznetsov, to let ENI know that he felt "deeply offended" by Finsider's attitude.[86]

With regard to Britain, the oddity of its position vis-à-vis the embargo was instead highlighted by an episode that occurred in April 1963, when NATO's General Secretary, Dirk Stikker, was informed by the US government that a British firm, South Durham Steel, was negotiating with the Soviets on the sale of large-diameter pipe. Although the UK had not accepted the embargo, the Americans warned them that this move might jeopardize the whole edifice. US diplomats contacted their British counterparts to settle the matter.[87]

The degree to which the embargo succeeded is not easy to determine conclusively. According to NATO documents, these and other similar attempts to break the embargo did not ultimately succeed. By 1963, France and Italy had refused a number of contracts; the West Germans had embargoed 203 kt of 40-inch pipes, despite orders having been placed before the Council's decision. Japan and Sweden also generally cooperated. Maintaining that the outcome of the embargo had been successful, the Council noted the furious reaction of the Soviet Prime Minister, Nikita Khrushchev, in a television speech on 27 February 1963, during which he vehemently attacked the embargo. In addition, the Soviets also complained to Germany, and the blockade was extensively covered in the Soviet media. Other sources contradict this analysis. Indeed, the embargo seems to have been successful only to a limited extent: the construction of the pipeline system was indeed delayed, but by only a year, from a scheduled completion date of late 1963 to actual completion in late 1964. The measure adopted by NATO was not able to stop Soviet oil exports to Western Europe either, as these continued to increase in the early 1960s. By 1970, SNE had been exporting wherever it encountered opportunity.[88]

Energy expert and former CIA officer, Robert Ebel, contends that Sweden, which was not a NATO member, continued to deal with the Soviets, and that small amounts of pipes were also delivered to the USSR by Italy and Germany. According to Ebel, the number of 40-inch pipes imported by the USSR may have been enough to complete Druzhba by late 1963, but that did not happen because of the Soviet Union's ongoing development program for natural gas production, which directed the bulk of 40-inch pipes to that use. This factor, not the embargo, Ebel maintains, explains why Druzhba was not finished until 1964. In addition, in order to frustrate the embargo and manufacture more 40-inch pipes, a number of Soviet pipe mills were converted from small- to large-diameter pipes. All in all, therefore, the embargo seems to have not so much affected Soviet production of 40-inch pipes as that of smaller diameters, which the USSR had to decrease to make room for larger-diameter pipes.[89]

Four years after the enforcement of the embargo, ECONAD itself admitted that its main, inadvertent consequence had been to stimulate the growth of Soviet pipe production. While this production still left much to be desired as far as quality was concerned, the Soviet Union could now use its own manufacturing capacity to implement any project that would be important either in strategic or in economic policy terms. The embargo lasted until November 1966, when the French and West German governments requested its cancellation, arguing that it had reached the end of its usefulness, and that the Soviet rolling mills had by then recovered their backlog.[90]

Conclusion

Were American and West European diplomats really acting in the interests of European security when trying to limit Soviet oil exports? Historian Geir Lundestad disagrees, maintaining that the US was more interested in perpetuating Europe's dependence on American national companies. His claim, I believe, is generally correct, but does not explain the whole picture. On the one hand, big economic interests were the elephant in the room at EEC and NATO discussions on trade restrictions with the Soviets: the plans and lobbying of oil companies, whether American or European, could not be referred to in the Alliance's discussions, but were obviously present, mostly cloaked in the guise of national security. It seems fair to say that national delegations acted as diplomatic proxies for oil interests in Western Europe, thus uniting in this transnational space efforts both to administer energy security and to slow down Soviet technological progress, to the benefit of Western oil producers.

As for Italy, ENI continued its struggle with the majors by mobilizing sympathetic Italian diplomats at NATO. Mattei, Ratti, and Ruffolo suggested that diplomats employ time-wasting tactics to forestall the approval of regulations that could damage the company. These tactics succeeded in delaying decisions on Soviet imports, and essentially neutralized the most dangerous proposals on the issue, whether advanced by NATO or European countries. The precious time gained by ENI allowed the company to further its business with the Soviet Union before new regulations were applied.

On the other hand, however, US military circles appeared genuinely concerned by the military implications of the Soviet oil strategy, and this anxiety may have been increased by nebulous and partial information on Soviet industrial capabilities that leaked through the Iron Curtain.[91] However, the American proposal that NATO establish an embargo on pipes was received with skepticism. The British delegation opposed the possibility for over a year. Cracks appeared in the British–American special relationship in the face of two radically different interpretations of security. Military and strategic considerations advanced by the US contrasted with the commercial and political reasons that were paramount to the British. Existing trade relations between the USSR and NATO country members caused a standstill in decision-making.

Oil pipe technology was the form in which national oil interests were embodied in the NATO debate. The winner of the debate would ultimately determine the Western Bloc's strategy vis-à-vis Soviet oil trade. The choices to be made about allowing or restricting the sale of certain kinds of pipes were neither purely technical nor purely political: they were instead technopolitical, in the sense that the technology and geopolitics of pipes became indistinguishable in the course of the eighteen-month debate on the Druzhba issue.

The game played at the Atlantic Alliance was not one with a simple solution: the technopolitical battle was fought through technical reports, but also over the possibility of distinguishing between strategic and non-strategic pipes or equipment. What an oil pipeline was—or was not—as a technological product became defined by the struggle to control or suppress commerce with the Soviet Union. As for Italy, the battle also included technological blackmail, in that an American firm threatened to deny the Italian national iron and steel company spare parts for the completion of one of its plants, should the Italians not consent to block their sales of pipes to the Soviets.

While there is little doubt that the pipe embargo represented a successful American attempt to alter the East–West trade policies of its European allies, whether the intended goal of jeopardizing Soviet pipeline plans was effective to the extent the Americans desired, is highly doubtful. But the pipeline issue may have only been a part of a larger strategy: as noted by Stent, the US government was aware that a number of its most important European allies were against the embargo measure, and its insistence on pushing it through NATO may have been a matter of principle, pursued in order to assert US predominance in the Atlantic Alliance in East–West trade.[92]

As for the debate at the EEC, the French position of defending its African oil on the Common Market clashed not only with Italy's position, but also with Dutch interests associated with Shell. So French influence did not ultimately succeed in the short term in shaping the debate toward the formulation of a strong Common Market policy. Both transnational debates were triggered and defined by the same objective of drafting a strategy on Soviet oil exports, and both revolved to a significant extent around discourses on Western economic security. But they were also marked by a number of differences.

Considering the objectives and scope of NATO's activities, it is not surprising that the military aspect of the Soviet pipeline system played a much more significant role for the Atlantic alliance than for the EEC. Moreover, while France's political leverage within the EEC was greater than that of its other members, the European Community—unlike NATO—was not subject to the hegemonic influence of a single country, which made finding a common line much harder. Ultimately, the French administration was unable to impose its perspectives on Algerian and Soviet oil on the EEC, whereas the US managed to impose the embargo.

Leaving aside Iceland and Finland, Soviet oil imports never reached a dangerous level in the West. The fear that a commodity that could be sold below cost would overrun the European market and bring the international oil cartel to its knees was also never fulfilled. It would be easy to maintain that Soviet exports did not develop beyond that threshold because of the policies enacted in response to the Soviet oil offensive. In fact, it would appear that this view was also held in oil economics circles in 1960, when a *World Petroleum* article contended that, because of its rapidly expanding industry, it was unlikely that the Soviet Union would deprive its own market of a precious source of energy.[93]

Debates in the EEC and NATO demonstrated that the focus of surveillance and security had shifted from oil prospecting to transportation and distribution. Security was a factor that shaped the definition of a new technological artifact, the pipeline, rather than being confined exclusively to geoscientific intelligence. Surveillance was present at the center of transnational relations with enemies and allies alike. Through the actions of supranational organizations, national governments attempted to force their allies into making their intentions transparent in a way they would not accept for themselves.

While demanding shared responsibility from their allies over industrial initiatives and, in short, overt surveillance, they nevertheless tried to conceal their own activities and to use intelligence provided by allies to adapt and redesign their own strategies. In the embargo debate, issues of metallurgy, as well as estimations of technical industrial capabilities, became the cornerstone on which powerful narratives were built and wielded as scientific weapons in strategies of attack and defense.

Notes

1 "Statement of position on the threat of Communist trade," Jan. 19, 1962, p. 2; folder (fd.) Pétrole soviétique; box (b.) 92.26/31; Fonds Total-CFP; Archives Historiques du Groupe ELF/Total, La Défense (AHTOTAL).

2 Joseph J. Ross, *Defining National Security: The Nonmilitary Aspects* (New York: Council on Foreign Relations Press, 1993); Prabhakaran Paleri, *National Security: Imperatives and Challenges* (New Delhi: Tata McGraw-Hill, 2008); Timothy Mitchell, "Carbon Democracy," *Economy and Society* 38, no. 3 (2009): 409.

3 "Committee of Economic Advisers (ECONAD), Sino-Soviet Bloc Oil on World Markets, Note by the Economic Service," Jul. 11, 1960, p. 1; Atlantic Community Committee (AC); AC/127-D/1; NATO Archives, Brussels (NATOA).

4 Trevor J. Pinch and Wiebe E. Bijker, "The Social Construction of Facts and Artefacts: Or How the Sociology of Science and the Sociology of Technology Might Benefit Each Other," *Social Studies of Science* 14 (August 1984): 399–441; Gabrielle Hecht, *The Radiance of France: Nuclear Power and National Identity after World War II*, 2nd edition (Cambridge, MA/London: MIT Press, 2009. 1st edition: 1998); Michael Thad Allen, and Gabrielle Hecht, eds., *Technologies of Power*; Dolores L. Augustine, *Red Prometheus. Engineering and Dictatorship in East Germany, 1945–1990* (Cambridge, MA: MIT Press, 2007).

5 Gabrielle Hecht, *Being Nuclear: Africans and the Global Uranium Trade* (Cambridge, MA/London: MIT Press, 2012).

6 Timothy Mitchell, *Carbon Democracy: Political Power in the Age of Oil* (New York: Verso, 2011); Thomas P. Hughes, *Networks of power: Electrification in Western Society, 1880–1930* (Baltimore, MD: The Johns Hopkins University Press, 1983.

7 Per Högselius, *Red Gas. Russia and the Origins of Europe's Energy Dependence* (New York: Palgrave Macmillan, 2013); Angela Stent, *From Embargo to Ostpolitik. The Political Economy of West Germany–Soviet relations, 1955–1980* (Cambridge: Cambridge University Press, 1981), 101.

8 Excerpt from the *Journal des Carburants*, Nov. 20, 1960; fd. Pétrole soviétique; b. 92.26/31; Fonds Total-CFP; AHTOTAL.

9 "Préoccupations à propos du pétrole soviétique," *Petroleum Press Service* XXIX, no. 11 (1962): 403.

10 Armelle Demagny, "France and the Project for a Community Oil Policy, from the Signature of the Treaty of Rome to the First Oil Shock," in *A Comparative History of National Oil Companies*, ed. Alain Beltran (Brussels: Peter Lang, 2010), 306–7.

11 Demagny, "France and the Project," 310.

12 Olivier Wormser, Direction des Affaires Économiques et Financières (DAEF), French Foreign Ministry (MAEF), to William Harpham, Minister Economic, Britemb Paris, Nov. 29, 1959; N. 85. DE-CE Papiers Directeur Olivier Wormser; Sous-série: Directeur—Wormser; Série: Affaires économiques et financières; Archives Diplomatiques du Ministère des Affaires Etrangères, La Courneuve (ADMAE).

"Recherche de protection pour le pétrole saharien," *Petroleum Press Service* XXVII, no. 1 (1960), p. 9.

13 "Recherche de protection pour le pétrole saharien," *Petroleum Press Service* XXVII, no. 1 (1960), p. 9.

14 Ibid., 10; Olivier Wormser, MAEF, to Hervé Alphand, French Embassy Washington, Dec. 2, 1959; N. 85. DE-CE Papiers Directeur Olivier Wormser; Sous-série: Directeur—Wormser; Série: Affaires économiques et financières; ADMAE (my translation).

15 "Note sur la réunion du 9 Décembre 1959," Dec. 9, 1959; fd. Écoulement du pétrole saharien; b. 92.26/7, Vincent Labouret; Fonds Total-CFP; AHTOTAL.

16 Ibid.

17 Olivier Wormser, MAEF—DAEF, to Jean-Marcel Jeanneney, Ministry of Industry, Dec. 12, 1959, p. 2; N. 85. DE-CE Papiers Directeur Olivier Wormser; Sous-série: Directeur—Wormser; Série: Affaires économiques et financières; ADMAE. The quote is from: Letter by Albonetti, Oct. 16, 1959; b. 92.26/40, Vincent Labouret; Fonds Total-CFP; ADMAE (my translation).

18 Letter by Albonetti, Oct. 16, 1959. Labouret was also a French diplomat, and was to be part of the French delegation at the Évian negotiations in 1962. CFP's habit of employing officials with a strong diplomatic background as political analysts is shown also by the hiring of René Massigli, a former French Ambassador in London, after his diplomatic career.

19 François de Laboulaye, CFP, to Francis de Baecque, Organisation commune des regions sahariennes (OCRS), "Observations au sujet de la note du 18 avril," May 2, 1961; fd. Sahara—Politique algérienne concernant le Sahara; b. 92.26/7 Vincent Labouret; Fonds Total-CFP; AHTOTAL.

20 Demagny, "France and the Project," 305. On Euratom and American foreign policy, see: John Krige, "The Peaceful Atom as Political Weapon: Euratom and American Foreign Policy in the Late 1950s," *Historical Studies in the Natural Sciences* 38, no. 1 (2008): 5–44. On EURATOM, see also: Jonathan E. Helmreich, "The United States and the Formation of EURATOM," *Diplomatic History* 15 no. 3 (1991): 387–410; Simone Turchetti, "A Most Active Customer. How the U.S. Administration Helped the Italian Atomic Energy Project to 'De-Develop'," *Historical Studies in the Natural Sciences* 44, no. 5 (2014): 470–502.

21 A similar group was also created at the Organisation for European Economic Cooperation. "Considérations sur les problèmes posés par les pétroles russes à l'économie européenne," Apr. 8, 1960; fd. Politique vis-à-vis des pays de l'Est; AN—b. 19800118/3, CEE/Hydrocarbures, 1960–1962; AN (FOIA n° 111 382).

22 Council of European Communities—General Secretary, "Note d'information—Assemblée Parlementaire européenne," Oct. 7, 1960; fd. Politique vis-à-vis des pays de l'Est; b. 19800118/3 CEE/Hydrocarbures, 1960–1962; AN (FOIA n° 111 382).

23 Unsigned note, Oct. 11, 1960; fd. CB8; b. 24; Presidenza Eugenio Cefis; Fondo ENI; ASENI. Guicciardi agreed his action with Esso Italiana's President, Vincenzo Cazzaniga.

24 "Accordo italo-sovietico," Nov. 23, 1960; and Giorgio Ruffolo, ENI, to Giuseppe Ratti, ENI; and Translation of a circular sent by SONJ to their affiliates on Nov. 3, 1960, Dec. 6, 1960; fd. 7E2; b. 2; Rapporti commerciali con l'estero; Estero; Fondo ENI; ASENI.

Note SDECE, "Derniers développements de l'activité de Mattei—Réactions qu'elle suscite," Aug. 18, 1961, secret/confidential, p. 3; sub-fd. Italie 1955/1979; fd. 1; b. 19900317/13; AN (FOIA n° 111 382).

25 In January 1958, a unified secretariat was created for the Councils of the three European Communities, led by the ECSC's general secretariat already in office, and named the General Secretariat of the Council of the European Communities. CECA High Authority/EEC Commission/ECSC Commission, "Note au

Conseil Special de Ministres—Propositions de premières mesures en vue d'une coordination des politiques énergétiques," Jan. 1961, very secret; fd. 2A89; b. 29; Relazioni esterne; Fondo ENI; ASENI.

26 Giorgio Ruffolo, ENI, to Sig. Giorgi and Sig. Carbone (Italian representatives at NATO Ad Hoc Study Group on Soviet Oil Policy), Dec. 29, 1960; fd. 7E2; b. 2; Rapporti commerciali con l'estero; Estero; Fondo ENI; ASENI.

27 Barbara Curli, *Il progetto nucleare italiano (1952–1964). Conversazioni con Felice Ippolito* (Soveria Mannelli: Rubbettino, 2000), 56, 58. The reactor became critical in 1962 and started to produce electric energy the following year. See also: Mauro Elli, "British First Nuclear Export: ENI's Atomic Power Station at Latina and Anglo-Italian Nuclear Cooperation," *Annales historiques de l'électricité* 9 (2011): 27–42; Turchetti, "Most Active Customer." See also: Leopoldo Nuti, *Gli Stati Uniti e l'apertura a sinistra. Importanza e limiti della presenza americana in Italia* (Bari: Laterza, 1999), 220–1; Leopoldo Nuti, *La sfida nucleare: la politica estera italiana e le armi atomiche, 1945–1991* (Bologna: Il Mulino, 2007). The quote is from: Giuseppe Ratti, "Appunto per l'Ing. Girotti," Oct. 17, 1960; fd. 482E; b. 264; Presidenza Raffaele Girotti; Fondo ENI; ASENI (my translation).

28 Bonomi, "Osservazioni sulla 'Nota all'attenzione del Consiglio Speciale dei Ministri,'" Mar. 4, 1961, confidential; fd. 2A89; b. 29; Relazioni esterne; Fondo ENI; ASENI. Olivier Wormser, MAEF, Note, "Pétrole," Jan. 13, 1961; N. 85. DE-CE Papiers Directeur Olivier Wormser; Sous-série: Directeur—Wormser; Série: Affaires économiques et financières; ADMAE. Council of European Communities—General Secretary, "Note d'information—Assemblée Parlementaire européenne," Jan. 31, 1961; fd. Politique vis-à-vis des pays de l'Est; b. 19800118/3 CEE/Hydrocarbures, 1960–1962; AN (FOIA n° 111 382).

29 "Le pétrole russe à la C.E.E.," *Pétrole Informations*, Apr. 5, 1961; sub-fd. Organismes officiels; fd. III. Réactions du monde occidental; b. 90.4/350, Ingérence russe dans l'industrie pétrolière; Fonds Total-CFP; AHTOTAL.

30 EEC Commission—General Direction of Economic and Financial Affairs, "Groupe d'experts pétroliers—Importations de pétrole brut et de produits raffinés en provenance des Pays de l'Est dans la Communauté," Apr. 27, 1961, confidential; fd. Politique vis-à-vis des pays de l'Est; b. 19800118/3 CEE/Hydrocarbures, 1960–1962; AN (FOIA n° 111 382). *Politique étrangère* 6 (1960); Rassegna stampa estera 1961, n. 31, Apr. 28, 1961; ASENI.

31 In fact, according to oil expert Robert Ebel, Soviet exports to the West started growing (+344.8 kt) already in 1951—the first year of the Five-Year Plan—against a deficit of 99 kt the year before. Ebel, *Communist Trade*, 33.

32 In 1957, exports to the West amounted to 821 kt, against over 5 Mt in 1960 (for Italy, the respective figures read 422 kt and 2.8 Mt).

33 Direction des Carburants, "Note pour le Comité Interministériel—Politique de la C.E.E. vis-à-vis du pétrole des Pays de l'Est," Jun. 27, 1961; fd. Politique vis-à-vis des pays de l'Est; b. 19800118/3 CEE/Hydrocarbures, 1960–1962; AN (FOIA n° 111 382).

34 "Pro-memoria," undated [TPQ: Apr. 1961]; fd. 7DA; b. 2; Rapporti commerciali con l'estero; Estero; Fondo ENI; ASENI. "Critique du commerce pétrolier Russo-Italien," *Petroleum Press Service* XXVIII, no. 8 (1961): 302–3.

35 Europe, Bulletin quotidien n. 1025, Jul. 11, 1961; sub-fd. Organismes officiels; fd. III. Réactions du monde occidental; b. 90.4/350 Ingérence russe dans l'industrie pétrolière; Fonds Total-CFP; AHTOTAL. Bobin, "La politique énergétique de la Communauté Européenne": Chronologie 1952–1970, undated [TPQ: 1970]; b. 86.12/20, Etienne Dalemont; Fonds Total-CFP; AHTOTAL. "Euromart Faces Red Oil Dilemma," *Journal of Commerce*, Oct. 19, 1961;

fd. III. Réactions du monde occidental, sub-fd. Organismes officiels—Réaction du Moyen-Orient; b. 90.4/350 Ingérence russe dans l'industrie pétrolière; Fonds Total-CFP; AHTOTAL. "CEE—Contingentamento importazioni di petrolio dall'URSS," Jun. 27, 1962; fd. 482E; b. 264; Presidenza Raffaele Girotti; Fondo ENI; ASENI. Nigel J. D. Lucas, *Energy and the European Communities* (London: Europa Publications, 1977), 35.

36 Quoted from: Premier Ministre—État-Major Général de la Défense Nationale—Division du Renseignement, "Note d'information—Aspects de la politique de l'E.N.I.," Jul. 16, 1962.

37 Giuseppe Ratti, "Missione a Mosca (4–6 Settembre 1962)," Sep. 7, 1962; and Giuseppe Ratti, Promemoria riservato al Dr. Cefis, "Operazione in abbinamento ENI-URSS," Nov. 8, 1962; fd. 482E; b. 264; Presidenza Raffaele Girotti; Fondo ENI; ASENI. "Projet d'accord pour la coordination des importations de pétrole brut et de produits pétroliers en provenance des Pays de l'Est dans la Communauté," Sep. 7, 1962; fd. Politique vis-à-vis des pays de l'Est; b. 19800118/3 CEE/Hydrocarbures, 1960–1962; AN. "La Commission de la C.E.E. et le régime pétrolier français," *Europe Énergie*, Sep. 25, 1962; b. 90.4/328, Vincent Labouret; Fonds Total-CFP; AHTOTAL.

38 Memorandum, "Accordo ENI-URSS del 4.XI.63—Riunione di Mosca per esaminare la situazione dell'accordo e per stabilire un programma di forniture sino al 1970 come da impegni assunti dalle parti," undated [TPQ: 1967]; fd. 5; b. 45; Iniziative industriali estero; Estero; Fondo ENI; ASENI.

39 Lucas, *Energy*, 36.

40 "ECONAD, Meeting held at the Permanent Headquarters on 20 July 1961, Decision Sheet," Aug. 4, 1961, confidential, p. 5; AC; AC/127-R/71; NATOA. "ECONAD, Report by the Ad Hoc Study Group on Soviet Oil Policy to ECONAD," May 23, 1961, confidential, pp. 6–12; AC; AC/127-D/68; NATOA. Frank Uhlig, "The Threat of the Soviet Navy," *Foreign Affairs* 20 (1951–1952): 449–52.

41 However, the functions of the two committees sometimes overlapped. The quote is from: "ECONAD, Date of the first meeting and programme of work—Note by the Chairman," Mar. 22, 1957, confidential, p. 2; AC; AC/127-D/1; NATOA.

42 "ECONAD, Sino-Soviet Bloc Oil on World Markets, Note by the Economic Service," Jul. 11, 1960, p. 1; AC/127-WP/56 (Revised), confidential; AC; AC/89-WP/67, confidential (later unclassified); NATOA. "ECONAD, Meeting held at the Permanent Headquarters on 21 July 1960, Decision Sheet," Jul. 22, 1960, p. 1; AC; AC/127-R/53, confidential; NATOA. "ECONAD, Study Group on Soviet Oil Policy, Note by the Chairman," Sep. 23, 1960, p. 1, 3; AC; AC/127-WP/64, confidential; NATOA. "Dix millions de tonnes de pétrole exportées par le bloc soviétique," *Petroleum Press Service* XXVI, no. 3 (1959): 111–12. On the ad hoc Study Group, see also: Bruna Bagnato, *Prove di Ostpolitik. Politica ed economia nella strategia italiana verso l'Unione Sovietica, 1958–1963* (Firenze: Olschki, 2003), 383ff.

43 "ECONAD, Recent Facts and Figures on Petroleum, Note by the Economic Service," Sep. 30, 1960, pp. 9, 11–13; AC; AC/127-WP/66, confidential; NATOA. D. L. Spencer, "The Role of Oil in Soviet Foreign Economic Policy," *American Journal of Economy and Society* 25, no. 1 (1966): 102.

44 Note Service de documentation extérieure et de contre-espionnage (SDECE), "L'activité de l'Ente Nazionale Idrocarburi (octobre 1959—octobre 1960)," Oct. 18, 1960, secret, p. 11; sub-fd. Italie 1955/1979; fd. 1; b. 19900317/13; Archives Nationales, Pierrefitte-sur-Seine (AN) (FOIA n° 111 382). Giorgio Ruffolo, ENI, to Guido Giorgi, and Carbone, Ministry of Industry, "Memorandum," Dec. 29, 1960; fd. 7E2; b. 2; Rapporti commerciali con l'estero; Estero; Fondo ENI; Archivio Storico ENI (ASENI).

45 Ashley Clarke, UK Embassy (Britemb) Rome, to Sir Paul Gore-Booth, K.C.M.G., Foreign Office, "Relations between Signor Mattei and the Western Oil Group," Aug. 11, 1960, secret; fd. RT 1532/10; b. FO 371/153362; The National Archives, Kew (TNA). John R. Jenkins, "Note on Soviet Bloc oil exports to the Free World," Sep. 16 September 1958; and Minute by A. B. Powell, May 19, 1960; b. POWE 33/2443; TNA. Sources as reported in: Niklas Jensen-Eriksen, "British government, business and the Soviet Cold War oil offensive, 1957–1964," (Paper presented at the 16th Annual Conference of the European Business History Association, and 1st Joint Conference with Business History Society of Japan, Paris, August 30—September 1, 2012), 8–9. François de Laboulaye, "Note pour M. Granier de Lilliac," Nov. 18, 1960, confidential; fd. Pétrole soviétique; b. 92.26/31; Fonds Total-CFP; AHTOTAL. Giorgio Ruffolo, ENI, to Guido Giorgi, and Carbone, Ministry of Industry, "Memorandum," Dec. 29, 1960; fd. 7E2; b. 2; Rapporti commerciali con l'estero; Estero; Fondo ENI; Archivio Storico ENI (ASENI).

46 Quoted from: Ruffolo to Giorgi and Carbone, "Memorandum," Dec. 29, 1960, p. 1 (my translation).

47 Premier Ministre—État-Major Général de la Défense Nationale—Division du Renseignement, "Note d'information—Aspects de la politique de l'E.N.I.," Jul. 16, 1962, secret/confidential, p. 10; sub-fd. Italie 1955/1979; fd. 1; b. 19900317/13; AN (FOIA n° 111 382). This is a very detailed report on ENI's history, activities, policies, and prospects, and on its dangers to France and the West.

48 Unsigned note [probably by Giorgio Ruffolo], undated [prob. late 1960]; fd. 7E2; b. 2; Rapporti commerciali con l'estero; Estero; Fondo ENI; ASENI. Mitchell, "Carbon Democracy," 409; Mitchell, *Carbon Democracy*, 39ff.

49 Italian Foreign Minstry (MAEI)—Direzione generale Affari politici (DGAE)—Ufficio I, "Appunto per il Signor Direttore General," undated [TPQ: Oct. 1960]; fd. 187E; b. 57; Assistente del Presidente per l'estero; Estero; Fondo ENI; ASENI.

The figures reported in this document (p. 11) and regarding total imports from the Sino-Soviet Bloc in 1959, are: West Germany $44.8 million, UK $27.1 million, France $13.3 million, Italy $12.9 million.

50 "ECONAD, Ad Hoc Study Group on Soviet Oil Policy, Meeting held at the Permanent Headquarters, 9 December 1960, Decision Sheet," Dec. 21, 1960, confidential, p. 2; AC; AC/127(O)R/1; NATOA. "ECONAD, Ad Hoc Study Group on Soviet Oil Policy, Meeting held at the Permanent Headquarters, 30 and 31 January 1961, Decision Sheet," Feb. 10, 1961, confidential, p. 2; AC; AC/127(O)R/2; NATOA.

51 "Ad Hoc Study Group on Soviet Oil Policy, Draft Report to the ECONAD," Mar. 28, 1961; AC; AC/127(O)-WP/2 (Revised); NATOA. "ECONAD, Report by the Ad Hoc Study Group on Soviet Oil Policy to ECONAD," May 23, 1961, confidential, pp. 2–6.

52 "ECONAD, Report by the Ad Hoc Study Group on Soviet Oil Policy to ECONAD," May 23, 1961, confidential, pp. 14–17.

53 Ibid., p. 17.

54 Ibid., pp. 23–5.

55 Ibid., p. 18.

56 "ECONAD, Ad Hoc Study Group on Soviet Oil Policy, Comments by the Italian Government on AC/127(O)WP/2 (Revised)," Apr. 28, 1961, confidential; AC; AC/127(O)WP/2 (Revised)/2; NATOA.

57 "ECONAD, Meeting held at the Permanent Headquarters on 20 July 1961, Decision Sheet," Aug. 4, 1961, confidential, pp. 3–4. The quote is from p. 4.

58 "ECONAD, Soviet oil and gas pipelines, Note by the Secretary," Oct. [2 or 3], 1961, secret, p. 5; AC; AC/127-D/83; NATOA.

59 Quoted from: "ECONAD, Report by the Ad Hoc Study Group on Soviet Oil Policy to ECONAD," May 23, 1961, confidential, p. 6.

60 "ECONAD, Soviet oil and gas pipelines, Note by the Secretary," Oct. [2 or 3], 1961, secret, p. 5, 7. The identity of the military representative is not specified in this document, but is revealed by other documentation. Besides *Druzhba*, scheduled to complete in 1964, the Soviet pipeline program included three more pipelines to Leningrad, to the Black Sea port of Tuapse, and to the Pacific Ocean at Nakhodka.

61 Ibid., pp. 7–14.

62 Simone Turchetti, "Sword, Shield and Buoys: A History of the Nato Sub-Committee on Oceanographic Research, 1959–1973," *Centaurus* 54, no. 3 (2012): 208, 224.

63 Patrick J. Haney, and Walt Vanderbush, *The Cuban Embargo: The Domestic Politics of an American Foreign Policy* (Pittsburgh: University of Pittsburgh Press, 2005); Peter Schwab, *Cuba: Confronting the U.S. Embargo* (New York: Palgrave Macmillan, 1999). On the radioisotopes embargo, see: Angela N. H. Creager, "Radioisotopes as Political Instruments, 1946–1953," *Dynamis* 29 (2009): 219–39; Sławomir Lotysz, "A 'Lasting Memorial' to the UNRRA? Implementation of the Penicillin Plant Programme in Poland, 1946–1949," *ICON: Journal of the International Committee for the History of Technology* 20, no. 2 (2014): 70–91; Hughes, *Networks of Power*.

64 Högselius, *Red Gas*, 188–90; Richard Aldous, *Reagan and Thatcher: The Difficult Relationship* (London: Random House, 2012), 121; Leopoldo Nuti, "Commitment to NATO and Domestic Politics: The Italian Case and Some Comparative," *Contemporary European History* 7, no. 3 (1998): 374.

65 *World Petroleum*, May 1963, p. 29: source as reported in Boris Rachkov, "Oil, Trade, and Politics," *International Affairs* 12 (1966): 17. "Statement of Position on the Threat of Communist Trade," Jan. 19, 1962, pp. 7–8.

66 "Les exportations aux pays communistes sont rendues plus faciles," *Petroleum Press Service* XXV, no 9: 347. On the history of CoCom, see: Michael Mastanduno *Economic Containment: CoCom and the Politics of East–West Trade* (New York: Cornell University Press, 1992).

67 "ECONAD, Meeting held at the Permanent Headquarters on 20 July 1961, Decision Sheet," Aug. 4, 1961, confidential, p. 4. I could not retrieve the name of the British delegate from the NATO archives. The Soviets had placed orders for 240 kt in Italy, 135 kt in Sweden and 420 kt in Germany. See: "Le réseau de pipelines U.R.S.S.-Europe de l'Est," *Petroleum Press Service* XXVIII, no. 6 (1961): 204; "Le potentiel d'exportation russe," *Petroleum Press Service* XXIX, no. 4 (1962): 127. "ECONAD, Ad Hoc Study Group on Soviet Oil Policy, Meeting held at the Permanent Headquarters, 30 and 31 January 1961, Decision Sheet," Feb. 10, 1961, confidential, p. 4. "ECONAD, Report by the Ad Hoc Study Group on Soviet Oil Policy to ECONAD," May 23, 1961, confidential, pp. 8–12.

68 Sir Frank Lee, "Russian Oil," Apr. 7, 1961; b. T236/6237; TNA. G. R. Walker, "Note of the meeting on 6 July 1961," Jul. 10, 1961; b. T236/6441; TNA. Sources as reported in Niklas Jensen-Eriksen, ""Red Oil" and Western Reactions: The Case of Britain," in Cold War Energy: A Transnational History of Soviet Oil and Gas, ed. Jeronim Perovic (London: Palgrave Macmillan, 2017), 127n63, 128n73.

69 "ECONAD, Meeting held at the Permanent Headquarters on 20 July 1961, Decision Sheet," Aug. 4, 1961, confidential, p. 4. I could not retrieve the name of the British delegate in the NATO archives. "ECONAD, Meeting held at the Permanent Headquarters on 19 October 1961," Oct. 28, 1961, secret, p. 5; AC; AC/127-R/76; NATOA.

70 "ECONAD, Corrigendum to AC/127-R/86 (dated 13th March, 1962)," Mar. 16, 1962, secret, p. 2; AC; Corrigendum to Decision Sheet AC/127-R/86;

NATOA. "ECONAD, Meeting held at the Permanent Headquarters on 22 March 1962, Decision Sheet," Mar. 29, 1962, secret, p. 5; AC; AC/127-R/87; NATOA. The British delegate was presumably A. K. Potters, who had taken part in all meetings from 1957 to 1959 with no interruptions. Unfortunately, retrieving the names of national ECONAD representatives after December 1959 from NATO archives proved impossible. The 'special relationship' is a phrase coined by Winston Churchill in 1946, and used to describe the exceptionally close political, diplomatic, cultural, economic, military, and historical relations between the United Kingdom and the United States. David Reynolds, "A 'and his Relationship'? America, Britain and the International Order Since the Second World War," *International Affairs* 62, no. 1 (1985–1986): 1–20.

71 "ECONAD, Meeting held at the Permanent Headquarters on 22 March 1962, Decision Sheet," Mar. 29, 1962, secret, p. 6.

72 "ECONAD, Meeting held at the Permanent Headquarters on 8 March 1962," Mar. 13, 1962, secret, p. 1; AC; AC/127-R/86; NATOA.

73 "ECONAD, Ad Hoc Study Group on Soviet Oil Policy, Comments by the Italian Government on AC/127(O)WP/2 (Revised)," Apr. 28, 1961, confidential; "ECONAD, Meeting held at the Permanent Headquarters on 20 July 1961, Decision Sheet," Aug. 4, 1961, confidential, pp. 3–4.

74 Ibid. p. 6.

75 Ibid. pp. 9–10.

76 Figures are reported from *Vneshnaia Torgovlia* [recte: *Vneshnyaya torgovlya*] *za 1963—god*, 237. Cited in: Stent, *From Embargo to Ostpolitik*, 101.

77 Stent, *From Embargo to Ostpolitik*, ch. 5; "ECONAD, Meeting held at the Permanent Headquarters on 22 March 1962, Decision Sheet," Mar. 29, 1962, secret, pp. 11–12.

78 Alain Beltran, and Jean-Pierre Williot, *Les routes du gaz. Histoire du transport de gaz naturel en France* (Paris: Cherche Midi, 2012), 109–13. See also: Högselius, *Red Gas*, for a history of East–West gas trading from the late 1960s to our days.

79 Quoted from: "ECONAD, Meeting held at the Permanent Headquarters on 22 March 1962, Decision Sheet," Mar. 29, 1962, secret, p. 12.

80 Ibid., p. 12.

81 "Soviet Pipeline System—Note by the Chairman of ECONAD," May 2, 1962, secret, passim; CM; C-M(62)51; NATOA. "Summary record of a meeting of the Council, held at the Permanent Headquarters on 17 May 1962," May 23, 1962, secret, pp. 11–13; CR; C-R(62)26; NATOA. "Summary record of a meeting of the Council, held at the Permanent Headquarters on 8 August 1962," Aug. 21, 1962, secret, pp. 9–11; CR; C-R(62)40; NATOA.

82 Quoted from: "ECONAD, Soviet Pipeline System, Draft Report to the Council, Note by the Secretary," Oct. 19, 1962, secret, p. 2; AC; AC/127-D/107/1; NATOA.

83 "ECONAD, Meeting held at the Permanent Headquarters on 7 March 1963, Decision Sheet," Mar. 13, 1963, secret, p. 1; AC; AC/127-R/106; NATOA. "Summary record of a meeting of the Council, held at the Permanent Headquarters on 20 March 1963," Mar. 27, 1963, secret, p. 23; CR; C-R(63)14; NATOA. Stent, *From Embargo to Ostpolitik*, 93–153, esp. 113–14.

84 Stent, *From Embargo to Ostpolitik*, 95–6.

85 Giuseppe Ratti, "Promemoria riservato per l'Ing. Mattei," Feb. 10 1962; and Giuseppe Ratti, "Promemoria riservato per l'Ing. Mattei," Feb. 12, 1962; fd. 482E; b. 264; Presidenza Raffaele Girotti; Fondo ENI; ASENI (the quote is from this document).

86 Ratti, "Promemoria riservato per l'Ing. Mattei," Feb. 12, 1962. Letter, Enrico Mattei, ENI, to Ernesto Manuelli, Finsider, Feb. 12, 1962; and Unsigned [prob. Giuseppe Ratti], "Note for the Foreign Minister [Antonio Segni],"

Feb. 1962; fd. CB8; b. 24; Presidenza Eugenio Cefis; Fondo ENI; ASENI. Giuseppe Ratti, "Colloquio con l'Ambasciatore Ortona sulla fornitura di tubi Finsider all'U.R.S.S.," Feb. 14, 1962; fd. 482E; b. 264; Presidenza Raffaele Girotti; Fondo ENI; ASENI. Letter, Ernesto Manuelli, Finsider, to Enrico Mattei, ENI, Mar. 7, 1962; fd. CB8; b. 24; Presidenza Eugenio Cefis; Fondo ENI; ASENI. The quote is from: Giuseppe Ratti, "Promemoria per l'Ing. Mattei," Mar. 30, 1962; fd. 482E; b. 264; Presidenza Raffaele Girotti; Fondo ENI; ASENI (my translation).

87 "Summary record of a meeting of the Council, held at the Permanent Headquarters on 24 April 1963," May 2, 1963, secret, p. 8; CR; C-R(63)21; NATOA. "ECONAD, Sale of large diameter pipe to Soviet Bloc countries—Addendum to the note by the French Delegation circulated as AC/127-WP/188," Oct. 6, 1966, secret, p. 1; AC; AC/127-WP/188/1; NATOA.

88 "Summary record of a meeting of the Council, held at the Permanent Headquarters on 24 April 1963," May 2, 1963, secret, p. 9; "ECONAD, Sale of large-diameter pipe to Soviet Bloc countries—Note forwarded by the Delegations of France and of the Federal Republic of Germany," Aug. 29, 1966, confidential, p. 1; AC; AC/127-D/220; NATOA. Ebel, *Communist Trade*, 184; Jonathan Stern, *Soviet Oil and Gas Exports to the West: Commercial Transactions or Security Threat?* (Aldershot: Gower, 1987), 27, 30.

89 Ebel, *Communist Trade*, 185, 231; "Lessons of an Ill-Fated Embargo," *Vneshnyaya torgovlya*, Dec. 12, 1966: 50–1: source as reported in Ebel, *Communist Trade*, 231.

90 "ECONAD, Sale of large diameter pipe to Soviet Bloc countries—Addendum to the note by the French Delegation circulated as AC/127-WP/188," Oct. 6, 1966, secret, p. 1; AC; AC/127-WP/188/1; NATOA. "ECONAD, Sale of large-diameter pipe to Soviet Bloc countries—Note forwarded by the Delegations of France and of the Federal Republic of Germany," Aug. 29, 1966, confidential, pp. 1–2. "ECONAD, Meeting held at the Permanent Headquarters on 8 September 1966 at 10.15 a.m.," Sep. 19, 1966, confidential; AC; AC/127-R/185; NATOA. "ECONAD, Sale of large diameter pipes to countries of the Soviet Bloc, Note by the Chairman," Sep. 21, 1966, secret; AC; AC/127-WP/190; NATOA. "ECONAD, Sale of large diameter pipes to Soviet Bloc countries, Draft Report by the Committee of Economic Advisers to the Council," Oct. 4, 1966, secret; AC; AC/127-WP/192; NATOA. "ECONAD, Meeting held at the Permanent Headquarters on 26 January 1966, Decision Sheet," Jan. 30, 1967, secret; AC; AC/127-R/194; NATOA.

91 Geir Lundestad, *The United States and Western Europe Since 1945* (Oxford: Oxford University Press, 2009); Högselius, *Red Gas*.

92 This thesis is defended in: Stent, *From Embargo to Ostpolitik*, 103.

93 "La Concurrence du pétrole russe" (extracts from the article appeared in the September issue of *World Petroleum*). Annex 2 to: Direction Générale Économie—Énergie, doc. n. 7395/60 f, "Le marché pétrolier d'aujourd'hui," Nov. 30, 1960; fd. Politique vis-à-vis des pays de l'Est; b. 19800118/3 CEE/Hydrocarbures, 1960–1962; AN.

Conclusion

Many of the debates that have been described in this work occurred in a geopolitical and economic context that was quite different from today's, notwithstanding frequent references to a new Cold War between Russia and the US, especially in relation to the ongoing Syrian civil war. There are nevertheless marked similarities with the current global hydrocarbon scene, as many of the arguments advanced at the time continue to be employed: Europe's energy vulnerability and need for a diversification of energy sources; its dependence on foreign hydrocarbon sources, with the Cold War dependency on Soviet oil being replaced by current dependency on Russian gas; but also the subordination of national governments' foreign affairs policies to energy company strategies, cloaked in the language of national security.[1] Understanding these recurring long-term themes in global oil dynamics therefore helps us to eschew presentist narratives of exceptionalism, and to interpret present-day oil policies in strong continuity with those of the recent past.

The aim of this book has been twofold. First, it has endeavored to explain the role played by the technoscientific understanding of oil in the development of diplomatic relations. Second, it has analyzed the links between oil prospecting and the national security apparatus in the context of the early Cold War. The focus of my analysis has been two European countries struggling to acquire some degree of energy autonomy from the oil multinational corporations that historically dominated the world market. The theoretical framework that I have adopted combines elements relating to American hegemony over European technoscience, the role of geoscientists as diplomats and intelligence-gathering agents, and the transnational diplomacy of natural resources. But it also takes into account recent trends in science and technology studies, revolving around the political materiality of technological artifacts.

In both the French and Italian cases, I have demonstrated the feedback loop between oil technoscience and national diplomacy in issues where scientific and technological information has been of critical importance. By doing so, I have exposed instances of the different dimensions of 'science diplomacy' highlighted in a 2010 report by the American Association for the Advancement of Science: science in diplomacy—informing foreign policy objectives with scientific advice; diplomacy for science—facilitating international scientific cooperation; and science for diplomacy—using scientific cooperation to improve international relations between countries.[2]

Technoscientific intelligence persuaded national authorities to endeavor to secure control of their own country's territory. In the case of Algeria, it also empowered the emerging political and diplomatic élite in their struggle for independence. It enabled national delegations within transnational organizations to substantiate their claims regarding oil imports, the construction of pipelines, and embargoes. But national diplomacies also advanced technoscience, especially by obtaining access to prospecting operations in unique locations, thus contributing to the generation of new technoscientific data. This work reveals the importance of covert surveillance operations focusing on the collection, use, and selective distribution of geophysical knowledge, and shows how these operations informed the work of diplomats on a national and a transnational level.

The examination of this interplay between technicians, diplomats, entrepreneurs, and intelligence agents, and the permeability of these categories, is one of the original insights in my account. Throughout this book we have met technicians acting as intelligence gatherers and diplomats, former secret agents with élite technical backgrounds turning into senior oil administrators, entrepreneurs turning into politicians and then into diplomats. The existence of these professionally hybrid figures is central to a balanced understanding of the complexity of history, as it helps to avoid simplistic categorizations of social actors into pre-assembled ideological or professional black boxes. In particular, in the cases I have analyzed, the actions of these hybrid figures may also help toward a reassessment of macro-themes in Cold War history. It is true, as Krige has argued, that the United States asserted its hegemony through the co-production of knowledge, but on many occasions hegemony was reliant on the secret information gathered by American nationals, and in any case it was repeatedly challenged by lesser powers. Intelligence invigorated diplomatic action and increased negotiating power.[3]

The investigation of geoscientific intelligence and diplomacy in a transnational setting required access to sources from a considerable number of countries. Thus, in terms of archival research my study was based on public and corporate archival materials kept in Belgium, France, Italy, the UK, and the US, and included classified documentation obtained through an FOI request to the French Ministry of Culture and Communication.[4] Multi-archive research gave me the invaluable opportunity to compare primary sources relating to particular issues (e.g. the Algerian War and Soviet imports); to cross-examine analyses of trading strategies between allies within the same international organizations; to fill in the gaps in one archive with information contained in others; and to recognize the role of secret services in the handling of sensitive information about allies' industrial and exploratory activities. As noted by historian Pierre-Yves Saunier, researching in different languages can help us to "become familiar with several archival systems and historiographical traditions and questions, to learn how to imagine the sources which can help to answer [one's] questions."[5]

In my work, I have endeavored to ground Ronald Doel's appraisal of scientists (and especially geoscientists) as policymakers, advisors, and intelligence agents in the analysis of oil prospecting and the development of oil technology in general. My argument has been that Doel's interpretation can be successfully applied to a context of indirect military relevance, which motivated national agencies to interact closely with private capital interests. While Doel writes of a 'science in black,' made of secret interconnections between scientists and public officials in order to serve national interests, in my work it is not so much interconnections that are secret, as the way in which science is handled. By this I mean that what matters here is less the covert funding of scientific activities for military purposes, or the secret affiliation of scientists to intelligence organization, than the use of confidentially acquired geoscientific data and the role of diplomats and technicians in getting hold of it: we may call it a 'science in grey.'[6]

Overall, this book adds to recent scholarly work that focuses on the evolution of technoscientific expertise in European states. The choice of Italy as one of my case studies was influenced by the literary presence of a 'myth' surrounding the national oil company, and the considerable availability of journalistic accounts and memoirs of former ENI executives that have helped to propagate this. Following a recent historiographical trend that, through the use of archival documentation, has begun to deconstruct the myth, this work is intended to contribute to this reassessment, especially by highlighting the role of less well studied figures than Enrico Mattei. While the ENI President's huge influence over the company's overall decision-making is hardly deniable, and appears clearly from non-Italian archives sources, uncovering the scientific and non-scientific activities of technicians and other staff in weaving diplomatic relations with 'politically sensitive' partners and in combating the free disclosure of geoscientific knowledge, again adds to the importance of the history of technology for a more accurate description of processual reality.

In the case of France, I have addressed the surprisingly limited awareness of the fine-grained dynamics of the history of national oil diplomacy. The existing literature provides an accurate chronology of key events, but lacks analysis of the agents of change. As a consequence, the powerful and dense personal networks in which such agents operated are often obscured. By including in my narratives technocrats like Guillaumat and Blancard, but also CGG technicians and American oil administrators operating within the Marshall Plan, I have contributed to the restoration of human agency in French oil history.

Oil Technoscience and Geopolitics

Throughout this book I have argued that oil technoscience was, and still is, a powerful weapon in the hands of state agencies and their oil companies. The investigation of oil prospecting methods and their application can reveal how governments, by making sure that national oil companies utilize these methods and knowledge, gain control of oil resources in the hope of achieving energy security. In Chapters 1 and 2, I demonstrated how, in the early postwar years, Italian and French geophysicists were dependent on American technologies: AGIP's reliance on WGC for most of its initial activities is a case in point, but French equipment also had to be purchased from the US. In addition, both the geophysical personnel of both countries had to be trained by foreign specialists, or hired from abroad. Although France and Italy pursued similar recovery strategies in the postwar years, their paths soon diverged.

For a number of structural and contingent reasons, although AGIP and ENI eventually managed to master imported techniques, Italian geophysics remained heavily dependent on American equipment and technology into the late 1960s. France, on the other hand, developed a series of institutions that helped to foster remarkable development in its own geophysical sector. This was not only the result of more effective planning; the prestige it had enjoyed since before the war was also a major factor, in stark contrast with governmental policymaking relating to the applied sciences in Italy. Furthermore, French agencies benefited from accumulated experience of exploration across the vast territory under the Hexagon's control.

US technological advantages during the early postwar period helped American and, to a lesser extent, British geoscientists to prospect or gather valuable intelligence on oil deposits in Italy and France. That in turn enabled the oil majors to assert—via their governments—their control over both countries' revenues. Italian and French administrations, however, also used geophysical knowledge as a political device. Geoscientific data, vital to the search for hydrocarbons, became a precious asset in the hands of French and Italian oil companies and diplomats alike. Foreign companies interested in pursuing exploration programs in Italy or the French Union could be directed to areas deemed less promising, or which required a substantial financial and technological effort, exceeding the capabilities of the national companies. While Mattei's political power and lobbying certainly played an important role in ENI's securing a monopoly over the Po Valley, ENI technicians had a crucial part in convincing him of the Italian valley's potential on geoscientific grounds.

Similarly, the BRP and CFP, while forming associations with other companies in the Algerian Sahara, managed to instigate a thorough exploration of a vast desert while not surrendering their rights over the area. After major discoveries in the area throughout the 1950s, French agencies set a series of requirements for foreign companies willing to commit their capital to Saharan exploration—such as training French technicians and passing geological and geophysical survey results to the BRP—that they were able to acquire a mass of data that they could then apply in further activities.

At a political level this management of geoscientific knowledge enabled France and Italy to resist British and American attempts to hand over the control of national oil markets to the oil majors. It also escalated conflict over the control of oil reservoirs in North Africa. Diplomats thus exchanged views and negotiated agreements on a variety of issues, including the formulation of mining legislation, the modalities of oil company access to national territories, and the actions and strategies of officials at the head of national oil companies, notably Mattei and the French technocratic elite led by Pierre Guillaumat.

However, what emerges from this work is that diplomats were as much concerned with oil as they were with the 'hidden hand' of states: national oil deals cannot really be understood unless one takes into account the secret collection of information on opposing interests and the oil knowledge they possessed. This is especially true for the results of oil prospecting, which were often concealed in negotiations and used secretly for a variety of purposes. In Chapter 2, I emphasized the action of Anglo-American geologists and geophysicists in inspecting AGIP's documentation when, in the late 1940s, the company's board decided to stimulate private prospecting in regions of the country previously abandoned. In the French case, I highlighted how a network of men with similar backgrounds in elite educational institutions and strong links with the secret services came together under Guillaumat's leadership and secured a leading position within France's public oil industry.

While the activities of foreign companies in French territories and beyond were closely monitored by the French secret services, foreign institutions were also conducting surveillance of French activities. An instance of the former was the 'intelligence-informed' strategy Guillaumat deployed when assigning exploration permits to foreign companies. He allocated them selectively, while retaining control of geoscientific knowledge, and taking advantage of US companies' geophysical expertise to train French technicians. As an example of the latter surveillance activities, I discussed in Chapter 3 how American diplomatic institutions such as the Consulate General in Algiers collected information on French prospecting and production from American technicians and trade agents working in Saharan oilfields. Such intelligence, once transmitted to the State Department, was then leaked to US companies interested in expanding operations to the Sahara and wanting updates on the situation. This was also true of Italy, once ENI had established its parallel diplomacy in Tunis to liaise with the FLN and help plan the future of the Algerian oil industry.

Opportunities for collecting geoscientific data on the Algerian subsoil were also fully exploited by Italian AGIP technicians, who used them as a currency of exchange with the Algerian independence fighters, thereby acquiring potential advantages for future concessions in the country. At the same time, the GPRA used intelligence passed to them by ENI to substantiate their claims over the whole of Algerian territory. The importance of the technoscientific element in the history of international relations is thus once more evidenced, as is the significance of a transnational framework to the production of scientific knowledge. Unable to insert ENI into Algeria as a direct and active player in oil exploration, its executives had to resort to other means to acquire data on that region: we have seen how part of this information was passed by the French technicians themselves to their Italian counterparts in the name of a long-standing collaboration. Commercial links thus became a vehicle for intelligence gathering.

Secret data collection on the activities and results of competitors also enabled companies to take grounded decisions on where to concentrate their exploration efforts in territories unexplored by them, but not by their allies and rivals, as well as to evaluate competitors' discoveries, their oil needs and/or shortages, and to shape their own strategies accordingly. Moreover, it brought them considerable savings in prospecting efforts, manpower, and money. These considerations clarify the significance of a history of intelligence about geoscientific knowledge.

The Midstream Shift and New Challenges for Security

In Chapter 4, I showed how a series of discoveries, facilitated by the introduction of new geophysical equipment, resulted in global oil overproduction, initiating a worldwide decline in geophysical exploration activity, except in the Soviet Union and parts of Africa. I argued that by the end of the 1950s overproduction prompted a temporary shift in the priorities assigned to sectors of the oil industry and brought new challenges for energy security. While in the second half of the 1940s and throughout most of the 1950s, the focus had been on the acquisition of new permits and concessions, it now shifted gradually to transportation infrastructures and to the wholesale marketing of crude: the key activities in the Euro–Asian oil sector now became building, controlling, and securing pipelines, in order to be the first to reach new consumption zones and thereby to ensure adequate outlets for oil. In the cases under study, this process, which I have termed the 'midstream shift,' occurred as soon as French agencies began to build their pipeline network from the Algerian oilfields to the Mediterranean coast, and ENI, with the support of the Italian government, decided to cross the red line and barter technology for oil with the Soviet Union. But it also reverberated heavily in Europe itself, with the battle of the pipelines that ENI ultimately lost to CFP and the majors, but which ultimately led to the rapid laying of a dense network of pipelines on the continent.

The midstream shift also brought about a shift in the kind of surveillance activities employed, vis-à-vis both allies and enemies: what mattered now was the covert accumulation of information on pipeline flow rates and routes, industrial muscle, and technological advances. Moreover, the industrial sectors involved in pipeline building—and oil tanker construction, since it should be recalled that maritime transportation constituted the largest alternative to pipelining—were not the same as those engaged in oil exploration, nor were the technologies employed in midstream sector activities the same as those used in the upstream sector.

One of the limitations of this work is exactly that, concentrating as it does on oil exploration, it only scratches the surface of the technosciences involved in oil transportation (in Chapter 5), and that it does not touch upon the downstream technologies of refining and distribution either. Also, while it focuses on pipelines as a means of transporting oil, it is silent on oil tanker technology and on the many security issues involved in maritime transportation (such as the importance of controlling the Suez Canal or the Strait of Hormuz). On the other hand, my aim was not to write a complete history of oil technology, but more modestly to show the role of the geosciences and geoscientists, and of material artifacts, in shaping that history.[7]

In France, the new possibilities provided by Algerian oil instigated a comprehensive transformation of the French market, manifested in the creation of an integrated public oil company. However, the Soviet project for a colossal pipeline system had to be dealt with in a different manner: neither Western states nor oil companies could directly interfere with Russian plans for the Soviet Bloc, so the only possible way to delay operations on Druzhba was to materially impede them. As several Western countries traded steel pipes and pipeline equipment with the USSR, this meant placing an embargo on those technologies. Whether European countries would agree was a different matter. The long NATO debate on a US-proposed embargo, which I discussed in Chapter 5, clarified their misgivings. My analysis of British–American confrontation on this issue demonstrates that the dispute, though eminently geopolitical in nature, was primarily fought through technical reports based on different evaluations of Soviet industrial capabilities and the specific qualities of Soviet oil.

Security was often brought to the fore in international exchanges: the meaning attributed to this concept, however, varied greatly from situation to situation, and from country to country. In the Italian case, protecting national security meant importing from the Soviets. For the French and the American oil majors, it meant exactly the opposite. The core technical point of the entire NATO debate was the definition of 'strategic' materials. As there was no pre-existing agreement about which kinds of pipe should be considered strategic and which not (Were gas pipes as strategic as oil pipes? How could the two be distinguished? Was equipment that could be used both for pipelines and other work strategic?), the definition of the term had to be negotiated. This, at times acrimonious, negotiation culminated in a controversial outcome, namely the acceptance of the embargo by all NATO members except the UK. In Chapter 5, I also discussed the consequences of American technological hegemony in the Italian–American dispute over the manufacture of pipes for the Soviet pipeline, which eventually obliged ENI to agree to a compromise and curtail its deliveries to the Russians.

Were the Soviets really threatening the Western oil market through their low oil prices during the 1950s to 1960s, as the British, American, and French companies maintained? Although Soviet activism in the oil industry generated widespread anxieties among both Middle-Eastern producers and Western oil majors, I think that the answer is no, an answer in which I seem to be supported also by Högselius's analysis of Soviet gas trade during the Cold War.[8] Instead, the generalized fear of market dumping appears to have been caused by the secrecy surrounding the actual state of the Soviet oil industry, coupled with the majors' consciousness that their artificially high prices and their strategy of scarcity production could easily be jeopardized by the new Soviet oil abundance.

The American oil expert formerly responsible for the CIA's Middle Eastern branch, Robert Ebel, commented in 1970 that Soviet Bloc oil sales had been economically motivated, and that oil "ha[d] purchased 'time': time, which otherwise would have been spent in the development of processes and in the accumulation of know-how to produce the advanced equipment and technology the Socialist Bloc was now gaining in barter for its oil."[9] Almost twenty years later, Jonathan Stern, at the time Head of the Energy and Environmental Programme at the Royal Institute of International Affairs in London, agreed with Ebel's evaluation. He has argued that Soviet exports, rather than being threats to security, were entirely reasonable commercial transactions. During long periods between 1960 and 1985, Stern reasoned, Soviet oil and gas deliveries proved more trustworthy and market-responsive than those of their competitors.[10]

Describing the formation of national narratives, and the ways these were strengthened, weakened, and modified throughout the development of the pipeline debate, clarifies the fragmentary and ambiguous nature of the Western alliance, and shows that, while US political influence certainly gave the Americans a hardly disputable hegemonic role within NATO, the US delegates had to come to terms with the imperatives of lesser partners in order to obtain quasi-unanimous acceptance of the embargo. This tweaking operation took a long time, as countries with large stakes in trade with the Soviets tried to delay a final decision as long as possible in order to minimize the consequences of the embargo.

Also, the embargo in its final formulation proved to be significantly watered down by comparison with the US's initial proposal, an outcome in which lesser NATO members played a crucial role. As Lino Camprubí has recently noted, "[c]ompetition between the two superpowers accounts for only part of the story": the history of the pipe embargo does nothing more than reinforce this argument about the importance of the third powers in Cold War history.[11] By emphasizing once again the processes of co-constructed hegemony within one of the Cold War's most influential transnational organizations, it nevertheless demonstrates with incredible clarity that the issue of pipe exports to the USSR did not prove to be just a question of the political hand wearing the technological glove as Halford Hoskins and Leon Herman claimed.[12] At NATO, no glove was needed, because pipe technology was not just a cover for oil politics. It was its essence.

Notes

1 Mathias Reymond, "European Key Issues Concerning Natural Gas: Dependence and Vulnerability," *Energy Policy* 35 (2007): 4169–76; Enrique Palazuelos and Rafael Fernández, "The Importance of Transnational Corporations in the Supply of Oil to Europe: Implications," *Energy Policy* 47 (2012): 270–81.

2 AAAS, *New Frontiers in Science Diplomacy* (London: The Royal Society, 2010), v–vi.

3 John Krige, *American Hegemony and the Postwar Reconstruction of Science in Europe* (Cambridge, MA/London: MIT Press, 2006).

4 Gabrielle Hecht, *Being Nuclear: Africans and the Global Uranium Trade* (Cambridge, MA/London: MIT Press, 2012).

5 Quoted from: Pierre-Yves Saunier, "Going Transnational? News from Down Under," *Historical Social Research* 31, no. 2 (2006): 126.

6 Ronald E. Doel, "Scientists as Policymakers, Advisors, and Intelligence Agents: Linking Contemporary Diplomatic History with the History of Contemporary Science," in *The Historiography of Contemporary Science and Technology*, ed. Thomas Söderqvist (Amsterdam: Harwood Academic, 1997), 215–44.

7 Caitlin Talmadge, "Closing Time: Assessing the Iranian Threat to the Strait of Hormuz," *International Security* 33, no. 1 (2008): 82–117.

8 Per Högselius, *Red Gas: Russia and the Origins of Europe's Energy Dependence* (New York: Palgrave Macmillan, 2013).

9 Quoted from: Robert E. Ebel, *Communist Trade in Oil and Gas* (New York/Washington/London: Praeger, 1970), 82.

10 Jonathan Stern, *Soviet Oil and Gas Exports to the West: Commercial Transactions or Security Threat?* (Aldershot: Gower, 1987), xi.

11 Lino Camprubí, "Resource Geopolitics: Cold War Technologies, Global Fertilizers, and the Fate of Western Sahara," *Technology and Culture* 56, no. 3 (2015): 697; Simone Turchetti, Néstor Herran, and Soraya Boudia, "Introduction: Have We Ever Been 'Transnational'? Towards a History of Science Across and Beyond Borders," in "Transnational History of Science," edited by Simone Turchetti, Néstor Herran and Soraya Boudia, special issue, *British Journal for the History of Science* 45, no. 3 (2012): 1–18; Simone Turchetti and Peder Roberts, "Introduction: Knowing the Enemy, Knowing the Earth," in *The Surveillance Imperative: Geosciences During the Cold War and Beyond*, edited by Simone Turchetti and Peder Roberts (London: Palgrave Macmillan, 2014), 1–19.

12 See p. 187 in this volume.

Bibliography

Archive Materials

Archives Diplomatiques du Ministère des Affaires Etrangères, La Courneuve (ADMAE)

Série: Amérique 1944–1952

Sous-série: États-Unis:
b. 245, Relations économiques et financières avec la France. Aide américaine;
b. 246, Relations économiques et financières avec la France. Aide américaine;
b. 247, Relations économiques et financières avec la France. Aide américaine;
b. 248, Relations économiques et financières avec la France. Aide américaine;
b. 249, Relations économiques et financières avec la France. Aide américaine;
b. 250, Commerce extérieur. Relations avec la France.

Série: Affaires économiques et financières

Sous-série: Coopération économique:
b. 327, DE-CE 1945–1960, Aide américaine.

Sous-série: Directeur–Wormser:
N. 85. DE-CE Papiers Dirécteur Olivier Wormser;
N. 94. DE-CE Papiers Dirécteur Olivier Wormser.

Série: Cabinet du Ministre:

Sous-série: Couve du Murville (1958–1968):
N.70.

Série: Direction d'Europe (Z-Europe)

Sous-série: Italie 1944–1970:
N. 288.

Série: Service de liaison avec l'Algérie

Sous-série: 1957–1966:
N. 45.

Archives Historiques du Groupe ELF/Total, La Défense (AHTOTAL)

Fonds ELF-ERAP

b. 07AH0008–110, Bureau de recherches pétrolières (BRP):
 fd. 411386, BRP—Dép. Exploration.
b. 07AH0024, Direction des hydrocarbures (DHYCA), anciennement Direction des carburants (DICA).
b. 07AH0168–6, REPAL—Correspondence;
b. 10AH0832–27, BRP;
b. 07AH0168–28, REPAL;
b. 10AH0832–13, BRP.

Fonds Total-CFP

b. 1 PRES-Président Victor de Metz:
 -2, Correspondence;
b. 3 SG/ Secrétariat général: archives de Vincent Labouret, diplomate détaché auprès du président-directeur général de la Compagnie française des pétroles (CFP):
 /2: fd. Études
b. 85.26/ Société nationale des pétroles d'Aquitaine (SNPA):
 /5, SPG;
b. 86.12/20 Etienne Dalemont;
b. 90.4/ Centre de documentation et de synthèse (CDS): économie et politique dans le monde:
 /102, Revues de presse;
 /108: fd. Pipe-line Edjeleh/La Skirra (Pourpalers préliminaires + attitude du F.L.N.
 /164, Négociations franco-GPRA et le Sahara:
  fd. Réactions des pays arabes aux Accords d'Évian.
 /328, Vincent Labouret;
 /350, Ingérence russe dans l'industrie pétrolière:
  fd. III. Réactions du monde occidental.
b. 92.10/ Compagnie française des pétroles (CFP), documents de sociéte:
 /1, CFP;
 /2, CFP;
 /3, CFP.
b. 92.13/ Participations de la Compagnie française des pétroles (CFP) dans différentes sociétés: historique et vie de la société:
 /8.
b. 92.26/ Compagnie française des pétroles (CFP), Proche-Orient, Afrique, Extrême-Orient, Europe, Amérique du Nord:
 /7, Vincent Labouret:
  fd. Commercialisation du pétrole saharien;
  fd. Écoulement du pétrole saharien;
  fd. Sahara—Politique algérienne concernant le Sahara;

/9, Vincent Labouret:
fd. Politique algérienne jusque fin 1962.
/31: fd. Pétrole soviétique;
/40, Vincent Labouret.
b. 92AA039, Rapports annuels de la Compagnie française des pétroles (CFP) et de différentes filiales (Hutchinson, Minatole, etc.):
fd. 13, CGG's yearly reports.
CFP Ordinary General Assembly (OGA) of Jun. 11, 1928;
CFP Extraordinary General Assembly of Mar. 20, 1929;
CFP OGA of Jun. 2, 1937;
CFP OGA of Jun. 22, 1938;
CFP OGA of Sep. 16, 1940;
CFP OGA of Jun. 30, 1942;
CFP OGA of Dec. 5, 1945;
CFP OGA of Jun. 26, 1946;
CFP OGA of Jul. 2, 1947;
CFP OGA of Jun. 27, 1949;
CFP OGA of Jun. 28, 1950;
CFP OGA of Jun. 26, 1951;
CFP OGA of Jun. 30, 1952;
CFP OGA of Jun. 30, 1953;
CFP OGA of Jun. 24, 1954.

Archives Nationales, Pierrefitte-sur-Seine (AN)

Versement 19900317, Relations internationals dans le secteur pétrolier:
b. 19900317/3, CEE/Hydrocarbures, 1960–1962:
fd. Politique vis-à-vis des pays de l'Est.
b. 19900317/8:
fd. 1;
fd. 2, Algérie 1957/64;
fd. 3, Algérie-Sahara.
b. 19900317/13:
fd. 1.
b. 19900317/20:
fd. 2, Frontières algéro-marocaines.
b. 19900317/21:
fd. 1, Frontières algéro-libyennes.
b. 19900317/24:
fd. 3.

Archives nationales d'outre-mer, Aix-en-Provence (ANOM)

Fonds Ministériels (FM)

Affaires algériennes (1873/1964):

b. 81F/966:
fd. Évacuation des pétroles sahariens;
fd. Le FLN et le pétrole saharien;
fd. Recherches de pétrole;
fd. Untitled.
b. 81F/1476:
fd. Examen du projet de décret par le Conseil d'État;
fd. Protection du Pipe-Line Hassi-Messaoud.
b. 81F/2060:
fd. Recherche pétrolière, attribution de concessions et de permis, affaires diverses, 1949–1957;
fd. Recherche pétrolière, correspondance, 1949–1955.
b. 81F/2064:
fd. Untitled.
b. 81F/2067:
fd. Politique du pétrole.
b. 81F/2068:
fd. Société nationale de recherches de pétrole d'Algérie.
b. 81F/2069:
fd. Bureau de Recherches de pétrole (B-R.P.);
fd. Untitled.

Archivio Scuola Superiore di Studi sugli Idrocarburi

Scuola Superiore di Studi sugli Idrocarburi: Anno accademico 1963–1964.

Archivio storico-diplomatico del Ministero degli Affari esteri, Rome (ASMAE)

Ambasciata d'Italia a Parigi, 1951–1958:
b. 74 (Algeria '57);
b. 81 (Algeria '58);
b. 82 (Algeria '58).

Direzione Generale Affari Politici, Ufficio I (1947–1960):
b. 43.

Telegrammi ordinari, Russia (Ambasciata Mosca), 1959:
vol. 42 arrivo (gen-mag);
vol. 43 partenza (gen-ago).

Telegrammi ordinari, Russia (Ambasciata Mosca), 1960:
vol. 59 arrivo (lug-dic).

Telegrammi ordinari, Russia (Ambasciata Mosca), 1961:
vol. 55 arrivo (gen-giu).

Archivio Storico ENI, Pomezia (Roma) (ASENI)

Fondo AGIP

DI.MI:
—Processi Verbali Assemblee: 59/1953–1959;
—Processi Verbali Assemblee: 5A/1959–1962.

Direzione Mineraria:
—Ricerche e produzione:
b. 7, fd. 7DA;
b. 201, fd. 2FF;
b. 260, fd. 36F;
b. 263, fd. 36B;
b. 275, fd. 37F;
b. 348, fd. 3EF;
b. 355, fd. 3FC.

Organi deliberativi, Verbali Consiglio di Amministrazione AGIP:
b. 1, fd. 14 (16/10/1935—6/3/1940);
b. 2, fd. 17 (Commissario Enrico Mattei, 30/4/1945—20/10/1945);
b. 2, fd. 18 (17/2/1945—9/8/1946);
b. 2, fd. 19 (9/8/1946—28/10/1947);
b. 3, fd. 1A (28/10/1947—27/5/1950);
b. 3, fd. 1B (27/5/1950—25/2/1954).

Organi deliberativi, Verbali Comitato esecutivo AGIP:
b. 16, fd. 3B (29/10/1945—24/9/1949).

Fondo ENI

Estero:
—Assistente del Presidente per l'estero:
b. 10, fd. 8B2;
b. 16, fd. A2A; fd. A3E;
b. 57, fd. 187E;
b. 76, fd. 20D6.

—Iniziative industriali estero:
b. 45, fd. 5.

—Rapporti commerciali con l'estero:
b. 2, fd. 7DA; fd. 7E0; fd. 7E2; fd. 7E6;
b. 73, fd. 2003.

Presidenza Eugenio Cefis:
b. 24, fd. CB8.

Presidenza Mattei:
b. 1, fd. 40;
b. 48, fd. 3E0;
b. 70, fd. 47F.
b. 75, fd. 150.

Presidenza Raffaele Girotti:
b. 264, fd. 482E.

Relazioni esterne:
b. 29, fd. 2A89;
b. 129, fd. 2F2B.

Fonti orali

Interview:
N. 47. Mario Pirani, b. 3, fd. 462B and fd. 462C.

Rassegna stampa estera

Vol. 1961;
Vol. 1962.

Archivio Tecnico-Scientifico ENI, San Donato Milanese

ENI U 1.018.801: Myron T. Kozáry, Algeria—Prospects of the Algerian Sahara, Geological Report no. 6.

Institut Français du Pétrole: Fonds documentaire, Rueil Malmaison (IFPFD)

Activités de l'Institut Français du Pétrole:
Rapport d'activité 1961 et programme pour 1962;

Activités de l'Institut Français du Pétrole:
Réalisations de 1946—Projets pour 1947 et les années suivantes;

Rapport annuel 1966.

National Archives and Records Administration, College Park, MD (NARA)

CIA Records Search Tool Database (CREST)

Record Group 59

African Lot, Bureau of African Affairs, Office of Northern African Affairs:
—Records Relating to Algeria, 1952–1962:
b. 1:
fd. A6 Petroleum;
fd. A8 Relations with Soviets and satellites;
fd. A8 FLN—French—Self-determination Negotiations, Jan. 61;

fd. R-8 Relation with USSR & Satellites.
—Records Relating to Morocco, 1955–1962:
b. 4:
fd. M-12, Mattei/Moroccan Oil Concession.

Central Decimal File, 1955–1959:
—French Africa:
b. 2569; b. 3378; b. 4603; b. 4604.
—France's International Politics:
b. 2622.
—Iran:
b. 4973; b. 4974.
—Italy:
b. 2021; b. 3617; b. 4826.

Central Decimal File, 1960–1963:
Italy: b. 1919, b. 2684, b. 2694, b. 2695

Records of the Office of Western European Affairs:
—Subject File Relating to France, 1944–1960:
Lot 61D30, b. 2:
fd. 16 Algeria-ARAMCO.

Subject Numeric Files, 1950–1954:
—French Africa:
b. 5006

Record Group 84

Records of the Foreign Service Posts of the Department of State, Italy:
U.S. Embassy, Rome Classified General Records, 1946–1964:
b. 89;
b. 128, fd. 511.12 Export–Import;
b. 129, fd. 523.1 Petroleum (January–June) 1962.

Record Group 469

Mission to Trieste, Entry 1394, Mission to Trieste: Office of the Director, Subject Files 1947–1950; b. 1, Petroleum.

The National Archives, Kew (TNA)

Foreign Office Files

b. FO 369/3504, War damage compensation to British and American oil interests in France, 1946;
b. FO 371/79500, Italian oil market: quota negotiations between major oil companies and Italian government. Code 22, file 1531;
b. FO 371/79503, Report of discovery of oil in the Po valley;
b. FO 371/99194, Italian oil imports;

b. FO 371/101772, Observations on the Fifth Annual Report of the French Bureau of Petroleum Research (BRP) concerning oil prospecting in France and French territories overseas;
b. FO 371/104606, 371/104616: Anglo–US efforts to settle the oil dispute with Persia;
b. FO 371/104617, 371/104619 to 371/104630: Efforts to stop Persia selling oil belonging to AIOC (Anglo-Iranian Oil Company);
b. FO 371/113125, Exploration for oil in Italy.
b. FO 950/31, War damage claims of British oil interests in France.
b. FO 371/153362, Oil industry:
fd. RT 1532/6;
fd. RT 1532/9;
fd. RT 1532/10;
fd. RT 1532/10 (A);
fd. RT 1532/17.
b. FO 371/145054, Visit to UK by President of ENI-AGIP of Italy:
fd. RT 1152.

Ministry of Power Files

Series: POWE 33/ Ministry of Technology, Petroleum Division, and Predecessors: Correspondence and Papers:

b. POWE 33/229, Italy: petroleum legislation.
b. POWE 33/1709, Iraq Petroleum Company: "red line" inter company agreement 31 July 1928.
b. POWE 33/2443, Import Licensing Committee: imports of petroleum products from Eastern Bloc.

Prime Minister's Office Files

b. PREM 3/243/8, Policy towards Italy and Italian government;
b. PREM 11/501, Representations to the Italian Government against attempts to import Persian oil.

Treasury Files

Series: T236/ Treasury: Overseas Finance Division: Registered Files (OF and 2OF Series):

b. T236/6237, Imports of Russian oil into UK;
b. T236/6441, Imports of Russian oil into UK.

NATO Archives, Brussels (NATOA)

—Atlantic Community Committee:

AC/89-WP/67; AC/89-WP/76 (Revised 1); AC/127-D/1; AC/127-D/68; AC/127-R/76; AC/127-R/106; AC/127-D/82; AC/127-D/82 (2nd Revise); AC/127-D/82 (Revise) 1; AC/127-D/82 (Revised); AC/127-D/83; AC/127-

D/83/1; AC/127-D/106; AC/127-D/107; AC/127-D/107/1; AC/127-D/220; AC/127-R/53; AC/127-R/71; AC/127-R/87; AC/127-R/97; AC/127-R/99; AC/127-WP/56 (Revised); AC/127-WP/64; AC/127-WP/66; AC/127-WP/78; AC/127-WP/85; AC/127-WP/188/1; AC/127(O)-WP/2 (Revised); AC/127(O) WP/2 (Revised)/2; AC/127(O)R/1; AC/127(O)R/2; Annex to AC/127-R/99; Corrigendum to Decision Sheet AC/127-R/86.

—Council Memoranda:
C-M(62)30; C-M(62)47; C-M(62)51; C-M(62)104.

—Council Records:
C-R(62)14; C-R(62)26; C-R(62)40; C-R(62)55; C-R(63)14; C-R(63)21.

Monographs, Journal Articles, Book Chapters

Abdesselam, Belaïd. *Le pétrole et le gaz naturel en Algérie. Comment les Algériens ont gagné la bataille de la récupération du pétrole et du gaz*. Algiers: ANEP, 2012.

Abraham, Itty. "Rare Earths: The Cold War in the Annals of Travancore." In *Geographies: Empire and Technopolitics in the Global Cold War*, edited by Gabrielle Hecht, 105–22. Cambridge, MA/London: MIT Press, 2011.

Accorinti, Giuseppe. *Quando Mattei era l'impresa energetica: io c'ero*. Matelica: Halley, 2006.

Adamson, Matthew. "Les *liaisons dangereuses*: resource surveillance, uranium diplomacy and secret French–American collaboration in 1950s Morocco." *The British Journal for the History of Science* 49, no. 1 (2016): 79–105.

Adamson, Matthew, Lino Camprubí, and Simone Turchetti. "From the Ground Up: Uranium Prospecting and Atomic Energy in Western Europe, 1945–1964." In *The Surveillance Imperative. The Rise of the Geosciences during the Cold War*, edited by Simone Turchetti and Peder Roberts, 23–44. London/New York: Palgrave, 2014.

Aga Rossi, Elena, ed. *Il Piano Marshall e l'Europa*. Roma: Istituto dell'Enciclopedia Italiana, 1983.

Ageron, Charles-Robert. *La guerre d'Algérie et les Algériens, 1954–1962*. Paris: Armand Colin, 1995.

Aïssaoui, Ali. *Algeria: The Political Economy of Oil and Gas*. Oxford: Oxford University Press, 2001.

Aldous, Richard. *Reagan and Thatcher: The Difficult Relationship*. London: Random House, 2012.

Allaud, Louis A., and Maurice H. Martin. *Schlumberger. The History of a Technique*. Hoboken: John Wiley & Sons, 1977.

Allen, Michael T., and Gabrielle Hecht, eds. *Technologies of Power. Essays in Honor of Thomas Parke Hughes and Agatha Chipley Hughes*. Cambridge, MA/London: MIT Press, 2001.

Amatori, Franco. "Entrepreneurial Typologies in the History of Industrial Italy (1880–1960): A Review Article." *Business History Review* 54, no. 3 (1980): 359–86.

Ambasciata d'Italia, and Istituto Italiano di Cultura di Algeri, eds. *Enrico Mattei e l'Algeria durante la Guerra di Liberazione Nazionale*. Algiers: Ambasciata d'Italia and Istituto Italiano di Cultura di Algeri, 2010.

———. *Il contributo dell'Italia alla costruzione dell'Algeria indipendente*. Algiers: Ambasciata d'Italia and Istituto Italiano di Cultura di Algeri, 2011.

Anderson, Irvine H. *ARAMCO. The United States and Saudi Arabia. A Study of the Dynamics of Foreign Oil Policy, 1933–1950*. Princeton: Princeton University Press, 1981.

Ardesi, Luciano. "La politica estera della Repubblica algerina, con particolare riferimento ai rapporti con gli stati maghrebini." In *Algeria. Il disastro e la memoria*, edited by Federico Cresti, special issue of *Oriente moderno* 22, no. 4 (2003): 1–22.

Augustine, Dolores L. *Red Prometheus. Engineering and Dictatorship in East Germany, 1945–1990*. Cambridge, MA: MIT Press, 2007.

Badel, Laurence, Stanislas Jeannesson, and N. Piers Ludlow, eds. *Les administrations nationales et la construction européenne. Une approche historique (1919–1975)*. Brussels: Peter Lang, 2005.

Bagnato, Bruna. "Une solidarité ambiguë: L'OTAN, la France et la guerre d'Algérie 1954–1958." *Revue d'histoire diplomatique* 4 (2001): 329–50.

———. *Prove di Ostpolitik. Politica ed economia nella strategia italiana verso l'Unione Sovietica, 1958–1963*. Firenze: Olschki, 2003.

———. *Petrolio e politica. Mattei in Marocco*. Firenze: Polistampa, 2004.

———. "La Pira, de Gaulle e il primo Colloquio mediterraneo di Firenze." In *Giorgio La Pira e la Francia. Temi e percorsi di ricerca. Da Maritain a de Gaulle*, edited by Pier Luigi Ballini, 99–134. Firenze: Giunti, 2005.

———. "L'Italia e la guerra d'Algeria: il governo, i partiti, le forze sociali e l'ENI di Mattei." In *Enrico Mattei e l'Algeria durante la Guerra di Liberazione Nazionale*, edited by Ambasciata d'Italia and Istituto Italiano di Cultura di Algeri, 23–39. Algiers: Ambasciata d'Italia and Istituto Italiano di Cultura di Algeri, 2010.

———. "L'Italia e la causa algerina: tra prudenza delle Istituzioni e solidarietà della società civile." In *Il contributo dell'Italia alla costruzione dell'Algeria indipendente*, edited by Ambasciata d'Italia and Istituto Italiano di Cultura di Algeri, 53–65. Algiers: Ambasciata d'Italia and Istituto Italiano di Cultura di Algeri, 2011.

———. *L'Italia e la guerra d'Algeria (1954–1962)*. Soveria Mannelli: Rubbettino, 2012.

Bagnato, Bruna, ed. *I diari di Luca Pietromarchi: ambasciatore italiano a Mosca, 1958–1961*. Firenze: Olschki, 2002.

Ballande, Henri. "Le Plan Marshall et le Pétrole." *Bulletin AFTP* 75 (1949): 3–24.

Bamberg, James H. *The History of the British Petroleum Company*, vol. 2: *The Anglo-Iranian Years, 1928–1954*. Cambridge: Cambridge University Press, 1994.

Barei, Geoffrey. "The Sakiet Sidi Youssef Incident of 1958 in Tunisia and the Anglo-American 'Good Offices' Mission." *Journal of North African Studies* 17, no. 2 (2012): 355–71.

Barrett, Ross, and Daniel Worden, eds. "Oil Culture: Guest Editors' Introduction." Special issue, *Journal of American Studies* 46, no. 2 (2012): 269–72.

Barry, Andrew. *Material Politics: Disputes Along the Pipeline*. Chichester: Wiley-Blackwell, 2013.

Barth, Kai-Henrik. "The Politics of Seismology: Nuclear Testing, Arms Control, and the Transformation of a Discipline." *Social Studies of Science* 33, no. 5 (2003): 743–81.

Bates, Charles C., Thomas F. Gaskell, and Robert B. Rice. *Geophysics in the Affairs of Man*. Oxford: Pergamon Press, 1982.

Bazzoli, Luigi, and Riccardo Renzi. *Il miracolo Mattei*. Milano: Rizzoli, 1984.

Beaufre, André. *The Suez Expedition*. London: Faber, 1969.

Bellini, Fulvio, and Alessandro Previdi. *L'assassinio di Enrico Mattei*. Milano: FLAN, 1970.

Beltran, Alain. "Pétrole et gaz: Nouvelles perspectives et outils de recherché." *Bulletin de l'IHTP* 84 (2004) [no page number reported], (http://www.ihtp.cnrs.fr/spip.phppercent3Farticle316&lang=fr.html).

Beltran, Alain, and Jean-Pierre Williot. *Les routes du gaz. Histoire du transport de gaz naturel en France*. Paris: Cherche Midi, 2012.

Benchikh, Madjid. *Les Instruments juridiques de la politique algérienne des hydrocarbures*. Paris: LGDJ, 1973.

———. "La nouvelle loi pétrolière algérienne: direction publique et économie de marché." *L'Année du Maghreb* II (2005–06) [no page number reported] (http://anneemaghreb.revues.org/103).

Berry, John A. "Oil and Soviet Policy in the Middle East." *Middle East Journal* 26, no. 2 (1972): 149–60.

Berstein, Serge, and Pierre Milza. *Histoire de la France au XXe siècle*, tome III: 1945–1958. Paris: Éditions Complexe, 1991.

Bertrand, Georges. "Histoire des recherches pétrolières en Aquitaine. Les premiers titres d'exploration." In *La recherche pétrolière française*, edited by Jean Prouvost, 99–113. Paris: Éditions du CTHS, 1994.

Bini, Elisabetta. *La potente benzina italiana. Guerra fredda e consumi di massa tra Italia, Stati Uniti e Terzo mondo (1945–1973)*. Roma: Carocci, 2013.

Boilley, Pierre. "OCRS/Royaume Sanussi de Libye: deux tentatives pour durer?." In *L'ère des décolonisations*, edited by Charles-Robert Ageron and Marc Michel, 359–68. Paris: Karthala, 1995.

Bolt, Bruce A. *Nuclear Explosions and Earthquakes. The Parted Veil*. San Francisco: Freeman and Company, 1976.

Bossuat, Gérard. *L'Europe occidentale à l'heure américaine*. Paris: Éditions Complexe, 1992.

———. *La France, l'aide américaine et la construction européenne, 1944–1954*. Paris: Comité pour l'histoire économique et financière de la France, 1997.

Bourdrel, Philippe. *La dernière chance de l'Algérie française. Du gouvernement socialiste au retour de De Gaulle, 1956–1958*. Paris: Albin Michel, 1996.

Bowker, Geoffrey C. *Science on the Run. Information Management and Industrial Geophysics at Schlumberger, 1920–1940*. Cambridge, MA/London: MIT Press, 1994.

Briatico, Franco. *Ascesa e declino del capitale pubblico in Italia. Vicende e protagonisti*. Bologna: Il Mulino, 2004.

Brogi, Alessandro. *L'Italia e l'egemonia americana nel Mediterraneo. 1945–1958*. Scandicci: La Nuova Italia, 1996.

———. *A Question of Self-Esteem: The United States and the Cold War Choices in France and Italy, 1944–1958*. Westport, CT: Praeger, 2002.

Brosio Manlio, and Federico Bacchetti, ed. *Diari di Mosca: 1947–1951*. Bologna: Il Mulino, 1986.

Bruni, Luigi, and Marcello Colitti. *La politica petrolifera italiana*. Roma: Giuffrè, 1967.

Bucarelli, Massimo. "All'origine della politica energetica dell'ENI in Iran: Enrico Mattei e i negoziati per gli accordi petroliferi del 1957" *Nuova rivista storica* XCIV, no. 2 (2010): 465–99.

Buccianti, Giovanni. *Enrico Mattei. Assalto al potere petrolifero mondiale.* Milano: Giuffrè, 2005.

Bush, Vannevar. *Science—The Endless Frontier. A Report to the President by Vannevar Bush, Director of the Office of Scientific Research and Development, July 1945.* Washington, DC: United States Government Printing Office, 1945.

Cahn, Jean-Paul, and Klaus-Jürgen Miller. *La RFA et la guerre d'Algérie (1954–1962).* Paris: Félin, 2003.

Calchi Novati, Giampaolo. "I rapporti fra FLN e Tunisia durante la Guerra di Liberazione: gli effetti del bombardamento di Sakiet Sidi Youssef." In *Algeria. Il disastro e la memoria*, edited by Federico Cresti, special issue of *Oriente moderno* 22, no. 4 (2003): 23–38.

Callon, Michel. "Eléments pour une sociologie de la traduction. La domestication des coquilles Saintjacques et des marins-pêcheurs dans la baie de Saint-Brieuc." *L'année sociologique* 36 (1986): 169–208.

Camprubí, Lino. "Resource Geopolitics: Cold War Technologies, Global Fertilizers, and the Fate of Western Sahara." *Technology and Culture* 56, no. 3 (2015): 676–703.

Cantoni, Roberto. "Breach of Faith? Italian–Soviet Cold War Trading and ENI's 'International Oil Scandal'." *Quaestio Rossica* 4 (2015): 180–98.

———. "The Enemy Underground: Geostrategic Intelligence and the War in Algeria." *History and Technology* 32, no. 1 (2016): 33–69.

———. "Transnational Reactions to the Soviet Oil Offensive (1960–2)." In *Cold War Energy: A Transnational History of Soviet Oil and Gas*, edited by Jeronim Perovic, 131–61. London: Palgrave Macmillan, 2017.

———. "What's in a Pipe? Transnational Negotiation of a 'Strategic' Item." *Technology and Culture* 58, no. 1 (2017): 67–96.

Cantoni, Roberto, and Leucha Veneer. "Underwater and Underground: Gatekeeping Oil Exploration during the Cold War." In *The Surveillance Imperative. The Rise of the Geosciences during the Cold War*, edited by Simone Turchetti and Peder Robert, 45–66. London/New York: Palgrave, 2014.

Catta, Emmanuel. *Victor De Metz. De la CFP au Groupe Total.* Paris: Total Edition Presse, 1990.

Centre de recherches sur l'Afrique méditerraneéenne, ed. "L'Algérie et les hydrocarbures." *Annuaire de l'Afrique du Nord* 4 (1966): 63–100.

Cereghino, Mario J., and Giovanni Fasanella. *Il golpe inglese. Da Matteotti a Moro: le prove della guerra segreta per il controllo del petrolio e dell'Italia.* Milano: Chiarelettere, 2011.

Chauveau, Sylvie, and Alain Beltran. *ELF Aquitaine. Des origines à 1989.* Paris: Fayard, 1998.

Chikhi, Abdelmadjid. "Gli Accordi di Evian." In *Enrico Mattei e l'Algeria durante la Guerra di Liberazione Nazionale*, edited by Ambasciata d'Italia and Istituto Italiano di Cultura di Algeri, 60–3. Algiers: Ambasciata d'Italia and Istituto Italiano di Cultura di Algeri, 2010.

Clarke, John I. "Saharan Oil." *Geography* 45, no. 1/2 (1960): 106–8.

———. "Economic and Political Changes in the Sahara." *Geography* 46, no. 2 (1961): 102–19.

Clavin, Patricia. "Introduction: Defining Transnationalism." *Contemporary European History* 14, no. 4 (2005): 421–40.

Clô, Alberto. *Oil Economics and Policy*. Boston/London: Kluwer, 2000.

Cloud, John. "Introduction: Special Guest-Edited Issue on the Earth Sciences in the Cold War." In "Earth Sciences in the Cold War," edited by John Cloud and Judith Reppy, special issue, *Social Studies of Science* 33, no. 5 (2003): 629–30.

Cobb, Howard. "Operations Research—A Tool in Oil Exploration." *Geophysics* 25, no. 5 (1960): 1009–22.

Cointet, Michèle. *De Gaulle et l'Algérie française*. Paris: Perrin, 1995.

Colitti, Marcello. *Energia e sviluppo in Italia. La vicenda di Enrico Mattei*. Bari: De Donato, 1979.

———. *ENI. Cronache dall'interno di un'azienda*. Milano: Egea, 2008.

Combaz, André. "Les premières découvertes de pétrole au Sahara dans les années 1950: le témoignage d'un acteur." *Comité Français d'histoire de la géologie*, 3ème série, T.XVI (2002) [no page number reported] (http://annales.org/archives/cofrhigeo/sahara.html).

Compagnie Générale de Géophysique. *CGG 1931–2006: 75 ans de passion*. Paris: Hachette Livre, 2006.

Connelly, Matthew. *A Diplomatic Revolution: Algeria's Fight for Independence and the Origins of the Post-Cold War Era*. Oxford: Oxford University Press, 2002.

Constant, Edward W. "Science in Society: Petroleum Engineers and the Oil Fraternity in Texas, 1925–1965." *Social Studies of Science* 19, no. 3 (1989): 439–72.

Cornet, Pierre. *Du mirage au miracle. Pétrole saharien*. Paris: Nouvelles Editions Latines, 1960.

Cottino, Gastone, Angela Pressenda, and Marcella Sarale. *Ricerca sulle Partecipazioni statali. 2. L'ENI da Mattei a Cefis. La politica del petrolio tra mito e realtà*. Torino: Einaudi, 1978.

Crawford, John M., William E. N. Doty and Milford R. Lee. "Continuous Signal Seismograph." *Geophysics* 25, no. 1 (1960): 95–105.

Creager, Angela N. H. "Radioisotopes as Political Instruments, 1946–1953." *Dynamis* 29 (2009): 219–39.

Curli, Barbara. *Il progetto nucleare italiano (1952–1964). Conversazioni con Felice Ippolito*. Soveria Mannelli: Rubbettino, 2000.

Dawkins, Richard. *The Selfish Gene*. New York/Oxford: Oxford University Press, 1976.

De Gaulle, Charles. *Memoirs of Hope: Renewal and Endeavour*. New York: Simon and Schuster, 1971.

Delavesne, Yves. "Développement récent des recherches de pétrole en Afrique." *Bulletin AFTP* 112 (1955): 365–80.

Demagny, Armelle. "France and the Project for a Community Oil Policy, from the Signature of the Treaty of Rome to the First Oil Shock." In *A Comparative History of National Oil Companies*, edited by Alain Beltran, 305–22. Brussels: Peter Lang, 2010.

Desaint, R., and H. Richard. "Évolution de l'activité géophysique de surface (pétrole)." *Geophysical Prospecting* 11, no. 2 (1963): 197–221.

De Sanctis, Riccardo. *Delitto al potere*. Roma: Samonà e Savelli, 1972.

Devaux-Charbonnel, Jean. *L'intervention de l'Etat dans la Recherche et dans l'Exploitation des gisements de pétrole*. Paris: IFP, 1951.

Dobrin, Milton B., and Stanley H. Ward. "Tools for Tomorrow's Geophysics." *Geophysical Prospecting* 10, no. 1 (1962): 433–52.

Doel, Ronald E. "Scientists as Policymakers, Advisors, and Intelligence Agents: Linking Contemporary Diplomatic History with the History of Contemporary Science." In *The Historiography of Contemporary Science and Technology*, edited by Thomas Söderqvist, 215–44. Amsterdam: Harwood Academic, 1997.

———. "Constituting the Postwar Earth Sciences: The Military's Influence on the Environmental Sciences in the USA after 1945." *Social Studies of Science* 33, no. 5 (2003): 635–66.

———. "The Earth Sciences and Geophysics." In *Companion to Science in the 20th Century*, edited by John Krige and Dominique Pestre, 391–417. London: Routledge, 2003.

———. "Does Scientific Intelligence Matter?" *Centaurus* 52, no. 4 (2010): 311–22.

Doel, Ronald E., and Allan A. Needell. "Science, Scientists, and the CIA: Balancing International Ideals, National Needs, and Professional Opportunities." *Intelligence and National Security* 12, no. 1 (1997): 59–81.

Dozon, Jean-Pierre. *Frères et sujets. La France et l'Afrique en perspective.* Paris: Flammarion, 2003.

Du Castel, Didier, Philippe Pierre-Adolphe, Max Mamoud, Max, and Georges-Olivier Tzanos. *Les aventuriers de la Terre.* Boulogne: La Sirène, 1995.

Duce, James T. "The Changing Oil Industry." *Foreign Affairs* 40 (1961–62): 627–34.

Dunlap, Henry F., and Curtis H. Johnson. "Research and Progress in Exploration." *Geophysics* 23, no. 2 (1958): 267–84.

Ebel, Robert E. *Communist Trade in Oil and Gas.* New York/Washington/London: Praeger.

Eckhardt, Engelhardt A. "Geophysical Activity in 1951." *Geophysics* 17, no. 3 (1952): 441–51.

Elli, Mauro. "British First Nuclear Export: ENI's Atomic Power Station at Latina and Anglo-Italian Nuclear Cooperation." *Annales historiques de l'électricité* 9 (2011): 27–42.

Ellwood, David W. "The Propaganda of the Marshall Plan in Italy in a Cold War Context." In *The Cultural Cold War in Western Europe, 1945–1960*, edited by Giles Scott-Smith and Hans Krabbendam, 224–36. London/Portland, OR: Frank Cass, 2003.

———. "Was the Marshall Plan Necessary?" In *Alan S. Milward and a Century of European Change*, edited by Fernando Guirao, Frances M. B. Lynch, and Sigfrido M. Ramírez Pérez, 179–98. New York: Routledge, 2012.

El Mechat, Samya. *Les États-Unis et l'Algérie. De la méconnaissance à la reconnaissance, 1945–1962.* Paris: L'Harmattan, 1996.

———. "Les États-Unis et la question coloniale en Afrique du Nord 1945–1962." *Outre-mers* 95 (358–9: 2008): 249–66.

Esposito, Chiarella. *America's Feeble Weapon: Finding the Marshall Plan in France and Italy, 1948–1950.* Westport, CT/London: Greenwood Press, 1994.

Eveno, Patrick, and Jean Planchais, eds. *La guerre d'Algérie.* Paris: La Découverte/Le Monde, 1989.

Faivre, Maurice. *Les archives inédites de la politique algérienne, 1958–1962.* Paris: L'Harmattan, 2000.

Fisher, William B., ed. *The Cambridge History of Iran*, vol. 1. *The Land of Iran.* London: Cambridge University Press, 1968.

Fleming, James R., ed. "Military Patronage and the Geophysical Sciences in the United States." special issue, *Historical Studies in the Physical and Biological Sciences* 30, no. 2 (2000).

Fleming, James R. *Fixing the Sky. The Checkered History of Weather and Climate Control.* New York: Columbia University Press, 2010.

Fontaine, Pierre. *La guerre froide du pétrole.* Paris: SCEL, 1956.

———. *La nouvelle course au pétrole.* Paris: Les Sept Couleurs, 1957.

———. *La mort étrange de Conrad Kilian, inventeur du pétrole saharien.* Paris: Les Sept Couleurs, 1959.

Foresta Martin, Franco, and Geppi Calcara. *Per una storia della geofisica italiana: la nascita dell'Istituto Nazionale di Geofisica (1936) e la figura di Antonino Lo Surdo.* Milano: Springer, 2010.

Forman, Paul. "Behind Quantum Electronics: National Security as Basis for Physical Research in the United States, 1940–1960." *Historical Studies in the Physical and Biological Sciences* 18, no. 1 (1987): 149–229.

Fosset, Robert. "Pétrole et gaz naturel au Sahara." *Annales de Géographie* 71, no. 385 (1962): 279–308.

Fourastié, Jean. *Les Trente Glorieuses, ou la révolution invisible de 1946 à 1975.* Paris: Fayard, 1979.

Frankel, Paul H. *Mattei. Oil and Power Politics.* London: Faber and Faber, 1966.

Frémeaux, Jacques. *Le Sahara et la France.* Paris: SOTÉCA, 2010.

Galison, Peter. "Secrecy in Three Acts." *Social Research* 77, no. 3 (2010): 941–74.

Galli, Giorgio. *La sfida perduta. Biografia politica di Enrico Mattei.* Milano: Bompiani, 1976.

———. *La regia occulta. Dal caso Mattei a Piazza Fontana.* Milano: Marco Tropea, 1995.

———. *Enrico Mattei: petrolio e complotto italiano.* Milano: Baldini Castoldi Dalai, 2005.

Gardner, Lloyd C. "Responses to John Lewis Gaddis, 'The Emerging Post-Revisionist Synthesis on the Origins of the Cold War.'" *Diplomatic History* 7, no. 3 (1983): 191–204.

Gasiorowski Mark J., and Malcolm Byrne, eds. *Mohammad Mosaddeq and the 1953 Coup in Iran.* Syracuse, NY: Syracuse University Press, 2004.

Gassner, Miriam. "Lokale Umwelt oder transnationale Chance? ENIs Reaktion auf die Proteste gegen die CEL-Pipeline in den 1960er Jahren." *Zeitschrift für Unternehmensgeschichte* 57, no. 1 (2012): 31–46.

Gavin, Francis J. "Politics, Power, and U.S. Policy in Iran, 1950–1953." *Journal of Cold War Studies* 1, no. 1 (1999): 56–89.

Germain-Jones, Donald T. "What Is Our Contribution?" *Geophysical Prospecting* 2, no. 3 (1954): 177–84.

Giannetti, Renato. *Tecnologia e sviluppo economico italiano, 1870–1990.* Bologna: Il Mulino, 1998.

Giannuli, Aldo. *La guerra fredda delle spie. L'ufficio affari riservati.* vol. I. Roma: Nuova Iniziativa Editoriale, 2005.

Gilmour, Andrew. "The state of seismic prospecting." *Geophysics* 15, no. 3 (1950): 395–9.

Ginsborg, Paul. *Storia d'Italia dal dopoguerra a oggi.* Milano: Einaudi Scuola, 1996.

Goldman, Marshal I. "The Soviet Union." In "The Oil Crisis: In Perspective." special issue, *Daedalus* 104, no. 4 (1975): 129–43.
Goldsmith, Christopher. "The British Embassy in Paris and the Algerian War: An Uncomfortable Partner?" In *France and the Algerian War, 1954–62: Strategy, Operations and Diplomacy*, edited by Martin S. Alexander and J. F. V. Keiger, 159–71. London/Portland: Frank Cass, 2002.
Grevsmühl, Sebastian V. *La Terre vue d'en haut. L'invention de l'environnement global.* Paris: Seuil, 2014.
Guderzo, Massimiliano, and Matteo Luigi Napolitano, eds. *Diplomazia delle risorse: le materie prime e il sistema internazionale nel Novecento.* Firenze: Polistampa, 2001.
Guidi, Francesco. "VII. A braccetto con geofisica e mitologia, fra il Lete e il giardino delle Esperidi." In *Documenti dell'Archivio storico*, vol. 3, *La memoria raccontata*, edited by ENI and APVE, 77–8. Roma/San Donato Milanese: ENI/APVE, 2012.
Guillen, Pierre. "Le déclin de la puissance italienne à la fin de la seconde guerre mondiale." *Relations internationales* 9 (1977): 3–23.
Guisnel, Jean. "Foccart, Elf et le sang noir de l'Afrique." In *Histoire secrète de la Ve République*, edited by Roger Faligot and Jean Guisnel, 133–43. Paris: La Découverte.
Hacker, Barton C. "Military Patronage and the Geophysical Sciences in the United States. An Introduction." *Historical Studies in the Physical and Biological Sciences* 30, no. 2 (2000): 309–13.
Hamblin, Jacob Darwin. *Oceanographers and the Cold War: Disciples of Marine Science.* Seattle: University of Washington Press, 2005.
Hammer, Sigmund. "Geophysical Activity in 1953." *Geophysics* 19, no. 3 (1954): 517–28.
Haney Patrick J., and Walt Vanderbush, *The Cuban Embargo: The Domestic Politics of an American Foreign Policy.* Pittsburgh: University of Pittsburgh Press, 2005.
Harbi, Mohammed, and Benjamin Stora. *La Guerre d'Algérie. 1954–2004, la fin de l'amnésie.* Paris: Robert Laffont, 2004.
Headrick, Daniel R. *Power over Peoples: Technology, Environments and Western Imperialism: 1400 to the Present.* Princeton, NJ: Princeton University Press, 2010.
Hecht, Gabrielle. "Technology, Politics, and National Identity in France." In *Technologies of Power. Essays in Honor of Thomas Parke Hughes and Agatha Chipley Hughes*, edited by Michael Thad Allen and Gabrielle Hecht, 253–94. Cambridge, MA/London: MIT Press, 2001.
———. "Rupture-Talk in the Nuclear Age: Conjugating Colonial Power in Africa." *Social Studies of Science* 32, n. 5/6 (2002): 691–727.
———. "Nuclear Ontologies." *Constellations* 13, no. 3 (2006): 320–31.
———. "A Cosmogram for Nuclear Things." *Isis* 98, no. 1 (2007): 100–8.
———. *The Radiance of France: Nuclear Power and National Identity after World War II.* 2nd edition. MA/London: MIT Press, 2009. 1st edition: 1998.
———. "The Power of Nuclear Things." *Technology and Culture* 51, no. 1 (2010): 1–30.
———. "Introduction." In *Entangled Geographies: Empire and Technopolitics in the Global Cold War*, edited by Gabrielle Hecht, 1–12. Cambridge, MA/London: MIT Press, 2011.

———. *Being Nuclear: Africans and the Global Uranium Trade*. Cambridge, MA/London: MIT Press, 2012.

Helmreich, Jonathan E. *Gathering Rare Ores, The Diplomacy of Uranium Acquisition, 1943–1945*. Princeton, NJ: Princeton University Press, 1986.

Héritier, Francis. "Histoire de l'exploration pétrolière en France." In *La recherche pétrolière française*, edited by Jean Prouvost, 13–33. Paris: Éditions du CTHS.

Heymann, Matthias, and Janet Martin-Nielsen. "Introduction: Perspectives on Cold War Science in Small European States." *Centaurus* 55, no. 3 (2013): 221–42.

Hitchcock, William I. *France Restored: Cold War Diplomacy and the Quest for Leadership in Europe, 1944–1954*. Chapel Hill, NC/London: University of North Carolina Press, 1998.

Hogan, Michael J. *The Marshall Plan: America, Britain, and the Reconstruction of Western Europe, 1947–1952*.Cambridge: Cambridge University Press: 1987.

Hogg, Jonathan, and Christoph Laucht, eds. "British Nuclear Culture." special issue, *British Journal for the History of Science* 45, no. 4 (2012): 479–669.

Högselius, Per. *Red Gas. Russia and the Origins of Europe's Energy Dependence*. New York: Palgrave Macmillan, 2013.

Horne, Alistair. *A Savage War of Peace: Algeria 1954–1962*. New York: Viking, 1978.

Hoskins, Halford L. *Problems Raised by the Soviet Oil Offensive*. U.S. Senate. Committee on the Judiciary. Washington, DC: United States Government Printing Office, 1962.

Hoskins, Halford L., and Leon M. Herman. *Soviet Oil in the Cold War*. U.S. Senate. Committee on the Judiciary. Washington, DC: United States Government Printing Office, 1961.

Hughes, Thomas P. *Networks of Power: Electrification in Western Society, 1880–1930*. Baltimore: John Hopkins University Press, 1983.

Iriye, Akira. "Transnational History." *Contemporary European History* 13, no. 2 (2005): 211–22.

Jacobini, Oreste. "La questione petrolifera mondiale e quella italiana, III parte, nota VI: La questione petrolifera italiana" (Roma, 1948). In *La questione petrolifera italiana. Studi di Oreste Jacobini tra primo e secondo dopoguerra. Documenti dell'Archivio storico*, vol. 1, edited by Pier Angelo Toninelli. Roma: ENI, 2006.

Jakosky, John J. "Whither Exploration." *Geophysics* 12, no. 3 (1947): 361–8.

Jensen-Eriksen, Niklas. "The Cold War in Energy Markets. British Efforts to Contain Soviet Oil Exports to Non-Communist Countries, 1950–1965." In *Le pétrole et la guerre/Oil and War*, edited by Alain Beltran, 191–208. Brussels: Peter Lang, 2012.

———. "'Red Oil' and Western Reactions: The Case of Britain". In *Cold War Energy: A Transnational History of Soviet Oil and Gas*, edited by Jeronim Perovic, 105–30. London: Palgrave Macmillan, 2017.

Jervis, Robert. "Cooperation Under the Security Dilemma." *World Politics* 30, no. 2 (1978): 167–214.

———. "Was the Cold War a Security Dilemma?" *Journal of Cold War Studies* 3, no. 1 (2001): 36–60.

Jonchay, Yves. "L'infrastructure de départ du Sahara et de l'Organisation Commune des Régions Sahariennes (O.C.R.S.)." *Revue géographique* 32, no. 4 (1957): 277–92.

Jones, H. J. "Central Office Processing of Seismic Data." *World Petroleum* 28, no. 3 (1957): 68–70.
Kablia, Dahou O. "Enrico Mattei e la Rivoluzione Algerina." In *Enrico Mattei e l'Algeria durante la Guerra di Liberazione Nazionale*, edited by Ambasciata d'Italia and Istituto Italiano di Cultura di Algeri, 18–21. Algiers: Ambasciata d'Italia and Istituto Italiano di Cultura di Algeri, 2010.
Kaplan, Lawrence S. *The Long Entanglement: NATO's First Fifty Years.* Westport, CT/London: Praeger, 1999.
Kauffer, Rémi. "L'or noir et la bombe: la face cachée des accords d'Évian." In *Histoire secrète de la Ve République*, edited by Roger Faligot and Jean Guisnel, 83–6. Paris: La Découverte, 2006.
Keohane, Robert O. "The United States and the Postwar Order: Empire or Hegemony?" *Journal of Peace Research* 28, no. 4 (1991): 435–9.
Kettle, Michael. *De Gaulle and Algeria, 1940–1960. From Mers El-Kébir to the Algiers Barracades* [sic]. London: Quartet Books, 1993.
Khelladi, Mohamed. "Testimonianza." In *Enrico Mattei e l'Algeria durante la Guerra di Liberazione Nazionale*, edited by Ambasciata d'Italia and Istituto Italiano di Cultura di Algeri, 57–8. Algiers: Ambasciata d'Italia and Istituto Italiano di Cultura di Algeri, 2010.
Kocher-Marbœuf, Éric. *Le Patricien et le Général. Jean-Marcel Jeanneney et Charles de Gaulle 1958–1969.* vol. I. Paris: Comité pour l'histoire économique et financière de la France, 2003.
Kolodziej, Edward A. *French International Policy Under De Gaulle and Pompidou. The Politics of Grandeur.* Ithaca/London: Cornell University Press, 1974.
Kovacs, Giorgio E. *Storia delle raffinerie di petrolio in Italia.* Roma: Colombo, 1994.
Krige, John. *American Hegemony and the Postwar Reconstruction of Science in Europe.* Cambridge, MA/London: MIT Press, 2006.
———. "The Peaceful Atom as Political Weapon: Euratom and American Foreign Policy in the Late 1950s." *Historical Studies in the Natural Sciences* 38, no. 1 (2008): 5–44.
———. "Hybrid Knowledge: The Transnational Co-production of the Gas Centrifuge for Uranium Eenrichment in the 1960s." In "Transnational History of Science," edited by Simone Turchetti, Néstor Herran and Soraya Boudia, special issue, *British Journal for the History of Science* 45, no. 3 (2012): 337–57.
Krige, John, and Kai-Henrik Barth, eds. "Global Power Knowledge. Science and Technology in International Affairs," special issue, *Osiris* 21, no. 1 (2006).
Latour, Bruno. *Science in Action: How to Follow Scientists and Engineers through Society.* Cambridge, MA: Harvard University Press, 1987.
Layat, C., A. C. Clement, G. Pommier, and A. Buffet. "Some Technical Aspects of Refraction Seismic Prospecting in the Sahara." *Geophysics* 26, no. 4 (1961): 437–46.
Leffler, Melvyn P. "National Security." *Journal of American History* 77, no. 1 (1990): 143–52.
Lerat, Serge. "La mise en valeur du gisement de gaz de Lacq." *Annales de Géographie* 66, no. 355 (1957): 260–7.
Leslie, Stuart W. *The Cold War and American Science: The Military-Industrial-Academic Complex at MIT and Stanford.* New York: Columbia University Press, 1993.
Leslie, Stuart W., and Robert Kargon, "Exporting MIT: Science, Technology, and Nation-Building in India and Iran." In "Global Power Knowledge: Science

and Technology in International Affairs," edited by John Krige and Kai-Henrik Barth, special issue, *Osiris* 21, no. 1 (2006): 110–30.

Levy, Walter J. "Economic Coopération [sic] Administration (E. C. A.)." *Bulletin AFTP* 73 (1949): 41–6.

Li Vigni, Benito. *La grande sfida. Mattei, il petrolio e la politica.* Milano: Mondadori, 1996.

Lo Bianco, Giuseppe, and Sandra Rizza. *Profondo Nero. Mattei, De Mauro, Pasolini. Un'unica pista all'origine delle stragi di stato.* Milano: Chiarelettere, 2009.

Loftus, John A. "Oil in United States Foreign Policy." *Vital Speeches of the Day* 12, no. 24 (1946): 755.

Lomartire, Carlo Maria. *Mattei. Storia dell'italiano che sfidò i signori del petrolio.* Milano: Mondadori, 2004.

Lombardi, Leonard V. "Notes on the Use of Multiple Geophones." *Geophysics* 20, no. 2 (1955): 215–26.

Lotysz, Sławomir. "A 'Lasting Memorial' to the UNRRA? Implementation of the Penicillin Plant Programme in Poland, 1946–1949." *ICON: Journal of the International Committee for the History of Technology* 20, no. 2 (2014): 70–91.

Lundestad, Geir. "Empire by Invitation? The United States and Western Europe, 1945–1952." *Journal of Peace Research* 23, no. 3 (1986): 263–77.

———. *The United States and Western Europe since 1945.* Oxford: Oxford University Press, 2009.

———. *The Rise and Decline of the American "Empire": Power and its Limits in Comparative Perspective.* Oxford/New York: Oxford University Press, 2012.

Lyons, Paul L. "The Future of Geophysics." *Geophysics* 20, no. 3 (1955): 503–15.

Maganga-Moussavou, Pierre-Claver. *L'aide publique de la France au développement du Gabon depuis l'indépendance (1960–1978).* Paris: Publications de la Sorbonne, 1982.

Magini, Manlio. *L'italia e il petrolio tra storia e cronologia.* Mondadori: Milano, 1976.

Maiocchi, Roberto. "Il ruolo delle scienze nello sviluppo industriale italiano." In *Storia d'Italia. Annali 3. Scienza e tecnica nella cultura e nella società dal Rinascimento a oggi*, edited by Gianni Micheli, 855–999. Torino: Einaudi, 1980.

Malek, Rédha. *L'Algérie à Évian. Histoire des négociations secrètes, 1956–1962.* Paris: Seuil, 1995.

Malti, Hocine. *Histoire secrète du pétrole algérien.* Paris: La Découverte, 2010.

Manzione, Joseph. "'Amusing and Amazing and Practical and Military': The Legacy of Scientific Internationalism in American Foreign Policy, 1945–1963." *Diplomatic History* 24 (2000): 21–55.

Martin, Guy. "Uranium: A Case-Study in Franco–African Relations." *Journal of Modern African Studies* 27, no. 4 (1989): 625–40.

Mastanduno, Michael. *Economic Containment: CoCom and the Politics of East–West Trade.* New York: Cornell University Press, 1992.

Maugeri, Leonardo. *L'arma del petrolio. Questione petrolifera globale, guerra fredda e politica italiana nella vicenda di Enrico Mattei.* Firenze: Loggia De' Lanzi, 1994.

Mayhew, Zeb. "A Review of Foreign Oil Production in 1960." *Journal of Petroleum Technology* 13, no. 4 (1961): 320–2.

McBride, James H. *The Test Ban Treaty: Military, Technological and Political Implications.* Chicago: Henry Regnery Company, 1967.

Melby, Eric D. K. *Oil and the International System. The Case of France, 1918–1969.* New York: Arno Press, 1981.
Mendershausen, Horst. "Dollar Shortage and Oil Surplus in 1949–1950." *Essays in International Finance* 11 (1950): 8–11.
Michon, Dominique. "Histoire de la sismique pour la recherche pétrolière." In *La recherche pétrolière française*, edited by Jean Prouvost, 217–33. Paris: Éditions du CTHS.
Milano, Rosario. *L'ENI in Iran (1962–1970).* Napoli: Giannini, 2013.
Miller, James E. "Taking Off the Gloves: The United States and the Italian Elections of 1948." *Diplomatic History* 7, no. 1 (1983): 35–56.
Milward, Alan S. *The Reconstruction of Western Europe, 1945–1951.* Berkeley: The University of California Press, 1984.
Mistry, Kaeten. "The Case for Political Warfare: Strategy, Organization and US Involvement in the 1948 Italian Election." *Cold War History* 6, no. 3 (2006): 301–29.
Mitchell, Timothy. "McJihad: Islam in the US Global Order." *Social Text* 20, no. 4 (2002): 1–18.
———. "Carbon Democracy." *Economy and Society* 38, no. 3 (2009): 399–432.
———. *Carbon Democracy: Political Power in the Age of Oil.* New York: Verso, 2011.
Morange, André, Alain Perrodon, and Francis Héritier. *Les grandes heures de l'exploration pétrolière du groupe ELF Aquitaine.* Boussens: Elf Aquitaine Éditions, 1992.
Morrison, L. S., and Robert Watson. "The Electronic Computer and Geophysics." *Geophysics* 26 (1): 40–4.
Murat, Daniel. *L'intervention de l'État dans le secteur pétrolier en France.* Paris: Technip, 1969.
Nash, Gerald D. *United States Oil Policy. 1890–1964.* Pittsburgh: University of Pittsburgh Press, 1968.
Needell, Allan A. *Science, Cold War and the American State: Lloyd V. Berkner and the Balance of Professional Ideals.* Amsterdam: Harwood Academic, 2000.
Nouschi, André. *Luttes pétrolières au Proche-Orient.* Paris: Flammarion, 1970.
———. *Pétrole et relations internationales de 1945 à nos jours.* Paris: Armand Colin, 1999.
———. "Un tournant de la politique pétrolière française: les Heads of Agreement de novembre 1948." *Relations Internationales* 44: 1985 [no page number reported].
———. *La France et le pétrole: de 1924 à nos jours* Paris: Picard, 2001.
Nuti, Leopoldo. "Commitment to NATO and Domestic Politics: the Italian Case and Some Comparative." *Contemporary European History* 7, no. 3 (1998): 361–77.
———. *Gli Stati Uniti e l'apertura a sinistra. Importanza e limiti della presenza americana in Italia.* Bari: Laterza, 1999.
———. *La sfida nucleare: la politica estera italiana e le armi atomiche, 1945–1991.* Bologna: Il Mulino, 2007.
Odell, Peter R. *An Economic Geography of Oil.* London: G. Bell and Sons, 1963.
Oreskes, Naomi, and Ronald E. Doel. "Physics and Chemistry of the Earth." In *The Cambridge History of Science.* vol. V: *Modern Physical and Mathematical*

Sciences, edited by Mary Jo Nye, 538–58. Cambridge: Cambridge University Press, 2002.

Oreskes, Naomi, and James R. Fleming, "Why Geophysics?" *Studies in History and Philosophy of Modern Physics* 31, no. 3 (2000): 253–7.

Painter, David S. "Oil and the Marshall Plan." *Business History Review* 58, no. 3 (1984): 359–83.

———. *Oil and the American Century: The Political Economy of U.S. Foreign Oil Policy, 1941–1954*. Baltimore: Johns Hopkins University Press, 1986.

———. "Oil, Resources, and the Cold War, 1945–1962." In *The Cambridge History of the Cold War*, edited by Melvyn P. Leffler and Odd Arne Westad, 486–507. Cambridge: Cambridge University Press, 2010.

Palazuelos, Enrique, and Rafael Fernández, "The Importance of Transnational Corporations in the Supply of Oil to Europe: Implications." *Energy Policy* 47 (2012): 270–81.

Paleri, Prabhakaran. *National Security: Imperatives and Challenges*. New Delhi: Tata McGraw-Hill, 2008.

Parra, Francisco. *Oil Politics. A Modern History of Petroleum*. New York: I. B. Tauris & Co, 2010.

Patrick, Homer G. "Geophysical Activity in 1955." *Geophysics* 22, no. 1 (1957): 89–103.

Patrick, Stewart. "Embedded Liberalism in France? American Hegemony, the Monnet Plan, and Postwar Multilateralism." In *The Marshall Plan: Fifty Years After*, edited by Martin Schain, 205–48. New York: Palgrave, 2001.

Péan, Pierre, and Jean-Pierre Séréni. *Les émirs de la République. L'aventure du pétrole tricolore*. Paris: Seuil, 1982.

Penrose, Edith T. *The Large International Firm in Developing Countries. The International Petroleum Industry*. London: George Allen and Unwin, 1968.

Penrose, Edith, and Ernest F. Penrose. *Iraq: International Relations and National Development*. London: Ernest Benn, 1978.

Perrodon, Alain. "Historique des recherches pétrolières en Algérie." In *La recherche pétrolière française*, edited by Jean Prouvost, 323–40. Paris: Éditions du CTHS, 1994.

———. *Histoire des grandes découvertes pétrolières. Un certain art de l'exploration*. Pau/Paris: Elf Aquitaine-Masson, 1995.

Perrone, Nico. *Mattei il nemico italiano: vita e morte del presidente dell'ENI attraverso i documenti segreti*. Milano: Leonardo Mondadori, 1989.

———. *Obiettivo Mattei. Petrolio, Stati Uniti e politica dell'ENI*. Gamberetti: Roma, 1995.

———. *Enrico Mattei*. Bologna: Il Mulino, 2001.

———. *Perché uccisero Enrico Mattei. Petrolio e guerra fredda nel primo grande delitto italiano*. Roma: Nuova Iniziativa Editoriale, 2006.

Philippon, André. "The French Example. The 1928s Laws. Longevity and Effectiveness of the Approach to Creating and Maintaining a National Oil Industry in a Consumer Country—Appearances and Realities." In *A Comparative History of National Oil Companies*, edited by Alain Beltran, 21–53. Brussels: Peter Lang, 2010.

Pietra, Italo. *Mattei: la pecora nera*. Roma: La Repubblica, 2002. 1st edition. Milano: Sugarco, 1987.

Pieuchot, Maurice, and Henri Richard, "Some Technical Aspects of Reflection Seismic Prospecting in the Sahara." *Geophysics* 23, no. 3 (1958): 557–73.

Pinch, Trevor J., and Wiebe E. Bijker. "The Social Construction of Facts and Artefacts: Or How the Sociology of Science and the Sociology of Technology Might Benefit Each Other." *Social Studies of Science* 14 (August 1984): 399–441.
Pirani, Mario. *Poteva andare peggio. Mezzo secolo di ragionevoli illusioni.* Milano: Mondadori, 2012.
Pizzigallo, Matteo. *Alle origini della politica petrolifera italiana (1920–1925).* Milano: Giuffrè, 1981.
———. *L'AGIP degli anni ruggenti (1926–1932).* Milano: Giuffrè, 1984.
———. *La politica estera dell'AGIP (1933–1940).* Milano: Giuffrè. 1992.
Polach, Jaroslav G. *EURATOM: Its Background, Issues and Economic Implications.* Dobbs Ferry: Oceana, 1964.
Polanyi, Michael. *The Tacit Dimension.* London: Routledge & Kegan Paul, 1967.
Pontecorvo, Bruno. "Neutron Well Logging." *Oil and Gas Journal* 40 (1941): 32–3.
Porch, Douglas. *The French Secret Services: From the Dreyfus Affair to the Gulf War.* New York: Farrar, Straus and Giroux, 1995.
Porter, Theodore M. *Trust in Numbers. The Pursuit of Objectivity in Science and Public Life.* Princeton, NJ: Princeton University Press, 1995.
Pozzi, Daniele. "Tra New York e Fornovo Taro: l'occasione mancata della Società petrolifera italiana (1945–1953)." *Imprese e Storia* 24 (2001): 361–408.
———. "L'industria degli idrocarburi in Italia: gli operatori privati e il problema dell'integrazione." In *Energia per il territorio: Enrico Mattei e l'industria del metano in Italia*, edited by Andrea Giuntini and Daniele Pozzi, 37–57. Lodi: Giona, 2003.
———. "L'introduzione della sismica a riflessione in Italia." In *Energia per il territorio: Enrico Mattei e l'industria del metano in Italia*, edited by Andrea Giuntini and Daniele Pozzi, 125–59. Lodi: Giona, 2003.
———. "Mattei e la 'vecchia' AGIP: tra ipotesi di continuità e rilancio strategico (1945–1948)." *Imprese e Storia* 27 (2003): 56–95.
———. "Techno-Managerial Competences in Enrico Mattei's AGIP: A Prolonged Accumulation Process in an International Network (1935–1965)." *Business and Economy History* 1 (2003): 1–32.
———. *Dai gatti selvaggi al cane a sei zampe. Tecnologia, conoscenza e organizzazione nell'AGIP e nell'ENI di Enrico Mattei.* Padova: Marsilio, 2009.
———. "Entrepreneurship and Capabilities in a 'Beginner' Oil Multinational: The Case of ENI." *Business History Review* 84 (2010): 253–74.
———. "The Natural Gas Industry in Italy Since Autarky Until ENI's Hegemony: 1935–1965." In *A Comparative History of National Oil Companies*, edited by Alain Beltran, 233–64. Brussels: Peter Lang, 2010.
Pozzi, Daniele, ed. *La leggenda del pioniere. Diario Mazzini Garibaldi Pissard. Documenti dell'Archivio Storico.* vol. 2. Roma: ENI, 2008.
Pressenda, Angelo, and Marcella Sarale. *Ricerca sulle Partecipazioni statali. II. L'ENI da Mattei a Cefis. La politica del petrolio tra mito e realtà.* Torino: Einaudi, 1978.
Prouvost, Jean ed. *La recherche pétrolière française.* Paris: Éditions du CTHS, 1994.
Pruessen, Ronald W. *John Foster Dulles: The Road to Power.* New York: Free Press, 1982.
Quartararo, Rosaria. *Italia e Stati Uniti: gli anni difficili, 1945–1952.* Napoli: Edizioni Scientifiche Italiane, 1986.

Rachkov, Boris. "Oil, Trade, and Politics." *International Affairs* 12 (1966): 14–20.

Rachline, Maurice. *Geophysical Prospecting and Oil Exploration.* Paris: CGG/Editions Atlas, 1998.

Randall, Stephen J. "Harold Ickes and United States Foreign Petroleum Policy Planning, 1939–1945." *Business History Review* 57, no. 3 (1983): 367–87.

———. *United States Foreign Oil Policy Since World War I: For Profits and Security.* 2nd edition. Montreal/London: McGill-Queen's University Press, 2005.

Reymond, Mathias. "European Key Issues Concerning Natural Gas: Dependence and Vulnerability." *Energy Policy* 35 (2007): 4169–76.

Reynolds, David. "A 'Special Relationship'? America, Britain and the International Order Since the Second World War." *International Affairs* 62, no. 1 (1985–86): 1–20.

Rioux, Jean-Pierre. *The Fourth Republic, 1944–1958.* Cambridge: Cambridge University Press, 1987.

———. *La Guerre d'Algérie et les Français.* Paris: Fayard, 1990.

Rioux, Jean-Pierre, and Jean-François Sirinelli. *La guerre d'Algérie et les intellectuels français.* Paris: Institut d'Histoire du Temps Présent, 1988.

Rocco, Tiziano. *I giacimenti gassiferi dell'Europa occidentale.* vol. II. Roma: Accademia Nazionale dei Lincei, 1959.

Roche, François. *TotalFinaElf: The French Major.* Paris: Le Cherche Midi, 2003.

Roger, Philippe. *L'ennemi américain. Généalogie de l'antiaméricanisme français.* Paris: Seuil, 2002.

Romm, Joseph J. *Defining National Security: The Nonmilitary Aspects.* New York: Council on Foreign Relations Press, 1993.

Rondot, Jean. "Les intérêts pétroliers français dans le Proche-Orient." *Politique étrangère* 17, no. 4 (1952): 267–91.

———. *La Compagnie Française des Pétroles. Du franc-or au pétrole-franc.* Paris: Plon, 1962.

Ross, Kristin. *Fast Cars, Clean Bodies: Decolonization and the Reordering of French Culture.* Cambridge, MA/London: MIT Press, 1995.

Roverato Giorgio. *Nuovo Pignone. Le sfide della maturità.* Bologna: Il Mulino, 1991.

Rutman, Gilbert. "Quelques éléments pour l'histoire de la Société nationale des pétroles d'Aquitaine (SNPA) de 1941 à 1976." In *La recherche pétrolière française*, edited by Jean Prouvost, 147–54. Paris: Éditions du CTHS, 1994.

Salut, Samir. "Politique nationale du pétrole, société nationales et 'pétrole franc.'" *Revue historique* 638, no. 2 (2006): 355–88.

Sampson, Anthony. *The Seven Sisters. The Great Oil Companies and the World They Made.* London: Hodder and Stoughton, 1975.

Sapelli, Giulio, and Francesca Carnevali. *Uno sviluppo tra politica e strategia. ENI (1953–1985).* Milano: Franco Angeli, 1992.

Saul, Samir. "REPAL, CFP and 'Oil-Paid-in-Francs.'" In *A Comparative History of National Oil Companies*, edited by Alain Beltran, 233–64. Brussels: Peter Lang, 2010.

Saunier, Pierre-Yves. "Going Transnational? News from Down Under." *Historical Social Research* 31, no. 2 (2006): 118–31.

———. "Learning by Doing: Notes about the Making of the Palgrave Dictionary of Transnational History." *Journal of Modern European History* 6, no. 2 (2008): 159–79.

Schain, Martin, ed. *The Marshall Plan: Fifty Years After.* New York: Palgrave, 2001.

Schlesinger, Arthur. *A Thousand Days: John F. Kennedy in the White House.* Boston: Houghton Mifflin, 1965.

Schvartz, Julien. *Sur les sociétés pétrolières opérant en France... Rapport de la commission d'enquête parlementaire (6 novembre 1974).* Paris: Union Générale d'Editions, 1974.

Schwab, Peter. *Cuba: Confronting the U.S. Embargo.* New York: Palgrave Macmillan, 1999.

Sèbe, Berny. "In the Shadow of the Algerian War: The United States and the Common Organisation of Saharan Regions (OCRS), 1957–62." *The Journal of Imperial and Commonwealth History* 38 (2: 2010): 303–22.

Smith, E. Timothy. "The Fear of Subversion: The United States and the Inclusion of Italy in the North Atlantic Treaty." *Diplomatic History* 7, no. 2 (1983): 139–56.

Smith, Neal J. "Geophysical Activity in 1962." *Geophysics* 28, no. 6 (1963): 1049–71.

Solari, Leo. *La polemica sugli idrocarburi.* Bologna: Il Mulino, 1955.

Soutou, Georges-Henri, and Alain Beltran, eds. *Pierre Gullaumat, la passion des grands projets industriels.* Paris: Institut d'Histoire de l'Industrie et Editions Rive Droite, 1995.

Spagnolo, Carlo. *La stabilizzazione incompiuta. Il Piano Marshall in Italia.* Roma: Carocci, 2001.

Spencer, D. L. "The Role of Oil in Soviet Foreign Economic Policy." *American Journal of Economy and Society* 25, no. 1 (1966): 91–107.

Squarzina, Federico. *Le ricerche di petrolio in Italia. Cenni storici dal 1860 e cronache dell'ultimo decennio.* Roma: Jandi Sapi, 1958.

Stent, Angela. *From Embargo to Ostpolitik. The Political Economy of West Germany-Soviet Relations, 1955–1980.* Cambridge: Cambridge University Press, 1981.

Stern, Jonathan. *Soviet Oil and Gas Exports to the West: Commercial Transactions or Security Threat?* Aldershot: Gower, 1987.

Stoff, Michael B. *Oil, War, and American Security: The Search for a National Policy on Foreign Oil, 1941–1947.* New Haven: Yale University Press, 1982.

Stora, Benjamin. *Histoire de la guerre d'Algérie (1954–1962).* Paris: La Découverte, 1993.

Styan, David. *France and Iraq. Oil, Arms and French Policy Making in the Middle East.* London/New York: I. B. Tauris & Co, 2006.

Talbott, John. *The War Without a Name. France in Algeria, 1954–1962.* London/Boston: Faber and Faber, 1980.

Talmadge, Caitlin. "Closing Time: Assessing the Iranian Threat to the Strait of Hormuz." *International Security* 33, no. 1 (2008): 82–117.

Thelen, David. "The Nation and Beyond: Transnational Perspectives on United States History." *Journal of American History* 86, no. 3 (1999): 965–75.

Thénault, Sylvie. *Histoire de la guerre d'indépendance algérienne.* Paris: Flammarion, 2005.

Thomas, Martin. *The French North African Crisis. Colonial Breakdown and Anglo-French Relations, 1945–62.* London: Macmillan, 2000.

Thorp, Willard L. "American Policy and the Soviet Economic Offensive." *Foreign Affairs* 35 (1956–7): 271–82.

Tonini, Alberto. "L'ENI alla ricerca di un partner arabo: Egitto e Iraq, 1955–62." In *Diplomazia delle risorse: le materie prime e il sistema internazionale nel Novecento*, edited by Massimiliano Guderzo and Matteo Luigi Napolitano, 205–24. Firenze: Polistampa, 2001.

———. *Il sogno proibito. Mattei, il petrolio arabo e le 'sette sorelle'*. Firenze: Polistampa, 2003.

Tremolada, Ilaria. *All'ombra degli arabi. Le relazioni italo-israeliane 1948–1956. Dalla fondazione dello Stato Ebraico alla crisi di Suez.* Milano: M&B, 2003.

———. *La via italiana al petrolio. L'ENI di Enrico Mattei e l'Iran (1945–1962).* Milano: L'Ornitorinco, 2011.

Tripp, R. Maurice. "'Geophysics in National Defense': An ESMWT Course Conducted at the Colorado School of Mines." *Geophysics* 10, no. 3 (1945): 432–3.

Tristani, Philippe. "L'Iraq Petroleum Company, les États-Unis et la lutte pour le leadership pétrolier au Moyen-Orient de 1945 à 1973." *Histoire, économie & sociéte* 29 (2010): 81–107.

Turchetti, Simone. *The Pontecorvo Affair. A Cold War Defection and Nuclear Physics*. Chicago: University of Chicago Press, 2012.

———. "Sword, Shield and Buoys: A History of the Nato Sub-Committee on Oceanographic Research, 1959–1973." *Centaurus* 54, no. 3 (2012): 202–31.

———. "In God We Trust. All Others We Monitor: Seismology, Intelligence and the Test Ban Negotiations, 1957–1963." In *The Surveillance Imperative. The Rise of the Geosciences During the Cold War*, edited by Simone Turchetti and Peder Roberts, 85–102. London/New York: Palgrave, 2014.

———. "A Most Active Customer. How the U.S. Administration Helped the Italian Atomic Energy Project to 'De-Develop.'" *Historical Studies in the Natural Sciences* 44, no. 5 (2014): 470–502.

Turchetti, Simone, and Peder Roberts. "Introduction: Knowing the Enemy, Knowing the Earth." In *The Surveillance Imperative: Geosciences During the Cold War and Beyond*, edited by Simone Turchetti and Peder Roberts, 1–19. London: Palgrave Macmillan, 2014.

Turchetti, Simone, Néstor Herran, and Soraya Boudia. "Introduction: Have We Ever Been 'Transnational'? Towards a History of Science Across and Beyond Borders." In "Transnational History of Science," edited by Simone Turchetti, Néstor Herran and Soraya Boudia, special issue, *British Journal for the History of Science* 45, no. 3 (2012): 1–18.

Uhlig, Frank. "The Threat of the Soviet Navy." *Foreign Affairs* 20 (1951–1952): 444–54.

Vaïsse, Maurice. "France and the Suez Crisis." In *Suez 1956*, edited by Wm. Roger Louis and Roger Owen, 131–43. Oxford: Clarendon, 1989.

———. *Vers la paix en Algérie. Les négociations d'Évian dans les archives diplomatiques françaises.* Bruxelles: Bruylant, 2003.

Van der Vleuten, Erik. "Toward a Transnational History of Technology Meanings, Promises, Pitfalls." *Technology and Culture* 49, no. 4 (2008): 974–94.

Van Melle, F. A., D. L. Faass, S. Kauffman, G. W. Postma, and A. J. Seriff. "Geophysical Research and Progress in Exploration." *Geophysics* 28, no. 3 (June 1963): 466–78.

Vellinger, Edmond. "Le rôle du Physicien dans l'Industrie Extractive du Pétrole." *Bulletin de l'Association française des techniciens du pétrole* 55 (1946): 3–26.

Verschave, François-Xavier. *La Françafrique: le plus long scandale de la République*. Paris: Stock, 1998.

———. *Noir silence: qui arrêtera la Françafrique*. Paris: Les Arènes, 2000.

Vidal-Naquet, Pierre. *Les Crimes de l'armée française en Algérie 1954–1962*. Paris: La Découverte, 2001.

Vietor, Richard H. K. *Energy Policy in America Since 1945. A Study of Business–Government Relations*. Cambridge: Cambridge University Press, 1984.

Vining, Margaret, and Barton C. Hacker, eds. *Science in Uniform, Uniforms in Science. Historical Studies of American Military and Scientific Interactions*. Plymouth: Scarecrow Press, 2007.

Votaw, Dow. *The Six-legged Dog. Mattei and ENI—A Study in Power*. Berkeley/Los Angeles: University of California Press, 1964.

Wall, Irwin M. "Jean Monnet, the United States and the French Economic Plan." In *Jean Monnet: The Path to European Unity*, edited by Douglas Brinkley and Clifford Hackett, 86–113. New York: Palgrave, 1991.

———. *The United States and the Making of Postwar France, 1945–1954*. Cambridge: Cambridge University Press, 1991.

———. *France, the United States and the Algerian War*. Berkeley/Los Angeles: University of California Press, 2001.

———. "The Marshall Plan and French Politics." In *The Marshall Plan: Fifty Years After*, edited by Martin Schain, 167–84. New York: Palgrave, 2001.

Wallis, W. E., and E. M. McNatt. "Selection of New Regions for Overseas Exploration." *Geophysics* 23, no. 2 (1958): 305–17.

Whidden, William R., ed. *Buried Flexible Steel Pipe: Design and Structural Analysis*. Reston: American Society of Civil Engineers, 2009.

Winter, Lea. "Fueling Oil Scarcity: Produced Scarcity and the Sociopolitical Fate of Renewable Energy." *Journal of International Affairs* 69, no. 1 (2015): 195–206.

Yates, Douglas A. *The Rentier State in Africa: Oil Rent Dependency and Neocolonialism in the Republic of Gabon*. Trenton/Asmara: Africa World Press, 1996.

———. "Life Stories and Family Histories of the French Oil Industry. The Rise and Fall of the Corps des Mines." In *A Comparative History of National Oil Companies*, edited by Alain Beltran, 54–67. Brussels: Peter Lang, 2010.

Yergin, Daniel. *The Prize: The Epic Quest for Oil, Money, and Power*. 2nd edition. New York: Simon & Schuster, 2009. 1st edition: 1991.

———. *The Quest: Energy, Security, and the Remaking of the Modern World*. London: Penguin, 2011.

Ziegler, Charles A., and David Jacobson. *Spying Without Spies: Origins of America's Nuclear Surveillance System*. Westport, CT: Praeger, 1995.

Other Published and Unpublished Sources

AAAS. *New Frontiers in Science Diplomacy*. London: The Royal Society, 2010.

Adamson, Matthew. *Nuclear Reach*. Unpublished manuscript.

Addresses—Ickes, Harold L., "An Oil Policy for the United States." Dec. 8, 1944; Chicago Council on Foreign Relations Records, Special Collections, b. 3, fd. 96; University of Illinois at Chicago.

AGIP Mineraria. *Relazione sulla attività svolta nell'anno 1953*. Milano: AGIP, 1954.

AGIP Mineraria. *Relazioni e bilancio al 31 dicembre 1956*. Roma: AGIP/CEDI, 1956.

Cantoni, Roberto. "Une étude de la prospection géophysique française du pétrole au Gabon entre la fin de la Seconde Guerre Mondiale et le premier choc pétrolier (1946–1973)." Master's thesis, Université Paris 7 'Denis Diderot', 2010.

Cassano, Emanuele, ed. "La Storia dei Gruppi Geofisici dell'AGIP." Working Paper, Associazione Pionieri e Veterani ENI, San Donato Milanese, 2008, (http://www.eageseg.org/download.php?f=0a3303d95dea6d87326ea2508b766c20).

CEDI. *Archivio storico. Verbali Comitato tecnico ricerche e produzioni (1948–1949)*. San Donato Milanese: Centro stampa AGIP, 1991.

CEDI. *Archivio storico. Verbali Comitato tecnico ricerche e produzioni (1950)*. San Donato Milanese: Centro stampa AGIP, 1992.

CEDI. *Archivio storico. Verbali Comitato tecnico ricerche e produzioni (1951)*. San Dona.o Milanese: Centro stampa AGIP, 1992.

CEDI. *Verbali Comitato tecnico ricerche e produzioni (1952)*. San Donato Milanese: Centro stampa AGIP, 1992.

CEDI. *Archivio storico. Verbali Comitato tecnico ricerche e produzioni (1953)*. San Donato Milanese: Centro stampa AGIP, 1993.

Deluchi, Lucio. "Storia dei Centri Elaborazione AGIP." Working Paper, Associazione Pionieri e Veterani ENI, San Donato Milanese, undated [TPQ 1992], (www.pionierieni.it/wp/wp-content/uploads/Centri_Elaborazione_Geofisica_Agip.pdf).

Foreign Relations of the United States, 1944, III, The British Commonwealth and Europe. Washington, DC: United States Government Printing Office, 1965.

Foreign Relations of the United States, 1945, IV, Europe. Washington, DC: United States Government Printing Office, 1968.

Foreign Relations of the United States, 1945, VIII, The Near East and Africa. Washington, DC: United States Government Printing Office, 1969.

Foreign Relations of the United States, 1946, V, The British Commonwealth, Western and Central Europe. Washington, DC: United States Government Printing Office, 1946.

Foreign Relations of the United States, 1947, III, The British Commonwealth and Europe. Washington, DC: United States Government Printing Office, 1972.

Foreign Relations of the United States, 1947, V, The Near East and Africa. Washington, DC: United States Government Printing Office, 1971.

Foreign Relations of the United States, 1948, III, Western Europe. Washington, DC: United States Government Printing Office, 1973.

Foreign Relations of the United States, 1952–1954, I, pt. 2, General: economic and political matters. Washington, DC: United States Government Printing Office, 1952–1954.

Foreign Relations of the United States, 1952–1954, V. pt. 1, Western European Security. Washington, DC: United States Government Printing Office, 1952–1954.

Foreign Relations of the United States, 1952–1954, VI, pts. 1 and 2, Western Europe and Canada. Washington, DC: United States Government Printing Office, 1986.

Foreign Relations of the United States, 1952–1954, XI, pt. 1, Africa and South Asia. Washington, DC: United States Government Printing Office, 1952–1954.

Foreign Relations of the United States, 1955–1957, XVIII, Africa. Washington, DC: United States Government Printing Office, 1955–1957.

Foreign Relations of the United States, 1961–1963, XIII, Western Europe and Canada. Washington, DC: United States Government Printing Office, 1994.

IFP. *Institut Française du Pétrole* (booklet). Paris: IFP, 1967.

IFP. *Institut Française du Pétrole* (booklet). Paris: IFP, 1969.

Jensen-Eriksen, Niklas. "British government, business and the Soviet Cold War oil offensive, 1957–1964." Paper presented at the 16th Annual Conference of the European Business History Association, and 1st Joint Conference with Business History Society of Japan, Paris, August 30–September 1, 2012.

Niccolini, Francesco, and Simone Cortesi. *Enrico Mattei. Vita, disavventure e morte di un cavaliere solitario*. Padova: BeccoGiallo, 2012.

Solaini, Luigi. "Lo stato della geofisica applicata in Italia"; Opening discourse of the Academic Year; Yearbook of the School of Higher Studies on Hydrocarbons, 1963–1964, p. 12–22; Archivio della Scuola Superiore di Studi sugli Idrocarburi (currently ENI Corporate University), San Donato Milanese.

Subcommittee on Multinational Corporations. "Multinational Oil Corporation and U.S. Foreign Policy, Report together with individual views, to the Committee of Foreign Relations, United States Senate, by the Subcommittee on Multinational Corporations." Washington, DC: United States Government Printing Office, 1975, (http://www.mtholyoke.edu/acad/intrel/oil1.htm).

Toninelli, Pier Angelo. "Energy supply and economic development in Italy: the role of the state-owned companies." Working Paper 146, University of Milano-Bicocca, Department of Economics, 2008.

US Federal Trade Commission. *The International Petroleum Cartel*, Staff Report to the Federal Trade Commission, released through Subcommittee on Monopoly of Select Committee on Small Business, U.S. Senate, 83d Cong., 2nd sess (Washington, DC: US Senate, 1952).

Varsori, Antonio. "Italy's European Policy." UNISCI Discussion Papers 25, Universidad Complutense de Madrid, January 2011 (http://revistas.ucm.es/ index.php/UNIS/article/download/UNIS1111130041A/26855).

Varvelli, Riccardo. "Il Campo di Bahrgan Sar (Persia, ora Iran 1957–1961)." Working Paper, Associazione Pionieri e Veterani ENI, San Donato Milanese, 2010, (http://www.pionierieni.it/wp/?p=2061).

Oral Sources

Author's interview with Francesco Guidi. San Donato Milanese, February 4, 2013.

Audio-Visual Sources

"Hocine Malti: L'histoire secrète du pétrole algérien." YouTube video, 1:02:54, from an interview given to Philippe Robichon (Berbère Télévision), posted by "abuhucem" on 14 July 2011, (http://www.youtube.com/watch?v=cGQOi9qDlRw).

Index

Achnacarry Agreement 53, 60, 71n82
Adamson, Matthew 10, 83
Adenauer, Konrad 186, 234
AGIP 9, 16, 18–20, 33–8, 40, 42–59, 61–4, 65n4, 65n6, 65n9, 66n16, 68n36, 68n43, 71n74, 71n75, 71n76, 71n82, 74n125, 74n127, 90, 110n35, 148, 178, 203n34, 216, 219, 250–1. *See also* AGIP Mineraria
AGIP Mineraria 141, 143, 147–8, 164n102, 174
AIOC 27n33, 46, 53–4, 57, 59, 61, 83, 93–4, 100, 102, 117n110, 122. *See also* Anglo-Persian Oil Company; BP
Algeria xii–xiii, 1, 9, 11–12, 15, 20, 22–3, 51, 77, 83, 91, 97, 99–103, 105–7, 114n89, 116n105, 168–70, 178, 182, 185, 187, 191, 199, 200n3, 201n14, 215–17, 226, 238, 248, 250–3; transport and marketing of Algerian oil 193–8; wartime Algeria 119–53, 157n39, 163n90, 163n92, 166n114, 167n125. *See also* Algerian War (of Independence)
Algerian War (of Independence) xii–xiii, 15, 22–3, 77, 105, 119, 121, 126–7, 148, 151, 194, 248
Allies xii, 1, 34–5, 38–42, 44, 63, 76, 85–6, 90
Alphand, Hervé 91, 133, 138
Anglo-American 12, 21, 34, 36, 38–44, 46, 57, 59–60, 63, 76–7, 81, 86, 199, 251. *See also* Allies
Anglo-Persian Oil Company 71n82, 78, 107n7
Anglo-Iranian Oil Company *see* AIOC
ANIC 35, 38, 54, 65n6, 66n16, 181
Arab nationalism 101, 126, 129, 141
ARAMCO 93–6, 113n78, 119, 127–9, 136, 150
Bagnato, Bruna 20, 121, 165n108, 166n122, 181, 204n49
Ball, George 191–2
Barry, Andrew 10, 212
bases (military) 41, 96, 125–6, 142, 149, 186
Bates, Charles 15, 173
Belkacem, Krim 146–7
Ben Bella, Ahmed 119, 150–1, 153n2
Bénézit, Jacques 99, 197
Berkner, Lloyd 7, 13
Berriane 98–9, 123
Bizerte (attack) 149, 186, 194
Blancard, Jean 91, 110n43, 127, 130, 136, 158n45, 145, 197–8, 249
Blum-Byrnes Agreement 89
Blum, Léon 87–9
Boldrini, Marcello 49, 53
Bolton, Ralph 46, 53–4, 56, 62
Bonnet, Henri 90–1
Boulahrouf, Taïeb 142, 144, 163n90
Bourguiba, Habib 119, 142, 149, 194
Bowker, Goeffrey 16, 85
BP 1, 2, 136, 147, 171, 185, 223, 229
Briatico, Franco 144, 150
Brosio, Manlio 166n122, 188–9
BRP 11, 18, 85, 87–8, 91–2, 97, 99–100, 102–5, 110n43, 111n44, 120, 123–4, 128, 130, 133–4, 137–8, 145, 149, 152, 170, 178, 187, 193, 196–8, 250–1
Bruderer, Willy 97, 148
Bush, Vannevar 6–7
Byrnes, James 36, 87, 89

Caltex 61, 91, 100, 103, 112n59, 117n110, 139
Camprubí, Lino 9–10, 254
Canada 90, 103, 200n3
Caviaga 38, 40, 43–5, 49

Cefis, Eugenio 151, 165n108, 167n126, 192, 204n57, 205
CEL 184, 188–9, 191, 196, 207n87
CEP (Compagnie d'exploitation pétrolière) 143–4
CFP 11, 18, 21, 30n62, 76–8, 80–1, 84–7, 89–90, 172, 187, 189, 193, 223, 240n18, 250, 252; in Algeria 97–9, 103–5, 136–8, 143, 216–17; in relation to the Red Line Agreement 93–5; on oil marketing 196–9
CFP(A) 99, 123–4, 135, 147–8, 197
CFR (Compagnie française de raffinage) 81, 91
CGG 28n50, 51, 79–80, 83–5, 90, 97–8, 124, 135, 148, 178, 180–1, 249
Chanderli, Abdelkader 138, 146
China 121, 142, 162n92, 182, 200n3, 212
Christian Democrats: French 87, 111n45, 137; German 232; Italian (DC) 8, 39, 42–3, 48, 54–6, 57–8, 63, 144, 182–3, 204n56
Churchill, Winston 41, 57, 66n18
CIA 48, 171, 182, 184, 192, 236, 254
CIP 34–5, 40, 42, 45–7, 52–3
Clarke, Ashley 58, 185
coal xi, 10, 38, 82, 86, 88–9, 95, 184, 197, 217, 218, 223
Colitti, Marcello 19, 38, 42
Common Market 182, 193, 196, 215–17, 219–20, 238
Communist 120, 126, 133, 142, 171, 211, 222–3, 226; French 87–8, 111n45; Italian 8, 39, 48–9, 69n63, 144–5
Connelly, Matthew 121, 126
confidential information *see* intelligence
Confindustria 54, 56
Corps des Mines 18, 82, 97, 178; corpsard 82–3, 91, 97, 99, 198
Cortemaggiore 49, 52–3, 56, 62, 92
CPA 105, 123, 135, 137
CREPS 105, 122–3, 127, 194
Crowley-Monnet Agreements 86
CTRP 49, 51. *See also* Technical Committee for Exploration and Production
Czechoslovakia 142, 212
Cuba xi, 172, 223, 228; Cuban missile crisis 24, 150

DC *see* Christian Democrats
Debré, Michel 142, 193–4
decolonization xii, 9, 15, 22, 27n30, 77, 122
De Gasperi, Alcide 33, 41–2, 48–9, 56, 65n5
DeGolyer Everette 92, 112n65, 169
DICA 80, 83–4, 87, 94, 102–3, 135, 145
Djebel Berga xii, 122–3, 155n12
Doel, Ronald xiii, 2, 4, 5, 7, 13, 16, 122, 249
Douglas Dillon, Clarence 127–8
Dulles, John Foster 125, 133
dumping 53, 56, 171, 224, 254
Dunn, James 48, 56

East Germany 188–9, 212
Ebel, Robert 170, 236
ECA 60–2, 90–1, 106, 192
École Polytechnique 18, 82, 178
ECONAD 222–3, 226–7, 229–31, 233, 236
ECSC (European Coal and Steel Community) 217, 240n25
Eden, Anthony 41, 57–8
Edison 58–9
Edjeleh 105, 122–5, 127–8, 143, 170, 193–5, 216
EEC 20, 23, 169, 172, 184, 189, 198, 225, 236, 238, 240n25; stance vis-à-vis Soviet oil imports 211–22
Egypt 129, 141–2, 157n39, 172, 181, 187, 192
Eisenhower, Dwight 13, 48, 58, 66n18, 125, 128, 132–3, 171
electrical exploration technique 13, 16, 47, 51–2, 78–80, 85, 108n12, 148
El Mechat, Samia 121, 133
embargo 23–4, 36, 91, 129, 133, 172, 185–7, 201n16, 212–13, 244n63; on pipes and pipeline equipment 226–38, 248, 253
ENI 11–12, 22–4, 52, 55, 57–8, 63–4, 68n47, 108n73, 83, 162n82, 162n85, 162n94, 164n101, 165n108, 166n114, 166n116, 169–70, 172, 174–5, 178, 180–1, 196–7, 199–200, 201n16, 203n48, 204n57, 208n95, 237, 243n47, 249–52, 254; accommodation with the majors 192; contacts with NATO Study Group 223–4, 226; in Algeria 122–3, 139, 141–53; historiography on 16–21; deals with the USSR 181–8, 231–2, 234–5; pipeline

battle 188–91; Soviet imports 216, 218–21, 223
ERP *see* Marshall Plan
Euratom 217, 240n20
Évian Agreements xiii, 146–7, 149–50, 153, 165n109, 167n125, 198, 240n18

Fascism 8, 33–4, 36, 38, 43, 81
Finsider 234–5
Fanfani, Amintore 182–5, 189, 204n56, 205n59, 207n93
FIAT 35, 61, 65n6
FLN 22, 119, 121–2, 128–30, 132–3, 136–9, 141–7, 149, 152, 153n2, 157n39, 163n90, 164n101, 193–4, 208n100, 216, 251
French Union 21, 77–8, 80, 87–8, 90, 91, 97, 99, 105–6, 178, 250

Gaillard, Félix 137, 142, 162n88
gas xii, 1, 2, 9, 11, 17, 22, 168, 180, 213–4, 227, 230–3, 236, 247, 253–4; in Algeria 105–6, 121–4, 130, 145, 148, 198; in France 77, 80, 88, 92; in Italy 35, 37–8, 49, 52–3, 56, 62, 64, 145, 151
Gaulle, Charles de xii, 18, 81–3, 87, 119, 137–8, 142, 144, 146, 149, 167n125, 181, 234
geology 3–5, 16–17, 33, 36–8, 43, 44–7, 49–51, 56, 59, 77, 92, 97–8, 102–4, 106, 114n91, 122–3, 127, 147–8, 154n8, 154n9, 172, 251. *See also* geosciences
geophysics xii–xiii, 3–5, 8–9, 12–17, 20–3, 33, 37–8, 43, 47, 49–52, 55, 61, 63–4, 65n4, 71n75, 71n76, 76, 78–9, 84–5, 90, 92, 97–9, 105–6, 112n65, 122–4, 126, 135, 141, 148, 151–2, 168–9, 173–6, 178, 180–1, 199, 248, 250–2. *See also* geosciences
geosciences xii, 3–4, 7, 12–5, 17, 20, 22, 24, 34, 43–7, 50–1, 57, 63–4, 77, 83, 97–8, 100, 123, 133–6, 138, 141, 147–8, 151–3, 197, 238, 247–53
Gerbella, Luigi 44–6, 68n40
Giorgi, Guido 223–4, 226
Goetze, Roger 91, 99, 104, 197
GPRA xiii, 138, 142–7, 149, 150, 152, 163n90, 166n116, 252
GPRF 81–3, 85–7, 102
gravimetry 36, 38, 47, 51, 78, 52, 78, 98, 108n11, 176
Grew, Joseph 33–4, 40–1, 85–6
Gronchi, Giovanni 44, 54, 68n40, 144, 183, 186–7
Guillaumat, Pierre 18, 76, 81–3, 94, 97, 99, 100–6, 107n2, 124, 134, 138, 144, 146, 152, 158, 181, 193, 198, 210n120, 249, 251
Gulbenkian, Calouste 78, 108n7
Gulf Oil 9, 27n33, 44–6, 56, 58–9, 94, 100, 102–3, 108n17, 117n110, 175, 192, 218, 228
Gurov, Evgeniy 182, 186

Hassi Messaoud 105, 122, 124, 135, 143, 147–8, 193–5, 216
Hassi R'Mel 105, 122, 124, 134–5, 148
Hecht, Gabrielle 7–8, 10, 15, 82, 203n35, 212
Högselius, Per 11, 213, 254
Hughes, Thomas 19, 212

IFP 50, 84–5, 123, 178, 191, 198, 201n14
IGY (International Geophysical Year) 13, 173
In Amenas 1, 194
intelligence xii, xiii, 2–4, 7, 9, 12–15, 18, 22, 34, 38, 41–5, 48, 51, 55, 59, 63–4, 71n76, 76–7, 83, 86, 94, 96–7, 99, 100–1, 103, 105–6, 122–5, 132, 134–7, 145, 147–8, 149–53, 170–1, 174, 182, 184, 196, 214, 223, 227, 230–1, 238, 247–52
IPC 21, 77–8, 85–6, 114n86; French relations with 89, 93–6
Iran 20, 52, 57, 73n104, 95–6, 108n13, 114n85, 114n88, 130, 141, 143, 150, 153, 162n82, 188, 200n3, 201n14, 203n48
Iraq xi, 18, 21, 30n64, 76–8, 81, 93, 95–6, 114n88, 130, 147, 153, 168, 200n3
Iron Curtain 211–12, 228, 237
Italian Geological Service 50–1, 180
Italian Social Republic 34, 40, 43

Jeanneney, Jean-Marcel 198, 216
Jervis, Robert 4, 11–12, 93

Kaplan, Léon 83, 100–1
Kennedy, John Fitzgerald 133, 146, 184, 191, 207n93
Khrushchev, Nikita 185–6, 235
Kilian, Conrad 97, 114n90, 114–15n91

Kirk, Alexander 33–4, 36, 40–1, 44–5, 65n5
Klaipėda 189, 191, 212
Kocher-Marbœuf, Eric 18, 91, 197–8
Krige, John 6–7, 21, 174, 248
Kuwait 76, 94, 168

Lacoste, Robert 127–8, 193–4
Law of 1928 on imports regulation 81, 89, 108n16, 197
Lejeune, Max 131, 140
Lerici Foundation 50, 180
Levy, Walter 60, 62, 90–1, 192
Libya 1, 38, 41, 83, 123, 127–9, 134, 138, 143, 149, 157n32, 170, 175, 178, 192–4, 196–7, 199, 200n3, 216
Loddo, Carmine 147–8
logging *see* well logging
Lombardo, Ivan Matteo 55–6
Lugrin 147, 149
Lundestad, Geir 49, 70n64, 236

Macmillan, Harold 172
magnetism 13, 79; magnetic recording 52, 124, 148, 173–4, 181; magnetometry 202n28
majors 10–12, 17, 19, 21–2, 30n59, 35, 39, 42, 44–6, 51–4, 57, 59–64, 73n108, 76, 78, 80–1, 83, 85, 89–93, 95–6, 103, 106, 108n8, 108n15, 119, 121–2, 124, 127, 132–4, 136–7, 139, 141, 143, 151–2, 167n126, 169–72, 181, 183–4, 186–9, 191, 192, 196–7, 199, 216–18, 222–6, 228–9, 237, 250–4
Manuelli, Ernesto 234–5
Marjolin, Robert 215, 217, 220
Marshall Plan 11, 249: in Italy 40, 48, 53, 59–63, 67n24; in France 87, 90–1, 112n59
Mattei, Enrico xii–xiii, 34; at AGIP, 43–9, 52–7, 63–4, 83, 219, 221, 223, 235, 237, 249–51; historiography on 17–20, 30n66, 31n73; Middle Eastern and North African operations 141–6, 148–52, 162n82; 164n101, 166n122, 167n126; international tensions 182–5, 188–9, 191–2, 196, 199, 207n93
Mediterranean (Sea) 10, 20, 23, 39, 41, 85, 93–4, 119–20, 130–1, 141–2, 144, 164n101, 191, 193–4, 222, 252
Métropole (European France) 21, 76, 80, 97
Metz, Victor de 30n62, 84, 93–4, 136, 172, 197–8
Middle East 11–12, 18, 20–3, 39, 53, 60, 62, 76–8, 81, 92–7, 100, 105, 124–5, 129, 136, 141, 149, 152, 168, 170–1, 175, 184, 191, 193, 195–7, 199, 215, 217, 224–5, 254
Mitchell, Timothy 10–11, 59, 134, 211–12
Moch, Paul 97, 102, 104, 127, 198
Mollet, Guy 119, 127–30, 133, 157n35
Monnet, Jean 87–8
Monnet Plan (Modernization and Equipment Plan) 88–90, 111n47
Montecatini 9, 35, 38, 40, 55–6, 59, 61, 65n6, 66n16
Morocco (-an) 9, 20, 101, 103, 119–20, 125–6, 132, 141–6, 149, 196
Mosaddegh, Mohammad 57, 95

NAC 222, 233–5
Nafta (Società Anonima) 36, 45
Nasser, Gamal Abdel 129, 157n39
NATO xi, xii, 7, 10, 16, 20, 23–4, 40, 115n97, 120, 125–6, 137, 142, 182, 184, 186, 189, 194, 208n94, 211–14, 217, 253–5; debate on Soviet oil imports and pipelines 221–32, 234–8, 245n70
NEDC 78, 94
Needell, Allan 2, 7, 122
Neo-Atlanticism 8, 142, 183, 185
Nixon, Richard 132–3
North Africa xii, 12, 20, 22, 77, 96–7, 100–2, 105, 108, 120–1, 123–8, 132, 134, 139, 141, 144–5, 149, 151–3, 157n39, 175, 184, 186, 215, 251
North Sea 9, 16, 175
Nouschi, André 83, 95, 107n3, 108n17
NSC 39, 48, 96, 185
nuclear 3, 4; 7–13, 15, 24, 27n30, 28n51, 82, 84, 97, 173, 182–3, 212, 215, 217–19; French nuclear program 130, 146, 149–50, 158n46, 203n35

OCRS 130–3, 146, 152
OPEC 171

Palewski, Gaston 142, 150, 186
Parentis 92, 106
Petretti, Arnaldo 42, 45–7, 49
photo-geology 98, 102, 123

Pineau, Christian 130, 133, 141–2, 194
pipe 10, 16, 23–4, 183, 212, 214, 222, 226–37, 253–5
pipeline xii, 6, 10, 15, 23, 76, 169, 172, 180, 184, 187–9, 191, 199, 248, 252; gas 38, 49, 52; Middle Eastern 94–5, 130; Algerian 137, 142, 158n47, 169, 172, 193–4, 199, 209n103, 209n105, 216; Soviet 10, 16, 23, 183, 187–9, 191, 211–3, 221–2, 226–30, 232–3, 235, 237–8, 244n60, 253–4
Pirani, Mario 145–7
playback centers 148, 173–5
Pontecorvo, Bruno 8–9, 47
Po Valley 12, 36–8, 43, 45–7, 49, 51–6, 58, 62, 73n108, 250
Pozzi, Daniele 16–17, 36, 44, 47, 51, 55
prospecting xii, 2–5, 8–10, 12–17, 21–3, 34, 36, 38, 43–4, 47–50, 54, 56, 58, 63–4, 73n108, 78–80, 83, 87, 89, 96–9, 101–2, 104–5, 116n98, 121–4, 127, 134–8, 147–53, 168–70, 172–3, 175–6, 178, 180–1, 183, 193, 197, 238, 247–52

Quaroni, Pietro 132, 140–1, 145, 182

Ramadier, Paul 88, 100
RAP 80, 87, 97, 105, 122, 127, 198
Rathbone, Monroe 218, 228
Ratti, Giuseppe 182–3, 205n57, 221, 237
Red Line Agreement 78, 93–6
re-exports 219–20, 224
refining xii, 144, 150–1, 189, 196–7, 208n94, 209n110; in Italy 36, 38, 40, 42, 46, 54, 60–2, 182, 185, 219, 223, 228; in France 76, 81, 98, 108–9n17, 112n59, 215
Reggane 130, 135, 158n46
Reinhardt, George Frederick reinhardt 149, 192
relabeling 182, 215, 219
REPAL 91, 97–100, 102–5, 123–4, 126, 134, 197–8
Rocco, Tiziano 37, 47, 50–1
Royal Dutch-Shell 27n33, 35–6, 42, 45–6, 53, 63, 71n82, 78, 80, 83, 85, 91, 93–4, 100, 107n7, 122–3, 132, 135, 146, 185, 197, 218, 220, 223, 229, 231, 238; attempts to enter Algeria 102–6
Rusk, Dean 186, 192
Sahara xii, 1, 9, 22, 97–9, 100, 103–6, 115n95, 120–4, 126–8, 131, 133, 136, 138–48, 178, 194, 196, 208n100, 250–1; territorial issues 146–7, 150–2, 167n125; resources 125, 129–30, 134–5, 137–8, 145, 147, 149, 150, 152, 169, 185, 195–9, 215, 225, 231, 251. *See also* OCRS; Saharan Oil Code
Saharan Oil Code 136, 138, 147, 150, 152, 161n74, 167n125
Sakiet Sidi Youssef 136
Saʿūd, Ibn 95, 129
Saudi Arabia 76, 93, 95–6, 112n59, 129, 168
Schlumberger 16, 29n54, 47, 51, 76, 79, 84–5, 108n12, 148, 178
Schuman, Robert 91, 125
SDECE xiii, 18, 83, 121–2, 130, 132–3, 136–8, 142, 145, 150, 163n90, 182, 188, 196, 251
secrecy 4, 13–14, 28n44, 83, 96, 254
security xii, 1–4, 8, 12–14, 23, 34, 39, 48, 61–2, 80, 86, 93, 96, 101, 121, 125–6, 130, 137, 152, 169, 172, 182, 184–8, 193–5, 198–200, 214, 218–19, 223–4, 226, 228, 236–8, 252–4; energy 2, 4, 6, 8, 11, 18, 21, 24, 45, 62–4, 77, 92, 94, 105, 129, 133, 169, 187, 214, 236, 250, 252; oil 4, 9, 36, 46, 53, 57, 64, 77, 94, 96, 105, 122, 153; national xi, 2, 6, 11, 12, 14, 17, 24n4, 39, 63, 77, 96, 98, 105, 107, 122, 125, 153, 168, 184, 211, 236, 247, 253
seismology 4, 13, 16, 36–8, 47, 50–2, 54, 65n4, 71n76, 79, 90, 92, 98, 102, 110n35, 115n94, 124, 126, 134–5, 148, 173–6, 178, 180; Panel on Seismic Improvement 173; reflection 16, 37, 92, 98, 112n65, 115n95, 135, 181; refraction 98–9, 115n95, 124, 148, 181
Selem, Antonio 52, 141
SEPL 187–9, 191
SFMG 175, 181
Shell *see* Royal Dutch-Shell
SIAP 36, 56
Sicily 41, 52, 58–9
Sinclair Oil 46, 134
SNE 181–3, 185–6, 192, 218, 221, 224, 234–6
SNPA 80, 89, 92
Socialists 48; French 87–8, 111n45, 131; Italian 39, 48–9, 144, 183

Society of Exploration Geophysicists 14, 50, 168, 175–6
SOCONY 27n32, 35–6, 42, 46, 61, 70, 80, 91, 93–5, 119, 139, 159n54, 223
SONJ 27n32, 35–6, 42–3, 45–6, 51, 53–5, 58–64, 70n72, 71n82, 78, 80, 91–5, 98, 100, 102–3, 106, 108n17, 119, 122, 127–8, 136–9, 143, 146, 159n54, 171, 188–9, 192, 199, 211, 218, 220–1, 223, 228
Soviet oil offensive 172, 183, 186–7, 200, 211, 217, 238
SPI 36, 38, 45, 54–5
Study Group on Soviet Oil Policy 223–6
Suez: Crisis 128–9, 133, 157n39; Suez Canal 22, 41, 253
surveillance 2, 4, 9, 12–13, 17–18, 22, 27n37, 39, 77, 86, 99, 102, 116n98, 142, 182, 211, 223, 226, 238, 248, 251–2

tanker 6, 33, 41, 60, 76, 86, 129, 172, 183, 191, 205n59, 222–3, 253
Technical Committee for Exploration and Production 61
technopolitics 7, 9–10, 12, 26n21, 27n30, 34, 45, 49, 63, 214, 229, 237
technoscience 5, 6, 8, 11, 15–16, 22, 50, 99, 122, 172, 178, 181, 183, 197, 201n14, 247–50, 252–3
telluric current method 51–2, 80, 84, 98, 173
Tenaille, Michel 97, 102, 115n91
Texaco 42, 80, 119, 122, 223
Thomas, John Elmer 44–5
Tiguentourine 1, 124
Togni, Giuseppe 55–6
transnational 2, 3, 5, 6, 9–12, 19, 21, 23–4, 50, 124, 135, 174, 184, 211–14, 217, 225–6, 236, 238, 247–8, 252, 255
Treaty of Rome 215–16, 219–20
Truman Doctrine 48–9, 69n58, 88, 101
Truman, Harry 6, 39, 53, 93, 96
Tunisia 41, 83, 100–1, 119, 125–6, 132, 136–7, 142, 144–6, 149, 193–4, 196
Turchetti, Simone 8, 10
Turkish Petroleum Company 76–8, 107n7

UN *see* United Nations
United Nations 48, 67, 125, 127, 130, 137–9, 141, 149, 182, 186, 228
US Consulate General in Algiers 22, 99, 125, 135, 138, 251

Vanoni, Ezio 49, 55–6, 58
Venezuela 104, 108n13, 134, 168, 171, 225

war damages 40, 46
well logging 29n54, 47, 51–2, 79, 85, 108n12, 148, 178
West Germany 61, 74n124, 115n97, 121, 172, 182–3, 185–6, 188–9, 191, 201n15, 213, 218, 222, 224–5, 229, 232–6, 243n49
WGC 9, 37–8, 46–7, 50–2, 54, 59, 64, 65n4, 71n74, 174, 250
World War II xi, xii, 4, 6, 8–10, 77, 80, 93, 102, 126, 130, 151, 174, 229
Wormser, Olivier 125, 145, 216

X-Mines 82, 84, 99

Yazid, Mohamed 128, 130, 138, 161n76
Yergin, Daniel 17, 25n7, 169

Zanmatti, Carlo 43, 49–51
Zarzaitine 124, 127
Zellerbach, David 62, 182, 189

For Product Safety Concerns and Information please contact our EU representative GPSR@taylorandfrancis.com
Taylor & Francis Verlag GmbH, Kaufingerstraße 24, 80331 München, Germany

www.ingramcontent.com/pod-product-compliance
Ingram Content Group UK Ltd.
Pitfield, Milton Keynes, MK11 3LW, UK
UKHW020017200926
475702UK00014B/1925
* 9 7 8 0 3 6 7 2 7 5 2 9 7 *